W9-ACG-511

Writers and their Background

MATTHEW ARNOLD

In the same series

ROBERT BROWNING edited by Isobel Armstrong
GEOFFREY CHAUCER edited by D. S. Brewer
S. T. COLERIDGE edited by R. L. Brett
JOHN DRYDEN edited by Earl Miner
ALEXANDER POPE edited by Peter Dixon
TENNYSON edited by D. J. Palmer

Writers and their Background

MATTHEW ARNOLD

EDITED BY KENNETH ALLOTT

OHIO UNIVERSITY PRESS · 1976

PRINTED BY OFFSET AND BOUND IN THE
UNITED STATES OF AMERICA
FOR OHIO UNIVERSITY PRESS, ATHENS, OHIO 1976
BY EDWARDS BROTHERS, INC., ANN ARBOR, MICHIGAN

LC 75-15339
ISBN 0-8214-0197-1

Contents

In Memoriam

KENNETH ALLOTT

1912–1973

But he is now by fortune foiled
No more; and we retain
The memory of a man unspoiled,
Sweet, generous, and humane.

The Contributors

PROFESSOR FRASER NEIMAN
College of William and Mary, Williamsburg, U.S.A.

PROFESSOR WILLIAM A. MADDEN
University of Minnesota, Minneapolis, U.S.A.

KENNETH ALLOTT
Late Andrew Cecil Bradley Professor of Modern English Literature, University of Liverpool

MIRIAM ALLOTT
Andrew Cecil Bradley Professor of Modern English Literature, University of Liverpool

PROFESSOR DAVID DELAURA
Professor of English, University of Pennsylvania, U.S.A.

PROFESSOR R. H. SUPER
Professor of English, University of Michigan, Ann Arbor, U.S.A.

PROFESSOR JAMES BERTRAM
Professor of English, Victoria University of Wellington, New Zealand

DR. PETER KEATING
Lecturer in English, University of Edinburgh

PROFESSOR BASIL WILLEY
Emeritus Professor of English, University of Cambridge

PROFESSOR WARREN ANDERSON
Professor in Comparative Literature, University of Massachusetts, U.S.A.

DR. JAMES SIMPSON
Lecturer in German, University of Liverpool

General Editor's Preface

THE STUDY OF LITERATURE is not a 'pure' discipline since works of literature are affected by the climate of opinion in which they are produced. Writers, like other men, are concerned with the politics, the philosophy, the religion, the arts, and the general thought of their own times. Some literary figures, indeed, have made their own distinguished contributions to these areas of human interest, while the achievement of others can be fully appreciated only by a knowledge of them.

The series, to which the present volume is an important addition, has been planned with the purpose of presenting major authors in their intellectual, social, and artistic context, and with the conviction that this will make their work more easily understood and enjoyed. Each volume contains a chapter which provides a reader's guide to the writings of the author concerned, a Bibliography, and Chronological Tables setting out the main dates of the author's life and publications alongside the chief events of contemporary importance.

When this volume was first projected my thoughts turned at once to Kenneth Allott who was acknowledged to be our foremost Arnold scholar and whose edition of Arnold's poetry had been universally admired. I was delighted when he accepted my invitation to be its editor and was impressed by the care and consideration he gave to the planning of its contents. Like everything else he did it was built on sound foundations. Then in the summer of 1973 his many friends learned with dismay of his unexpected death, at the height of his powers and with so much still to give to his generation.

It was with a deep sense of gratitude that I heard from his widow, Professor Miriam Allott, that she was ready to take over the work that her husband had left unfinished. I express not only my own indebtedness but that of the publishers and the contributors to this volume for her readiness to do this at a time when she faced so many personal and professional difficulties. It was, of course, a very fitting solution to our problems, for Miriam and Kenneth Allott were fellow workers with the same scholarly standards, who knew each other's minds and shared each other's interests. It is gratifying to their friends that the University of Liverpool has also recognized this by appointing Miriam Allott to succeed her husband in the Andrew Cecil Bradley Chair of English.

And so it comes about that the volume which Kenneth Allott planned and of which he was the first editor is now presented as a tribute to his memory. We hope this book comes near the high standards he would have expected, not only because of our admiration for him as a scholar but also because of our affection for him as a friend.

R. L. Brett

Prefatory Note

I MUST EXPLAIN THAT at the time of my husband's death in May 1973, the planning and organization of this book were completed and most of the contributions were ready for the press. What remained to be done included the standardizing of the footnotes, the compiling of the Bibliography and the Chronological Tables, and, most seriously, the completing of my husband's own projected contribution, the chapter on Arnold's narrative and dramatic poems. It is characteristic of his fastidiousness in such matters that my husband had written many different drafts of the chapter, none of which satisfied him and all of which—except for an excellent prolegomenon, which is printed below—he destroyed. He had in fact worked during a period of some two years on the undertaking. He had wished, as he says in one of his surviving notes, to look at Arnold's poetry 'as if for the first time'. His hope was to write about the poetry freshly and with attention to the art with which it was composed as well as to the various shades of its meaning, believing that over recent years the latter had perhaps too frequently received attention at the expense of the former.

After a good deal of hesitation, I decided to take up work on the chapter myself and to make an attempt, however inadequate, to sustain the discussion along lines suggested in the introductory pages and in various of my husband's rough notes: my own notes to the chapter try to indicate as exactly as possible the nature and extent of my indebtedness to this and other of my husband's unpublished Arnold writings, and in fairness to his special knowledge and individual style to give some idea of where my own contribution begins and ends. The personal and professional difficulties which stood in the way of getting on with the chapter as quickly and as well as one wanted to in the circumstances must be held responsible for holding up the publication of this book for so long. I cannot express warmly enough my gratitude to everyone concerned for their patient sympathy, and I want to thank especially those of my fellow-contributors who helped me with the final preparations: particularly David DeLaura who worked on the Bibliography; Peter Keating, who tracked down numerous references for me; and James Simpson, my colleague at the University of Liverpool, who read over and corrected the most recent additions to the typescript. I should like to thank Mr. Nicholas Shrimpton, the colleague with whom I share our course on Victorian Literature at Liverpool (where he also formerly worked with my husband), for his valuable suggestions about points of detail in the chapter which I completed and, furthermore, for gallantly coming to our aid at page-proof stage when Matthew Arnold had to contend with the rival claims of our sessional examining. My chief anxiety now is that all the good work which has been put into this book by its distinguished contributors should not have been damaged by my own unlooked-for share in its preparation.

MIRIAM ALLOTT

	The main events in Arnold's life	*Events of literary and intellectual importance in Arnold's lifetime*	*Events of historical importance in Arnold's lifetime*
1822	(24 December) Born at Laleham-on-Thames, eldest son of Rev. Thomas Arnold and Mary Arnold (*née* Penrose)	Thomas Hughes born Shelley dies Byron's *The Vision of Judgment* *Sunday Times* started	George IV King
1828	(August) Arnold's family move to Rugby on his father's appointment as Headmaster of Rugby School	D. G. Rossetti and George Meredith born Carlyle's 'Essay on Burns' Lockhart's *Life of Robert Burns* Leigh Hunt's *Lord Byron and his Contemporaries* Sir John Malcolm's *Sketches of Persia*	Wellington Prime Minister
1831	(January) Pupil of his uncle, Rev. John Buckland, at Laleham until December 1832 Reads Virgil's Eclogues (August) Visits Lake District for the first time	William Hale White ('Mark Rutherford') born Peacock's *Crotchet Castle* Founding of the British Association	
1832		Walter Scott and Goethe die Tennyson's *Poems*	Reform Act
1833	(May) Herbert Hill, a cousin of Southey, engaged by Dr. Arnold as a tutor for his sons	Arthur Henry Hallam dies Keble's 'National Apostasy' sermon (14 July) Beginning of the Oxford Movement Carlyle's *Sartor Resartus*	Factory Act Abolition of Slavery
1834	(July) Fox How (near Ambleside) completed and becomes the permanent holiday home of the Arnolds in the Lakes Wordsworth a neighbour and frequent visitor	William Morris born Coleridge and Charles Lamb die Lytton's *Last Days of Pompeii*	New Poor Law Houses of Parliament burnt Peel becomes Prime Minister (after dismissal of Whigs)
1835		Samuel Butler born Browning's *Paracelsus* *Sketches by Boz* Vigny's 'Chatterton'	Whigs return; Melbourne Prime Minister
1836	First attempts at writing verse	William Godwin dies *Pickwick Papers* appears	

1836 (*cont.*)	(September) With his brother Tom enters Winchester College, his father's old school, as a Commoner	in monthly parts to Nov. 1837 Emerson's *Nature*	
1837	Wins verse-speaking prize at Winchester with a speech from Byron's *Marino Faliero* (August) First visit to France (September) Removed from Winchester and enters the Fifth Form at Rugby	Constable dies Swinburne born Carlyle's *French Revolution, Lectures on German Literature* *Oliver Twist* Hallam's *Literature of Europe* Hawthorne's *Twice-Told Tales*	Accession of Queen Victoria
1838	(January) First number of the manuscript *Fox How Magazine*, which he brought out twice a year with his brother Tom's help until January 1842 Fifth Form prize for Latin verse (August) Removed to the Sixth Form under his father	Thomas Arnold's *Early History of Rome* (concl. 1843) Carlyle's *Lectures on the History of Literature* *Nicholas Nickleby* Lady Charlotte Guest's *Mabinogion* Lyell's *Elements of Geology*	Committee on Trades Unions London and Birmingham Railway Negro Emancipation completed
1839		Walter Pater born Winthrop Mackworth Praed dies Carlyle's *Chartism* Harriet Martineau's *Deerbrook* Shelley's *Poetical Works*, ed. Mrs. Shelley	Penny Postage Act Birmingham Riots Royal Commission on Police First Factory Inspectors' Report
1840	(June) School prizes for English essay and English verse His prize poem, 'Alaric at Rome', printed at Rugby (November) Wins open scholarship to Balliol College, Oxford.	Thomas Hardy, J. A. Symonds and Zola born Browning's *Sordello* Darwin's *Voyage of H.M.S. Beagle*	Marriage of Queen Victoria and Prince Albert New Zealand annexed P. and O. incorporated
1841	(June) Shares school prizes for Latin essay and Latin verse (August) His father appointed Regius	Newman's Tract 90 Carlyle's *Heroes, Hero-Worship, and the Heroic in History* Emerson's *Essays: 1st*	Fall of Whigs; Peel Prime Minister Factory Committee Handloom Weavers' Committee

1841 (*cont.*)	Professor of Modern History at Oxford (October) Goes into residence at Oxford Beginning of intimacy with A. H. Clough Impressed by Newman's preaching at St. Mary's, but little affected by the ideas of the Oxford Movement	*Series* (2nd Series 1844) Hugh Miller's *Old Red Sandstone* *Punch* started	
1842	(March) *Proxime accessit* for Hertford Latin Scholarship (12 June) Sudden death of his father of heart disease at Rugby	William James born Thomas Arnold's *Study of Modern History* Browning's *Bells and Pomegranates* (nos. 2, 3) Tennyson's *Poems*	Income Tax Ashley's Act (Women and Children in Mines) Chartist Riots Hong Kong annexed
1842–5	Reads and is influenced by Carlyle, Emerson, and George Sand; a little later by Goethe and Spinoza Member of the 'Decade', undergraduate society similar to Cambridge 'Apostles'		
1843	Newdigate prize-poem *Cromwell* printed	Henry James, Edward Dowden and F. W. H. Myers born Southey dies Wordsworth Poet Laureate Borrow's *Bible in Spain* Carlyle's *Past and Present* *A Christmas Carol, Martin Chuzzlewit* Lytton's *Last of the Barons* Ruskin's *Modern Painters,* I [ii, 1846; iii–iv, 1856; v, 1860] Herbert Spencer's *Proper Sphere of Government*	Newman leaves St. Mary's Rebecca Riots Smoke abatement committee
1844	A. P. Stanley's *Life and Correspondence of Thomas Arnold* (November) B.A. Second Class in 'Greats'	Robert Bridges and Andrew Lang born William Beckford and Thomas Campbell die Barnes's *Poems of Rural Life in Dorset Dialect* E. B. Browning's *Poems* Disraeli's *Coningsby*	

1844 (*cont.*)		Kinglake's *Eothen* Patmore's *Poems* Thackeray's *Luck of Barry Lyndon*	
1845	(February–April) Temporary assistant-master at Rugby (28 March) Elected Fellow of Oriel College, Oxford	George Saintsbury and Sidney Colvin born Thomas Hood dies Newman joins the Church of Rome (9 October) Carlyle's *Cromwell* Disraeli's *Sybil* Lewes's *Biographical History of Philosophy* (concl. 1846) Newman's *Essay on the Development of Christian Doctrine* Poe's *Tales of Mystery and Imagination*	Potato failure
1846	(July) Visits France and meets George Sand at Nohant (December) Visits Paris at the end of the month to see Rachel act; remains there until 11 February 1847 Probably begins to read Senancour and Sainte-Beuve at this time	F. H. Bradley born Elizabeth Barrett and Robert Browning marry *Dombey and Son* George Eliot's translation of Strauss's *Leben Jesu* George Grote's *History of Greece* I–II (concl. 1856) Lear's *Book of Nonsense*	Potato famine Repeal of Corn Laws Russell Prime Minister
1847	(April) Private Secretary to the Marquis of Lansdowne, Lord President of the Council and Whig elder statesman (November) His brother Tom emigrated to New Zealand in the hope of finding 'Liberty, Equality, Fraternity'	Alice Thompson (Mrs. Meynell) born Bohn's 'Antiquarian Library' and 'Scientific Library' inaugurated *Wuthering Heights*; *Agnes Grey*; *Jane Eyre* (by 'Ellis, Acton and Currer Bell') Disraeli's *Tancred* Emerson's *Poems* Froude's *Shadows of the Clouds* Tennyson's *The Princess* Thackeray's *Vanity Fair* Marx's Communist Manifesto	Fielden's Factory Act Bank crisis Franklin expedition First use of chloroform
1848	(February) His brother	Branwell and Emily	European revolutions

1848 (*cont.*)	William Delafield leaves Oxford to go out to India as an Ensign in the Bengal Army of the East India Company (September) Visits Switzerland and meets 'Marguerite' at Thun (November) Clough publishes *The Bothie of Toper-na-Fuosich* after resigning his Oriel Fellowship in October because of his conscientious difficulties about religious subscription	Brontë die Chateaubriand dies 'Acton Bell's' *Tenant of Wildfell Hall* Mrs. Gaskell's *Mary Barton* Keats's *Life, Letters and Literary Remains,* ed R. Monckton Milnes Kingsley's *Yeast* Newman's *Loss and Gain* Thackeray's *Pendennis* Founding of the Pre-Raphaelite Brotherhood Bohn's 'Classical Library' inaugurated	Gorham Case Public Health Act
1849	(February) Publishes *The Strayed Reveller, and Other Poems* (September) Visits Switzerland and meets 'Marguerite' for the second and last time	Edmund Gosse and W. E. Henley born Hartley Coleridge, Maria Edgeworth, Ann Brontë and Edgar Allan Poe die Dickens starts *Household Words* Layand's *Nineveh and its Remains* 'Currer Bell's' *Shirley* Clough's *Ambarvalia* (with Thomas Burbidge) *David Copperfield* Froude's *Nemesis of Faith* Macaulay's *History of England* Melville's *Mardi* and *Redburn* Ruskin's *Seven Lamps of Architecture*	Punjab annexed
1850	(23 April) Death of Wordsworth (June) Publishes 'Memorial Verses' in *Fraser's Magazine* (August) His eldest and favourite sister, Jane ('K'), is married to W. E. Forster His own courtship of Frances Lucy Wightman interrupted because of lack of worldly prospects His brother Tom (at	Robert Louis Stevenson born Balzac dies Tennyson Poet Laureate; publishes *In Memoriam* Wordsworth's *The Prelude* R. Browning's *Christmas Eve and Easter Day* Carlyle's *Latter-Day Pamphlets* Emerson's *Representative Men* Hawthorne's *The Scarlet Letter* Leigh Hunt's *Autobiography*	Papal aggression Gold in California

1850 (*cont.*)	Hobart, Tasmania) and William (at Lahore in the Punjab) also marry during the year	Kingsley's *Alton Locke* *The Germ* (four nos., Jan.–April; Rossetti and others)	
1851	(15 April) Appointed Inspector of Schools by Lord Lansdowne (10 June) Marries Frances Lucy, daughter of Sir William Wightman, Justice of the Queen's Bench, at Hampton (September–October) Delayed honeymoon on the Continent (France, Italy, Switzerland) during which he visits the Grande Chartreuse (11 October) Begins work as school-inspector From this time forward spends much time in travelling both on inspectorial duties and for some years as Marshal to Judge Wightman on circuit	Mary Augusta Arnold (Mrs. Humphry Ward) and Andrew Cecil Bradley born J. M. W. Turner dies Borrow's *Lavengro* E. B. Browning's *Casa Guidi Windows* Carlyle's *Life of John Sterling* Coleridge's *Poems*, ed D. Coleridge Melville's *Moby Dick* Meredith's *Poems* Ruskin's *Pre-Raphaelitism* and *Stones of Venice*, Vol. I (ii–iii, 1853) W. von Humboldt's *The Spheres and Duties of Government* translated by R. Coulthard	French *coup d'état*: Louis Napoleon Emperor Palmerston dismissed Great Exhibition Repeal of window tax Livingstone reaches Zambesi
1852	(October) Publishes *Empedocles on Etna, and Other Poems*	George Moore born Thomas Moore dies *Bleak House* Hawthorne's *The Blithedale Romance* Melville's *Pierre* Newman's *Scope and Nature of University Education* (later, *The Idea of a University*) Tennyson's 'Ode on the Death of Wellington' Thackeray's *Henry Esmond*	Derby Prime Minister; Disraeli Chancellor of Exchequer Aberdeen Prime Minister; Gladstone Chancellor of Exchequer Cholera Report Drainage and Sewerage of Towns Report
1853	(November) Publishes *Poems. A New Edition* (a selection from his two earlier volumes, with a critical preface and, among new poems, 'Sohrab and Rustum' and 'The Scholar-Gipsy')	'Bohn's British Classics' inaugurated Charlotte Brontë's *Villette* Mrs. Gaskell's *Ruth* and *Cranford* Haydon's *Autobiography* Kingsley's *Hypatia* Lewes's *Comte's Philosophy* Harriet Martineau's	Crimean War, 1853–6

1853 (*cont.*)		*Philosophy of Comte* (transl.) Thackeray's *The Newcomes* A. R. Wallace's *Travels on the Amazon* Charlotte Yonge's *Heir of Redclyffe*	
1854	(December) Publishes *Poems, Second Series* (a further selection from his two earlier volumes, 'Balder Dead' being the only important new poem; title-page dated 1855)	Marie Corelli born J. E. Lockhart and John Wilson ('Christopher North') die *Hard Times* Coventry Patmore's *Angel in the House*, Part I (ii, 1856; iii, 1860; iv, 1862) W. B. Scott's *Poems* Thoreau's *Walden* Charlotte Yonge's *The Little Duke*	Working Men's College founded
1855	(April) Publishes 'Stanzas from the Grande Chartreuse' in *Fraser's Magazine* (May) Publishes 'Haworth Churchyard' in *Fraser's Magazine*	Charlotte Brontë and Mary Mitford die R. Browning's *Men and Women* R. Burton's *Pilgrimage to El-Medinah and Mecca* *Little Dorrit* Mrs. Gaskell's *North and South* Kingsley's *Westward Ho!* Lewes's *Life of Goethe* Tennyson's *Maud and Other Poems* Trollope's *The Warden* Whitman's *Leaves of Grass*	Palmerston Prime Minister Fall of Sebastopol *Daily Telegraph* started
1856		Oscar Wilde, G. B. Shaw and William Archer born Hugh Miller dies Carlyle's *Collected Works* George Eliot's *Scenes of Clerical Life* (in *Blackwood's Magazine*; separately 1857) Emerson's *English Traits* Kingsley's *The Heroes* Ruskin's *Modern Painters* iii–iv (see 1843) Stanley's *Sinai and Palestine*	Peace of Paris Speke on Victoria Nyanza Bombardment of Canton
1857	(5 May) Elected Professor of Poetry at Oxford	Joseph Conrad and George Gissing born	Indian Mutiny Divorce Act

	(August) Visits Switzerland with his wife (14 November) Inaugural lecture, 'On the Modern Element in Literature' at Oxford (the first Professor of Poetry to lecture in English; re-elected at the end of his first term of five years) (December) Publishes *Merope* (title-page dated 1858)	Alfred de Musset dies Borrow's *Romany Rye* Charlotte Brontë's *The Professor* Mrs. Gaskell's *Life of Charlotte Brontë* E. B. Browning's *Aurora Leigh* Buckle's *History of Civilisation in England*, vol. I (ii, 1861) T. Hughes's *Tom Brown's Schooldays* Kingsley's *Two Years Ago* G. A. Lawrence's *Guy Livingstone* Livingstone's *Missionary Travels in South Africa* Miller's *Testimony of the Rocks* D. M. Mulock, *John Halifax, Gentleman* R. Spencer's *Essays, Series 1* (ii, 1863; iii, 1874) Thackeray's *The Virginians* Trollope's *Barchester Towers*	
1858	(February) Settles at 2, Chester Square, London ('. . . it will be something to unpack one's pormanteau for the first time since I was married, now nearly seven years ago') (August–September) On a walking holiday in Switzerland with his friend Theodore Walrond	Carlyle's *Frederick the Great* Goethe's *Poems and Ballads* translated by Aytoun and Martin Clough's *Amours de Voyage* L. J. Cory's *Ionica* (vol. II, 1877) Farrar's *Eric, or Little by Little* Gladstone's *Studies on Homer* Hogg's *Life of Shelley* Mansell's *Limits of Religious Thought* Morris's *Defence of Guinevere* Trelawny's *Recollections of the last days of Shelley and Byron* Trollope's *Dr. Thorne* and *The Three Clerks* Dickens begins his public readings	Defeat of Palmerston; Derby Prime Minister Property qualification for M.P.s removed Jews admitted to Parliament India transferred to the Crown

1859	(March–August) Abroad in France, Holland and Switzerland as Foreign Assistant Commissioner to the Newcastle Commission on elementary education (9 April) Death of his brother William at Gibraltar (August) Publishes *England and the Italian Question*	Lady Gregory, Francis Thompson, Conan Doyle, A. E. Housman and Havelock Ellis born De Quincey, Leigh Hunt, Lord Macaulay and Henry Hallam die Darwin's *Origin of Species* *Tale of Two Cities* Fitzgerald's *Rubáiyat of Omar Khayyám* George Eliot's *Adam Bede* Lewes's *Physiology of Common Life* Meredith's *Ordeal of Richard Feverel* Mill's *On Liberty* Tennyson's *Idylls of the King* (Enid, Vivien, Elaine, Guinevere) Trollope's *The Bertrams*	War of Italian Liberation Garibaldi in Sicily Franco-Austrian War Derby defeated; Palmerston Prime Minister Gladstone Chancellor of the Exchequer Livingston on Lake Nyassa
1860		James Barrie born Bright's *History of the Church A.D. 313–457* Collins's *Women in White* *Great Expectations* Emerson's *The Conduct of Life* George Eliot's *The Mill on the Floss* Peacock's *Gryll Grange* (*Fraser's Magazine*; separately 1861) W. C. Roscoe's *Poems and Essays*, ed R. H. Hutton Swinburne's *The Queen Mother, Rosamond. Essays and Reviews*, ed H. B. Wilson (Wilson, F. Temple, M. Pattison, R. Williams, Baden Powell, C. W. Goodwin) *Cornhill Magazine* started (Thackeray editor until 1862) Wilberforce–Huxley debate at British Association meeting at Oxford	Cobden Treaty with France Annexation of Savoy Garibaldi in Sicily and Naples Discovery of the source of the Nile
1861	(January) Publishes *On*	G. L. Dickinson,	Victor Emmanuel

1861 (*cont.*)	*Translating Homer* (May) Publishes *The Popular Education of France* (with the introductory essay 'Democracy') (13 November) Death of Clough at Florence	Rabindranath Tagore, Maurice Hewlett and Walter Raleigh born E. B. Browning dies George Eliot's *Silas Marner* T. Hughes's *Tom Brown at Oxford* Mill's *Representative Government* and *Utilitarianism* (*Fraser's Magazine*; separately 1863) Müller's *Science of Languages* Palgrave's *Golden Treasury* (revised and enlarged 1896) Reade's *The Cloister and the Hearth* Stanley's *History of the Eastern Church* Trollope's *Framley Parsonage* Mrs. Henry Wood's *East Lynne*	King of Italy American Civil War (1861–5) Lincoln President of U.S.A. Prince Albert died Elementary Education: Newcastle Commission Elementary Education: Revised Code
1862	(March) Risks official hostility by publishing in *Fraser's Magazine* 'The Twice Revised Code' attacking Robert Lowe's new method of distributing government grants for education ('Payment by Results'). Publishes *On Translating Homer; Last Words*	Henry Newbolt, Eden Phillpotts and M. R. James born Borrow's *Wild Wales* E. B. Browning's *Last Poems*, ed R. Browning Clough's *Collected Poems*, with F. T. Palgrave's Memoir Colenso's *The Pentateuch Examined* (concl. 1879) Collins's *No Name* Derby's translation of *Homer* (*Cornhill Magazine*; separately 1863) George Eliot's *Romola* Meredith's *Modern Love* Christina Rossetti's *Goblin Market and Other Poems* Ruskin's *Unto this Last* Spencer's *A System of Synthetic Philosophy: First Principles*	Colenso controversy Lancashire Cotton Famine (until 1864)

1863		Thackeray and R. Whately die Conington's translation of Horace's *Odes* Gardiner's *History of England*, vols I–II (concl. 1883) Mrs. Gaskell's *Sylvia's Lovers* Huxley's *Man's Place in Nature* Kingslake's *Invasion of the Crimea*, vols I–II (iii–iv, 1868; v, 1875; vi, 1880, vii–viii, 1887) Le Fanu's *The House by the Churchyard* Lyell's *Antiquity of Man* Renan's *La Vie de Jésus*	Lincoln's Gettysburg Address
1864	(June) Publishes *A French Eton.* Most of his work from now on appears in magazines before being published in book form	W. S. Landor, John Clare and Nathaniel Hawthorne die Browning's *Dramatis Personae* *Our Mutual Friend* (monthly parts 1864–5; collected 1865) Mrs. Gaskell's *Cousin Phillis and Other Tales* Le Fanu's *Uncle Silas* Praed's *Poetical Works*, ed D. Coleridge Tennyson's *Enoch Arden* Trollope's *The Small House at Allington* and *Can You Forgive Her?*	Geneva Convention Schleswig-Holstein Public Schools Commission
1865	(February) Publishes *Essays in Criticism* (First Series) (April–November) Abroad in France, Italy, Germany and Switzerland as Foreign Assistant Commissioner to the Taunton (*Schools Enquiry*) Commission	Yeats, Rudyard Kipling and L. Housman born Mrs. Gaskell dies Clough's *Letters and Remains* Lecky's *Rise and Influence of the Spirit of Rationalism in Europe* *Alice in Wonderland* Ruskin's *Sesame and Lilies* Swinburne's *Atalanta in Calydon* Whitman's *Drum-Taps* *Fortnightly Review* started	Abraham Lincoln assassinated Fenian Conspiracy Insurrection in Jamaica Union Rating Act

1866	(March) Applies unsuccessfully to be appointed a Charity Commissioner (April) Publishes 'Thyrsis', his elegy on Clough, in *Macmillan's Magazine*	H. G. Wells and Gilbert Murray born Peacock, John Keble and Jane Welsh Carlyle die Collins's *Armadale* E. S. Dallas's *The Gay Science* Mrs. Gaskell's *Wives and Daughters* George Eliot's *Felix Holt* Kingsley's *Hereward the Wake* Ruskin's *Crown of Wild Olive* Swinburne's *Poems and Ballads, 1st Series* Trollope's *The Belton Estate* *Contemporary Review* started	Hyde Park riots Suspension of Habeas Corpus Act (Ireland)
1867	(April) Applies unsuccessfully for the Librarianship of the House of Commons (June) Publishes *On the Study of Celtic Literature* (July) Publishes *New Poems* (including 'Empedocles on Etna', reprinted at Browning's wish, for the first time since 1852) From this time forward writes very little verse, is increasingly widely known for his controversial social and religious writings	Arnold Bennett, G. W. Russell, Lionel Johnson and John Galsworthy born Baudelaire dies Bagehot's *English Constitution* Carlyle's *Shooting Niagara* (in *Macmillan's Magazine*) Froude's *Short Studies on Great Subjects* I (ii, 1871; iii, 1877; iv, 1883) Morris's *Life and Death of Jason* Pater's *Essay on Winckelmann (Westminster Review)* Thackeray's *Collected Works* Trollope's *Last Chronicles of Barset* and *The Claverings*	Reform Act Disraeli Prime Minister Trial of Fenians at Manchester Marx's *Kapital*, I
1868	(January) Death of his infant son Basil (April) Moves to Byron House, Harrow (November) Death of his eldest son Thomas, aged sixteen, then a Harrow schoolboy	Louisa Alcott, *Little Women* Browning's *The Ring and the Book* Collins's *The Moonstone* Dilke's *Greater Britain* George Eliot's *Spanish Gypsy* Morris's *Earthly Paradise* I (II, 1869) Queen Victoria's *Leaves*	Prosecution of Governor Eyre Abyssinian Campaign Gladstone Prime Minister

1868 (*cont.*)		*from a Journal of our Life in the Highlands* F. J. Furnivall founds The Ballad and Chaucer Societies Royal Historical Society founded	
1869	(January) Publishes *Culture and Anarchy*, his chief work in social criticism (June) Publishes the first collected edition of his *Poems* (two volumes) Applies unsuccessfully for appointment as one of the three Commissioners under the Endowed Schools Act (October) Publishes his essay on *'Obermann'* in *The Academy* (13 October) Death of Sainte-Beuve (November) Publishes his essay 'Sainte-Beuve' in *The Academy*	Laurence Binyon born Lamartine dies Blackmore's *Lorna Doone* Clough's *Poems and Prose Remains, with Selection from Letters*, ed by his wife Lecky's *History of European Morals* Mill's *On the Subjection of Women* Tennyson's *Holy Grail and Other Poems* Trollope's *Phineas Finn* *Nature* and *The Academy* started	Irish Church Act Vatican Council Girton College founded
1870	(May) Publishes *St. Paul and Protestantism* (June) Receives the Honorary Degree of D.C.L. at Oxford Promoted Senior Inspector of Schools during this year	T. Sturge Moore and Hilaire Belloc born Charles Dickens dies *Mystery of Edwin Drood* Disraeli's *Lothair* Emerson's *Society and Solitude* Huxley's *Lay Sermons* Morris's translation (with E. Magnússon) of *The Volsunga Saga* Rossetti's *Poems* Ruskin's *Lectures on Art* Spencer's *Principles of Psychology* Brewer's *Dictionary of Phrase and Fable*	Franco-German War, 1870–1 Irish Land Act Fenian Amnesty Elementary Education Act First School Board Election—Mrs. Garrett Anderson and Miss Emily Davies elected Civil Service thrown open
1871	(February) Publishes *Friendship's Garland*, a series of letters 'half serious, half playful' on English life and culture	J. M. Synge, W. H. Davies, Erskine Childers and Marcel Proust born George Grote dies Darwin's *Descent of Man*	Tichborne Case Voysey Case Founding of Newnham College Abolition of religious

1871 (*cont.*)	originally contributed to the *Pall Mall Gazette* (1866–7, 1869–70) (August) Visits France and Switzerland with his wife and his son Richard	George Eliot's *Middlemarch* (in parts; collected 1872) Hardy's *Desperate Remedies* R. H. Hutton's *Essays* Jowett's translation of *The Dialogues of Plato* Lear's *Nonsense Songs and Stories* *Through the Looking Glass* Meredith's *Harry Richmond* Ruskin's *Fors Clavigera* (concl. 1887) Swinburne's *Songs before Sunrise* Whitman's *Democratic Vistas* and *Passage to India*	tests at Oxford, Cambridge and Durham
1872	(February) Death of his son William Trevenen, aged eighteen	Bertrand Russell and Max Beerbohm born E. D. Maurice and C. J. Lever die Browning's *Fifine at the Fair* Forster's *Life of Dickens* Hardy's *Under the Greenwood Tree* Macdonald's *The Princess and the Goblin* Winwood Reade's *The Martyrdom of Man* Tennyson's *Gareth and Lynette*; collected *Poems*	Ballot Act
1873	(February) Publishes *Literature and Dogma*, the most important of his writings on religion (February–May) Spends a holiday leave from school-inspection with his wife in Italy (June) Moves to Pains Hill Cottage, Cobham, Surrey (30 November) Death of his mother at Fox How	Walter de la Mare born John Stuart Mill, Bulwer Lytton and Samuel Wilberforce die J. C. Maxwell's *Treatise on Electricity and Magnetism* Mill's *Autobiography* Morley's *Rousseau* Pater's *Studies in the Renaissance* J. F. Stephen's *Liberty, Equality, Fraternity* Leslie Stephen's *Essays on Freethinking and Plain Speaking* Stubbs's *Constitutional History of England* (concl. 1878)	Remington type-writer manufactured

1873 (*cont.*)		Trollope's *Phineas Redux* and *The Eustace Diamonds* Tyndall's *Lectures on Light*	
1874		Maurice Baring, G. K. Chesterton, Somerset Maugham and Gertrude Stein born Farrar's *Life of Christ* Green's *Short History of the English People* Greville's *Memoirs* I (ii, 1885; iii, 1887) Hardy's *Far from the Madding Crowd* Jevons's *Principles of Science* Lewes's *Problems of Life and Mind* Stephen's *Hours in a Library* Series I (ii, 1876; iii, 1879) Thomson's *The City of Dreadful Night* (in *National Reformer*, March–May; separate, with other poems, 1880) D. Wordsworth's *Recollections of a Tour in Scotland* (1803), ed Shairp	Ashantee War Indian famine Disraeli Prime Minister Public Worship Regulation Act
1875	(November) Publishes *God and the Bible*, a review of objections to *Literature and Dogma*	Charles Kingsley and Sir Charles Lyell die Martin's and Aytoun's *Life of the Prince Consort* Morris's translation of Virgil's *Aeneid* and (with E. Magnússon) *Three Northern Love-Stories from Icelandic* W. B. Scott's *Poems*, etc. Swinburne's *Essays and Studies* Symonds's *Renaissance in Italy* Tennyson's *Queen Mary* Trollope's *The Way We Live Now*	Visit of Prince of Wales to India Acts for Amending Labour Laws
1876	(9 June) Death of George Sand (December) Reprints 'The New Sirens' in *Macmillan's Magazine*	G. M. Trevelyan born Harriet Martineau and John Forster die Thomas Arnold's edition of *Beowulf*	Bulgarian Atrocities

1876 (*cont.*)		F. H. Bradley's *Ethical Studies* Bridges's *The Growth of Love* Fitzgerald's translation of Aeschylus's *Agamemnon* George Eliot's *Daniel Deronda* H. James's *Roderick Hudson* Melville's *Clarel* Spencer's *Principles of Sociology* i (ii, 1882; iii, 1896) L. Stephen's *English Thought in the Eighteenth Century* Swinburne's *Eretheus* Tennyson's *Harold* Trevelyan's *Life of Macaulay* Trollope's *The Prime Minister*	
1877	(February) Declines re-nomination for the Professorship of Poetry at Oxford (March) Publishes *Last Essays on Church and Religion* (April–May) Portrayed as 'Mr. Luke' in W. H. Mallock's *The New Republic* (June) Publishes his essay 'George Sand' in *The Fortnightly Review* (November) Declines nomination for the Lord Rectorship of St. Andrew's University	Walter Bagehot dies H. James's *The American* Mallock's *The New Republic* H. Martineau's *Autobiography* Meredith's *Idea of Comedy* (*New Quarterly Magazine*; separately 1897) Patmore's *The Unknown Eros and Other Poems* A. Sewell's *Black Beauty* Swinburne's *Charlotte Brontë* *Truth* and *Nineteenth Century* started Ibsen's *Pillars of Society*	Queen Victoria becomes Empress of India Annexation of Transvaal Russo-Turkish War, 1877–8
1878	(June) Publishes *Selected Poems of Matthew Arnold* (Golden Treasury Series)	John Masefield and Edward Thomas born G. H. Lewes dies C. & M. Cowden Clarke's *Recollections of Writers* Grove's *Dictionary of Music* (completed 1889) Hardy's *The Return of the Native* H. James's *Watch and Ward*	Berlin Congress Afghan War

<table>
<tr><td>1878
(cont.)</td><td></td><td>Keats's Letters to Fanny Brawne, ed H. B. Forman
Lecky's History of England in the 18th Century (to 1890)
Martin's translation of Heine's Poems and Ballads
M. Müller's Origin and Growth of Religion
Morley's Diderot and the Encyclopaedists
Senior's Conversations with Thiers, Guizot, and Other Persons during the Second Empire
Stanley's Through the Dark Continent
L. Stephen's Samuel Johnson [the first in the English Men of Letters Series]
Stevenson's An Inland Voyage
Swinburne's Poems and Ballads, 2nd Series
Trollope's Is he Popenjoy?
Wallace's Tropical Nature</td><td></td></tr>
<tr><td>1879</td><td>(c. March) Publishes Mixed Essays
(August) Publishes his selected Poems of Wordsworth</td><td>E. M. Forster and Harold Monro born
Bagehot's Literary Studies, ed R. H. Hutton
Balfour's A Defence of Philosophic Doubt
Bridges's Poems
Huxley's David Hume
H. James's Daisy Miller, The Europeans, Hawthorne
Lang's and Butcher's translation of the Odyssey
Meredith's The Egoist
Morley's Edmund Burke
Pattison's Milton
Ibsen's A Doll's House</td><td>Zulu War</td></tr>
<tr><td>1880</td><td>(12 May) Attends the reception in London given in honour of Cardinal Newman by the Duke of Norfolk 'because I wanted to have spoken once in my life to Newman'</td><td>Lytton Strachey and Alfred Noyes born
George Eliot dies
Baring-Gould's Mehalah
George's Progress and Poverty
Hardy's The Trumpet Major
Shorthouse's John Inglesant
L. Stephen's Alexander Pope</td><td>Gladstone Prime Minister
Bradlaugh's Claim to Affirm</td></tr>
</table>

1880 (*cont.*)	(September) Visits Switzerland and Italy on holiday Contributes three essays—'Introduction' (later called 'On the Study of Poetry'), 'Thomas Gray' and 'John Keats' to T. H. Ward's *The English Poets* W. E. Forster, Arnold's brother-in-law, appointed Chief Secretary for Ireland by Gladstone. (Resigned 1882, shortly before the Phoenix Park Murders)	Tennyson's *Ballads and Other Poems* L. Wallace's *Ben Hur*	
1881	(June) Publishes his selected *Poetry of Byron* (18 July) Death of A. P. Stanley, Dean of Westminster	P. G. Wodehouse and Lascelles Abercrombie born Carlyle, Disraeli and George Borrow die Carlyle's *Reminiscences*, ed J. A. Froude Conway's *Carlyle* Cox's *Introduction to the Science of Comparative Mythology* H. James's *The Portrait of a Lady* 'Mark Rutherford's' *Autobiography of Mark Rutherford* Morley's *Life of Cobden* C. Rossetti's *A Pagent, and Other Poems* D. G. Rossetti's *Ballads and Sonnets* Swinburne's *Mary Stuart, A Tragedy* Wilde's *Poems* *Revised Version of the New Testament* Ibsen's *Ghosts*	Irish Land Act Married Woman's Property Act
1882	(January) Publishes 'Westminster Abbey', his elegy on Stanley, in *The Nineteenth Century* (March) Publishes *Irish Essays*	James Joyce, James Stephens and John Drinkwater born Darwin, D. G. Rossetti, Trollope, Emerson and Longfellow die	Phoenix Park Murders Bombardment of Alexandria

1882 (*cont.*)		Anstey's *Vice Versa* Besant's *All Sorts and Conditions of Men* Froude's *History of the First Forty Years of Carlyle's Life* (his *Carlyle's Life in London*, 1884) Morley's *Reminscences, chiefly of Oriel and the Oxford Movement* Stevenson's *Familiar Studies of Men and Books, Treasure Island, New Arabian Nights* Swinburne's *Tristram of Lyonesse, and Other Poems*	
1883	(August) Accepts Civil List pension of £250 a year 'in public recognition of service to the poetry and literature of England' (October) Arrives in the U.S.A. to begin a lecture-tour lasting until March 1884	Edward Fitzgerald dies Bradley's *Principles of Logic* Jane Welsh Carlyle's *Letters and Memorials*, prepared by T. Carlyle, ed J. A. Froude Carlyle's correspondence with Emerson Galton's *Inquiries into Human Faculty* Macdonald's *The Princess and Curdie* O. Schreiner's *The Story of an African Farm* Shaw's *An Unsocial Socialist* Sidgwick's *Political Economy* Trollope's *Autobiography*	Fabian Society founded
1884	Becomes Chief Inspector of Schools	James Elroy Flecker, Hugh Walpole and J. C. Squire born Charles Reade and Mark Pattison die Dixon's *Odes and Eclogues* Cross's *Life of George Eliot* Moore's *A Mummer's Wife* Rogers's *Six Centuries of Work and Wages* Toynbee's *Industrial Revolution* Twain's *The Adventures of Huckleberry Finn* Oxford English Dictionary begins to appear (completed 1928)	Royal Commission on Housing of the Poor Franchise Bill

1884 (*cont.*)		Revision version of the Old Testament	
1885	(June) Publishes *Discourses in America* (*c.* August) Publishes three-volume collected edition of *Poems* (Library Edition) (October) Again declines re-nomination for the Professorship of Poetry at Oxford (in spite of a memorial from Oxford heads of colleges and tutors, and another from four hundred under-graduates). 'Everyone is very kind as one grows old . . .' (November–December) Abroad in Germany for the Royal Commission on Education	D. H. Lawrence and Ezra Pound born Monckton Milnes dies Burton's translation of *The Arabian Nights* (privately printed; revised 'for household reading', 1887–8) Haggard's *King Solomon's Mines* J. Martineau's *Types of Ethical Theory* Meredith's *Diana of the Crossways* Pater's *Marius the Epicurean* Ruskin's *Praeterita* (concl. 1889) *Dictionary of National Biography* (ed L. Stephen until 1891, Sidney Lee 1891ff.)	Fall of Khartoum Salisbury Prime Minister
1886	(February–March) Abroad again in France, Switzerland and Germany for the Royal Commission on Education (30 April) Retires from Inspectorship of Schools (May–August) Second visit to U.S.A.	Lennox Robinson and Siegfried Sassoon born Dowden's *Life of Shelley* Froude's *Oceana* Hardy's *Mayor of Casterbridge* H. James's *The Bostonians* and *The Princess Casamassima* Kipling's *Departmental Ditties* Maine's *Popular Government* D. G. Rossetti's *Collected Works*, ed W. M. Rossetti Stevenson's *Dr. Jekyll and Mr. Hyde*, *Kidnapped* and *The Merry Men and Other Tales* Stubb's *Lectures on the Study of History* Swinburne's *A Study of Victor Hugo* and *Miscellanies* Tennyson's *Locksley Hall, sixty years after, Promise of May, and Other Poems* Ward's *Psychology* Shelley Society founded	Gladstone Prime Minister Home Rule Bill Liberal split Salisbury Prime Minister Lord Randolph Churchill's resignation

1887		Rupert Brooke and Edith Sitwell born Carlyle's *Early Letters* and *Correspondence with Goethe*, ed Norton Darwin's *Life and Letters, with Autobiography*, ed F. Darwin Conan Doyle's *A Study in Scarlet* Haggard's *Allan Quartermain* Hill's edition of Boswell's *Life of Johnson* Lang's *Myth, Ritual and Religion* 'Mark Rutherford's' *Revolution in Tanner's Lane* Pater's *Imaginary Portraits* Saintsbury's *Elizabethan Literature* Swinburne's *Locrine, a Tragedy*, *The Question*, *Selections from Poems*	Queen's Jubilee Trafalgar Square riots Independent Labour Party
1888	(15 April) Dies suddenly of heart failure at Liverpool while awaiting the arrival of his married daughter from America (November) Posthumous publication of *Essays in Criticism* (Second Series)	T. S. Eliot and Katherine Mansfield born Edward Lear dies Allingham's *Poetical Works* Doughty's *Travels in Arabia Deserta* Hardy's *Wessex Tales* H. James's *The Reverberator* and *Partial Portraits* Kipling's *Soldiers Three* and *Plain Tales from the Hills* Moore's *Confessions of a Young Man* Morris's *Dream of John Ball* Quiller Couch's *Troy Town* Rogers's *Economic Interpretation of History* Stevenson's *Black Arrow* Wilde's *The Happy Prince and Other Tales* Wordsworth's *The Recluse* Yeats's *Fairy and Folk Tales of the Irish Peasantry*	Death of William, German Emperor Parnell Commission

1: *A Reader's Guide to Arnold*

FRASER NEIMAN

I

IN THE 1970s we cannot quite yet say of Matthew Arnold as Dr. Johnson could of Shakespeare, 'He has long outlived his century.' Nor would we wish to write that he has begun 'to assume the dignity of an ancient, and claim the privilege of established fame and prescriptive veneration'; for the language of Johnson, whose sanity, reasonableness, and humaneness Arnold frequently recalls, suggests an embalming and entombment from which Arnold perennially escapes. His sense for life was triumphant although his capacity for melancholy was profound. His commitment to the force of mind compelled him to engage vigorously in diverse issues of his century, and the vivacity with which he expressed his concern has been a cause for freshly discerning appraisals through at least three generations of critical readers since his death in 1888.

Born in 1822, Arnold as a young man poignantly articulated in his verse the dilemma of the romantic idealist confronted in an iron age with conflicting, shifting, and disintegrating values; he emerged from his deeply-felt poetic questing to assert the transforming power for society of intelligence employed in the service of reason; for almost a decade in his middle years he stressed his increased personal sense of the noumenal in human experience, of the 'something not ourselves' that he believed gave coherence and continuity to civilization; in his late years he closely observed and commented on England's unhappy relations with Ireland, and, having returned from a successful lecture tour in the United States, he prepared for the press two final books of criticism expressive of his sense of the profound relation between literature and life. Although emphasis, tone, and media altered during forty active public years, Arnold continuously enjoined 'Two blending duties, harmonis'd in one': the individual interior search for sanctions of action, and the obligation to act for the civilizing of society.[1] For Arnold, as for Milton, the poet must assume responsibilities as a citizen. Arnold began his inaugural lecture in 1857 as Professor of Poetry at Oxford with an anecdote of the Buddha that expressed his own sense of responsibility. The Buddha enjoined his disciple: 'Go then, O Pourna; having been delivered, deliver; having been consoled, console; being arrived thyself at the farther bank, enable others to arrive there also.'[2] These words also convey Arnold's intuition that social and intellectual gains begin in the 'buried life' of the individual.

In professional or public roles Arnold was variously a poet, the private secretary to a Liberal peer, an Inspector of Schools, a commissioner in the examining of educational systems at home and on the Continent, a Professor of Poetry at Oxford, a reviewer of books for numerous periodicals, a literary critic, a critic of social, political, and religious issues, a critic of England's relations with Italy in 1859, with Ireland in the 1880s, and an interested observer of the mental climate of the United States. To note the chapter headings of this volume is to perceive only a few of the plausible directions from which he may be approached, for, in addition, Arnold and Celtic literature, Arnold and education, Arnold and France, Arnold and race, Arnold and the Romantics, Arnold and the social classes, Arnold and the United States have all been the subject of extended and enlightening investigation.[3] Moreover, the juxtaposition of Arnold in comparative studies with such fellow countrymen as Burke, Carlyle, John Stuart Mill, John

[1] 'Quiet Work', *PW*, 1 (see Bibliography). The reading of the line quoted is that of 1849.

[2] 'On the Modern Element in Literature', *CPW*, I, 19. This edition (see Bibliography) will be completed in eleven volumes, of which the tenth was published in 1974.

[3] R. Bromwich, *Matthew Arnold and Celtic Literature: A Retrospect 1865–1965*, Oxford 1965; W. F. Connell, *The Educational Thought and Influence of Matthew Arnold*, London 1950; F. J. W. Harding, *Matthew Arnold the Critic and France*, Geneva 1965; F. E. Faverty, *Matthew Arnold, the Ethnologist*, Evanston, Illinois 1951; L. Gottfried, *Matthew Arnold and the Romantics*, London 1963; P. J. McCarthy, *Matthew Arnold and the Three Classes*, New York and London 1964; J. H. Raleigh, *Matthew Arnold and American Culture*, Berkeley, California 1957.

Henry Newman, and Walter Pater further indicates points at which his thought derives from, or illuminates, or influences that of diverse individuals who shaped the Victorian world of mind and feeling.[1] Dispraised by F. H. Bradley who thought his relation of happiness to virtue to be 'clap-trap', by Lytton Strachey who thought he shared a Victorian 'innate incapacity for penetration' of anything, by T. S. Eliot who thought him in philosophy and theology 'an undergraduate; in religion a Philistine', by Alan Tate who found his analytical powers 'simple', his critical theory, in comparison with that of Coleridge, 'elementary', Arnold remains central to our apprehension of his age, and to our own critical experience.

In an early letter to his sister Jane, presumably in reaction to *The Strayed Reveller and Other Poems* (1849), Arnold wrote, '. . . a person who has any inward completeness can at best only like parts of them; in fact such a person stands firmly and knows what he is about while the poems stagger weakly & are at their wits end'.[2] The Hamlet-like irresoluteness suggested in that final phrase by the poet's identification of himself with his poems also manifested itself in the constructive sympathy with which he could enter into the powerful sentiment of Burke and Newman for the order of tradition, into the Romantic epistemology of Wordsworth and Carlyle for the authority of feeling, as well as into the scepticism of Lucretius or of nineteenth-century religious doubters. Arnold's dilemma was that he recognized the world of Hegel and that of Spinoza. His sense for the relative and the flux finds expression in poems of estrangement and alienation—'The

[1] R. C. Tobias, 'Matthew Arnold and Edmund Burke', University Microfilms, Ann Arbor, Michigan 1958; E. Alexander, *Matthew Arnold and John Stuart Mill*, New York and London 1965; D. J. DeLaura, *Hebrew and Hellene in Victorian England: Newman, Arnold, and Pater*, Austin, Texas, and London 1969; K. Tillotson, 'Matthew Arnold and Carlyle', Warton Lecture on English Poetry, *Proceedings of the British Academy* XLII, 1956, 133–53, repr. in G. and K. Tillotson, *Mid-Victorian Studies*, 1965; W. A. Madden, *Matthew Arnold: A Study of the Aesthetic Temperament in Victorian England*, Bloomington, Indiana 1967; E. Alexander, *Matthew Arnold, John Ruskin and the Modern Temper*, Columbus, Ohio 1973.

[2] *Unpublished Letters of Matthew Arnold*, 18. W. E. Houghton and G. R. Stange plausibly assign the letter to 1849 in *Victorian Poetry and Poetics*, Boston 1959, 547, n 10.

Forsaken Merman' comes to mind, and 'To Marguerite—Continued'. His sense for the relative and the flux provides half the impulse for the quest in poems like 'The Scholar Gipsy' or 'Thyrsis', and for the tragic contingency of 'Tristram and Iseult' or 'Sohrab and Rustum'; it lies behind the gloom of 'Dover Beach'. But the affirmations of the poems of quest and tragic contingency, and of 'Dover Beach', express Arnold's concomitant insight into human values that transcend change. Ultimately Arnold found a stabilizing centre in his conviction of the absoluteness of ethical values. More compassionate than Stoicism, more aesthetically generous than a puritanical Protestantism, Arnold's conviction led him to emphasize his awareness in interrelated ways: for example, in the importance of choosing an 'excellent' human action for poetry, of recognizing the 'moral effects' of the 'grand style' in criticism, and in perceiving, in the sphere of human relations, that 'conduct, not culture, is three-fourths of human life'.[1] This is his Plotinian centre where, to borrow Yeats's lines, '. . . all the gyres converge in one', where 'all the planets drop in the Sun'.

Arnold's centrality to our understanding of his age resides partly in the range of his interests, partly in the seriousness with which he sought answers to his questionings, and partly also in his feeling for the unitary character of European culture. 'He has assimilated certain continental ways of looking at things,' the young Henry James said of him in 1884; 'his style has a kind of European accent.'[2] Arnold possessed in a more flexible way than his eminent father the humanizing quality of cosmopolitanism that he thought distinguished Dr. Thomas Arnold of Rugby from the insularity and parochialism of 'his set'. The names of Goethe, Heine, George Sand, Sainte-Beuve enter as familiarly into his writings as those of Wordsworth or Byron or Shelley or Keats, or those of Homer, Sophocles, Lucretius, or Marcus Aurelius; and in December 1887 he published a review of Tolstoy's contemporary *Anna Karenina* (1875–6), a novel congenial to him in showing 'the failure of science to tell a man what his life means'.[3] Arnold's interest in authors remote from him in time or in place was in what, at least in the 1960s, would have been called their 'relevance'. For him, to be relevant was to be 'modern', for modernity has more to do with a cast of mind, with

[1] *Literature and Dogma, CPW*, VI, 407.

[2] 'Matthew Arnold', *English Illustrated Magazine*, I, January 1884, 242.

[3] *Essays in Criticism, Second Series, Works*, IV, 211.

sanity and cosmopolitanism, than with chronology. He insisted in 1857 in the inaugural lecture at Oxford that Thucydides is more modern than Sir Walter Raleigh, because he used a language that expressed the greater critical intelligence manifest in Periclean Athens than in Elizabethan England.[1] There is of course more than a little gamesmanship in Arnold's comparison here, and there is an element in this lecture of the polemical that enlivens much of his criticism; but in essence he is arguing that those writers, comprising a timeless community, are modern who through intelligence free a man from his local prejudices whether of manners or of cosmologies.

Arnold's gamesmanship in the essays comprises a large element of their interest for the reader. His strategies rejoiced, when they did not exasperate, many of his contemporaries, as they do us. Sometimes they did both. Yet the reader will not go far in Arnold who does not enjoy the games, who cannot perceive, for example, in 'The Function of Criticism at the Present Time', the weight for Arnold's severe indictment of society that resides in his play with the phrase 'Wragg is in custody' (*CPW*, III, 273). And the reader who will not be amused in the same essay by Arnold's sport with the grotesquerie of Anglo-Saxon names—'Higginbottom, Stiggins, Bugg!'—or in *Culture and Anarchy* with Mrs. Gooch's Golden Rule—'Ever remember, my dear Dan, that you should look forward to being some day manager of that concern!'—or who feels chauvinistic outrage at Arnold's occasional condescension, must remain at the threshold of Arnold's work. Happily the modern reader has an admirable guide to Arnold's resources of rhetoric in John Holloway's *The Victorian Sage* (1953), the publication of which twenty years ago marked a fresh direction in the critical approach to Victorian prose.[2]

[1] *CPW*, I, 26. With a different strategy at work Arnold praised Elizabethan England saying, 'If England were swallowed up by the sea tomorrow, which of the two, a hundred years hence, would most excite the love, interest, and admiration of mankind,—would most, therefore, show the evidences of having possessed greatness,—the England of the last twenty years, or the England of Elizabeth, of a time of splendid spiritual effort, but when our coal, and our industrial operations depending on coal, were very little developed?' *Culture and Anarchy, CPW*, V, 97.

[2] *The Victorian Sage: Studies in Argument*, London, 1953. See also Geoffrey

Although a sharpened awareness of strategies will increase the pleasures of the reader, it is only candid to admit in Arnold failures of tone—and occasional failures of sensitivity. We may think, for an example, of the imperious exhortation, quoted from Dante's Ulysses, that concludes his address at the Ipswich Working Men's College: 'Consider whereunto ye are born! Ye were not made to live like brutes, but to follow virtue and knowledge.'[1] Or for a second instance, there is Arnold's uneasiness about the popular, as contrasted with the 'higher', literature and art of France in the 1880s, which elicited the prim remark: 'And therefore, even though a gifted man like M. Renan may be so carried away by the tide of opinion in France where he lives, as to say that Nature cares nothing about chastity, and to see with amused indulgence the worship of the great goddess Lubricity, let us stand fast, and say that her worship is against nature, human nature, and that it is ruin.'[2]

On the other hand, hardly have we read with some uneasiness in *Culture and Anarchy* how the 'self-confident liberalism of the last thirty years' may have been conquered by 'the sentiment of Oxford for beauty and sweetness', or how 'the sterner self of the Populace likes bawling, hustling, and smashing; the lighter self, beer. But in each class there are born a certain number of natures with a curiosity about their best self . . . ; for the pursuit, in a word, of perfection,' and wondered how far culture is to be equated with an academic amenity, when we

Tillotson, 'Matthew Arnold's Prose: Theory and Practice' in *The Art of Victorian Prose*, ed G. Levine and W. Madden, New York 1968. Section III of Tillotson's essay is included in *Matthew Arnold: A Collection of Critical Essays*, ed D. J. DeLaura, Twentieth Century Views, Englewood Cliffs, New Jersey 1973.

[1] 'Ecce, Convertimur ad Gentes', *Last Essays on Church and Religion*, *CPW*, IX, 19.

[2] 'Numbers', *CPW*, X, 159–60 (*Discourses in America*, *Works*, IV, 309). My own copy of this essay bears the marginal injunction—or was it only an *aide mémoire*?—of a Bryn Mawr College student of 1904, 'Must stand ag Lubricity.'

William Allingham recorded in his diary (8 August 1880) a remark of Tennyson: 'I was asked by some one in London, "Shall I ask M.A.?" I said I didn't much like dining with Gods!' *William Allingham's Diary*, ed Geoffrey Grigson, Fontwell 1967, 288.

are recalled to the force of Arnold's humane social sympathy. Quoting the awesome self-serving texts *'Be fruitful and multiply'* and *'The poor shall never cease out of the land'*, Arnold grimly continues, 'Thus Hebraism is conducted to nearly the same notion as the popular mind and as Mr. Robert Buchanan, that children are *sent*, and that the divine nature takes a delight in swarming the East End of London with paupers. Only, when they are perishing in their helplessness and wretchedness, it asserts the Christian duty of succouring them, instead of saying, like the *Times*: "Now their brief spring is over; there is nobody to blame for this; it is the result of Nature's simplest laws!"' (*CPW*, V, 217). And we may recall his concern with 'the many' in the essay 'Equality' (1878): 'No individual life can be truly prosperous, passed, as Obermann says, in the midst of men who suffer; *passée au milieu des générations qui souffrent'* (*CPW*, VIII, 289).

Logan Pearsall Smith, an admiring young disciple who discovered Arnold upon arriving at Harvard College in 1884, attests to his sense of Arnold's humaneness and his derisiveness in language, his urbanity and his harsh ridicule towards evangelicalism and Dissent. He concludes his balanced summary with the interesting reflection: ' . . . what delighted me most of all was his attribution of an arrogant superiority, an exclusive kind of distinction to that culture, that sweetness and light, which now for the flimsiest reasons I believed that I had attained. But it was not only the attainment of culture for oneself, but the diffusion of it, which Matthew Arnold preached, and this part of his doctrine was most of all an inspiration to me.'[1]

A few months after Arnold's 'Culture and Its Enemies' (soon to be revised as 'Sweetness and Light', the first chapter of *Culture and Anarchy*) appeared in the *Cornhill Magazine* (July 1867), Frederic Harrison responded to the tone of preciosity in the essay. In a shrewdly witty satire, 'Culture: A Dialogue' in the *Fortnightly Review* (November 1867), the innocent visitor Arminius meets the insouciant Arnoldian reporter of their encounter:

'But how does it [culture] recognize these [human ideals],' he

[1] *Unforgotten Years*, Boston 1939, 125. Smith completed his own cosmopolitan acculturation as a friend of Henry James, Jr., and George Santayana, and as brother-in-law to Bertrand Russell and Bernard Berenson.

asked helplessly, evidently now striking at random, 'if it has neither system, method, nor logic?'

'By Insight,' I replied triumphantly; 'by its own inborn sensibility to beauty, truth, and life.'

'But if a man is born without it?' he asked.

'God help him then,' I rejoined, 'for I cannot'; and as Arminius was still silent, I hummed gaily to myself, 'Sordid, unfeeling, reprobate, degraded, spiritless outcast'; and indeed there are but too many in that plight.[1]

Frederic Harrison himself saw well beyond the invitation that Arnold afforded for satire. He understood his important talent for phrasemaking—phrases more numerous, he noted, even than Disraeli's, 'more simple and apt' than Carlyle's. 'The very name of Matthew Arnold', he said, 'calls up to memory a set of apt phrases and proverbial labels which have passed into our current literature, and are most happily redolent of his own peculiar turn of thought. How could modern criticism be carried on were it forbidden to speak of "culture", of "urbanity", of "Philistinism", of "distinction", of "the *note* of provinciality", of "the great style"?'[2] Harrison understood the importance of Arnold's phrases beyond their mere currency. 'They are', he said, 'generative, efficient, and issue into act.'

For the present generation of readers literary criticism is the area in

[1] *The Choice of Books and Other Literary Pieces*, London 1886, 109. Arnold wrote to Lady de Rothschild, 30 October 1867, 'You will be amused, as I have been, with Mr. Harrison's answer to me in the *Fortnightly*. It is scarcely the least vicious, and in parts so amusing that I laughed till I cried.' *Letters*, I, 372.

The other classic contemporary satire of Arnold's occasional over-refinement of tone is W. H. Mallock's *The New Republic; or Culture, Faith, and Philosophy in a Country House*, 1877. In the guise of Mr. Luke, Arnold is made to say, 'It is true that culture sets aside the larger part of the New Testament as grotesque, barbarous, and immoral, but what remains, purged of its apparent meaning, it discerns to be a treasure beyond all price' (*The New Republic*, ed J. M. Patrick, Gainesville, Florida 1950, 23–4).

[2] *Tennyson, Ruskin, Mill and Other Literary Estimates*, London and New York 1899, 111. Harrison must have meant the 'grand style'.

which the greatest number of Arnold's phrases continue to be generative, efficient, and active. To follow the reverberations of phrases that have entered into our critical consciousness would be to write a large chapter in the history of modern criticism. The echoes, combinations, and directions are so numerous in the way of approval, or extension, or refutation, that we wonder what literary criticism could do without them. The title itself of 'The Function of Criticism at the Present Time' has reverberated through the titles of books or essays by T. S. Eliot, Alan Tate, F. W. Bateson, F. R. Leavis, to a sound of finality in Robert Langbaum's 'The Function of Criticism, Once More', in each case evoking Arnold's presence.[1]

But let us take one example of the redirections. In the second lecture for his Oxford series *On Translating Homer* (1861) Arnold proposed as the main critical effort of modern Europe 'to see the object as in itself it really is'. Employing a characteristic strategy of quoting himself, he gave further currency to the phrase by making it conspicuously the point of departure for the essay in the *National Review* (1864) that became so importantly 'The Function of Criticism at the Present Time' in the collective *Essays in Criticism* (1865). Perhaps the phrase owed something by way of origin to Sir Joshua Reynolds's *Discourse VII* (1776) to the Royal Academy: 'It is necessary that at some time or other we should see things as they really are . . . '; perhaps it owed something to Carlyle's comment that in time Schiller's 'love of contemplating or painting things as they should be, began to yield to the love of knowing things as they are'.[2] But it is the context that Arnold gave to the phrase that promotes its vitality.

Walter Pater opens the second paragraph of his familiar Preface to

[1] 'The Function of Criticism' (1923) in *Selected Essays, 1917–1932*, 1932; 'The Function of Criticism' in *Reason in Madness*, New York 1940; 'The Function of Criticism at the Present Time', *Essays in Criticism*, III, 1953, 1–27; 'The Responsible Critic, or the Function of Criticism at Any Time' (1953), in *A Selection from Scrutiny*, ed F. R. Leavis (2 vol, Cambridge 1968); *Yale Review*, LIV, 1965, 205–18, rpt. in *The Modern Spirit*, New York 1970. Eliot's title *The Use of Poetry and the Use of Criticism*, 1933, provides another echo.

[2] *The Discourses*, ed Austin Dobson, The World's Classics, London and New York 1907, 93. *The Life of Schiller*, in *The Works of Thomas Carlyle*, Edinburgh Edition, 30 vol, New York 1903–4, XXV, 84.

his *Studies in the History of the Renaissance* (1873): '"To see the object as in itself it really is," has been justly said to be the aim of all true criticism whatever'; and then he moves into his own subjectively relativistic variation, 'and in aesthetic criticism the first step towards seeing one's object as it really is, is to know one's own impression as it really is, to discriminate it, to realize it distinctly'. A little later H. G. Wells combined this concept with the formulas in praise of Sophocles in Arnold's sonnet 'To a Friend'. In his essay on the fiction of George Gissing, he remarked, 'To see life clearly and whole, to see and represent it with absolute self-detachment, with absolute justice, above all with evenly balanced sympathy, is an ambition permitted only to a full-grown man.'[1] Again, T. E. Hulme's well-known formulation in 'Romanticism and Classicism' (1913–14) of the criteria of excellence in art—in opposition in part to Arnold's emphasis on the importance of the choice of the subject—begins: 'There are then two things to distinguish, first the particular faculty of mind to see things as they really are, and apart from the conventional ways in which you have been trained to see them.'[2] And working out his own epistemology in 'The Noble Rider and the Sound of Words' (1942) Wallace Stevens stimulates the reader to retrospective comparison with his proposition, 'Reality is things as they are'.[3]

One might further observe that Stevens concludes this essay with another interesting echo—Arnold's phrase 'the instinct of self-preservation in humanity' from 'The Modern Element in Literature' (*CPW*, I, 29). Arnold employed his phrase to support a rather fantastic explanation for the survival of the works of Aristophanes and the loss of those of Menander. Stevens appears to have adopted it for his definition of the force of mind: 'It is the imagination pressing against the pressure of reality. It seems, in the last analysis, to have something to do with our self-preservation; and that, no doubt, is why the

[1] 'The Novels of Mr. George Gissing', *Contemporary Review*, LXII, August 1897, 195, quoted by G. N. Ray, 'H. G. Wells Tries to Be a Novelist', in *Edwardians and Late Victorians*, ed R. Ellmann, English Institute Essays, New York 1966, 112–13.

[2] *Speculations: Essays on Humanism and the Philosophy of Art*, ed Herbert Read, 1924, 133.

[3] *The Necessary Angel: Essays on Reality and the Imagination*, Vintage Edition, New York 1965, 25.

expression of it, the sound of its words, helps us to live our lives.' Here the context for the phrase is Stevens's conviction of the need for the poet sensitively to make 'affirmations of nobility' and of the relation of poetry to life lived, as well as life perceived. Thus the reader is brought round to Arnold's critical concern not only with 'things as they really are', but with two other vexed and vexing issues, namely, his concept of poetry as a 'magister vitae', or a 'criticism of life', and with the importance of the subject in poetry.

Arnoldian critical phrases infuse modern criticism, bringing his thought into account in exploring issues even when he is not invoked as a supporting witness. Thus a few years ago Murray Krieger pursued some interrelations in his essay 'The Critical Legacy of Matthew Arnold: or, The Strange Brotherhood of T. S. Eliot, I. A. Richards, and Northrop Frye'.[1] The brotherhood is of course not so strange, since Arnold will only with conscious effort be excluded from the work of any English or American critic who possesses a strong sense for the continuity of human society. But there is a touch of charming irony when Susan Sontag pleads for an anti-Arnoldian criticism that will 'reveal the sensuous surface of art without mucking about in it', yet ends her plea with the evocation of Arnold's ghost by allusion to his most famous critical essay: 'The function of criticism should be to show *how it is what it is*, even *that it is what it is*, rather than to show *what it means*.'[2]

In his own phrasing and for his own critical and polemic purposes, Arnold formulated in language that we still cannot resist, critical issues of sincerity, style, form, content, reality, literature and life, that make him a continuing and effective agent. In his essay 'Literature as Knowledge' (1941) Alan Tate said regretfully, 'Arnold is still the great critical influence in the universities, and it is perhaps not an exaggeration of his influence to say that debased Arnold is the main stream of popular appreciation of poetry.'[3] Among the achievements of the New Criticism is its stimulation of a re-examination of Arnoldian critical issues. Sometimes anguished and acrimonious in the process, the

[1] *Southern Review*, new series, V, spring 1969, 457–74; rpt. in *The Modern Spirit: Essays on the Continuity of Nineteenth- and Twentieth-Century Literature*, New York 1970.

[2] *Against Interpretation and Other Essays*, New York 1966, 14.

[3] *On the Limits of Poetry*, New York 1948, 19.

forced reassessment has left Arnold in a central position as poet and critic.

Arnold's niece, Mrs. Humphry Ward, tells how Arnold and his wife on 5 May 1857 came to London from Hampton to await at Charing Cross Station the telegraphed news of the polling at the Oxford Convocation for the Poetry Chair. About 4 p.m. they received from Theodore Walrond a message that has its engaging import for us and for Arnold's future: 'Nothing certain is known, but it is rumoured that you are ahead.'[1]

II

Like the children in the later Victorian intellectual family of Leslie Stephen, the children of Dr. Arnold made an early identification with the adult world through playing at publishing. Clive Bell reports that the Stephen children were devising their 'Hyde Park Gate News' when Virginia was nine; the young Arnolds had their 'Fox How Journal'. Matthew earlier and independently of the other Arnolds is said to have printed by hand his first 'book' for presentation to his father on 15 October 1830.[2]

Arnold's first published works are his two prize poems 'Alaric at Rome', which he recited at Rugby in 1840, and which he chose never to reprint after its Rugby publication, and *Cromwell*, the Newdigate prize poem at Oxford in 1843. This poem likewise Arnold did not himself reprint, although it was included anonymously in *Additions to Prize Poems* (Oxford 1846), and published in a second edition in London in

[1] *A Writer's Recollections*, 2 vol, New York and London 1918, I, 74.

[2] H. F. Lowry, *Matthew Arnold and the Modern Spirit*, Princeton, New Jersey 1941, 5.

The publication of *Buckler* (see Bibliography, p. 319 below) has added greatly to the knowledge of Arnold's close and careful relations with his publishers. The Tinker and Lowry *Commentary* and Allott's edition of the *Poems* (see Bibliography) provide further information on the printing of the poems. In his definitive *Complete Prose Works of Matthew Arnold*, R. H. Super gives for each work an introduction to its intellectual and publishing background, as well as a collection of successive texts, and full annotation. This section of 'A Reader's Guide' provides, then, only a brief chronology of the principal books by Arnold published in his lifetime.

1863. Designed to be read in the Sheldonian Theatre at the Commemoration exercises for the founders of the University, the reading was a casualty to the undergraduate tumult characteristic of the Encaenia ('that absurd scene' Arnold called it in a letter to his mother in 1866), and the Convocation was dissolved.[1] 'What business took place', the *Times* reported on June 29, 'was transacted in dumb show.'

Arnold published his first book of verse, *The Strayed Reveller, and Other Poems*, in 1849. He concealed his identity from the public with the pseudonym 'A'. His friend James Anthony Froude, whose autobiographical novel *The Nemesis of Faith* (1849) was the occasion of his resigning in the same year his fellowship at Oxford, commented on 6 March to Arthur Hugh Clough, 'I admire Matt—to a very great extent. Only I don't see what business he has to parade his calmness and lecture us on resignation when he has never known what a storm is, and doesn't know what he has to resign himself to. . . .'[2]

Roger L. Brooks has pointed out in his article in *Library* (1961) that Arnold contributed to the bibliographical myth of the scarcity of this volume through a note in *Macmillan's Magazine* for December 1876. Reprinting 'The New Sirens' at that time, Arnold said, 'It was published in 1849 in a small volume without my name, was withdrawn along with that volume, and until now has never been reprinted.' Brooks, however, reported eighty-five surviving copies in 1963. Moreover, C. B. Tinker and H. F. Lowry indicate that the withdrawal was not immediate, for *The Strayed Reveller* continued to be advertised as for sale at the end of Arnold's next book, *Empedocles on Etna, and Other Poems* (1852).

The second book likewise identified the author only as 'A'. Important for its content, not for its sales, *Empedocles on Etna*, which reprinted none of the earlier poems, gives evidence of Arnold's great creative activity from 1849 to 1852, for in addition to the long title poem, the volume includes 'Tristram and Iseult' as well as the 'Switzerland' series, 'Memorial Verses', 'The Buried Life', 'Lines Written in Kensington Gardens', and 'Stanzas in Memory of the

[1] *Poems*, 13. For remarks on the T. J. Wise facsimile and the Wise forgery of *Cromwell*, see *Commentary*, 321. Tinker and Lowry indicate (*Commentary*, 325) that the 'real trouble' at the 1843 convocation arose over the awarding of a D.C.L. to the American Minister, Edward Everett.
[2] Cited in *Letters to Clough*, 127 n3.

Author of "Obermann"'. Again sales were slow. Arnold said in the notes to his *New Poems* (1867) that fewer than fifty copies were sold. But this did not deter Longman from bringing out in 1853 under Arnold's own name what was called 'A New Edition' of *Poems*. The nine new poems included 'Sohrab and Rustum' and 'The Scholar-Gipsy'; the designation 'New' edition was justified by the selection of twenty-six poems from the earlier book—among them 'The Strayed Reveller', 'Mycerinus', 'Tristram and Iseult', and 'The Forsaken Merman'. In April Arnold had written to his sister 'K' touching 'Sohrab and Rustum', 'I am occupied with a thing that gives me more pleasure than anything I have ever done yet . . .'; and in May he wrote to his mother expressing satisfaction that his poetry was getting to be known: 'Miss Blackett told Flu [Arnold's wife] that Lord John Russell said, "in his opinion Matthew Arnold was the one rising young poet of the present day"' (*Letters*, I, 29, 30).

The importance of *Poems* (1853) was decisive. Arnold intended to include in it, as Tinker and Lowry indicate, 'all that he cared to acknowledge as his own'; it made public two important new poems; it included a Preface that, although it is not quite a farewell to the writing of poetry, nevertheless marks the beginning of Arnold's role as a major critic. Arnold esteemed the Preface sufficiently to reprint it in the 1854 and 1857 editions of *Poems*, although he did not include it in either series of *Essays in Criticism*. The occasion for the Preface was Arnold's decision to justify his exclusion of 'Empedocles on Etna' from the new collection. Aristotelian in its emphasis on the importance in a poem of 'the action itself, its selection, and construction', the Preface is the occasion also for renouncing the indulgence of a Romantic melancholy and for reinforcing, in 'the confusion of the present times', Schiller's affirmation, 'All art is dedicated to Joy, and there is no higher and no more serious problem than how to make men happy' (*CPW*, I, 2).

A second edition of *Poems* (1854) differed only in the addition of one poem rescued from the 1852 book; a third (1857) contained one new poem. The so-called Second Series of *Poems* (1855) added only 'Balder Dead' and the lyric 'Separation'; otherwise it was composed of revivals from 1849 and 1852. In 1858 Arnold published his academic tragedy *Merope*. On 15 August 1861 Arnold wrote to his mother, 'Tell Fan I must finish off for the present my critical writings between this and forty, and give the next ten years earnestly to poetry. It is my last chance' (*Letters*, I, 142). But with the exception of 'Stanzas from the Grande Chartreuse' (*Fraser's magazine*, 1855). 'Thyrsis' (*Macmillan's Magazine*, 1866), 'Dover Beach', which Kenneth Allott believed was finished by 1851, and 'Rugby Chapel', which was completed by 1860, 'Palladium' and 'Obermann Once More', the 1853 volume of *Poems* represents with a few exceptions the end of the poetic accomplishment that matters.

Arnold's hope persisted beyond 1861. Early in February two years later, he planned six articles with a possible additional one on Joubert and two lectures for Oxford: 'And then there is inspecting. So I have plenty to do. After the summer I mean to lie fallow again for some time, or to busy myself with poetry only' (*Letters*, I, 183). The wished-for ten years were given to other endeavours.

New Poems (1867) contained little that was new, but it reinstated, at Robert Browning's urging, 'Empedocles on Etna'. *New Poems* (1868) was only a new edition. Meanwhile in the United States Ticknor and Fields issued in 1856 a *Poems*, combining as Roger L. Brooks has shown, the 1853 and 1855 volumes, retaining the 1853 preface.

An efficient and practical negotiator with his publishers, Arnold arranged his verse in the categories Narrative and Elegiac and Dramatic and Lyric for a two-volume edition of *Poems* in 1869. For the two-volume 'New and Complete Edition' of 1877 he grouped the poems as Early Poems, Narrative Poems, and Sonnets and Lyric, Dramatic, and Elegiac Poems. 'The poems, as a body of doctrine, gain greatly', Arnold told Alexander Macmillan in May 1869, 'by their new and regular classification.'[1] It is not clear precisely what Arnold meant by his reference to the poems as 'a body of doctrine'. Yet it is certain that at the age of forty-six he thought of his poems as embodying the feelings and intellectual attitudes of a generation, that in his poems from 1849 to 1867 he had caught an image of the *Zeitgeist*. He commented to his mother on June 5, 'My poems represent, on the whole, the main movement of mind of the last quarter of a century, and thus they will probably have their day as people become conscious to themselves of what that movement of mind is, and interested in the literary productions which reflect it' (*Letters*, II, 9). It seems quite probable that the reinstatement of 'Empedocles' owed as much to his

[1] Buckler, 38.

own sense of its expressiveness of the age as to Browning's admiration.

In 1878 Macmillan in London, and Harper and Brothers in New York, issued the highly successful *Selected Poems of Matthew Arnold*. Published in the summer, a new edition was required in England in October 1878; 'We have under 700 out of the 3000', Macmillan reported early in February 1879 (*Buckler*, 51). Arnold arranged for another collected *Poems* in 1881, and again in 1885 for a three-volume edition with three groupings: Early Poems, Narrative Poems, and Sonnets; Lyric and Elegiac Poems; Dramatic and Later Poems. In 1890 Frederick Macmillan completed arrangements with Arnold's widow for the one-volume *Poetical Works of Matthew Arnold* that remained standard for many years.

Through the interest of his employer Lord Lansdowne, President of the Privy Council, Arnold was appointed to an Inspectorship of schools on 14 April 1851; he retired in April 1886. It is salutary to remember that his very active career as man of letters was accomplished in recreative hours won from the continuous and often grinding responsibilities of examining students, teachers, and school conditions, and reporting his findings. Surviving notebooks remind us how rudimentary much was that he was obliged to record. In 1855 at the Limehouse Wesleyan School for boys he observed: 'desks on no regular plan [;] insufficient but repaired walls & ceiling whitewashed. class-room roof has been raised windows made, and ventilation greatly improved. drainage good. a good supply of books has now been obtained [.]' At Margate on 22 July 1857 he noted: '21 boys in cards. only 1 could parse an easy sentence. many had left for summer work. 10 write in copybooks. languid school. 3 new windows. new fittings. new offices[.] slight increase in numbers.' Perhaps it confirmed an intuition about English parochialism to hear the singing at 'Lam and Fla R.S.' (1863):

Of all the tongues from east to west
I love my native tongue the best.

Perhaps it confirmed a sense of the responsibilities of society to note for a General Report (1864): 'parents make farmers of children on Exam$^{\underline{on}}$[.] 4erly payments—cannot be insisted on because the next S. is competing for the child—Ld Hertford at Sudborne—voluntary subscriptions—parents in Bow making 15^{s}/ a week as Dock-Labourers will give 8^{d}/ a week for a child's schooling: well but this is more than they should have to give: it clips their civilization on some other side.'[1] F. G. Walcott in his study *The Origins of 'Culture and Anarchy'* (1970) traces the development of Arnold's social thought to the insights gained through his professional tasks.

It was amidst routine pressures of official employment that Arnold achieved his own identity and celebrity. On 31 July 1861 he said, 'I find people are beginning to know something about *me* myself'—but he added that he was still more often known as his father's son (*Letters*, I, 139).

We can hardly guess what influence Arnold would possess in the present century had he not won in 1857 the election to the Chair of Poetry at Oxford, and in 1862 election for a second five years. (He declined to stand a third time, in favour of younger men.) We would have *England and the Italian Question* (1859), a curiosity of his political interests in 1859, and the major reports stemming from his work on the Newcastle and other commissions: *The Report to the Education Commission—Confidential Edition* (1860) that was republished as *The Popular Education of France* (1861), *A French Eton; or, Middle Class Education and the State* (1864), *Schools and Universities on the Continent* (1868), *Higher Schools and Universities in Germany* (1874)—but what else?[2] The obligations of the professorship and the renewed associations with Oxford stimulated major writings, while the prestige of the chair undoubtedly helped to make marketable the periodical essays that were revised into a succession of notable books for almost thirty years. Numerous title-pages identify Arnold as Professor of Poetry, or Formerly Professor of Poetry in the University of Oxford.

Arnold's inaugural lecture at Oxford in the Sheldonian Theatre took place on 14 November 1857. 'On the Modern Element in Literature'

[1] W. B. Guthrie, 'Matthew Arnold's Diaries, The Unpublished Items: A Transcription and Commentary', 4 vol, unpublished University of Virginia dissertation, 1957, II, 126, 170, 423, 426. Available on University Microfilms, 1959.

[2] Possibly one should add *Reports on Elementary Schools, 1852–1882*, ed F. R. J. Sandford, 1969. *England and the Italian Question* has been reprinted with an introduction by M. M. Bevington, Durham, North Carolina 1953.

began a series on this general topic. He hoped to publish the series in book form, but the project was never entirely completed. In fact, the inaugural lecture itself, first printed in *Macmillan's Magazine* in February 1869, was not collected in a book in Arnold's lifetime. However, the lecture on Homer that he delivered on 3 November 1860, an 'off lecture' as he called it, was followed by two others; the three were published as *On Translating Homer* in 1861. The immediate stimulus for the subject was F. W. Newman's recent translation of the *Iliad*, but as R. H. Super shows in his valuable introduction (*CPW*, I, 238–40), the greater issue of the theory of Homeric origins lay in the background of Arnold's interest in the subject and in that of his audience. His success in urbanely defining the elements of Homeric style, and the limitations of that of Newman and other English translators, brought cheers from his Oxford audience at the third lecture, and an impenitent response from Newman in *Homeric Translation in Theory and Practice* (1861). Arnold replied in a fourth Oxford Lecture. 'As I get into it', he said shortly before its delivery on 30 November 1861, 'it interests me and amuses me' (*Letters*, I, 153). The lecture was printed in the spring of 1862 as a small separate book, *On Translating Homer; Last Words*. Ralph Waldo Emerson once remarked to William Allingham, 'Dr. Wendell Holmes . . . said he could find nothing to read; everything appeared to him *slow*. I said, "I have a book at home which is not slow," and lent him Matthew Arnold on Homer. He said he could read any quantity of books like that'; Lionel Trilling in a more contemporary way has commended the series as one of Arnold's 'finest performances, with an athletic quality in which austerity and elegance combine'.[1]

Arnold's official if intermittent connection with Oxford was a source of great satisfaction both in the way of sentimental recollection and of intellectual stimulation. Yet his audience, however responsive, was circumscribed. In an assessment of his larger aims, Arnold wrote to his sister Jane on his birthday, 24 December 1859, that his 'line of endeavour' was 'to inculcate *intelligence* . . . upon the English nation as what they most want' (*Letters*, I, 111). The University of Oxford was a small part of the nation that he hoped to influence. A few years later, anticipating the publication of *Essays in Criticism*, and contemplating a further essay on Alexandre Vinet, a French liberal theologian, Arnold said, 'If I can do Vinet to my mind it will be a great thing, and I shall

[1] *William Allingham's Diary*, 217; *Matthew Arnold*, New York 1939, 167.

have reached the Dissenters and the middle class; then I shall stop for the present' (21 January 1865, *Letters*, I, 247).

Before he was done even with the lectures on Homer, however, Arnold's professional duties pulled him into the protracted controversy over the crucial social issue of state aid to education. Nevertheless, the lectures at Oxford continued sporadically. By January 1865 Arnold was preparing a selection from them for Macmillan, together with some essay-length reviews of books, to appear as *Essays in Criticism*. He told his mother on 21 January, '. . . I think the moment is, on the whole, favourable for the Essays; and in going through them I am struck by the admirable riches of human nature that are brought to light in the group of persons of whom they treat, and the sort of unity that as a book to stimulate the better humanity in us the volume has' (*Letters*, I, 246–7). At the end of February Alexander Macmillan reported a 'brisk and encouraging sale'—'something over 400' (*Buckler*, 70). Sales did not remain brisk, but they were continuous. The first edition was sold out by 1 July 1868; a second appeared in 1869, a third in 1875, and a fourth in 1884. Meanwhile, independently and apparently without Arnold's advance approval, Ticknor and Fields brought out in Boston an edition that included 'A French Eton' and the lectures on Homer, followed by a second and a third in 1866. All of the pieces in *Essays in Criticism*, but especially the two placed strategically at the beginning—'The Function of Criticism at the Present Time' and 'The Literary Influence of Academies'—stress those values of 'curiosity', 'disinterestedness', intelligence, urbanity, and cosmopolitanism that synthesized Arnold's past critical effort and foretold his continuing one. He took a natural pleasure in reaching a widened public. In November he wrote to his sister Fan, 'The *North American Review* for July had an article on me which I like as well as anything I have seen. There is an immense public there, and this alone makes them of importance' (*Letters*, I, 309).

On the Study of Celtic Literature was the next book derived from Oxford lectures. It was, however, even more circumscribed in interest than the lectures on Homer. George Smith, Thackeray's successor as editor of the *Cornhill Magazine* and in 1865 founding editor of the *Pall Mall Gazette*, published the lectures individually in the *Cornhill* shortly after each was delivered and in 1867 as a book. 'The appearance of the book is beautiful,' Arnold told his publisher; 'I cannot tell you how much I like it' (*Buckler*, 84). Super's introduction to these essays relates Arnold's interest in his subject both to his visit to Brittany in 1859 when he reflected thoughtfully on his maternal connections with the Cornish Celts, and to his later political writings on Ireland (*CPW*, III, 490–8).

Arnold's final lecture in his professorship was given on the afternoon of 7 June 1867. He appears to have thought originally of a literary subject, perhaps Propertius. Pressures of work led him to decide upon the topic 'Culture and Its Enemies', which he was planning as an essay for the *Cornhill Magazine*. He wanted, he said, to make the lecture 'as pleasing to my audience and as *Oxfordesque* as I could' (*Buckler*, 85). The Oxfordesque element is in part expressed in the vein of Arnold's praise: 'On this last time that I am to speak from this place, I have permitted myself, in justifying culture and in enforcing the reasons for it, to keep chiefly on ground where I am at one with the central instinct and sympathy of Oxford. The pursuit of perfection is the pursuit of sweetness and light. Oxford has worked with all the bent of her nature for sweetness, for beauty; and I have allowed myself today chiefly to insist on sweetness, on beauty, as necessary characters of perfection' (*CPW*, V, 502). George Smith printed the lecture in the *Cornhill* for July; but on 15 June when Arnold returned his corrected copy he had added that he had in mind another paper 'to say several things which need to be said in accompaniment to what has been said here' (*Buckler*, 86). The thoughts were developed to constitute both *Culture and Anarchy: An Essay in Political and Social Criticism* (1869) and its facetiously sportive by-product *Friendship's Garland* (1871), the latter being assembled from a series of letters to the *Pall Mall Gazette*. *Culture and Anarchy* remains together with the two series of *Essays in Criticism* at the heart of Arnold's continuing vitality. Arnold himself hoped for much from the book. He wrote on 12 June 1869, 'You will see that it will have considerable effect in the end, and the chapters on Hellenism and Hebraism are in the main, I am convinced, so true that they will form a kind of centre for English thought and speculation on the matters treated in them' (*Letters*, II, 11). The public response may initially have been smaller than he hoped, but a second edition was printed in 1875, a third in 1882, and in 1883 an edition combining *Culture and Anarchy* with *Friendship's Garland*.

Arnold's estimate of the importance of his distinction between

Hebraism and Hellenism has been borne out. His habit of rhetorical antitheses—culture and anarchy, literature and dogma, dissolution and renovation, epochs of concentration and epochs of expansion—is expressive of an intelligence that sought meaning through the dialectic of the mind and the dialectic of history, and found at least clarity. D. J. DeLaura's *Hebrew and Hellene in Victorian England* (1969) richly explores the centrality of this antithesis for an understanding of the interrelatedness of the thought of John Henry Newman, Arnold, and Walter Pater. The serious reader who is willing to approach *Culture and Anarchy* in its complexity is ready for DeLaura's important book, which bears equally upon Arnold's major writings in the seventies: *St. Paul and Protestantism* (1870), *Literature and Dogma* (1873), *God and the Bible; A Review of Objections to 'Literature and Dogma'* (1875), and *Last Essays on Church and Religion* (1877).

Douglas Bush has recently reminded us that on 12 October 1869 Arnold wrote to his old Oxford friend Frederick Temple, newly appointed Bishop of Exeter. In his letter of congratulation Arnold remarked, 'In the seventeenth century I should certainly have been in orders, and I think if I were a young man now, I would take them.'[1] It is true that Arnold's early letters to Clough often reflect a jaunty religious scepticism. In 1850 he declared, as he returned to a reading of Locke on Human Understanding, '. . . my respect for the reason as the rock of refuge to this poor exaggerated surexcited humanity increases and increases' (*Letters to Clough*, 116). Nevertheless, the same letter expresses his feeling for the 'vivifying atmosphere' of Spinoza. Arnold's search for 'the spark from heaven', like that of his gipsy scholar, was continuous. He said in 1865, 'No one has a stronger and more abiding sense than I have of the "daemonic" element—as Goethe called it—which underlies and encompasses our life' (3 March, *Letters*, I, 249). A variety of other powerful forces, deriving from Arnold's perceptions about himself and the intellectual development of his age, entered into the making of those books. Notable among them were I think his strong sympathy for the humanizing power of the great historical religions, his conviction of the cultural impoverishment in arrogant religious separatism ('The Dissidence of Dissent and the

[1] *Matthew Arnold: A Survey of His Poetry and Prose*, Masters of World Literature Series, New York and London 1971, 172–3; quoted from *Memoirs of Archbishop Temple*, ed E. G. Sandford, 1906, I, 278.

Protestantism of the Protestant Religion' was the abrasively triumphant motto of the *Nonconformist*), his reading of the great historically revisionist views of the Bible stemming from the 'higher criticism', and the death in 1868 of two young sons. 'And Tommy's death in particular,' he said, 'was associated with several awakening and epoch-marking things' (*Letters*, I, 401).

In a generation less sympathetic to the Victorians than the present, the four main religious writings of Arnold were regarded as arid products of his years 'in the wilderness'. Eliot's influential rejection of Arnold's religious position had wide acceptance. Signal stages in the return of these books to thoughtful consideration have included Trilling's examination in his *Matthew Arnold* (1939), the discussion by Basil Willey in his *Nineteenth Century Studies: Coleridge to Matthew Arnold* (1949), and the extensive and vigorous study by William Robbins in *The Ethical Idealism of Matthew Arnold* (1959).

There were by-products also of Arnold's central concerns in the 1870s. For Arnold the educative power of religion as opposed to the educative power of science is its appeal to the part of our humanness that responds to feeling and imagination, and he knew of the Hawley Square Chapel at Margate where there were sung the 'animating' lines of Miss Emma Tatham,

> *My Jesus to know, and feel his blood flow,*
> *'Tis life everlasting, 'tis heaven below.* (*CPW*, III, 98)

This was very different from the 'glow', 'the boundless exhilaration', the 'energy and magnificence' that infused the final chapters of *Isaiah*, and from Arnold's own feeling for religion. He edited in 1872 a small selection, *A Bible-Reading for Schools; The Great Prophecy of Israel's Restoration*, and in 1875 a revised version of the book, *Isaiah XL–LXVI, With the Shorter Prophecies Allied to It*. The later text included an introduction that expresses succinctly Arnold's matured conviction about meaning in history, a conviction about its expressiveness of the inviolability of moral law that enters so emphatically into writings of his last ten years. 'In my belief', he said, 'the unique grandeur of the Hebrew prophets consists, indeed, not in the curious foretelling of details, but in the unerring vision with which they saw, the unflinching boldness and sublime force with which they said, that the great unrighteous kingdoms of the heathen could not stand, and that the world's salvation lay in a recourse to the God of Israel' (*CPW*, VII, 67). This is the Hebraic version of the Hellenic affirmation in *Oedipus Tyrannus* of laws in whom the god is mighty and does not grow old, which Arnold entered in his *Note-Books* (430). A corrected version of *Isaiah of Jerusalem* was published, again by Macmillan, in 1883.

Four anthologies of individual British authors followed *Isaiah XL–LXVI.* The first of these was a selection from Samuel Johnson's *Lives of the Poets*, which Macmillan published in 1878. Apparently Macmillan proposed it with a view to its use in schools, but Arnold countered with a broader purpose, saying, 'Let us not aim at a *school-book*, but rather at a literary book which schools can and will use' (*Buckler*, 126). *The Six Chief Lives from Johnson's Lives of the Poets*, augmented by including Macaulay's 'Life of Johnson', was reprinted in 1879, in 1881, and in a new edition in 1886. In 1879 Macmillan published in the Golden Treasury Series Arnold's immensely successful selection *Poems of Wordsworth*, and in 1881 for the same series his *Poetry of Byron*. In 1880 Arnold's continuous interest in Irish affairs and his admiration for the political insights of Edmund Burke prompted him to bring together Burke's *Letters, Speeches and Tracts on Irish Affairs*, also for Macmillan.

The selecting and arranging of works of others might suggest a diminishing of Arnold's own creativeness. I think it should be seen as an evidence of his confidence in the educative power of literature, and, as a corollary, of his way of countering what seemed to him to be the growing and threatening claims of 'science' to be primary in modern culture. In 'A French Critic on Milton' (1877) he remarked, 'Human progress consists in a continual increase in the number of those who, ceasing to live by the animal life alone and to feel the pleasures of sense only, come to participate in the intellectual life also, and to find enjoyment in the things of the mind' (*CPW*, VIII, 169). For Arnold the way to the better society was the inward change of each individual member. The beneficent inward change related not to the Englishman's pleasure in the simple freedom to do as one likes, but in the things of the mind. He said, 'One must, I think, be struck more and more the longer one lives, to find how much, in our present society, a man's life of each day depends for its solidity and value on whether he reads during *that* day, and, far more still, on what he reads during it'

(*NB*, 9). It was in this sense that he assembled the reflective entries that comprise so much of his published *Note-Books*, and I believe it was an element in his approach to the anthologies.

Early in 1879 under the title *Mixed Essays* Arnold published a collection whose main interest today is probably its inclusion of 'Democracy' and 'Equality' and 'Falkland'. The first of these was revived from its original place in 1861 as the introduction to the specialized *Popular Education of France*. Here it serves together with 'Equality' to epitomize much of Arnold's social thought. Lionel Trilling chose both of these political essays for his influential anthology *The Portable Matthew Arnold* (1949). 'Falkland' has gained recent attention, for it holds an important place in the argument of John P. Farrell's thoughtful essay 'Matthew Arnold's Tragic Vision'.[1]

In 1880 Smith, Elder in London and Macmillan in New York brought out an interesting selection chosen by Arnold himself with the title *Passages from the Prose Writings of Matthew Arnold.*[2] Perhaps the book was thought of as a companion to the highly successful *Selected Poems*. Taken but not wrenched from their original context, the extracts in the diversity of topics and the brightness of phrasing confirm the younger Henry James's finely perceptive tribute in the *English Illustrated Magazine* for January 1884: 'All criticism is better, lighter, more sympathetic, more informed, in consequence of certain things he has said. He has perceived and felt so many shy, disinterested truths that belonged to the office, to the limited speciality, of no one else; he has made them his care, made them his province and responsibility. This flattering unction Mr. Arnold may, I think, lay to his soul—that with all his lightness of form, with a certain jauntiness and irresponsibility of which he has been accused—as if he affected a candour and simplicity almost more than human—he has added to the interest of life, to the charm of knowledge, for a great many of those plain people among whom he so gracefully counts himself' (245).

By 1882 Arnold had assembled enough essays for one more somewhat miscellaneous collection, *Irish Essays and Others*. The final essential book published during his lifetime was *Discourses in America* (1885), comprising 'Numbers', 'Literature and Science' and 'Emerson',

[1] *PMLA*, LXXXV, January 1970, 107–17. Included in DeLaura, *Matthew Arnold: A Collection of Critical Essays*, 99–118.

[2] Edited by W. E. Buckler in 1963.

the lectures that he gave during his extensive and successful tour of the eastern United States in 1883–4. G. W. E. Russell was once told by Arnold that this was 'the book by which, of all his prose-writings, he should most wish to be remembered' (*Letters*, II, 280, n 2). 'Literature and Science' had been Arnold's Rede Lecture at Cambridge University in 1882, and his response to Thomas Henry Huxley's Birmingham lecture of 1880 on science and culture, defined by Huxley in narrowly belletristic terms. This was the classic version in Victorian England of the 'two cultures' debate in our age. Arnold wrote to his friend Charles Leaf from Boston: 'Here in New England every one is full of the Education question, and of the contest between letters and science more particularly; and all the country places want to hear me on Literature and Science. When I get to the great towns I have to give the lecture on Numbers' (6 December 1883, *Letters*, II, 236). Two other books resulted from the American visit. In 1887 *General Grant*, a long and desultory review of Grant's memoirs, was reprinted from *Murray's Magazine*. In the month of his death, April 1888, the *Nineteenth Century* published Arnold's essay 'Civilization in the United States', and in the same year the small Boston publisher Cupples and Hurd issued *Civilization in the United States: First and Last Impressions of America.* In addition to a reprinting of the review of Grant's memoirs, the book contained 'A Word about America' (1882), 'A Word More about America' (1885), and the title essay. 'Civilization in the United States' regained some attention through being included in E. K. Brown's *Representative Essays of Matthew Arnold* in 1936, and again in the standard anthology of C. F. Harrold and W. D. Templeman, *English Prose of the Victorian Era* (1938). The three best essays of the book are included with an appreciative introduction in Kenneth Allott's *Five Uncollected Essays of Matthew Arnold* (1953). Although on the one hand its call for 'elevation' and 'beauty' sounds less Hellenic than *fin de siècle*, its final affirmation leaves no doubt about Arnold's religious and ethical sincerity: '"Except a man be born *from above*, he cannot have part in the society of the future"' (Allott, *Five Uncollected Essays*, 65).[1]

[1] The reader interested in Arnold and America should consult Raleigh, *Matthew Arnold and American Culture* and the unpublished Yale University dissertation of C. H. Leonard, 'Arnold in America: A Study of Matthew Arnold's Literary Relations with America and of His Visits to This Country in 1883 and 1886', 1932; available on University Microfilms

Modern judgment does not confirm Arnold's preference for *Discourses in America*. On the other hand the book he was assembling at his death remains, together with *Essays in Criticism* (1865) and *Culture and Anarchy*, one of the three central works. At the end of the 1870s, T. Humphry Ward, who had married Arnold's niece Mary Augusta, proposed a major anthology *The English Poets* (1880), with a general introduction and prefatory essays by various writers on the poets included. Reluctant at first because of other pressures, Arnold consented to do the introduction and prefaces for Gray and Keats. Macmillan's partner G. L. Craik asked in January 1888, 'Is it not time for you to make a volume of collected papers?' (*Buckler*, 75). Arnold gave an immediate favourable response—a 'purely literary volume' as a companion to the 1865 volume, to be called *Essays in Criticism, Second Series*. He proposed to include the essays on Gray and Keats, the introductions to the Golden Treasury editions of Wordsworth and Byron, a speech on Milton, reviews of Edward Dowden's recent *Life of Percy Bysshe Shelley*, and essays on Tolstoy and Amiel, whose diary had been recently translated by Mary Augusta Ward. The general introduction for Ward's *English Poets* became the leading essay 'The Study of Poetry'. Arnold died suddenly on 15 April 1888, but his widow and his son Richard carried through the project, and the book appeared with a brief prefatory note by Arnold's friend John Duke, Lord Coleridge. Like the first series of essays, the second series expresses judgments, creates phrases, and raises critical issues that continue to enliven and illuminate literary debate.

Arnold's great authority of statement and his readiness to throw down an intellectual challenge are never more striking than in the memorable opening statement of 'The Study of Poetry': '"The future of poetry is immense, because in poetry, where it is worthy of its high destinies, our race, as time goes on, will find an ever surer and surer stay. There is not a creed which is not shaken, not an accredited dogma which is not shown to be questionable, not a received tradition which does not threaten to dissolve. Our religion has materialised itself in the fact, in the supposed fact; it has attached its emotion to the fact, and now the fact is failing it. But for poetry the idea is everything; the rest

(1965). *General Grant* was reprinted with Mark Twain's response by S. Y. Simon, Carbondale, Illinois 1966.

is a world of illusion, of divine illusion''' (*CPW*, IX, 161). One is already at the starting point for twentieth-century discussions of religion and poetry, science and poetry, sincerity and poetry, poetry and belief, and the nature of the 'supreme fiction'.

III

Thales said, 'Time is the wisest of things, for it finds out everything' (*Poems*, 616–17). Not without the persistent aid of modern scholarship, however, has Time recovered poems, letters, essays, and reviews by Arnold, so that the canon may now be regarded as virtually complete. The once useful 'de Luxe' edition in fifteen volumes of *The Works of Matthew Arnold* (London, 1903–4) has been superseded, except for the last three volumes containing the Russell edition of the letters, by two important editions of the poems and a monumental edition of the prose. The primary need for any reader of Arnold, then, is to know the current standard editions.

The standard edition of the poems is *The Poetical Works of Matthew Arnold* (1950), edited by C. B. Tinker and H. F. Lowry. As the basic text the editors chose that of Macmillan's final and so-called Popular edition of 1890. Variant readings from successive printed editions and manuscripts are given, together with Arnold's prefaces of 1853 and 1854. Tinker and Lowry order the poems in the final categories that Arnold gave them: Early Poems, Narrative Poems, Sonnets, Lyric Poems, Elegiac Poems, Dramatic Poems, and Later Poems. They also include ten poems that Arnold chose not to reprint in any edition, but oddly they do not include the six unpublished poems and fragments given in their earlier companion volume *The Poetry of Matthew Arnold: A Commentary* (1940). This edition of the poems provides the text for S. M. Parrish's *A Concordance to the Poetical Works of Matthew Arnold* (1959).

The other major text for the verse is *The Poems of Matthew Arnold* (1965), edited by Kenneth Allott for F. W. Bateson's series of Longmans Annotated English Poets. Allott gives some variant readings, and includes the prefaces, but the great merit is the abundance of annotation. Allot's wealth of detailed knowledge about Arnold makes his headnotes and footnotes invaluable. The edition is more complete for it includes the poetry that Tinker and Lowry did not reprint from their *Commentary* as well as a few pieces that have appeared in biographical or other studies, such as 'Lines written on the Seashore at Eaglehurst', which I. E. Sells first published in her *Matthew Arnold and France* (1935) and 'Lines written on first leaving home for a Public School' that N. Wymer printed in his *Dr. Arnold of Rugby* (1953), and, finally, verses not previously printed in book form, notably the twenty-four lines restored to 'The River'. Another great merit is the arrangement of the poems in the known or estimated order of composition. Whatever Arnold meant by thinking that his poems gained 'as a body of doctrine' by his classification, the modern reader is probably more interested in following his development as a poet.[1]

One could wish that Allott might have included his own preface to *Matthew Arnold: A Selection from His Poems* (1954) in the Penguin Poets series, for that lively introduction, in the form of a dialogue, addresses itself thoughtfully to the grounds of Arnold's withdrawal from the writing of poetry.[2]

The *Commentary* of Tinker and Lowry also provides useful background for individual poems. It is co-ordinated with their edition of *The Poetical Works*. The authors had access to the great collection of Arnold materials in the Yale University library, and in particular the so-called Yale Manuscript—a collection of notes, proposed subjects, and fragments relating to Arnold's poetic interests—and the Yale Papers, which include letters, manuscripts, and notebooks. There is useful discussion of source material, but little literary criticism as one understands the term today.

Generations of readers will owe a debt to R. H. Super for his editing of *The Complete Prose Works of Matthew Arnold* (1960–), which will be completed in eleven volumes. Like Allott's edition of the poems, Super's arrangement follows the chronological order of publication of

[1] T. B. Smart lists the contents of Arnold's individual books of poems in his *Bibliography of Matthew Arnold*, 1892, rev. 1904. Alan Roper conveniently lists the contents of the volumes of 1849, 1852, 1853, and 1867 in *Arnold's Poetic Landscapes*, Baltimore, Maryland 1969.

[2] Included under the title 'Matthew Arnold' in *Victorian Literature, Selected Essays*, ed R. O. Preyer, New York and London 1967, 103–20. Allott also touches the withdrawal from the writing of poetry in 'A Background for "Empedocles on Etna"', *Essays and Studies*, ed S. Potter, 1968, 80–100; this essay is slightly abridged in DeLaura, *Matthew Arnold: A Collection of Critical Essays*, 1973, 55–70.

the individual essays. The titles of the individual volumes in this edition are those of the editor. Thus, *On the Classical Tradition* comprises the prefaces of 1853 and 1854 to the *Poems*, the inaugural lecture at Oxford (1857), the Preface to *Merope* (1858), *England and the Italian Question* (1859), and *On Translating Homer* (1861–2). The reader must therefore have a general knowledge of the chronology of Arnold's work to find what he seeks, at least until the final volume is available. But the utility of chronological presentation is very great, for chronology makes possible a logical presentation of the large number of essays, reviews, and letters to editors that were never reprinted by Arnold or, in many instances, not publicly acknowledged by him. Super gives variant readings and illuminates with full explanatory notes the very great number of obscure and constantly fading topical references the reader encounters on almost every page of Arnold. *Friendship's Garland*, his *jeu d'esprit*, needs to be almost as thickly annotated as *The Dunciad*. Super's comprehensive introductory note to each essay is itself a reader's guide to its genesis and publishing history, its relation to other writings by Arnold, and to modern scholarship.

But it is not to be supposed that the general reader will have read all the poems of Arnold, or more than a few of the classic essays, before wishing to know more about him. He will very probably have been introduced to Arnold in a selective anthology like that of John Bryson or of Trilling, or he may simply, like Mrs. Ramsey, 'have turned and felt on the table beside her for a book' and found it to be, as did Mrs. Ramsey, *The Oxford Book of English Verse*. I think that the reader who seeks to increase his knowledge of Arnold will very logically, and with the greatest pleasure, begin with *The Letters of Matthew Arnold to Arthur Hugh Clough* (1932), with its penetrating biographical introduction and its enduring annotation by Lowry. It is a book to which the interested reader will constantly return. Its publication marked a turning point in the study of Arnold, and of Clough. Arnold is never more exuberant than in these letters, never more spontaneous. They are widely topical in subject, sometimes wonderfully outrageous in their honest response to persons, books, ideas, and they are fruitful in the critical insights they provide for Arnold's conception of the poetic office. It would not be easy to find, for example, a statement in one of Arnold's critics that leads in so many directions of Arnold's thought as this: 'For in a *man* style is the saying in the best way *what you have to say*. The *what you have to say* depends on your age. In the 17th century it was *a smaller harvest than now*, and sooner to be reaped: and therefore to its reaper was left time to stow it more finely and curiously. Still more was this the case in the ancient world. The poet's matter being *the hitherto experience of the world, and his own*, increases with every century' (65).

If interest in Arnold's letters continues, the reader should next explore the two-volume *Letters of Matthew Arnold 1848–1888* (1895) edited, with some supervision by Arnold's widow and sisters, by G. W. E. Russell. More sedate than the letters to Clough, and edited to convey an image, they remain nevertheless indispensable to understanding Arnold's thought and activity. A major source for the biographer of Arnold, they are in the absence of a full biography the reader's best approach to the sensibilities that Arnold showed to a private world: his enthusiasm for fishing, his 'passion for clear water', his delight in the spontaneous ('I saw a little duck of a girl running about stark naked (the best costume for her) at Maddaloni yesterday, who made me think of my Nell'), and his endurance in misfortune. And they confirm his impatience with pretence: 'It was the faithful who knelt in general, but then it was in general only the faithful who were presented. That old mountebank Lord – dropped on his knees, however, and mumbled the Cardinal's hand like a piece of cake.'[1]

For thirty-seven years Arnold kept a series of small diaries or note-books that have survived, and are among the papers at the Yale University library. Although to some readers they may be forbidding, it is appropriate to mention them together with the letters because they

[1] May 1865, *Letters*, I, 274; 15 May 1880, *Letters*, II, 169. *Unpublished Letters* (see Bibliography, p. 319 below) contains a few important letters. Buckler's *Matthew Arnold's Books* is excerpted from some three hundred letters to and from Arnold's publishers. *Matthew Arnold's Letters, A Descriptive Checklist*, ed A. K. Davis, Jr., Charlottesville, Virginia 1968, lists more than 2,600 published and unpublished letters to some five hundred correspondents. Professor Davis published his checklist with the hope of uncovering additional letters before the project of publishing a collective edition was begun. This extensive and difficult task is being undertaken by Cecil Y. Lang of the University of Virginia. During the years before the letters are finally published the Davis checklist remains a useful aid.

are, in a special sense, personal writings. In 1902, Arnold's daughter the Hon. Eleanor Wodehouse (afterwards Lady Sandhurst) published a small selection as *Matthew Arnold's Notebooks*. In 1952, however, H. F. Lowry, Karl Young, and W. H. Dunn edited a major portion of the diaries in *The Note-Books of Matthew Arnold*, a work both valuable and incomplete. The published note-books contain lists of books Arnold read or planned to read, and sometimes of articles he planned to write, from 1852 to 1888, but the greater part of the book consists of extracts, some repeated year after year from the diaries, or from 'general note-books', of memorable and gnomic sayings, generally in the language of the original, from, among others, Goethe and à Kempis, Voltaire and Plato, George Sand and Jesus, the Book of Proverbs and the *Pall Mall Gazette*. A few entries have immediate relevance to some work in progress by Arnold, but most are meditations to stimulate meditation. They comprise a uniquely private book. J. L. Lowes is said to have remarked, certainly with considerable if unintended ambiguity, that 'he was not sure "that anything which Arnold left is of more worth"' (*NB*, ix). J. Hillis Miller in a widely known essay on Arnold proposes that the repetitions express a strategy of role-playing in society. 'If he could go often enough', Miller writes, 'through the act of writing down a solemn and constructive quotation from some wise man of the past, Bishop Wilson or Isaiah or Epictetus, he might come to believe in the quotation and be made over in its image.'[1] Miller thinks the strategy fails, because Arnold 'is never able to conquer his coldness', because his own anxieties, like those of 'a bad actor', show through the persona of Sophocles or of Spinoza. I believe that the uncommitted reader who comes upon *The Note-Books* will find a more discerning, certainly a more sympathetic, insight in Lionel Trilling. 'For all the sophistication of his mind,' Trilling observes, 'he had what must seem to us an almost primitive belief in "wisdom". The written phrase that enshrined the discovered truth was almost magical to him. "Sayings" meant more to him than we can easily understand. . . . It was as if he were obeying as literally as he might the commandment to fasten the truth upon the doorpost of his house and upon his hand and to set it as a frontlet between his eyes. Such was his belief in the power of thought, in the strength of the human continuity, in the possibility of the

[1] *The Disappearance of God: Five Nineteenth Century Writers*, Cambridge, Massachusetts 1963, 242.

community of mind.'[1] Moreover, Arnold's unquenched sense of the noumenal left him open to epiphanies. I do not know in what other sense one can read the letter referred to earlier written soon after the death of two of his sons: 'And Tommy's death in particular was associated with several awakening and epoch-marking things. The chapter for the day of his death was that great chapter, the 1st of Isaiah; the first Sunday after his death was Advent Sunday, with its glorious collect, and in the Epistle the passage which converted St. Augustine' (24 December 1868, *Letters*, I, 401).

The Note-Books comprise only a selection of the diary entries. Kenneth Allott made a significant addition to our knowledge of the young Arnold in his essay 'Matthew Arnold's Reading-Lists in Three Early Diaries', for he added annotation and interpretation to the listings, showing their bearing on the thesis of Arnold's continuity of sensibility rather than his fragmentedness.[2]

In his Prefatory Note to the 1895 edition of Arnold's letters, G. W. E. Russell said, 'It was Matthew Arnold's express wish that he might not be made the subject of a Biography.' Nevertheless, biographical materials accumulate as letters are uncovered, family journals are read, contemporary records of friends are interpreted to support theses. Speculation about the identity of Marguerite will not be quenched. Interaction with other minds will be explored. With each increment of information, with the final ordering of the canon, with a definitive edition of the letters in prospect, the impulse to override the wish becomes stronger, while the passage of time has already overcome the argument for reticence. In the spring of 1971 Park Honan of the University of Birmingham reported that he was at work on a biography of Arnold.[3] A biography of the stature of W. J. Bate's *John Keats* would be a great service to Arnold and a pleasure to readers.

Meanwhile, where shall the reader turn for a general interpretation of Arnold so that he may order what he already knows? *Matthew*

[1] *The Portable Matthew Arnold*, Viking Portable Library, New York 1949, 4–5.

[2] *VS* II, March 1959, 254–66. Guthrie's 'Matthew Arnold's Diaries' includes detailed expense accounts and extensive notes on Arnold's school inspecting; its potential use is considerable for the biographer.

[3] 'A Note on Matthew Arnold in Love', *VN*, spring 1971, 11.

Arnold, A Study (1947) by E. K. Chambers carries the authority of an eminent name; but although it is factually useful, it is perfunctory in a way that will not encourage a reader. He will make a far better start, among the recent shorter introductions, with Douglas Bush's sympathetic *Matthew Arnold: A Survey of His Poetry and Prose* (1971). Bush writes from his own wide and deep knowledge of English intellectual and literary traditions, and in this case out of the context of the troubled end of the past decade, when 'extreme revolutionary zeal seems to be attended by anti-intellectual, anticultural intolerance and a false notion of "relevance"' (xv). He writes also from a conviction that Arnold never speaks with greater immediacy than in such embittered times.

Another book with which to extend one's knowledge of Arnold similarly emerged from a decade of distress, of international duplicity, of the seeming failure of reason. First published on the threshold of World War II, Lionel Trilling's distinguished *Matthew Arnold* (1939, revised 1949), which he called a 'biography of Arnold's mind', retains its great authority and its vitality. The crucial *Letters of Matthew Arnold to Arthur Hugh Clough* was in print, and although Trilling said he had 'consulted almost no unpublished material', his basic insights have not been made less valid by subsequent discoveries.

Although biographical details enter only to trace Arnold's intellectual development, Trilling's book has considerable status as a biography. So likewise does Louis Bonnerot's detailed *Matthew Arnold, Poète: Essai de biographie psychologique* (1947). For their purposes Trilling and Bonnerot emphasize, respectively, the prose and the poetry, but both writers pursue a unified image and have produced comprehensive studies.[1]

Trilling and Bonnerot wrote at the beginning of a generation more sympathetic to the Victorians than were the 'age' of Lytton Strachey and the 'age' of T. S. Eliot, and they contributed to that greater understanding; but they wrote on the verge of a period of extraordinary productivity both of literary criticism and of academic scholarship. Even the most general reader must share some sympathy with the speaker in 'Stanzas in Memory of the Author of "Obermann"',

[1] Bonnerot's study has been translated into English but awaits a publisher. See *Arnold Newsletter*, I, spring 1973, 5.

Like children bathing on the shore,
Buried a wave beneath,
The second wave succeeds, before
We have had time to breathe.

He hopes to locate Arnold's fixed 'place' in criticism, and all is contention; he tracks with the scholar the calm springs of Arnold's 'buried life' and discovers *Angst* and a 'bad actor'; he finds in himself some sympathy for the Forsaken Merman's Margaret only to be instructed that, by an 'exquisite irony', she is a Judas figure. He had even learned to doubt that Arnold smothered his gift in order to become his 'father's forum', only to be instructed that 'the poet abandoned the role of a merman in love with a girl for the role of Headmaster of Victorian England'. How shall the reader find his way through the *selva oscura* so vigorously cultivated by modern academic activity?

More fortunate than Dante, he has two judicious guides at hand to overcome his inevitable dismay. F. E. Faverty's 'Matthew Arnold' in *The Victorian Poets: A Guide to Research* (ed Faverty, 2nd edn, 1968) provides a lucid descriptive commentary on almost half a century of bibliographical and critical writings on Arnold down to 1966. *Victorian Prose: A Guide to Research* (1973), edited by D. J. DeLaura, contains a comprehensive chapter on Arnold by the editor. DeLaura's descriptive and balanced evaluative comments are often more extensive than Faverty's, reach further back towards Arnold's contemporaries for many comparative estimates, and bring the commentary down to 1972. These guides inevitably discuss critical work on both the prose and the verse of Arnold, although there is a leaning in emphasis.

Yet the extensiveness of these guide-books may itself deter the 'common reader'. There is help in the recent book on Arnold in the series, Twentieth Century Views. *Matthew Arnold: A Collection of Critical Essays* (1973), edited by DeLaura, is a convenient introduction, chiefly through contemporary scholars, to important ways in which he invites our interest. It is regrettable that most of the selections are abridged, although this does not diminish their distinction or representativeness. The book reflects the shift from the 'new' criticism of the 'autonomous verbal structure' to a criticism of works as they relate to the integrity of the writer's achievement.[1]

[1] Mr. DeLaura generously permitted me to read in manuscript his chapter

The selection begins outside the contemporary frame, but inevitably, with T. S. Eliot. His 'Arnold and Pater' taught a generation to think of Arnold as the probable ancestor of the fading American Humanism of the 1920s, and of Arnold's having been within his own time the prophet of the gospel of Walter Pater. Eliot taught us to discern an increasing anaemia in Arnold's meaning of culture, and to become believers when, persuaded by so much wit, we learned from Eliot that 'When we take *Culture and Anarchy* in one hand, and *Literature and Dogma* in the other, our minds are gradually darkened by the suspicion that Arnold's objection to Dissenters is partly that they do hold strongly to that which they believe, and partly that they are not Masters of Arts at Oxford' (DeLaura, *A Collection*, 13–14). When Eliot told us in his Norton lectures, *The Use of Poetry and the Use of Criticism* (1933), that 'The Forsaken Merman' was a charade, we found it a charade, and when told that 'Sohrab and Rustum' was 'less fine' than *Gebir*, we read *Gebir*. But especially, when assured that Arnold 'had no real serenity, only an impeccable demeanour,' that 'Perhaps he cared too much for civilisation, forgetting that Heaven and earth shall pass away, and Mr. Arnold with them, and there is only one stay'—when so assured, we failed to recognize the voice of the father in the son. Like Arnold's, Eliot's suavely ironic criticism has not been sterile, but in Frederic Harrison's words 'generative' and 'efficient'. Two important studies of Arnold are products of the stimulus of Eliot's remarks on Arnold and Pater. W. A. Madden's *Matthew Arnold: A Study of the Aesthetic Temperament* (1967) and DeLaura's *Hebrew and Hellene in Victorian England* call for the attention of the serious reader.

Eliot's presence extends into other essays in DeLaura's collection, for the debate on the validity of Arnold's religious thought continues into the selections from Vincent Buckley's *Poetry and Morality* (1959) and A. O. J. Cockshut's *The Unbelievers* (1964). And Eliot's reservations about Arnold will give the reader a context for the chapter from Miller's notable exploration of this central theme of the Victorian age, *The Disappearance of God* (1963). It is not necessary to be wholly convinced by Miller's interpretation of Arnold's role-playing, of Arnold's acquiescence in being nothing, of the final image of an Arnold wanly

on Arnold. *Victorian Prose: A Guide to Research* has now appeared and is published under the sponsorship of the Modern Language Association of America.

hoping for a symbolic return of God, at some infinitely distant time, to this world, in order to recognize that Miller has raised questions about Arnold's social and spiritual beliefs that cannot be reviewed without taking Miller's reading into account.

A Collection of Critical Essays also includes the final chapter, 'The Use of Elegy', from A. D. Culler's study of Arnold's poetry, *Imaginative Reason* (1966). Written with grace and with scholarly authority, *Imaginative Reason* is the fullest modern essay on the poetry. It integrates critical interpretation with an assured understanding of Arnold's life and thought. Some readers may resist as too schematic the tendency to order Arnold's experience in tripartite arrangements, of which the grouping of poetic imagery is the forest glade, the burning plain, and the wide-glimmering sea. Although Culler's book is a commentary on the major poems, it is also like Trilling's a 'biography of the mind'.

Culler's study does not quite usurp the field, and the reader who is interested in recent criticism of Arnold's poetry should soon come to know three other works of more limited range. W. S. Johnson's 'essay in criticism', *The Voices of Matthew Arnold* (1961), applies to the poems Eliot's suggestion in 'The Voices of Poetry' (1953) that the poet may be heard as he ruminates, as he modifies his voice for a particular audience, as he speaks through a *dramatis persona*. G. R. Stange's *Matthew Arnold, The Poet as Humanist* (1967), written before Culler's book was available, makes interpretive, and not very heavily documented, comments on individual poems. By its arrangement it is a useful critical companion to the Tinker and Lowry *Commentary*. Alan Roper in *Arnold's Poetic Landscapes* (1969) organizes his interpretations in a way similar to that of Culler, but the context is more the tradition of English landscape poetry than the background of Arnold's intellectual development.

Sooner or later the reader whose interest in Arnold develops will require bibliographical aids. Thomas Burnett Smart first published his *Bibliography of Matthew Arnold* in 1892. It was included in somewhat revised form in volume fifteen of the 'de Luxe' edition of *The Works* (1904), where it is probably most readily available. Super's *Complete Prose Works* will soon constitute the inclusive chronology for all the prose and its publishing history, but Smart's *Bibliography* will continue to be useful for his listing of the contents of the separate volumes of Arnold's poems and for its synoptic table of their contents. Super has contributed the reliable bibliography of Arnold's publications and studies of Arnold in *The New Cambridge Bibliography of English Literature*, edited by George Watson (1969, III). *Bibliographies of Twelve Victorian Authors* (1936, reprinted 1968), edited by T. G. Ehrsam, R. H. Deily, and R. M. Smith, is useful up to and including 1934. Listings of materials on Arnold with occasional brief comment, and frequent reference to their reception especially in scholarly journals, are provided by *Bibliographies of Studies in Victorian Literature for the Thirteen Years 1932–1944*, edited by W. D. Templeman (1945), *Bibliographies of Studies in Victorian Literature for the Ten Years 1945–1954*, edited by Austin Wright (1956), and *Bibliographies of Studies in Victorian Literature for the Ten Years 1955–1964*, edited by R. C. Slack (1967). Annual bibliographies, from which the three preceding volumes are the periodic compilations, currently appear in the June issue of the quarterly *Victorian Studies*. From 1933 to 1957 they were published annually in the May issue of *Modern Philology*. The semi-annual *Victorian Newsletter*, edited by W. E. Buckler, includes a 'selected' list, briefly annotated; and the annual survey in the journal *Victorian Poetry*, edited by R. C. Tobias, will be expanded to include poetry and prose. An *Arnold Newsletter* began publication in spring 1973 under the editorship of N. H. Bishop of Eastern Michigan University. Embracing all the Arnolds and their circle and appearing at a time when diaries and letters of the Arnold women remain unpublished, and when the preparation of a biography and an edition of the letters are in prospect, the *Newsletter* provides a forum for communication and understanding. A newsletter is the last refinement of scholarship, where it is not the beginning of fresh synthesis, new assessments, new configurations, and an aid to major undertakings. There is scope for all of these activities, for Arnold had commanding qualities of mind that endure: objectivity, sanity, clarity, and responsibility.

Eliot once deprecatingly objected, 'The vision of the horror and the glory was denied to Arnold, but he knew something of the boredom.'[1] Despite the deprecation there is insight in the remark, so far as it relates to the public figure of the poems and the essays. And much more recently, in a lecture at Canterbury, George Steiner made the arresting suggestion that Voltaire and Matthew Arnold between them 'may be

[1] *The Use of Poetry and the Use of Criticism*, Cambridge, Massachusetts 1933, 98–9.

said to date and define the generations of cultural promise.'[1] They really believed that 'the humanities humanize'. Steiner locates them at the historical extremes of the cultural optimism of the Enlightenment. Arnold indeed has his strong admiration for reason. Although certainly no pantisocratic enthusiast, Arnold never, like the anti-intellectual Wordsworth, disparaged the 'false secondary power/By which we multiply distinctions'. His optimism was persistent; he wrote in January 1879 to his sister Fan, '. . . Maine and Lecky both said to me, only yesterday, that the work I was doing by forcing the question of middle-class education and civilisation upon people's thoughts was invaluable, and that they were heartily with me' (*Letters*, II, 153–4). But Steiner implies that Arnold too naïvely believed in cultural promise, that modern experience shows that in Bluebeard's Castle there are doors he could not afford to open; and one must confess that 'beauty and charm' and 'mildness and sweet reasonableness' are better as descriptions of Blake's images of innocence than as charms against Auschwitz and Buchenwald. Admittedly, Arnold never quite achieved the ardent expression of Blake's 'mental strife'. Nevertheless, the intellectual qualities of Arnoldian optimism reach as far back as the rationale for Socrates's questioning, and the responses of a Trilling or a Bush confirm their viability in a later century.

[1] *In Bluebeard's Castle*, 1971, 61.

2: *Arnold the Poet:*

(i) Lyric and Elegiac Poems

WILLIAM A. MADDEN

MATTHEW ARNOLD was persuaded very early in his career that he would never be a popular poet, and history was to prove him right. But it sometimes happens that a poet who fails to attract a wide audience enjoys an important compensatory advantage in never being totally neglected, and such has been the case with Arnold. The large and sophisticated body of commentary on his poetry, covering more than a century of critical opinion, bears witness to his enduring, if limited, reputation as a poet.[1]

About the exact nature of Arnold's achievement, however, there has been considerable disagreement. Arthur Hugh Clough, his closest and poetically most knowledgeable friend, raised what was to be a persistent objection when reviewing Arnold's first two volumes, *The Strayed Reveller, and Other Poems* (1849) and *Empedocles on Etna, and Other Poems* (1852). Clough thought he detected a 'pseudo-Greek inflation' in the poems, a 'straining after the rounded Greek form' which could vitiate the style even of a Milton. The major flaw, in Clough's view, was Arnold's 'turning and twisting his eyes, in the hope of seeing things as Homer, Sophocles, Virgil, or Milton saw them', instead of 'accepting them as he sees them, and faithfully depicting accordingly'.[2] The related charge of academicism also arose early and has usually reflected a belief that Arnold's poetry appeals primarily to bookish readers. James Anthony Froude, another friend with whom Arnold discussed his poetic

[1] F. E. Faverty documents the steady growth of Arnold's reputation as a poet in the present century in *The Victorian Poets: A Guide to Research*, Cambridge, Mass. 1956 (rev. edn. 1968), 116–21.

[2] 'Recent English Poetry', *North American Review*, LXXVII, July 1853, 24, 18.

plans, complained of Arnold's parading calmness and urging resignation in his poetry when 'he only knows the shady side of nature out of books'.[1] Finally, more recent critics have been bothered by Arnold's poetic diction, which they see not as classical or academic, but as 'poetical' in a pejorative sense.

What hostile critics have generally overlooked—and it has been the main achievement of the best Arnold criticism to recognize—is the remarkable sensibility which informs the 'classical' themes and images and the traditional diction of Arnold's poems. They embody what Arnold called a 'state of mind' (*Letters*, I, 52) to which he repeatedly attached the epithet 'modern'. What he meant by the latter term he explained in the Preface to his third volume, *Poems* (1853), when describing the protagonist of one of his major works, 'Empedocles on Etna'. 'I intended to delineate the feelings of one of the last of the Greek religious philosophers, one of the family of Orpheus and Musæus, having survived his fellows, living on into a time when the habits of Greek thought and feeling had begun fast to change, character to dwindle, the influence of the Sophists to prevail. Into the feelings of a man so situated there entered much that we are accustomed to consider as exclusively modern . . . the calm, the cheerfulness, the disinterested objectivity have disappeared; the dialogue of the mind with itself has commenced; modern problems have presented themselves; we hear already the doubts, we witness the discouragement, of Hamlet and of Faust' (*CPW*, I, 1). Both as a critic and as a man, Arnold felt obliged to resist the debilitating consequences of the modern dialogue of the mind with itself; it produced, he said, 'a state of feeling unknown to less enlightened but perhaps healthier epochs—the feeling of depression, the feeling of *ennui*' (*CPW*, I, 32). In his criticism Arnold would defend the poetic ideals which led him to withdraw *Empedocles* precisely because it gave expression to such feelings, but as a poet he was faithful to his inner experience, giving to the modern dialogue of the mind with itself and the feelings which it induced a distinctive and original poetic voice.

The modernity of Arnold's sensibility can be traced to the combination of experiences which entered into his spiritual and intellectual history. The earliest and most lasting influence in his life was that of his father, Dr. Thomas Arnold, Headmaster of Rugby,

[1] Letter to Clough, 6 March 1849, cited in *Letters to Clough*, 127, n 3.

whose ardent latitudinarian Christianity and sophisticated historical sense affected almost everything the son was later to write, but whose energetic practical nature, almost wholly devoid of poetic sensitivity, rendered him incapable of understanding his son's innate temperament. Arnold's later analysis of the relationship between Lamennais, a religious educator with a temperament much like Dr. Arnold's, and a youthful disciple to whom Arnold was greatly attracted, Maurice de Guérin, suggests some memory on Arnold's part of his own relationship with his father: 'Lamennais never appreciated Guérin,' he wrote; 'his combative, rigid, despotic nature, of which the characteristic was energy, had no affinity with Guérin's elusive, undulating, impalpable nature, of which the characteristic was delicacy' (*CPW*, II, 23). Whereas the father worried over his eldest son's (as he put it) flitting from flower to flower, the son responded by going up to Oxford an insouciant, foppish dandy totally unlike, it seemed, the usual serious Rugby boy.

But whatever Dr. Arnold's limitations, there were important benefits to the future poet in being the son of his famous father. One was Thomas Arnold's friendship with his Grasmere neighbour, the elderly poet Wordsworth, in whose shadow Arnold grew up. The younger poet's feeling for nature, and his need to find in poetry both joy and moral profundity, were Wordsworthian in origin. Even when the young Arnold rebelled against his great predecessor, the themes and poetic strategy of his poetry were influenced by his almost filial sense of Wordsworth's greatness. The other benefit of Arnold's childhood education was Thomas Arnold's devotion to the classics. Although his father characteristically preferred the historians and Matthew the poets, the latter's love for the classics can be traced to his early exposure to Greek and Roman literature under the intelligent and vigorous tutelage of his father. Shortly before his death Arnold would recall how he had discovered his love of poetry and his poetic vocation when he encountered Virgil's Fourth Eclogue at Rugby at the age of nine. He thereafter regarded the Latin poet as his first poetic master.[1]

[1] Arnold recollected the experience two years before his death in a letter to Sidney Colvin, cited by E. V. Lucas, *The Colvins and Their Friends*, New York 1928, 193. For Arnold's general debt to classical literature see W. D. Anderson, *Matthew Arnold and the Classical Tradition*, Ann Arbor 1965.

The more direct contribution of his father to Arnold's education had to do with a philosophy of history and with moral habits. Thomas Arnold's admiration for the cyclical view of history developed by Vico and Niebuhr contributed important elements to Arnold's mature outlook as a poet and as a critic: a belief in historical recurrence, which made possible the use of figures and events from past history as analogues for modern experience; the conviction that philosophical and religious forms are relative to the age which produces them; and a belief that the age called for a reintegration of poetry and religion.[1] In the moral sphere Thomas Arnold's influence stemmed less from his explicit Evangelical Christian morality than from his encouraging in his children a conscientious habit of inwardness, practised as a moral discipline in self-knowledge and self-possession. Matthew indicated his sense of the nature and importance of this part of his debt to his father in a letter to his favourite sister, Jane, after their father's death. Describing himself as experiencing 'a kind of spiritual lethargy', and as being generally subject to 'periods of spiritual eastwind', Arnold said he struggled against such susceptibilities by recalling how his father and Jane had been the 'most faithful witnesses' among all the people he had known 'of the reality & possibility of that abiding inward life which we all desire most of us talk about & few possess'.[2] In an early notebook he entered the prophetic comment, 'The disease of the present age is divorce from self,'[3] anticipating the search for wholeness and self-possession which was to be one of the central themes of his poetry.

What Arnold's poetic career might have been had his father been more sympathetic towards its early manifestations, or had Dr. Arnold lived longer, we cannot know. What happened was that, having been made Professor of Modern History at Oxford shortly after Matthew

[1] Vico's influence is explored by Paul W. Day, 'Matthew Arnold and the Philosophy of Vico', *University of Auckland Bulletin*, 70, *English Series* 12, 1964. In his 1853 Preface Arnold links Niebuhr with Goethe as one of the great modern minds (*CPW*, I, 14).
[2] The undated letter is probably from the winter of 1849–50, according to A. Dwight Culler, who cites it in full in *Imaginative Reason: The Poetry of Matthew Arnold*, New Haven and London 1966, 134.
[3] *Poems*, 142 n. Kenneth Allott's critical and explanatory notes in this edition constitute an illuminating commentary on the poems.

matriculated there in the fall of 1840, Thomas Arnold died, suddenly and unexpectedly, in the spring of 1842. Matthew's immediate reaction was a sense of loss of the intellectual guidance he might have had if his father had lived, and perhaps also, judging by several early poems, a sense of the transience of human life and of the injustice of fate. The death of his father was followed by a period of extraordinarily heavy reading, when Arnold was in his mid-twenties, which resulted in his quietly shedding his childhood Christianity in favour of an austere stoicism. The religious denudation which he experienced in the process produced profound emotional disturbances that found direct poetic expression in 'Stanzas from the Grande Chartreuse' and 'Dover Beach' and help to explain the melancholy that permeates his poetry generally. 'I cannot conceal from myself', Arnold wrote in his notebook, 'the objection which really wounds & perplexes me from the religious side,' namely, that 'the service of reason is freezing to feeling, chilling to the religious moods' [*sic*]; and he added the revealing comment: 'feeling & the religious mood are eternally the deepest being of man, the ground of all joy & greatness for him'.[1] The vital connection, for someone raised as Arnold had been, between the writing of poetry and faith in some religious doctrine he explained to Clough: 'If one loved what was beautiful and interesting in itself *passionately* enough, one would produce what was excellent without troubling oneself with religious dogmas at all. As it is, we are *warm* only when dealing with these last—and what is frigid is always bad' (*Letters to Clough*, 143).

The extent of Arnold's readings can be estimated from his reading-lists, which included Plato, Sismondi, Cousin, Descartes, Bacon, Lucretius, Berkeley, Humboldt, Montesquieu, Schelling, Plotinus, Plutarch, Herder, Kant, Michelet, and Aristotle.[2] These lists did not include the works of imaginative literature which Arnold was also reading at the time—Emerson, George Sand, Goethe, Carlyle, the *Bhagavad Gita*, and others—that were as varied as his philosophical and historical readings. The preponderance of philosophical and historical studies is explained by Arnold's need to find some viable alternative to the Christianity which he had lost, but so far as Arnold the poet was

[1] *Commentary*, 270.

[2] The reading-lists for the important years 1845–7 appear in K. Allott, 'Matthew Arnold's Reading-Lists in Three Early Diaries', *VS*, II, 1959, 254–66.

concerned they had an adverse effect. He told Clough in 1853 that he felt immensely 'what I have (I believe) lost and choked by my treatment of myself and the studies to which I have addicted myself' (*Letters to Clough*, 136).

But there was a more favourable consequence of the readings in that Arnold believed that they equipped him with a modern European perspective from which he could judge his English contemporaries and immediate predecessors as not knowing enough. One thing they did not know was that nature, rather than being adapted to the mind of man, as Coleridge and Wordsworth had passionately believed, was absolutely indifferent to human desires, a conviction which Arnold developed, through Goethe's mediation, from his reading of Spinoza. The other important thing which the Romantics and most of his contemporaries did not know, Arnold believed, was the relativist view of history which he had initially learned from his father and later apotheosized, again under the influence of Goethe, in the concept of a *Zeitgeist.* What men thought, and what a poet had to say, Arnold became convinced, was not a personal affair but a *donnée* of the Time-Spirit, a phenomenon as impersonal as Nature itself. Moreover, viewed in a larger perspective, history was essentially tragic, governed by unknown powers beyond man's comprehension, one of those 'uno'erleap'd Mountains of Necessity' (*PW*, 7) which hemmed man in and prevented him from attaining complete happiness.

The final phase of Arnold's spiritual history, so far as it affected his poetry, centred around his temporary relaxation of his youthful stoicism when he was in his late twenties, under the pressure of a liaison with a young woman towards whom he felt for a time a strong romantic attraction. Little is known about Marguerite—as Arnold poetically named her—or about the history of their troubled relationship, except that she occasioned a serious crisis which had to do with Arnold's deepest sense of himself and of his duty and destiny.[1] The evidence is that in the mid-forties, prior to meeting 'Marguerite' and partly perhaps as a result of his discovery of George Sand's novels, Arnold developed a strong imaginative interest in romantic passion. His lasting

[1] Evidence indicating that 'Marguerite' was Mary Claude, an intimate friend of Clough's sister, Anne, is reviewed in P. Honan, 'A Note on Matthew Arnold in Love', *Victorian Newsletter*, No. 39, Spring 1971, 11–15; but see also James Bertram, 'Arnold and Clough', p. 186 n and n below.

admiration for George Sand testifies to the impact which her novels had at a critical moment. They seem to have suggested to Arnold a possible way of recovering the warmth and joy of which his religious disillusionment had deprived him: if a mutually self-fulfilling union with another were possible, one need not endure the desiccating loneliness of stoic self-dependence, nor lose one's identity through immersion in ordinary social life. As the 'Switzerland' sequence of poems indicates, the result of this testing of his revived hopes was to confirm Arnold in the conviction that man 'hast been, shalt be, art, alone' (*PW*, 181) his return, by the time he was thirty, to a more secure but more resigned stoicism, and the commencement of his career as a critic.

The collective effects of these formative experiences during Arnold's most productive period as a poet, roughly the period from 1843 to 1853, were clearly decisive in determining the kind of poetry he would write. Given the conclusions of modern thought, he was convinced that the decline of belief in the old Christianity was inevitable and that as a result poetry would have to become a complete *magister vitae* by 'including . . . religion with poetry, instead of existing as poetry only' (*Letters to Clough*, 124). For this purpose, he told Clough, a new type of poetry was required: 'The language, style and general proceedings of a poetry which has this immense task to perform must be very plain, direct and severe, and it must not lose itself in parts and episodes and ornamental work, but must press forwards to the whole' (*Letters to Clough*, 124). For poetic models of a plain and direct style suitable for handling the fulness of modern intellectual experience Arnold looked to modern German poetry and especially to Goethe.[1] For models of well-constructed poetic works that subordinated parts to the whole, he looked to the Greeks, especially to Homer and Sophocles, and to the two English poets who came closest to achieving the effect of Greek poetry, Milton and Wordsworth.

Arnold's ostensible classicism and traditional poetic diction were thus consciously chosen vehicles for expressing a 'modern' state of mind and

[1] G. R. Stange touches on Arnold's debt to Goethe and Heine for his 'Hellenic' metres, and suggestively links Arnold's 'Switzerland' lyrics to the *Liedercyklus*, a form of love poem developed by Heine and other German poets early in the century. See *Matthew Arnold: The Poet as Humanist*, Princeton 1967, 17 n and 222.

feeling which might be identified as post-Romantic. The central initiative of the English Romantic poets had been their effort to transfigure the analytical reason and scepticism of the eighteenth-century Enlightenment into the imaginative vision and joy of a new dispensation. While Arnold held to the Romantic conception of poetry's function—poetry, he said, echoing Wordsworth and Schiller, was to give joy—he told Clough privately that 'if the imagination would apprehend some joy[,] it comprehends some bringer of that joy' (*Letters to Clough*, 63), and Arnold's critical intelligence led him to conclude very early that the post-Romantic mind could not honestly conceive of any such bringer. In his poetry the 'excursive' power of the poetic imagination no longer attains joy; rather each 'going out' from the self only confirms the fated Otherness of an 'unmating' reality, and the imagination returns upon itself leaving the poet either in confirmed dejection or in a renewed resolve to be self-dependent. Judiciously modifying the earlier poetry of England and Germany as well as of classical antiquity, Arnold thus composed poems which described what it felt like to live in the middle of the nineteenth century for anyone endowed with the sensibility of a poet and the intelligence of the 'unintoxicated honest' (*Letters to Clough*, 103).

The document which may best serve as Arnold's manifesto as a poet is 'The Strayed Reveller', the title poem of his first volume of poetry in which he describes his task, and his misgivings, as an aspiring poet. The poem might be described as a lyric masque. The first half creates a frieze-like tableau, with a wooded glen in the background and the three statuesque figures of a white-necked Youth, the golden-haired Circe, and the dark-featured Ulysses in the foreground, which provides the frame for the central 'action' of the poem, the Youth's experiences during the day just ending. The Youth explains to Circe—it is evening when the poem opens—that he had that morning descended from the upland mountain slopes which were his home and where he had been accustomed to hearing 'Pan's flute-music', with the intention of joining in the Bacchic 'rout' in the valley town below. On the way to the communal festival, being distracted, he says, by the sight of Circe's palace, he entered the palace, and drank from a bowl on the altar a liquor which produced in his soul a 'wild, thronging train/ Of eddying forms' which he perceived all day long 'Without pain, without labour'.

The Youth's departure from his mountain home and his drinking of Circe's wine indicate an initiation rite of some kind, but the nature of the initiation is not immediately clear. The description of the wine is ambiguous: it is both beautiful ('red, creaming') and dangerous ('dark seeds'). The Youth's departure from his home in the morning marks a decisive break with the world of childhood, but before he can join the Bacchic revelry of the townspeople he is deflected by the sight of the beautiful palace which, as the poem unfolds, takes on something of the quality of a Palace of Art. The wine is thus in one aspect the intoxicating power of the poetic imagination which enables the Youth to participate in the life of the community vicariously, from the detached perspective provided by the portico of Circe's palace, which stands on a hill opposite to Bacchus's temple. The danger which threatens him as a burgeoning poet is not that of succumbing to the actual frenzy of the unrestrained passionate life of the Centaurs and Maenads, but rather one of enjoying in imagination, 'Without labour, without pain', the beautiful forms of life. This is the darker aspect of the wine: its tempting the Youth to succumb to the attraction of beautiful forms for their own sake, to live the life which Arnold would later describe as the peculiar temptation of the born poet, the endless pursuit of experience simply 'to feel what it is all like' (*CPW*, II, 31).

The wisdom necessary to warn the young poet of the inadequacy of his desire to enjoy life without pain, that is, aesthetically, is provided by the figures of Ulysses and of the aged Centaur, Silenus. Ulysses notices that the Youth's fawn-skin is half untied, and 'Smear'd with red wine-stains'. The later image is suggestive both of dissoluteness and of a wound; Ulysses' own 'short coat' is also stained, but it is 'travel-tarnished', the emblem of his heroic life and of the experience and wisdom that make him immune to Circe's enchantments. ('The favour'd guest of Circe', the Youth calls him.) When Ulysses, identifying the Youth as a poet by his sweet voice, asks him if he learned his songs by following some older bard 'By age taught many things,/ Age and the Muses', the Youth replies by repeating what he had learned from Silenus during his trance. His reply is, in effect, a corrective to the superficial view of the poetic life implied by Ulysses, a heroic activist who fails to understand the true nature, the wound, of the poetic vocation.

The dual aspect of the Youth's trance-vision is central to the poem's meaning. What he painlessly *sees* in his soul are images of the unfettered, free, sensual life of Bacchic revelry:

> *Sometimes a wild-hair'd Maenad—*
> *Sometimes a Faun with torches—*

But what he is *told* during his trance by 'old Silenus', who comes 'at noon' with his own Bacchic garland 'drooping', is that the wise bards not only, like the Gods, 'see' the whole range of human and creaturely existence, but they must 'feel', 'share', and 'bear' its attendant sufferings, as the Gods do not. When the wise bards behold the Centaurs, they empathetically experience not only the 'maddening wine' that swells the Centaurs' 'large veins to bursting', but also the moral consequences of a wine-maddened Dionysiac life, described in some of the most powerful lines Arnold ever composed:

> *. . . in wild pain*
> *They feel the biting spears*
> *Of the grim Lapithæ, and Theseus, drive,*
> *Drive crashing through their bones; they feel*
> *High on the jutting rock in the red stream*
> *Alcmena's dreadful son*
> *Ply his bow; such a price*
> *The Gods exact for song . . .*

As a 'strayed' reveller, the Youth has already abandoned direct participation in the life of Bacchic revelry; thanks to Circe's magic wine, he can participate vicariously in that life from the detached perspective of the imagination. But as Ulysses' presence and Silenus's words and drooping garland indicate, if the Youth is to fulfil his true vocation as a poet he must be prepared to learn, through imaginative participation in the suffering of all living things, to sing the wisdom which only such participation brings.

'The Strayed Reveller' is a fine poem in itself as well as an important document for understanding Arnold's poetic career. Arnold's original free-verse metrical form, modelled on German translations of Greek lyrics, is capable of an impressive variety of effects: Ulysses' candid but formal speech; the Youth's importunate pleas for more wine; Circe's insinuating invitation to drink; and the contrasting visions of the serene Gods and the suffering bards. The poem also shows Arnold's imagination to have been penetrated by the world of classical myth and its personae, whose import is not, of course, that of Homer's figures but of aspects of Arnold's poetic self, in which the Dionysian element is present but already contained by a lofty moral vision of the wise poet's task. There is a strong sense of what Keats called the 'chameleon element' necessary in great poetry, of the poet's need to go out of himself in a discipline of sympathy and participation, but the poem also presents the youthful poet as terrified by the anticipated pain of creative activity in a tragic universe presided over by absent indifferent Gods. Going out of the self entails not only pain but the possibility of a total loss of moral identity implicit in the Youth's lack of a centre. Arnold feared such outgoing movements because he was convinced that neither nature, nor history, nor the Gods reveal their secrets, that the only light available to man had to be found within, a fact which explains the difficulty which he experienced, evident in the other 1849 lyrics, in trying to realize the vision of the wise bard in his own poetry.

The major themes of Arnold's mature poetry are already present in the 1849 volume—the need for stoic detachment, the existence of a buried self, the primacy of universal law over personal desire, the inadequacy of romantic love, the transiency of human life, the exhaustion produced by inner division—but the variety of poetic strategies with which Arnold experimented indicates an uncertainty as to how to treat these themes poetically. After the volume was published he told his sister not to look for wholeness or consistency in it; the poems were fragments, he said, because he was fragments (*Unpublished Letters*, 18). Nevertheless, the poems provide a valuable record of Arnold's initial creative struggles, and occasional successes, that promised greater work to come. The most satisfying pieces, in addition to the quasi-dramatic title poem, are the narrative poems. But the lyric poems have their own interest, ranging from the introductory sonnet 'Quiet Work' to an extended conversation poem, 'Resignation', which concludes the volume and employs the poetic mode in which Arnold would compose his finest lyric and elegiac poems.

The least successful 1849 lyrics are those in which Arnold attempted to distance and objectify personal thoughts and feelings through the use of remote mythological or historical personae. Unlike the personae of 'The Strayed Reveller' and the narrative poems, those of the lyric poems are either indistinctly realized ('A Modern Sappho' and 'To Fausta'), or too obviously serve as mouthpieces for a point of view that clashes with the traditional associations which attach to them (the monk in 'Stagirius', Haemon and the Greek chorus in 'Fragment of an "Antigone"'). The poems in which Arnold drops the mask and gives direct expression to his thought and feeling, either in reflective poems recommending stoic detachment, or in lyric poems expressing the pain and deprivation which that stoicism exacted, are more successful. In terms of number, the dominant genre is the sonnet, of which there are eleven. Of these, 'Quiet Work' and 'To a Friend' occupy positions of honour apart from the remaining nine, being placed first and third respectively in the 1849 arrangement, and before the title-poem. Both strike the stoic note which dominates the volume as a whole. The contrast developed in the octet of 'Quiet Work' between the unity, silence, and enduringness of nature's 'ministers', and the multiplicity, noise and transiency of human life, is resolved in the elevated language of the sestet, with its subtle interplay of consonants, the even spread of the stress, the caesural variations, and the biblical echo of 'Labourers':

> *Yes, while on earth a thousand discords ring,*
> *Man's fitful uproar mingling with his toil,*
> *Still do thy sleepless ministers move on,*
>
> *Their glorious tasks in silence perfecting;*
> *Still working, blaming still our vain turmoil,*
> *Labourers that shall not fail, when man is gone.*

The repetitions of 'still', and its emphatic syntactical inversion in the penultimate line, carry the dual association of quiet and enduringness, embodying in the language itself the central lesson of 'two duties kept at one' elicited from nature by the speaker. Similarly, 'To a Friend' moves from the tortured syntax and diction of the opening line, awkward but appropriate to the anxious mood of the auditor being addressed by the speaker ('Who prop, thou ask'st, in these bad days my mind?'), through an ascending series of statements praising in turn Homer, Epictetus and Sophocles, culminating in the extended tribute in the sestet to Sophocles—'Who saw life steadily, and saw it whole'—in language that poetically expresses the balanced serenity which it recommends.

Each of the other sonnets, like 'Quiet Work', has a stoic base and, like 'To a Friend', celebrates a superior man who is self-possessed and whole (Shakespeare, the Duke of Wellington, Emerson), or dismisses those who are not so and will not allow others to be (Butler, the passing crowd, an Independent Preacher, Cruikshank, Clough). Modified Petrarchan sonnets in form, in substance they are egotistical in the Miltonic-Wordsworthian manner, the speaker confidently or angrily presenting positive or negative examplars of nature's stoic lesson as formulated in the introductory poem 'Quiet Work'. Although Arnold's sonnets lack qualities generally present in the great English sonnets—intellectual complexity, ironic tension, a sudden reversal or expansion—they have their own peculiar power, developing a simple, straightforward argument in elevated language, accompanied by a chastened imagery appropriate to the speaker's posture of self-contained stoic detachment.

Closely allied to the sonnets in theme, 'In Utrumque Paratus' argues against attempting to determine man's origins and to derive one's morality accordingly. In six stanzas of varying trimeters and pentameters that create a subtle but finely controlled rhythm, the intellectual arguments are clearly articulated, from the opening description of a neo-platonically generated universe to the shocked cry of the materialist who arrogantly subscribes to an evolutionary view that would place man at the summit of existence, only to reach the solipsistic conclusion: '*I, too, but seem*'.

That Arnold paid a severe psychological price for his hard-won stoicism is also evident in the 1849 poems. Two lyrics expressing his emotional deprivation are less successful as fully achieved poems than the stoic poems just discussed, but they contain passages of considerable power. 'The Voice', composed in a stanzaic form reflecting Shelley's influence, expresses a romantic melancholy modified by the firmness of the stoicism with which the speaker resists it. The poem is marred by a stiffly imitative, slightly bathetic opening stanza, but the remaining two stanzas are very nearly flawless, the concluding lines being among Arnold's purest lyric utterances on the pain endured by a man striving to attain a state of serene self-possession:

O unforgotten voice, thy accents come,
Like wanderers from the World's extremity,
Unto their ancient home!

In vain, all, all in vain,
They beat upon my ear again,
Those melancholy tones so sweet and still.
Those lute-like tones which in the bygone year
Did steal into mine ear—
Blew such a thrilling summons to my will,
Yet could not shake it;
Made my tost heart its very life-blood spill,
Yet could not break it.

Morally convinced of the need to exert the will in a habit of inward resistance, Arnold found that the renunciations entailed left him profoundly sad, as though some essential and attractive part of life itself were being sacrificed.

A poem which originated in the same psychic materials, 'The New Sirens: A Palinode', presents a young poet (not unlike the Strayed Reveller of the title poem) who has been lured from his mountain home by the sound of the Sirens' music and, having dwelt with them for a time, is about to decide to reject what now seems the inescapable transiency of the pleasures and excitements which their way of life offers. The poem's emotional power, and the intellectual confusion which led Arnold to describe it as a 'mumble', derive from Arnold's ambivalence regarding the decision and the emotional desolation it involved, confusedly but movingly expressed in beautifully varied eight-line trochaic stanzas. The poem concludes with the speaker's *requiescat* for his abandoned hopes.

The lesser lyrics which appeared later fall into the pattern established by the 1849 volume: either they express a 'lyric cry' rooted in painful feelings, verging at times on despair, or they give voice to the will to endure and resist these painful facts of life in poems like the sonnets and 'In Utrumque Paratus', which employ what might be called the lyric mode of Nobler Rhetoric. The later lyrics are consistently superior to those of 1849. Some—among them 'Requiescat', 'Growing Old', the sonnet 'Youth's Agitations', 'The Progress of Poesy', 'Self-

Dependence', 'A Wish', 'Palladium'—are admirable poems in a minor key, and they contribute significantly to our sense of Arnold's overall poetic achievement. But they do not, by themselves, account for the stature Arnold enjoys as a poet. To understand this we must look to the major lyrics and to the elegies.

In his search for a lyric mode adequate to the expression of the inner drama of his experience, Arnold seems at first to have deliberately resisted using a species of lyric in which his English Romantic predecessors had composed most of their greatest works. One of the achievements of the Romantic movement had been the discovery of a type of lyric poem which aspired to be simultaneously subjective and objective. Wordsworth's 'Lines Composed a Few Miles above Tintern Abbey is a notable instance of the type, which M. H. Abrams has aptly named the greater Romantic lyric because of its derivation from the Greater Ode ('pindaric') of eighteenth-century English poetry; *The Prelude*, as Abrams observes, is an expansion of it on an epic scale.[1] Its characteristics suggest its relevance to Arnold's major lyrics and elegies: 'Some of the poems are called odes, while the others approach the ode in having lyric magnitude and a serious subject, feelingfully meditated. They present a determinate speaker in a particularized, and usually a localized, outdoor setting, whom we overhear as he carries on, in a fluent vernacular which rises easily to a more formal speech, a sustained colloquy, sometimes with himself or with the outer scene, but more frequently with a silent human auditor, present or absent. . . . In the course of this meditation the lyric speaker achieves an insight, faces up to a tragic loss, comes to a moral decision, or resolves an emotional problem.'[2] Arnold's initial reluctance to adopt the greater Romantic lyric was probably related to a self-conscious effort to resist the English habit, too much encouraged, he thought, by Wordsworth, of 'thinking aloud, instead of making anything' (*Unpublished Letters,* 17). Of the three greater Romantic lyrics in the 1849 volume, two are consciously anti-Wordsworthian. It seems that Arnold discovered the form in

[1] M. H. Abrams, 'Structure and Style in the Greater Romantic Lyric', *From Sensibility to Romanticism: Essays Presented to Frederick A. Pottle*, ed F. W. Hilles and H. Bloom, New York 1965, and repr. in *Romanticism and Consciousness*, ed H. Bloom, New York 1970, 203.
[2] Abrams, 201.

which he was to compose his finest lyric poems when he adopted it with the intention of countering views which Wordsworth had expressed in similar poems.

Lionel Trilling and later critics have persuasively argued that 'To A Gipsy Child by the Sea-Shore' is a conscious attack on Wordsworth's view of childhood expressed in his Immortality Ode.[1] The landscape setting is localized by the poem's sub-title, 'Douglas, Isle of Man', but the particularities of the scene are slight. Brief allusions to the 'cluster'd pier', the 'swinging waters', the seabirds hovering above the pier, and the movement of distant sails on the horizon, serve mainly to heighten by their brightness and motion the dark contemplative gloom and motionless gaze of the Gipsy-Child, whose eyes absorb the speaker's full attention and convey to him a 'soul-searching vision' beyond any he has ever experienced. In stark contrast to Wordsworth's child, trailing clouds of glory and apparelled in celestial light, Arnold's Gipsy-Child is marked by the majesty of grief rather than of joy, his consciousness of a 'soiled glory' and a 'trailing wing' foreshadowing the vanity of human hopes. The weakness of the poem is that the Child is made to bear more visionary knowledge and conscious suffering than it persuasively can (that it 'proceed'st to live' despite its gloom imposes a self-awareness that the child's age will hardly support), yet the poem has sustained concentration and dignity. The speaker is awakened, in his attempt to comprehend the child's sad, inadvertent gaze, to a memorable statement of man's sense of tragic alienation in a seemingly bright and beautiful universe.

The other greater Romantic lyric of 1849, 'Resignation: To Fausta', is composed of relaxed iambic tetrameter rhyming couplets in language adapted to the conversational context established by the sub-title. Its place-revisited structure parallels Wordsworth's 'Lines Composed a few Miles above Tintern Abbey', but the theme and structure of the poem differ radically from those of Wordsworth's. Whereas 'Tintern Abbey' concentrates upon the instinctive joy which the speaker had found in nature five years earlier, and re-finds on a higher level in the 'holier love' which produces the 'joy of elevated thoughts', Arnold's

[1] Lionel Trilling, *Matthew Arnold*, New York 1955 (first edn, New York 1939), 89–90. For a fuller account of Arnold's relationship to Wordsworth see Leon Gottfried, *Matthew Arnold and the Romantics*, Lincoln, Nebraska 1963, 6–74.

speaker concentrates upon a 'general life' whose 'secret is not joy, but peace':

> *whose dumb wish is not missed*
> *If birth proceeds, if things subsist;*
> *The life of plants, and stones, and rain.*

If he could lend a voice to the turf, hills, stream, and rocks, they would 'Seem to bear rather than rejoice', for nature's life, like man's, suffers from 'The something that infects the world', the line with which the poem concludes. The speaker addresses his sister, not as a visionary poet but as her fellowman and brother, out of a settled stoic conviction that not even the poet, whom Fausta believes to be more than man because he feels more deeply and sees more widely, can escape the general lot. The poet's superiority consists not in his escaping the common lot of man, as Fausta thinks, but in his possessing a 'quicker pulse' and energy which he subdues in order to scan, 'with sad lucidity of soul', that general life of which man is a part.

The interest of 'Resignation' is not confined to its greater Romantic lyric structure or its anti-Wordsworthian view of nature. As the concluding poem in *The Strayed Reveller* volume it serves as something of a palinode to the title poem: it marks Arnold's rejection of the way of the wise bard who suffers what he sings. Not only does the speaker identify himself with those, who, like Fausta, have been deprived of the poet's 'rapt security', but his description of the poet's vision eliminates entirely the element of pain that is so prominent in 'The Strayed Reveller'. As described in 'Resignation' the poet is not a participant in the tragic sufferings of human and creaturely life; he beholds, in the detachment of his 'rapt security', uniformly pleasant things, or at least undisturbing ones: a ruler in a great-historied land, the beautiful eyes of a woman, a 'happy group' returning home after the day's toil through 'shining streets', and the beneficent aspects of nature—the pastures and woody hills, the cuckoo and stream and wet grass, of a quiet pastoral landscape. The note of withdrawal, of a diminution both of involvement and of energy, is unmistakable. Arnold was still to write his finest poems, but the shadow of his future abandonment of poetry appeared unusually early, in the significantly titled 'Resignation'.

A more favourable portent of 'To A Gipsy Child' and 'Resignation' was their foreshadowing the much finer greater Romantic lyrics published in subsequent volumes. Two important 1852 lyrics, 'The Buried Life' and 'The Future', approach but do not quite attain to that mode. They differ from the greater Romantic lyric proper in that they are not based upon localized experience, and the landscape imagery is excogitated rather than observed. In 'The Buried Life' the speaker addresses a silent, indeterminate beloved in a mood of profound melancholy induced by his sense of men as 'alien to the rest/ Of men, and alien to themselves'. The poem develops around the speaker's question whether even lovers must remain alienated; as the speaker seeks to answer his own question, the recurring image is that of the 'unregarded river of our life' flowing indiscernibly in the deepest self, up from which flow 'nameless feelings' that 'course on for ever unexpress'd'. It is possible but rare, the speaker concludes, that the hand, eyes, and voice of a beloved will enable a man momentarily to 'become aware of his life's flow', with the result that:

> *An air of coolness plays upon his face,*
> *And an unwanted calm pervades his breast.*
> *And then he thinks he knows*
> *The hills where his life rose,*
> *And the sea where it goes.*

The poem thus presents an image of the individual psyche, alienated from the stream of its buried life, but possibly able ('*thinks* he knows') to get a glimpse of it momentarily under the influence of another's love.

'The Future' employs the same mental landscape in a 'pindaric' that subordinates that landscape to a similar mood of a felt present alienation, relieved by the hope that the River of Time will eventually carry man to fulfilment. The speaker declares early in the poem that 'As is the world on the banks,/ So is the mind of man', reflecting Arnold's conviction that the *Zeitgeist* determines how men think and feel in the successive stages of history. As the River flows down from its mountainous source, the calm of earlier ages is lost, and modern man finds himself on a plain, 'our minds/ Are confused as the cries which we hear'. Some believe that the earlier mountain quiet has forever fled, that the din can only become worse, but Arnold is able to suggest a tentative hopefulness, evoking through the rhythm and imagery of the coda a serenity that the poem desiderates. As the 'river of Time' flows on, becoming wider and statelier, 'haply' it

> *may strike*
> *Peace for the soul of the man on its breast—*
> *As the pale waste widens around him,*
> *As the banks fade dimmer away,*
> *As the stars come out, and the night-wind*
> *Brings up the stream*
> *Murmurs and scents of the infinite sea.*

As in 'The Buried Life', the central image, tone, and mood are adroitly manipulated so that a river which at first appears to take its own way, carrying the human race with it, is transfigured by the language into an image of tentative hope suggesting that, despite his present alienation, man may someday be at peace with himself and with the universe, the outward and inward Rivers becoming one in the process.

What makes 'The Buried Life' and 'The Future' quintessentially Arnoldian is not their lyric form but their poetic exploitation of the image of water. If we can assume, with Gaston Bachelard, that a poet's essential temperament is most clearly reflected in his preference among the four basic elements of all imaginative experience: earth, air, fire, and water, then Arnold may be described as a poet of water.[1] Citing Arnold's remark in a letter to Clough that water seemed to him 'the Mediator between the inanimate and man', the authors of the *Commentary* go on to observe: 'The letters abound in references to the beauty of running water: he has a "perfect passion" for "divine" rivers and clear streams, and the dry water-courses in the Apennines end "by becoming a positive pain" to him. He was reconciled to his inability to visit Greece by the realization that he could go there only in summer, when the rivers would be at their lowest.'[2] It is not surprising, therefore, that in giving a poetic account of his deepest experiences Arnold should exploit the manifold aspects of water in the form of sea, lake, fountain, and ocean, as well as of river and stream. He attaches to water, which cools, purifies, and mirrors, but also segregates, engulfs,

[1] Gaston Bachelard, *The Psychoanalysis of Fire* (*La psychanalyse du feu*, Paris 1938), trans. A. C. M. Ross, Boston 1964, with a Preface by Northrop Frye.
[2] *Commentary*, 81.

and carries away, deep subjective impulses for which it provides a repertoire of poetic symbols. When elements of fire, air, or earth appear in the poems, they frequently share some quality of water. Arnold's favourite astronomical image is not the sun, but the moon and the stars, both felt as quiet, cool, and pure, and frequently seen as reflected in a sea or lake as though partaking of their qualities. Air likewise fascinates in so far as it is light, cool, pure, and gentle ('sweet virgin air' [*PW*, 236]), while the earth is most delightful when it is dewy and shaded, cool and flowery ('Moor'd to the cool bank in the summer-heats' [*PW*, 257]). Negative values are conveyed in the poems through images antipodal to those of water: the desert, the burning plain, the fever of passion, the volcano, the noise of cities, the furnace of the world, the noon-day heat. Empedocles' fiery death in a volcano, for example, is balanced by Callicles' retreat to a happier landscape:

> *. . . where Helicon breaks down*
> *In cliff to the sea,*
>
> *Where the moon-silver'd inlets*
> *Send far their light voice . . .*

In 'Palladium', a brief but curiously powerful poem, the buried self is associated both with a 'plashing' crystal stream as well as with the major image in Arnold's poetry of the buried self, the moon. Like the moon, Arnold's poetic self follows its own 'remote and spheréd course' (*PW*, 181), apart, cool, silent, shedding a beautiful light, moving and illuminating the waters of his buried self. His finest lyric poems exhibit a masterful manipulation of these central symbols in poems structured on the model of the greater Romantic lyric embodying the unique qualities of his individual poetic temperament.

The specifically poetic success of Arnold's greater Romantic lyrics has received extended analysis and it may therefore be helpful to concentrate instead upon their place and function within Arnold's total corpus.[1]

[1] In his selection *The Portable Matthew Arnold*, New York 1949, 40, Lionel Trilling argues that Arnold's poems succeed with us 'out of all proportion to their specifically poetic success'. A number of recent articles and several recent books, notably Alan Roper's *Arnold's Poetic Landscapes*, Baltimore 1969, have demonstrated how carefully 'made' Arnold's poems were. When he fails, as I think he does in the frequently

While the poems individually express a *state* of mind, as a group they express what Arnold called the 'main movement of mind of the past quarter of a century' (*Letters*, II, 9). The central image of the poetry, the River of Life (outward and inward), reflects Arnold's pervasive time-consciousness, his sense of life as a journey. And several of the greater Romantic lyrics employ the place-revisited structure of 'Resignation', a structure dependent upon a sense of time, of movement and change. Read from this perspective, the major lyrics and elegies contain a dramatic element absent from 'The Buried Life' and 'The Future'. As a group, they constitute an extended, coherent, and poetically realized autobiography of the poet's mind comparable to, though inevitably quite different from, *The Prelude* or *In Memoriam*. Like the latter poems, they provide what Robert Langbaum has called a 'narrative or drama of experience', of which the basic structure is 'a series of dramatic lyrics connected in biographical sequence'.[1] As though to emphasize the nature of the road which he had spiritually travelled in his poetry, Arnold placed side by side at the end of his 1867 volume the two greater Romantic lyrics which may be taken as establishing the two poles of his spiritual autobiography, 'Stanzas from the Grande Chartreuse' and 'Obermann Once More', between which the other major lyrics and elegies can be located as successive milestones along the road of Arnold's quest for self-possession and wholeness.

In the journey which begins with 'Stanzas from the Grande Chartreuse', we find a speaker whose central experience is already behind him. Afloat on the 'sea of life', he finds himself wandering between two worlds, one dead and the other powerless to be born, and in near-despair is seeking respite in the shelter of the medieval Carthusian monastery. The Grande Chartreuse serves in the poem as a symbol of the speaker's childhood, and that of Europe generally, when the Christian faith was not yet an exploded dream, when 'rigorous teachers' had not yet 'seized his youth' and 'purged its faith, trimmed its fire', the faith, that is, of Arnold's childhood Protestant Christianity, and the fire of Romantic rebellion

---

anthologized companion poems 'The Youth of Nature' and 'The Youth of Man', it is because the making is inferior. Labelled 'pindarics' by Arnold, the two poems are in fact flawed greater Romantic lyrics that fail despite fine isolated passages.

[1] Robert Langbaum, *The Poetry of Experience: The Dramatic Monologue in Modern Literary Tradition*, New York 1957, 58.

which as a young man he had found appealing in Byron, Shelley, and Senancour. In approaching the abbey the speaker crosses the Dead Guier, whose mists and torrents he sees and hears, in order to enter the death-in-life world of the monks; the abbey itself is deathly, its fountains 'icy', its corridors 'humid', and the white habits of the monks and the yellow tapers on the altar suggestive of a sepulchre. The poem is Arnold's sad farewell to Christianity and to Romantic defiance of the modern world; the fire of religious faith and of passionate rebellion must give way to the white star of intellectual honesty. Significantly, the Grande Chartreuse is the one place on Arnold's spiritual map which he does not revisit in his elegies. There can be no question of going back.

The 'Switzerland' poems originally appeared as isolated lyrics, but Arnold's poetic instinct led him to arrange them eventually into a sequence which, when read as a single poem (as their common title suggests), constitutes a variant of the greater Romantic lyric. The poems concern a loss of another kind, perhaps the mature Arnold's psychologically most damaging loss. The sequence opens with the speaker's tormented account of his romantic attraction to a woman called Marguerite, from whom he is separated and whose image threatens to fade ('A Memory-Picture'), develops through several poems that express the pain of the inner division caused by the conflicting calls of love and duty, and ends with the speaker's rejection of Marguerite, whose memory nevertheless persists, with diminishing force, for ten more years. In providing his first serious experience of romantic love, Marguerite compelled Arnold to put to the test of reality its imaginative attraction as he had vicariously experienced it in the novels of George Sand. The landscape setting of the poems indicates the depth of Arnold's emotional involvement: moon, stars, boon mountain air, the river Aar, the nearby lake and strand, the poplar-lined street in the Alpine town, the bridge over the flowing stream, all become vital parts of the speaker's passion, inextricably bound up with it in the poet's imagination and deeply rooted in his unconscious preferences.

As the images suggest, Marguerite's attraction for Arnold was not merely or even primarily sexual; it was the much more profound attraction of his possibly being able to abandon his chosen, lonely, autonomous stoic self and finding a more complete, more fulfilling life through union with another in a perfectly satisfying environment. The dilemma thus posed involved Arnold in an identity crisis; his true self was in danger of fleeing from itself as a strategy for survival. The crisis leads to the speaker's discovering both an inner prohibition ('I hear a God's tremendous voice:/ "Be counsell'd and retire"') and the freedom which that prohibition implies ('Stay with me, Marguerite, still!'). Undecided whether the attraction he experiences offers complete fulfilment or represents a form of madness, the speaker both loves and fears having to choose, both fears nearness and dreads isolation in relation to the woman. Although in his disturbed state he offers Marguerite a variety of reasons for his decision to reject romantic love as a way of finding his true self (a God's tremendous voice, Marguerite's different past, her fickleness, the speaker's own unstable 'feminine' feverishness, the 'unplumbed, salt, estranging sea', 'time's current strong', unknown 'guiding Powers'), they all arise out of a central conviction that 'the something that infects the world' makes complete happiness unattainable in this life. Real despair, the poems say in effect, is not to know that one is in despair: once one recognizes his despair, he can take the first step towards true freedom and self-possession, the way of obedience to necessity and resignation, and that is the step which the 'Switzerland' poems show Arnold to have taken.

Poetically, Arnold resolved his dilemma by transfiguring the actual Marguerite into an imaginative symbol. The 'Switzerland' poems particularize the real Marguerite in considerable detail—she has blue eyes, a clear voice, lilac kerchief, an arch chin and smile, ash-coloured hair—but these attractive qualities are mixed with more questionable ones, notably an apparent fickleness, and Arnold feels compelled to say farewell to her. Yet he retains the image of another Marguerite, 'my Marguerite', as the poetic symbol of the qualities for which his true self most deeply longs:

How sweet, unreach'd by earthly jars
My sister! to maintain with thee
The hush among the shining stars,
The calm upon the moonlit sea.

In a lyric related to the Marguerite experience entitled 'A Dream', the 'dashing river of Life' carries the dreamer away from the Swiss Alps and the real Marguerite, through 'burning plains,/ Bristled with cities', to the sea, where the transfigured Marguerite, we can assume, will be waiting for an Arnold freed of his torment and indecision.

'The Terrace at Berne', a greater Romantic lyric set apart from the rest of the 'Switzerland' poems by its separation in time, was written ten years after Arnold's decision to withdraw. It is a place-revisited poem in which an older and calmer speaker reflects on what may have happened to the real Marguerite in the intervening years. Once again situated in the Swiss landscape with which Marguerite is indelibly associated, the speaker speculates whether she will once more rush to greet him, or whether she has fallen into dissolute ways or is perhaps dead, or whether, finally, she lives but has had her 'being re-arranged,/ Pass'd through the crucible of time'. There is a momentary stirring of the old emotions, against which the speaker expresses a remembered sense of loss, but he is resigned to the real Marguerite's fate, whatever it may be, because she no long matters. Arnold's willingness to envision her as a prostitute, criticized by some readers, is not a reflection of the speaker's self-righteousness, but a poetic statement of his complete detachment from the mortal Marguerite.

The Alpine landscape of the 'Switzerland' poems has two levels: in the foreground, the lower Alps where the affair is conducted, with the nucleus of lovely images which that landscape evoked; and the higher Alps, in the background, with their 'vast seas of snow', misty clouds, and thunderous torrents, to which, in his retreat from Marguerite, the speaker is carried by autumn storm-winds that are the image of his tormented soul. 'Stanzas in Memory of the Author of *Obermann*', Arnold's third and last poem of loss and retreat, opens with an allusion to the same autumn storm-winds, describes his meditation on his experience in the solitude of the higher Alps, and closes with his farewell to Senancour, the French author of *Obermann*, in whose Alpine forest and stoic books of meditation he had, for a time, sought refuge not only from Marguerite, but, as Arnold told Clough in a letter, from the modern *Zeitgeist* as well (*Letters to Clough*, 95). Thus the poem takes us a step further along the path of Arnold's quest, providing an account of a fateful decision, again painful and reluctant but not so much so as the Marguerite decision, to abandon the mountain loneliness and icy despair of Senancour and to enter into society and the modern world. The speaker tells Senancour that although he must depart, he leaves half of his life in the Alps, that half, we may infer, which craved a detached, calm, self-possession like Senancour's in which nature's calming voice could be heard undefiled by man's uproar, the life of a natural anchorite awaiting death in calm resignation. The speaker assures Senancour that although he must go into the world he will be spiritually faithful by keeping himself unspotted by it.

The landscape element in 'Stanzas in Memory of the Author of *Obermann*' plays a relatively minor part in the poem's evolution, the focus being on Senancour himself and upon the 'wounded human spirit', the agony and the 'fever' which burn in the pages of his books beneath 'the calm they feign'. He thus emerges as an Empedoclean figure, outwardly calm and even icy, but inwardly afire, whose Alpine solitudes are no more suitable as haunts for a poet than Empedocles's fiery Etna crater. A poet, Arnold has decided, must not tell 'too deep' secrets, because the world will not listen; he must watch, not share, human strife and suffering. This view was anticipated, as we have seen, by 'Resignation', and we can now see why Arnold adopted it: the pain of sharing was simply too great, and even were it not, to embody the 'unstrung will' and 'broken heart' in poetry only alienates the world. In Arnold's definitive poetic statement of the poet's dilemma, 'Empedocles on Etna', one also detects a note of defeat, not for Arnold the man but for Arnold the poet. The interest of 'Stanzas in Memory of the Author of *Obermann*' is as a poetic record of Arnold's strategy for living in the modern world: he will be in it, but not of it.

What it was like to live in that world Arnold describes in a sequence of major lyrics and elegies that take him to the end of his spiritual journey and of his career as a poet. 'Lines: Written in Kensington Gardens' presents a speaker in flight from the 'girdling city's hum' who seeks relief in nature. One of Arnold's most perfectly articulated lyric monologues, the poem moves with mounting tension at two levels: the level of visual exploration of the garden landscape, and the level of the speaker's growing consciousness of his apartness from the serenity and self-renewing life of nature that he discovers there, culminating in the desperate concluding prayer:

Calm, calm me more! nor let me die
Before I have begun to live.

The speaker feels simultaneously calmed and depressed by the overpowering presence of nature's separate life, seemingly invulnerable to man's busyness and heedless of his deepest longings. The danger the speaker feels is not that of being carried away by passion, or of icy despair, but of a spiritual death inflicted by life in a modern city.

The short series of love lyrics grouped under the title 'Faded Leaves' marks a similar painful moment of transition between the elegies of retreat and loss and the major elegies of recovery and hope. Although something of the Marguerite experience still reverberates in portions of 'Faded Leaves', the poems as a group are emotionally less intense and poetically less impressive than 'Switzerland'. As the title indicates, they express a more conventional, more domesticated, but hardly less tormented love, the speaker turning to the woman (some and perhaps all of the poems are addressed to Arnold's future wife, Frances Lucy Wightman) rather than to nature in search of surcease from his restless loneliness. The shifting landscapes of the poems—a pier at Calais, the Thames, the Rhine valley—reflect the speaker's restless wanderings, providing random settings for lyric statements of the speaker's desperate need for a sustaining and comforting companionship of the kind described in a related lyric, 'Euphrosyne':

Two bleeding hearts,
Wounded by men, by fortune tried,
Outwearied with their lonely parts,
Vow to beat henceforth side by side.

Faded Leaves expresses a need for such an 'existential' love, as J. Hillis Miller has named it,[1] the love of those who have shed romantic illusions in favour of a more realistic, more resigned companionship of mutually pledged fidelity in an infected world.

It is to the latter kind of love that the speaker in 'Dover Beach' refers. Situated in a particularized landscape and dramatic context, the speaker appeals to his beloved for loving fidelity as the one stay of humanity in a world which seems beautiful, but in reality has 'neither love, nor joy, nor light,/ Nor certitude, nor peace, nor help for pain'. In this most famous of his lyrics Arnold invests two of his major poetic

[1] J. H. Miller, *The Disappearance of God: Five Nineteenth-Century Writers*, Cambridge, Mass. 1963, 251.

images, the sea and calm moonlight, with an almost unbearable melancholy. The irregular lines and rhymes of the first three stanzas give way in the concluding stanza to regularity of metre and rhyme in beautifully varied iambic pentameters summing up the human predicament:

> *And we are here as on a darkling plain*
> *Swept with confused alarms of struggle and flight,*
> *Where ignorant armies clash by night.*

The interplay of visual and auditory images, the gradual deepening of the speaker's perception, the spatial and temporal displacement—from England in the present, to the Aegean in Sophocles' age, back through medieval Europe, to England again—the shift in focus from sea to land, together with the flawless language and varying verse rhythm, express and vindicate the speaker's determination to recognize the terror of the truth and at the same time to assert the power of human love to transcend blind fate.[1]

The germinating occasion of 'Dover Beach' was in all likelihood Arnold's brief stay with his wife at Dover during their abbreviated honeymoon in 1851. His marriage that year and his assumption of the responsibilities of a school inspectorship and of a family marked his irrevocable entrance into society and the modern *Zeitgeist*. The three final personal elegies indicate that he nevertheless succeeded, in some part of himself, in keeping himself 'unspotted'. Whereas the Obermann poem concerned his flight from solitude into society, 'The Scholar-Gipsy' and 'Thyrsis' present momentary withdrawals from society into solitude as occasions of self-renewal. The poems originate in the same nucleus of experiences and memories: the Cumnor landscape around Oxford, Glanvil's story of a seventeenth-century Oxford scholar, Arnold's memory of the happy days spent in that landscape with his youthful friend and fellow-poet, Clough, and the echoes in his auditory imagination of the rhythms and occasionally the language of

[1] *Matthew Arnold: 'Dover Beach'*, ed J. Middlebrook, Columbus, Ohio 1970, contains a convenient collection of essays on 'Dover Beach' by various hands.

Keats's great Odes. Nevertheless, the poems differ in important ways, marking two distinct phases in Arnold's spiritual evolution.[1]

'The Scholar-Gipsy' is the greater of the two poems. The first part concentrates upon the Cumnor landscape, recreating Glanvil's historical figure as a *genius loci* who has kept himself unspotted while awaiting the spark from heaven to fall. The second part transfigures the Scholar-Gipsy into a symbol of immortal youth and hope whose single-minded pursuit and quiet self-possession stand as a devastating indictment of the hurry, disease, and endless fluctuations of life in the modern world. The poem moves correspondingly from landscape description to moral reflection, from the natural rhythms of the seasons to the hurry and aimlessness of modern society, and from lyric celebration to the dialectical tensions between purpose and wandering, self-possession and emptiness, permanence and transience, joy and ennui, culminating in the coda of the final two stanzas in which another, more ancient, shy and earnest quester flees across the sea to escape another society of intruding bustlers. On the strength of his dream-vision the speaker succeeds in fleeing for a time the dispiriting modern age to a poetic country of the mind where he can refresh his spirit and renew his hope. The original 'Oxford scholar poor' is dead, but the poem translates him into the realm of myth and poetry, a compelling image of a spiritual state which remains uninfected by the disease of modernity. 'The Scholar-Gipsy' brings together some of the major images of Arnold's poetry in a comprehensive rendering of his central poetic themes: the Cumnor flowers, the cool bank of the Thames, the moonlit stream, the dewy grass, the quiet bower, through which the Scholar-Gipsy moves as a titulary figure, an image of Arnold's own buried self.

Ostensibly an elegy on Clough, 'Thyrsis' re-evokes 'The Scholar-Gipsy' landscape as Arnold attempts to prove to himself that his Muse has not yet gone away. But while 'Thyrsis' derives much of its power from its association with its earlier companion poem, the focus is changed. The speaker is as much concerned with whether his 'pipe is lost' as he is with the loss of his friend, Thyrsis. The season is winter, the time is evening, and the speaker is oppressed by his consciousness of the happier times and seasons of his youth: 'Where is the girl . . .

[1] A thorough analysis contrasting the two poems is provided by J. P. Curgenven in a series of six articles in *Litera*, Istanbul, II–VI, 1955–9.

Where are the mowers . . . They are all gone'. His pervading sense of change, of 'some loss of habit's power', makes death seem for a moment as welcome to him 'as a friend': he would rather join Thyrsis than mourn him. This nostalgic and regressive movement is reversed by the appearance of a troop of jovial Oxford hunters, from whom the speaker flees and as a consequence suddenly sees a 'signal-elm', the symbol to both Thyrsis and the speaker during their happy youth of the Scholar-Gipsy and his immortal quest. Thus reassured, both of his poetic power and of the existence of the Scholar-Gipsy, the speaker is prepared to 'roam on' until he dies.

Like Marguerite and the Scholar-Gipsy, Clough-Thyrsis undergoes a metamorphosis in the poem: the real Clough, the Clough who 'of his own will' abandoned the Scholar-Gipsy country and whose pipe took on a troubled note because he allowed himself to become involved in human strife, Arnold dismisses; 'Thyrsis', *his* Clough, the figure whose words conclude the poem—'Our scholar travels yet the loved hill-side'—he retains through the power of the poetry. The controlling image is that of the Tree, however, which together with 'the mountain-tops' where the 'throne of Truth' abides, suggests a fundamental refocusing of Arnold's attention, away from the Cumnor landscape and 'The coronals of that forgotten time', the moon and 'the cuckoo's parting cry/ From the wet field', with which Arnold's poetic temperament had its deepest affinities, towards the austerer world of willed moral effort, with its mountains and high white star of Truth, which engaged Arnold's intelligence and will but never his imagination.

'Obermann Once More' is Arnold's farewell both to his past and to poetry, but there is no sadness in it. The poem consists mostly of a sustained lecture by a ghostly Senancour, a Senancour *transfiguré* as Sainte-Beuve called him,[1] who urges his former disciple to stop grieving for the past and to place his hope in the future. The controlling image of Senancour's speech is again the River of Life, but significantly altered: it is a specific historical river, one that has broken up the ice which had for centuries frozen Europe in a deathlike stasis and is now carrying mankind towards a world of a more firmly based, less illusory, hope and joy. Senancour's advice to the speaker is to reject despair and solitude:

[1] *Commentary*, 271.

> '*What still of strength is left, employ*
> *That end to help attain:*
> One common wave of thought and joy
> Lifting mankind again!'

The Speaker accepts the advice, but

> . . . *with aspect marr'd,*
> *Shorn of the joy, the bloom, the power*
> *Which best befit [the] bard.*

The image of the quiet Alpine dawn with which the poem concludes is an analogue for the speaker's new-found contentment and hope, but the absence of inner tension, the colourless and prosaic language, the delivery of a message to himself through the mask of an unrecognizable Senancour, give to 'Obermann Once More' an air of being *voulu*, a moral preachment from which the vital images of Arnold's poetry are absent. Arnold the poet has completed the account of his spiritual history in a poem that is, not altogether inappropriately, versified prose.

It is easier for us than it was for Arnold to recognize that despite the difference in theme and tone between his poetry and that of his Romantic predecessors, he wrote out of the same cultural predicament. His attacks upon his Romantic predecessors in his letters and early criticism were attempts, largely unconscious, to evade the dilemma of the Romantic poet, to get away from the only kind of poetry that it was possible for a modern poet to write, described by Yeats when he wrote: 'The reason for putting our actual situation into our art is that the struggle for complete affirmation may be, often must be, that art's chief poignancy.'[1] The desire to affirm, to animate, ennoble, and give joy was certainly present in Arnold's poetic nature, and we may even believe that he eventually attained some measure of joy in his life. But in his best poetry it is the struggle to affirm, not affirmation, that we feel, and when Arnold himself came to see this, he gave up writing poetry. Even when he goes out of himself in narrative or drama, the egotistical element is there, described by R. H. Hutton as a 'clear, self-contained, thoughtful, heroic egotism',[2] and lends Olympian dignity

[1] Richard Ellmann, *The Identity of Yeats*, New York 1954, 240.
[2] R. H. Hutton, *Essays Theological and Literary*, 2 vol 1880, II, 260.

and grace to poems that are in fact profoundly sad and personal. The term 'elegiac', so frequently used to characterize Arnold's poetry, is therefore appropriate if understood in Coleridge's sense as identifying the form of poetry 'natural to the reflective mind', which may treat of no subject for its own sake but 'always and exclusively with reference to the poet himself'.[1] In his finest lyric and elegiac poems Arnold's personal note finds direct expression in poems as intimate as any in the English language.

[1] Quoted from 'Table-Talk' in J. M. Murry, *The Problem of Style*, 1960 (first edn 1922), 37.

3: Arnold the Poet:

(ii) Narrative and Dramatic Poems

KENNETH AND MIRIAM ALLOTT[1]

MATTHEW ARNOLD'S ATTEMPTS at grouping his poems in the several collected editions of his poetry between the first in 1869 and the last to be published in his lifetime in 1885 conjure up images of a man distractedly packing and repacking a suitcase without ever making a neat job of it or satisfying himself that he had done so. His taxonomic problems sprang from his obduracy in holding that there could be no improvement 'upon the classification adopted by the Greeks for kinds of poetry', that the Greek 'categories of epic, dramatic, lyric, and so forth' possess 'a natural propriety' requiring us to adhere to them permanently. This claim is really an expression of Arnold's conservative bent, which grew more rigid with the years, as

[1] As I pointed out in the Prefatory Note, my husband left a fair copy of his opening argument. Pages 70–7 are therefore in his own words exactly as he left them, up to the closing remarks about 'Tristram and Iseult'. I take over at this point, still following the initial guidance and of course incorporating information from surviving rough notes and from his edition of Arnold's poems. For the detailed analysis of individual poems which follows I must assume sole responsibility, although again I have benefited from *Poems*, and also from the corrections which he made in his working copy in preparation for a future edition. The interpretative comments on 'Empedocles on Etna' lean heavily on unpublished lectures on Arnold delivered by him at Liverpool University and elsewhere. Direct quotations from his published and unpublished materials are indicated in the notes below, which are of my own compiling throughout (there were indications in his fair copy of the points which he wished to annotate, and these I have followed to the best of my ability).

its appearance in his Wordsworth essay of 1879 indicates:[1] two years earlier, in the second collected edition of his poetry in 1877, he had discovered that he could not in fact adhere strictly to the Greek kinds and had added to the narrative, elegiac, lyric and dramatic categories of 1869 the new un-Greek category of 'Early Poems'. His use of the new category was disingenuous. Into it he dropped alongside genuinely early pieces later poems which it puzzled him to classify convincingly. With the problem he had experienced in arranging his poems in 1877 still worrying him he did admit in the Wordsworth essay that 'it may sometimes seem doubtful to which of two categories a poem belongs', but this momentary entertainment of an honest doubt, which should have led him to reconsider his whole position, was immediately smothered by the rash assertion that 'there is to be found in every good poem a strain, a predominant note, which determines the poem as belonging to one of these kinds rather than the other'.[2] This assertion is contradicted by our experience of both Romantic and Victorian poetry (including Arnold's own). Inevitably it led Arnold into evasiveness and inconsistency. For example, the treatment of 'Resignation' in the collected edition of the poems is evasive. Placed last as a confession of faith or testament in *The Strayed Reveller* (1849), it was a lyric to Arnold in 1869, but was then tagged as an early poem in 1877, probably because it seemed to him on further reflection to contain too much argument for a lyric and yet was not to be described plausibly as a dramatic, narrative or elegiac poem. Shrugging off the difficulty of classification in this instance led to inconsistency in the treatment of other poems. For example, if 'Resignation' is not a lyric poem, then neither is 'Epilogue to Lessing's Laocoön', which adopts a similar method of procedure, but it remains one after 1869 because Arnold, we must suppose, could not feel comfortable about labelling 'early' a piece first published in *New Poems* (1867).

It would be tedious to record all Arnold's chopping and changing about the proper disposition of the poems in his collected editions, but we should be aware how often he was in two or more minds about a poem's 'predominant note'. Four lyric poems of 1869 were sensibly transferred in 1877 to the group of the elegiac poems (where they were to remain), but one understands very well Arnold's original hesitation in

[1] *CPW*, IX, 36–55.
[2] *CPW*, IX, 43.

classifying, for example, 'Heine's Grave', which is a lay sermon and a 'sort of poetical pendant' to his Heine essay (as Arnold called it in offering it in 1863 to George Smith for the *Cornhill*), with 'Memorial Verses' or 'Rugby Chapel', which are elegies in a more straightforward sense in spite of their inclusion of critical and homiletic material. 'The Strayed Reveller' was a narrative poem in 1869, a dramatic poem apparently in 1877, finally a lyric poem. (Yet it consists entirely of the speeches of three characters and has prefixed to it a stage-direction announcing the time and place of the action and the presence 'on stage' when the poem opens of two of these characters, Circe and the intoxicated Youth.) 'The Church of Brou' was also a narrative poem in 1869, presumably because Part I, The Castle, tells a story in ballad fashion, although Part II, The Church, is a lyric and Part III, The Tomb, an elegy. On Arnold's terms 'The Church of Brou', like 'Resignation', cannot be a good poem since no amount of quibbling will enable us to find in it a predominant strain or note, but when he suppressed Parts I and II in 1877 it was for their topographical inaccuracy, not because he recognized them to be inferior to Part III and out of key with it. The elegiac third part, now entitled 'A Tomb among the Mountains', was not put among the elegies but rather absurdly kept its old position with the other narrative poems. Then Arnold must have decided that he had as much right to situate his church of Brou in alpine scenery as Shakespeare had to supply Bohemia with a sea-coast. The poem was restored to its former tripartite shape and dismissed to a place among the early poems. It is not in Arnold's comparatively short poetic life an early composition. It was published first in *Poems* (1853), Arnold's third collection, with 'Sohrab and Rustum' and 'The Scholar-Gipsy', and, although conceived earlier, was probably written in the autumn of 1852 when at Clough's bidding he was revising and adding to 'Tristram and Iseult' to make what was then an unfamiliar story more intelligible.[1]

The double dealing to which Arnold was driven in trying to group his poems is a forcible reminder that when he composed most of them in the 1840s and 1850s the neo-classical idea of fixed literary kinds, each one clearly differentiated from all the rest, already had no more real

[1] See *Poems*, 214 n, *Letters to Clough*, 47–8, and (for Clough's comments in his review) C. Dawson, *Matthew Arnold: The Critical Heritage. The Poetry*, London and Boston 1973 (referred to below as *Dawson*), 72.

authority than the notion of the immutability of species was to have for botanists and zoologists after Darwin. For better or worse, it had finally lost that authority in the Romantic period. A. C. Bradley's useful *aperçu* in 'The Long Poem in The Age of Wordsworth', namely, that 'the whole poetic spirit of the time'—a time which he extended to cover the Victorians—was 'lyrical in tendency', should persuade us how radically stock notions of the nature of narrative and dramatic poetry have to be modified when the poet's interest shifts to 'emotions, thought, will'.[1] To speak of modification is to speak as neutrally as possible ('distortion' and 'transformation' would be the opposed party-cries). If Shelley's 'Alastor' and Keats's 'Isabella' are so 'strongly tinged with the lyrical' that in them 'the balance of outward and inward is lost', which in plain English means that Shelley could not be bothered with his story (making the best of things, Mrs. Shelley wrote that 'Alastor' 'ought rather to be considered didactic than narrative') and that Keats, as Arnold said in his 1853 Preface, spoilt the story he borrowed from Boccaccio, it has still to be recognized that in other Romantic narrative poems 'strongly tinged with the lyrical', for example, Coleridge's 'The Ancient Mariner' and Keats's 'The Eve of St. Agnes', not only is the balance of outward and inward better kept but the lyrical element permits an intensity of correspondence between feeling and event that is both new and satisfying. We approve of these poems as successful hybrids. In their poetic practice the Romantics cross-bred the neo-classical kinds to such effect that by Arnold's time a good poem might well be lyric, dramatic and elegiac simultaneously. 'Everything', as Bagehot once said, 'runs into everything else.'

To realize that the kinds run into each other in the Victorian period is to knock on the head one loosely expressed commonplace about Arnold's poetic achievement to which many readers might be tempted to give a casual assent. 'Arnold's poetry,' wrote the late D. G. James, 'the poetry we all know almost by heart, is elegiac. He longed to create in narrative and drama, but he failed: it would not do.'[2] There is, of course, a shadowy truth behind these words (Arnold was never, I think, interested in storytelling), but the statement itself will not do.

1. A. C. Bradley, 'The Long Poem in the Age of Wordsworth', *Oxford Lectures on Poetry*, 1965 [first edn 1909], 182–3.

2. D. G. James, *Matthew Arnold and the Decline of English Romanticism*, Oxford 1961, 103.

James is speaking first of the poetic note ('elegiac') and then without change of voice of poetic kinds ('narrative and drama'). But the elegiac note in Matthew Arnold's poetry is not confined to the elegiac poems, nor is it to be found in all of them. It is absent or all but absent from 'Heine's Grave'. Again, the poetry 'we all know almost by heart' does not include for example 'Stanzas in Memory of Edward Quillinan', officially an elegy, whereas it does include the Cadmus and Harmonia episode from the dramatic poem 'Empedocles on Etna' and the Oxus coda from the narrative poem 'Sohrab and Rustum'. At this point one cannot escape restating that the frequency of the elegiac note reflects Arnold's native melancholy. It is obvious that a vein of melancholy resisted and explored rather than simply indulged is a main component of Arnold's poetic nature, and that when he mastered the discontent of 'the mobile, straining, passionate, poetic temperament' in the interests of 'morality and character' (though the mastery was never to be complete) the poetry slowed to a trickle and then disappeared. Arnold himself uses this image to illustrate the course of individual poetic development in the late lyric 'The Progress of Poesy': the youth strikes the rock and water gushes forth; the man 'mature with labour' cuts a channel for 'the bright stream', but the channel is now completely dry.[1] The lyric has a clear autobiographical point even if it was intended to have a wider application and to be emblematic of the fate of the Romantic poet. To translate, there is a time when inspiration flows freely, but the poet may be unable to take full advantage of it because he is still technically immature; there is a time when inspiration is dead and the poet has enough self-knowledge not to be deceived by the mere wish to create. Between times there is an indefinite interim during which technical mastery serves a fitful and always declining inspiration. This means, then, in reply to those who think like D. G. James, that there are different sorts of success and failure on the way up and the way down, and that failure is too broad and indiscriminate a concept if it must blanket both 'Empedocles on Etna' and *Merope*, both 'Sohrab and Rustum' and 'St. Brandan'. 'Empedocles on Etna' and 'Sohrab and Rustum' are for different reasons failures if the critical sights are high enough, but to separate out the stronger and weaker parts of the work of any poet who is not one of the supreme

[1] *Poems*, 540–1.

creators—and that means all Victorian poets—one must cut more finely.

These preliminary remarks bear directly on the way in which we see Arnold's narrative and dramatic poems, but what is most obvious is too often overlooked. In the earlier narrative pieces such as 'Mycerinus', 'The Sick King in Bokhara' and 'Tristram and Iseult', and in 'Empedocles on Etna', we find Arnold tacitly accepting the freedom bestowed on him by Romantic practice and working effectively—although until 'Empedocles on Etna' for the most part with poetic skills not fully developed—in the mixed or hybrid kinds which the classical purist in him was later to deny had any right to exist. In such later major narrative poems as 'Sohrab and Rostum' and 'Balder Dead', which have a high degree of poetic finish, and in *Merope*, we discover him attempting to write against the grain of the age and against the inclinations of a part of himself that he was seeking to suppress, and these works, widely as they differ in merit, are in consequence all shaded by an inevitable artificiality. There is in fact a discontinuity in Arnold's poetic life, analogous to the line of a geological fault in a landscape, although the scenery, so to speak, has a family likeness on both sides of the broken and tilted streak. The discontinuity is glaring between 'Empedocles on Etna', the culmination of Arnold's earlier poetic development and his most ambitious poem, and *Merope*, the most open application of the critical doctrines of the 1853 Preface, but it can also be traced very obviously in contrasting Arnold's earlier and later narrative poems. The strata tilted as a result of a decision, although it would be more exact to speak of it as a series of decisions in the same way as there are premonitory rumblings and after-shocks in an earthquake. The earliest rumble was probably the decision to leave 'half of his life' behind him in Switzerland with Senancour (and Marguerite) in the autumn of 1849, but the main shock belongs to the spring of 1851 when Arnold accepted appointment to the uncongenial post of school inspector to be able to marry. *'Je connais Arnold'*, Sainte-Beuve wrote in 1860, *'il nous aimait beaucoup dans sa jeunesse . . . c'était un Français et un peu romantique égaré là-bas. C'était piquant chez le fils du respectable Arnold, le grand réformateur de l'instruction publique en Angleterre. Depuis il s'est marié, s'est réglé, et, dans ses pensées, il reste fidèle au culte des anciens et de l'art.'*[1] It is not necessary to explain Arnold's decision

[1] Letter of 27 October 1860, *Correspondance Générale de Sainte-Beuve*, ed J. Bonnerot, 1961, XI, 629.

psychologically in detail, but it must be accepted that it occurred and that it was defeat for his poetic self. The change in him had something to do with his 'settling down' and shouldering responsibilities (including that of marriage), with discovering that he was more like his father than he had once believed, with recognizing his divided nature and giving the ethical Teuton more play and the imaginative Celt less because he had begun to distrust what T. S. Eliot calls the 'genuine feelings of unrest, loneliness and dissatisfaction' which were the mainspring of his best poetry.[1] Yeats tells us,

> *The intellect of man is forced to choose*
> *Perfection of the life or of the work . . .*

Arnold chose life because after 'Empedocles on Etna' he was often unable and when able unwilling to face again the pangs and perils of poetic creation ('an actual tearing of oneself to pieces, which one does not readily consent to'[2]). But he chose sadly and reluctantly however bold the face he showed to Clough when the latter expressed his liking for 'The Scholar Gipsy':

> Homer animates—Shakespeare animates—in its poor way Sohrab and Rustum animates—the Gipsy Scholar at best awakens a pleasing melancholy, But this is not what we want.
> The complaining millions of men
> Darken in labour and pain—
> what they want is something to *animate* and *ennoble* them—not merely to add zest to their melancholy or grace their dreams—I believe a feeling of this kind is the basis of my nature—and of my poetics.[3]

He was more circumspect with Sainte-Beuve. When the French critic after studying the 1853 Preface objected in 1854 that in his view modern subjects were superior in interest to those drawn from earlier times, Arnold merely urged that sometimes '*œuvres de cabinet et d'étude*', to which 'Sohrab and Rustum' belonged, were the only sort of poems

[1] 'Matthew Arnold', *The Use of Poetry and the Use of Criticism* (1933), repr. in D. J. DeLaura's *Matthew Arnold: A Collection of Critical Essays*, Twentieth Century Views, Englewood Cliffs, N.J. 1973, 17.
[2] *Letters*, I, 63.
[3] Letter of 30 November [1853], *Letters to Clough*, 146.

possible.[1] Had he said 'now possible for me' after his rejection of the morbid exhaustion produced by poetic creation, he would have spoken with precision. 'Empedocles on Etna' was, as I have said elsewhere, 'like the crisis of a long and punishing illness from which the patient recovers to lead a diminished life'.[2] The art of the later narratives and *Merope* is the art nourished by a diminished life.

At the most cursory inspection there is a formal difference between 'Mycerinus', 'The Sick King in Bokhara', 'Tristram and Iseult' and 'The Church of Brou' on the one hand and 'Sohrab and Rostum' and 'Balder Dead' on the other. For example, if we compare 'Tristram and Iseult' with 'Balder Dead', which are both tripartite, we note that the latter is written throughout in blank verse and maintains a single tone whereas the former not only has a different metrical form for each part but varies metrically in the first two parts; Part I alternates between five-beat speeches for the present and equivalenced octosyllabics for the narratives of the Breton bard, both rhymed irregularly, and Part II begins with quatrains in trochaic pentameter for the speeches of Tristram and Iseult of Cornwall and then switches to the equivalenced octosyllabics, sometimes introducing rhyming couplets (not to mention several three-beat lines). In 'The Church of Brou', which is also tripartite, Part I reflects Arnold's feeling for 'the rapidity and grace' of Heine's ballad-form which he had imitated in 'The Neckan' (though his quatrains now find a closer counterpart in Tennyson's 'The Lord of Burleigh'); Part II consists of five eight-line stanzas (rhyming a b c a b c d d) in which the rhythm of Tennyson's 'The Lady of Shalott' is 'suggested but not actually reproduced';[3] and Part III is in five-beat rhyming couplets varying metrically between iambs and trochees. A similar formal difference separates 'Sohrab and Rustum' from 'Mycerinus' and 'The Sick King in Bokhara', none of which is broken into separate parts. 'Sohrab and Rustum' is again written throughout in blank verse, though

[1] Letter of Sainte-Beuve to Arnold, 6 September 1854, *Correspondance Générale* (*ed. cit.*), IX, 433; repr. in *Unpublished Letters*, 68–70. For Arnold's reply, 29 September 1854, see L. Bonnerot, *Matthew Arnold, Poète*, Paris 1947, 522.

[2] Kenneth Allott, 'A Background for "Empedocles on Etna"', *Essays and Studies*, ed Simeon Potter, 1968, 96–7; repr. in D. DeLaura's *Matthew Arnold: A Collection of Critical Essays*, *ed. cit.*, 67.

[3] See *Poems*, 299.

the verse form compasses more than the single tone of the less personal 'Balder Dead', whereas of the other two narratives 'Mycerinus' begins in the regular six-line stanza (a b a b c c) used—to very different ends—by Wordsworth in 'Laodamia' and finishes in blank verse, while 'The Sick King in Bokhara' begins in irregular rhyming verse paragraphs for the earlier speeches of Hussein, the Vizier and the King and ends in regular quatrains (a b a b), the change occurring in the middle of Hussein's account of the Mullah's story.

If we turn from these narratives and 'narrative lyrics' to 'Empedocles on Etna', which Arnold described in his heading as 'A Dramatic Poem' (as Byron described *Manfred*) and to *Merope: A Tragedy*, which was designed to give readers 'a specimen of the world created by the Greek imagination', we see that the 'dramatic' colouring in the earlier poem owes a great deal to its metrical variations, whereas all such variation is rigorously excluded from *Merope*: 'You are not in the least bound to like her', Arnold wrote defensively in February 1858 when his 'Greek' play was being greeted with mixed feelings, 'as she is calculated rather to inaugurate my Professorship with Dignity than to move deeply the present race of *humans*'.[1] *Merope* is in blank verse throughout for the principal speeches, broken only by the strophes and antistrophes of the chorus where an attempt is made to preserve the classical symmetry of Greek choric style. In 'Empedocles on Etna', on the other hand, the metrical variations signal and help to define the complex feelings which shape the poem. Act I i is in blank verse for the explanatory speeches given to Callicles and Pausanias and so is Act I ii for the not yet highly charged exchanges between Empedocles and Pausanias, but the metre begins to change at I ii 36–75 for Callicles's first song, which opens with a twenty-line descriptive introduction—celebrating delight in the physical world—in irregularly stressed unrhymed verse (though five-beat lines still predominate) and continues with a chant—celebrating the importance of traditional wisdom—which is in four-beat lines and has an irregularly patterned rhyme scheme (I ii 57–75). Empedocles's long despondent meditative recitative (on 'modern thought'[2]), which follows at I ii 77–426, runs to seventy-one

[1] *Letters*, I, 60.

[2] W. E. Houghton, '. . . in the two acts of the play, respectively, Arnold saw the possibility of portraying both "modern thought" and "modern feeling"', 'Arnold's "Empedocles on Etna"', *VS*, June 1958, 316–17.

stanzas, each consisting of two hexameters broken to form a quatrain rhyming a b a b and an unbroken hexameter which rhymes with the corresponding unbroken hexameter in the following stanzas. At its conclusion, Callicles resumes his irregularly rhymed joyful chant (I ii 427–60) and the Act closes with the blank verse exchanges between Empedocles and Pausanias. In Act II the metrical variations continue to draw attention to the personal conflict which brings together in the poem the contrasted figures of the young serene poet and the poet-philosopher who has left behind youth and joy and his poetic self. Empedocles's melancholy soliloquy (II 1–36), which is now concerned with 'modern feeling' and is uttered at the charred summit of Etna, is in blank verse broken by Callicles's two songs heard from 'below' through the violent eruptions of the volcano. The first song, in praise of music, is Pindaric in subject but fashioned to suggest the symmetry of a Greek tragic chorus ('The metre of the Song is balanced like strophe and antistrophe: two quatrains followed by two groups of twenty [-two] lines matching both in rhyme scheme and line length');[1] the second, which uses the fable of Apollo and Marsyas to record the cruel price of being a poet, consists of two matching quatrains followed by two passages of unequal length in rhymed trochaic tetrameter. Taking its cue from Callicles's closing lament for the slain Marsyas,

> *Ah, poor Faun, poor Faun, poor Faun! ah, poor Faun!* . . .,

Empedocles's subsequent renouncement of his symbols of intellectual and poetic power is cast in free verse, beginning,

> *And lie thou there,*
> *My laurel bough!*
> *Scornful Apollo's ensign, lie thou there!* . . .,

and his soliloquy from this point until his suicide (ll. 194–416) moves between blank verse and free verse through 'a descending and ascending series of short lines',[2] with variations between two-beat and three-beat

[1] P. Baum, 'Empedocles on Etna', *Ten Studies in the Poetry of Matthew Arnold*, Durham, N.C. 1958, 125. See also *Poems*, 178.
[2] P. Baum, *op. cit.*, 127.

lines. After he has leaped into the crater, Callicles continues to sing from the fertile wooded region below, and this final song, with its quatrains and mixed iambic and trochaic lines, catches something of the metrical effect of the Fourth Spirit's song in Byron's *Manfred* but closes with a characteristically Arnoldian cadence as it invokes the 'calm' often sought for in the poems and rarely found, or if found then accompanied by regret that its price is the loss of intense feeling.

'Can anyone doubt the conscious planning and secure execution?' asks Paull Baum of the management of Callicles's last song in his short commentary on 'Empedocles on Etna', which is intended to go a little way (it is only a little way) towards redressing a balance. For his handling of metre, says this author in his introduction, 'Arnold has never had his just deserts'.[1] It is not possible here to take further the task of rendering to Arnold his 'just deserts' for his command of metre, but the flexibility in the earlier narratives and in 'Empedocles on Etna' glanced at above signals the freedom of movement permitted before the strata tilted. In the interval between the publication of 'Tristram and Iseult', 'Empedocles on Etna' and the Marguerite poems, which together reflect the seismic shocks making first for the discontinuity in his poetic life and ultimately for its final cessation in the 1860s, and the appearance of *Merope* in 1858, Arnold set about impeding this freedom of movement with a deliberation which makes us read W. H. Auden's declaration that 'he thrust his gift in prison till it died' not as a poetic flourish but as the strict truth in a nutshell.[2] Reacting against the tensions produced by the conflict between the analytical reason on the one hand and moral intuition, feeling and imagination on the other—this struggle between the 'head' and the 'heart' is the key to Victorian romanticism—he turned to another order of poetry altogether. 'You may often have heard my sinews cracking under the effort to unite matter', he had said in a letter to Clough, written either late in 1847 or early in 1848.[3] Ten years later, when discussing the reception of *Merope*, he wrote to his sister, 'People do not understand what a temptation there is if you cannot bear anything *not*

[1] *Op. cit.*, 130, xi.

[2] The general direction of the argument in this paragraph, together with some of the phrasing, is indebted to one of a series of unpublished lectures on Arnold given by Kenneth Allott in the University of Liverpool.

[3] *Letters to Clough*, 65.

very good to transfer your operations to a region where form is everything. Perfection of a kind may be attained or approached without knocking yourself to pieces.[1] He had settled for—and bravely defended—the 'faultily faultless' form of what has been labelled his unread and unreadable quasi-Greek tragedy. As a half-way house to this reliance on form was his insistence, first formulated in his 1853 Preface, on the choice of a subject which was in itself good and therefore self-sustaining. It was this that he tried for in 'Sohrab and Rustum' and 'Balder Dead'. But the distinction here is that while both are good subjects by external criteria, it is the first only that engages the feelings. Both are well told, both are firmly constructed, both are disciplined in style, both make use of Homeric-Miltonic similes. But the truth is that 'Sohrab and Rustum' relates itself to Arnold's own situation and therefore receives a blood-transfusion of vitality. Where the feelings are more sedate, as they are in 'Balder Dead', the poem has all the minor merits, but remain mediocre ('*La médiocrité est un extrème vice en la poésie*', says Du Bellay). The earlier narratives or 'narrative lyrics'—'Mycerinus', 'The Sick King in Bokhara', 'The Forsaken Merman' and 'Tristram and Iseult'—do not belong to this attempt to avoid 'tearing oneself to pieces' and their subjects invariably relate themselves to Arnold's own situation. It is with these pieces and with 'Empedocles on Etna' that this discussion is chiefly concerned, the poems on the other side of the geological fault being looked at principally from the point of the poetic self whose tones are heard with increasing faintness as time goes on until they die out altogether.

Arnold's friend, James Anthony Froude, who wrote about him to Charles Kingsley on the day after the publication of *The Strayed Reveller and Other Poems*, saw little sign that he had been 'torn to pieces' by poetic creation: 'I admire Matt—to a very great extent. Only I don't see what business he has to parade his calmness and lecture us on resignation when he has never known what a storm is, and doesn't know what he has to resign himself to—I think he only knows the shady side of nature out of books.'[2] But Froude was in the middle of his own 'storm'. His confused and troubled autobiographical novel, *The Nemesis of Faith* (1849), a central document in the literature of England's 'crisis of faith', appeared in the same week as *The Strayed*

[1] *Letters*, I, 62–3.

[2] Cited in *Letters to Clough*, 127 n.

Reveller (when it stirred up further trouble for its author), and his reaction is the more understandable in that Arnold's 'crisis of faith' seemed to have occurred quietly off stage. The unorthodoxy is in the poems from the start and is apparently taken for granted, the issues now being the intellectual and emotional difficulties of 'how to live' in its presence. What we now know about Arnold's personal and literary experience in the early 1840s persuades us that his choice of the story of Mycerinus from the second book of Herodotus, of the Sick King from Captain Sir Alexander Burnes's *Travels into Bokhara* (1834) and of the Merman from Hans Andersen (via Mary Howitt and George Borrow) was in each case the result of an impulse to discover through the reworking of a series of fictional events an answer to emotional disquiet.

'Mycerinus' is an indictment of heavenly injustice, answering Wordsworth's 'Laodamia' to which it draws attention by its metrical imitation. The subject had been associated in Arnold's mind since 1831 with the personality of his father, who had set it that year as the subject for a Rugby prize poem, so it is hard not to link his renewed interest in it with Dr. Arnold's death in 1842 and the warning that he had inherited a similar weakness of the heart. (One early reviewer found the story 'a kind of apotheosis of despair; it looks as though suggested by a father's fate. At the same time it seems almost a profession of atheism.')[1] In Herodotus, Mycerinus's father, the Egyptian King Cheops, has been throughout a lengthy reign an unjust and impious ruler. On his death Mycerinus's sense of shock and wrong is aroused by a divine decree that he has only six years to live notwithstanding his desire to rule his people justly and well. He abandons good deeds and defiantly gives himself up to revelry by night and day, thus doubling the length of his allotted span. His bitterness finds expression in the stanzaic part of Arnold's poem (ll. 1–86), which opens with rhetorical verve:

> *Not by the justice that my father spurned,*
> *Not for the thousands that my father slew,*
> *Altars unfed and temples overturned,*
> *Cold hearts and thankless tongues, where thanks are due;*
> *Fell this dread voice from lips that cannot lie . . .*

[1] Unsigned notice in the *English Review*, March 1850: see *Dawson*, 131.

The single 'crime' was that he

> *. . . sate obedient, in fiery prime*
> *Of youth, self-governed, at the feet of Law . . .*

The poem ended originally with the twenty-line blank verse passage (ll. 79–99) beginning, 'So spake he half in anger, half in scorn', which is a colourful reworking of the straightforward description in Herodotus of the young king's nightly revelry. The passage was thought by many early readers to be Tennysonian, though it closes in fine panache with an individual variation of a well-known Shelleyan image which pictures the rays of the moon—the moon is always associated in Arnold with calm—'splintered' night after night by the lamplit branches of trees.[1] But in the twenty-seven lines of blank verse which were added later Mycerinus suffers a sea change from a defiantly hedonistic youth to an 'Egyptian Marcus Aurelius' who, for all his appearance of gaiety, is a Stoic in disguise. 'It may be', as Arnold cautiously puts it in order to effect his transition, he

> *Took measure of his soul and knew its strength,*
> *And by that silent knowledge, day by day*
> *Was calmed, ennobled, comforted, sustained . . .*

Arnold's early study of Stoicism belongs to the years 1846–8, when he was reading Senancour and Epictetus; we know too that his self-protective pose of dandyism in his early days at Oxford and in London deceived even close members of his family—a sister was taken by surprise by 'the knowledge of life and conflict . . . *strangely like experience*' displayed in this first volume of poems, and she added, '"Mycerinus" struck me most perhaps, as illustrating what I have been speaking of'.[2] 'I will write historically,' Arnold once wrote to his friend Clough in order to clear up a misunderstanding (this was in February 1853), 'as I can write naturally in no other way.' By 'historically' he meant 'chronologically', and if we read his poems in chronological order—and we have at least a broadly correct idea of this order—we can see the truth of this. The order helps us to understand

[1] See *Poems*, 31 n.

[2] Quoted in Mrs. Humphry Ward, *A Writer's Recollections*, 1918, 44.

more easily the differences between the poems, not only in their thinking but also in the art with which they are composed. As it turns out, the preponderance of recent studies of Arnold as a poet are almost exclusively interpretative and perhaps some of the differences in interpretation might have been avoided if Arnold's art, including his ordering and adaptation of his source material in his narrative and dramatic poems, had been looked at more closely.

'Mycerinus', we may say then, reflects stages in the conflict of feeling experienced by Arnold in the 1840s and the composing of the poem forms part of his effort to bring the conflict under control. The process continues, served by an increased command of poetic skills, in 'The Sick King in Bokhara', where the sights are now set on man's feeling for moral law even when this runs against his own interest (the Mullah in the poem has reminded readers of Raskolnikov in his search for punishment as a moral need).[1] William Rossetti, an early reviewer, found the poem 'the most simple and lifelike' of the narratives in the 1849 volume. It was 'full of life' again for R. H. Hutton in 1872, who admired it 'as . . . painting the richness and stateliness, and also the prostration and fatalism, of Oriental life'.[2]

The 'prostration' of the King, the Vizier and the Mullah takes its rise from Captain Burnes's stress in *Travels into Bokhara* (1834) on the fever to which he and his companions succumbed in the parching land.[3] In Arnold the malaise is as much spiritual as physical, and becomes in effect an extension of the idea suggested to him by Burnes's reference elsewhere in the book to 'the rigour of the Mohammedan law which is enforced in Bokhara'. This passage must have 'penetrated' him sharply when he came upon it, for the poem which it inspires carries on the themes of 'Mycerinus', where the 'Law' is at first external, divinely sanctioned and repudiated, and later, in the lines which are chronologically closer to 'The Sick King', self-imposed as a moral necessity.

The Mullah with whom Arnold's Sick King has to deal is a figure composed from the 'Moolah' who 'had violated the law' and the 'son who had cursed his mother', both of whom, according to Burnes, begged successfully for punishment and were executed, although in the

[1] Cp. Lionel Trilling, *Matthew Arnold*, 1970 [first edn 1939], 104–5.

[2] *Dawson*, 62, 227.

[3] Arnold's sources for the poem are set out in *Poems*, 75–6.

first case the king was reluctant to act: he threw the first stone as a gesture, but ordered his officers to let the man escape if he should make the attempt. The account stops here. In Arnold's narrative the Mullah, stricken with fever, secretes a pitcher filled with water from 'a little pool', one of Bokhara's meagre sources of water (the dryness of the land is another detail from Burnes and accords with the 'burning plain' which readers have seen as one of the characteristic regions in Arnold's poetic landscape).[1] When the Mullah finds that his mother and brothers have stolen his pitcher and drained it dry, he turns and curses them,

> *. . . being fevered, sick*
> *(Most unblest also) . . .*

'Now do right!' he urges the king, whose unwillingness and pity he resists until he is brought before the priests and condemned to death by stoning. The King gives his secret order to let him escape and himself casts the first stone 'softly' (Arnold's biblical echo is probably intentional), but the Mullah kneels on, praising Allah 'With a great joy in his face' while the officers fling the stones until he is dead. The ensuing dialogue between the King and the Vizier, who—less fortunate in this respect than the Mullah—are still afflicted by 'sickness', conveys their common weariness beneath the weight of unintelligible laws, although the one acquiesces in them and the other is restive. The quatrains, with which Arnold follows the irregular verse paragraphs used for the 'narrative' part of the poem, rise honourably to the task of meeting the difficult demands laid on them to preserve their ballad style while differentiating shades of feeling and at the same time engaging in a complicated moral debate (the syntax breaks down under the strain only at ll. 205–8; see *Poems*, 83). The Vizier's acceptance of his non-Christian law,

> *But who, through all the length of time,*
> *Could bear the burden of his years,*
> *If he for strangers pained his heart*
> *Not less than those who merit tears?*

[1] 'Borrowing phrases which Arnold himself employs we may call these regions the Forest Glade, the Burning or Darkling Plain, and the Wide Glimmering Sea'—A. Dwight Culler, *Imaginative Reason: The Poetry of Matthew Arnold*, 1966, 4.

> *Fathers we must have, wife and child,*
> *And grievous is the grief for these;*
> *This pain alone, which must be borne,*
> *Makes the head white, and bows the knees.*
>
> *But other loads than his own*
> *One man is not well made to bear . . .*,

is as heavy-hearted as the young king's restless grief, guilt and compassion.

> *O Vizier, thou art old, I young!*
> *Clear in these things I cannot see.*
> *My head is burning, and a heat*
> *Is in my skin which angers me.*
>
> *But hear ye this, ye sons of men!*
> *They that bear rule, and are obeyed,*
> *Unto a rule more strong than theirs*
> *Are in their turn obedient made . . .*

The poor look wistfully towards his 'silken raiment', his 'cherries served in drifts of snow' and his many riches, but his pain remains because, as he says in the poem's most contorted stanza, 'from all time/ The Law is planted . . .' which decrees that his will must not be satisfied. He goes on,

> *And I have meat and drink at will,*
> *And rooms of treasures not a few.*
> *But I am sick, nor heed I these;*
> *And what I would, I cannot do.*
>
> *Even the great honour which I have*
> *When I am dead, will soon grow still;*
> *So have I neither joy, nor fame—*
> *But what I can do, that I will.*

What he 'can do' is to lay the body of the Mullah in his own tomb, which is built near an apricot grove on the road to Samarcand

(Arnold's well-known delight in resonant and exotic foreign names finds early expression in his poems of 1847–8):

> *Bring water, nard, and linen rolls!*
> *Wash off all blood, set smooth each limb!*
> *Then say: 'He was not wholly vile,*
> *Because a King shall bury him.'*

The close of the story is again Arnold's own invention, and readers have seen in it a faint foreshadowing of Part III, The Tomb, in 'The Church of Brou', where the lovers find the rest and permanence unattainable in life in the 'chiselled broideries rare' of the marble tomb which bears their sculptured effigies. But the Keatsian contrasts of warmth and cold, colour and paleness, which are a central feature of this elegiac passage, arise from the new experience of emotional conflict most directly expressed in Arnold's first love poems written in 1848–9. Love, as we can see from the Marguerite poems and from 'Faded Leaves', so far from stilling the troubled questions about existence which are asked directly or indirectly throughout the 1849 volume, merely leads to their being posed in a new form and with a growing anxiety about the divided self. The experience of love strengthens the sense of impermanence:

> *. . . Time's current strong*
> *Leaves us fixed to nothing long . . .*[1]

It reminds the sceptical nature of the burden of its own scepticism:

> *. . . happier men . . . at least*
> *Have* dreamed *two human hearts might blend*
> *In one, and were through faith released*
> *From isolation without end . . .*

Its momentary drawing together of two people merely brings home more keenly than before the sense of this isolation—

[1] For this and the following passages from Arnold's love poems see *Poems*, 109, 122, 124, 120, 125.

Yes! in the sea of life enisled . . .
We mortal millions live alone!—

and it does so because it fails to ensure either the longed-for communion with the other or a clearer understanding of the self:

Far, far from each other
Our spirits have grown;
And what heart knows another?
Ah! who knows his own . . .

At its best, that is at its least disturbing as in 'Dover Beach' (which it is generally agreed concerns Arnold's wife 'Flu' and not Marguerite), love becomes what a recent writer—in an irreverent *jeu d'esprit* entitled 'The Dover Bitch'[1]—has called 'a sort of mournful cosmic last resort'. These linked feelings do nothing to alleviate the conception of a pitiless law governing the lonely existences of men:

A God, a God their severance ruled!
And bade betwixt their shores to be
The unplumbed, salt, estranging sea . . .

It is with these love poems that 'The Forsaken Merman', 'Tristram and Iseult' (both published in the 1852 volume) and 'The Church of Brou' (published in 1853 but apparently designed for the 1852 volume) are closely associated, so that the need to strike 'a balance between the inward and the outward' is still more pressing than in 'Mycerinus' and 'The Sick King in Bokhara', one symptom of the need being the writer's persistent search for a suitable dramatic frame for his personal themes. As it turned out, the formal method which best helped to effect a satisfying 'intensity of correspondence between theme and event' in these 'narratives or narrative lyrics' was not the half-narrative, half-dramatic manner which had been used with some success in 'The Sick King in Bokhara', and which was resorted to more awkwardly in 'Tristram and Iseult', but the individual variety of dramatic monologue adopted for 'The Forsaken Merman'. Arnold was not again to find

[1] A. Hecht, 'The Dover Bitch; A Criticism of Life', DeLaura's *Matthew Arnold: A Collection of Critical Essays, ed. cit.*, 54.

such success with this device in a narrative poem, but it is worth remarking that the form—which is the age's single most impressive poetic innovation and would be seen at its most resourceful six years later in Browning's *Men and Women* (1855)—can be linked in certain respects with the appearance in the 1830s and 1840s of the fictionalized autobiography, which enabled many writers, non-novelists among them (for example Carlyle, Froude and Newman), to explore pressing personal troubles in disguise.

'The Forsaken Merman' was admired by the early reviewers of the 1840s and 1850s and is still one of Arnold's best known and most widely anthologized poems. Arnold's 'Tennysonian' qualities were again remarked upon: besides being 'fantastic', as W. E. Aytoun put it in his characteristically 'sceptical, patronising and facetious' review of 1849, it 'had further the disadvantage of . . . reminding us of . . . Alfred's early extravaganzas', namely 'The Merman' and 'The Mermaid' (both of 1830), and there are of course verbal and descriptive echoes.[1] But the same reviewer found it 'by far the best poem' in the 1849 volume, with power not only of 'imagery and versification, but of actual pathos'. It was 'the gem of the book' for Charles Kingsley, surpassing Tennyson's '"Merman and Mermaid" in simple naturalness and a certain barbaric wildness of metre and fancy' and producing a strong impression by the correspondence between its themes and its formal innovations.[2]

Arnold's method of telling his story of loss and separation contrasts strikingly with the sparse straightforward versions of the legend which he found in Hans Andersen and in George Borrow's review of J. M. Thiele's *Danske Folksagen*, which is his principal source. Borrow relates how Grethe, the only child of poor parents in Jutland (she is Agnes in Hans Andersen, and some have attributed Arnold's variation—he calls her Margaret—to his feeling for Marguerite), is drawn to the bottom of the sea by a merman and lives for many years as his wife and the mother of their four children until one day, when she has 'forgotten all she knew of religion', the sound of the church bells coming down through the water from her former home fills her with melancholy longing. The merman leads her back to the land, begging her to return

[1] For Arnold on having 'Tennyson so in one's head, one cannot help imitating him sometimes' see *Commentary*, 83.

[2] *Dawson*, 54, 42.

after the service, but though he calls her three times, urging finally, 'Grethe, Grethe! will you come weeping quick? your children are crying for you', she does not reply and, weeping bitterly, he sinks back into the sea while 'ever after' she stays with her parents (*Poems*, 95–6).

Arnold retells this story, with the suppression of some original details and the invention of several new ones, through the Merman's lamenting address to his children, making full use of the freedom allowed by this device for the expression more than one at a time of the different 'voices of poetry'.[1] The Merman speaks as the bereft husband and the father of children who are 'wild with pain', the loss and pain belonging at first to the immediate present—it was 'only yesterday' that she left—so that the opening of the poem is a 'lyric cry':

> *Call her once before you go—*
> *Call once yet!*
> *In a voice that she will know:*
> *'Margaret! Margaret!'*
> *Children's voices should be dear*
> *(Call once more) to a mother's ear;*
> *Children's voices, wild with pain—*
> *Surely she will come again!*
> *Call her once and come away;*
> *This way, this way!*
> *'Mother dear, we cannot stay!*
> *The wild white horses foam and fret.'*
> *Margaret! Margaret! . . .*

As the lament unfolds so does the narrative. We learn that the action moves between the sea and the human town, and that 'yesterday', when Margaret's husband and children had crossed the sand and downs to 'The little grey church on the windy hill' and had gazed at her through 'the small leaded panes', she was already rapt away from them into her native world:

[1] W. Stacy Johnson says of T. S. Eliot's *The Three Voices of Poetry* (1953), 'He does, however, suggest that there may be fewer or more voices than three, and that these may be intermixed in any one poem—as they are, certainly, in Arnold', *The Voices of Matthew Arnold*, Yale 1961, ix.

But, ah, she gave me never a look,
For her eyes were sealed to the holy book!
Loud prays the priest: shut stands the door.
Come away children, call no more! . . .

Time passes to a later 'present' (ll. 85–107) and afterwards to the melancholy future on which the poem closes, so that Arnold's Merman is simultaneously an involved spectator and an omniscient narrator through whose agency we learn first that Margaret at her spinning wheel 'in the humming town' sings 'most joyfully' but at other times grieves for 'the cold strange eyes of the little Mermaiden'; and then that in coming years the sound of the wind and waves on stormy nights will trouble her, while on calm nights the Merman himself will rise with the children to gaze longingly at the Church and 'the white sleeping town' only to sink again mournfully into the sea, singing of faithlessness and loss.

Through the Merman's tones can be heard those of yet another voice: that of the poet who laments the painfulness of love and the irreducible conflict between two kinds of existence, one of them free, untamed and pagan, the other ordered and orthodox but inimical to passionate intensity of feeling. It is not simple pleasure in narrative embroidery for its own sake which makes Arnold alter the legend so that Margaret grieves on the land as her husband and children grieve in the sea. His reworking makes it clear that the separation between the 'land' and the 'sea' is a condition of the exile and loneliness at the centre of the poem, and his additional pictorial details heighten the difference between the two regions, whose symbolic function recalls the use of the opposed worlds of Thrushcross Grange and Wuthering Heights in the novel by the writer whom of the three Brontë sisters he most admired.[1] To his own 'Brontëan' contrasts of storm and calm he adds contrasts of colour: the 'little town' is 'white-walled' as well as decorous, the church on the 'windy shore'—it is situated like a bastion on the edge of the rival world—is 'grey'; in the Merman's magic world (for which Arnold took some pictorial hints from Byron[2] as well as Tennyson), the 'great winds' blow and the 'wild white horses play, on the surface of 'the clear green sea', while in the Merman's

[1] See 'Haworth Churchyard', ll. 92–100 (*Poems*, 395).

[2] *Poems*, 99.

palace far below is a 'ceiling of amber', 'pavement of pearl' and a 'red-gold throne'. The movement of feeling, from the wildness of the opening to the resigned melancholy of the close when the impossibility of reconciling the two worlds has to be accepted, is reflected in the rhythmical variations of the Merman's irregular chant, which is probably Arnold's finest individual melodic invention (he uses this 'chant' for the first time in 'The Strayed Reveller' and, as we have already seen, uses it again for the songs of Callicles). Here its flexibility accommodates the lyricism of the lines already quoted; the evocation of the wildness of the seascape in the predominantly four-stressed lines at the start,

> *Come, dear children, let us away;*
> *Down and away below!*
> *Now my brothers call from the bay,*
> *Now the great winds shoreward blow,*
> *Now the salt tides seaward flow;*
> *Now the wild white horses play,*
> *Champ and chafe and toss in the spray . . . ;*

and finally, in the concluding three-stress lines, the melancholy resignation imaged in the still landscape, which is white now because lit by the moon, so that the poem closes with the poet's favourite emblem of wished-for calm.

If, as readers have felt, the final lines of 'The Forsaken Merman' suggest some flagging of imaginative energy (the diction and syntax want their former suppleness), this is due less, perhaps, to the very much reduced pitch of feeling than to the always precarious hold on poetic élan, incandescence and ease of manner which is Arnold's principal poetic weakness. His triumphs lie 'in his feeling for poetic decorum, his command of tone and temper, his emotional honesty and his capacity in a few poems, of which "The Forsaken Merman" is one example, to rise above his self-consciousness to poetic expression as unimpeded as the best of Tennyson's'.[1] These virtues of 'decorum' and 'command of tone and temper' distinguish 'The Neckan', the short ballad in regular quatrains composed some years later, probably in 1852–3, which was designed as a companion-piece to 'The Forsaken

[1] Kenneth Allott, unpublished lecture.

Merman' (the two pieces were printed together in all collections from 1855 onwards), even if these virtues are preserved at the expense of the striking metrical resource and imaginative lyricism of the earlier poem. 'The Neckan' wins affection for its formal accomplishment, its sustained sorrowing 'note' and its decorous management of pictorial detail—the gold of the harp, the green of the seas and the white of the priest's surplice recall the similar but less understated use of these colours in the rival worlds of 'The Forsaken Merman'. But 'The Neckan' courts the dangers risked by any sequel which tries to draw freshly on an already closely worked imaginative vein. Arnold came upon the Swedish legend of the Neckan in Benjamin Thorpe's *Northern Mythology* (1851) and was taken by its resemblance to the story which he had already used, though now it is the non-human partner who in his turn longs to possess a human soul and who leaves his wife and their children at the bottom of the Baltic Sea to sit on the headlands singing his 'plaintive song'. More importantly, although Arnold has not yet 'transferred his operations to a region where form is everything', it is not the struggle with contradiction which occupies him so much as the careful ordering of his quatrains to capture 'his plaintive note, his note of melancholy' from the poetry of Heinrich Heine, which he was reading in 1852 and which he praised in his essay of 1865 for its 'incomparable' magic and its mastery of 'a ballad-form which has more rapidity and grace than any of ours'.[1] His concentration upon the sadder parts of the tale is partly in response to this interest, though it is also true that the Christian 'optimism' of lines 53–6, 61–4 was a later interpolation (see *Poems* 282, 284). In other words, Heine's melancholy and the sorrowful plight of his Neckan were both still sufficiently 'penetrating' emotionally to lend imaginative vitality to his ballad, which remains at a long distance from 'Saint Brandan', the narrative poem lying far on the other side of the geological fault in his poetic landscape (the poem was composed in 1859 or 1860), which is also written in quatrains and based on a legend with a Christian theme. 'St. Brandan . . . is not a piece which satisfies me', wrote Arnold, and we can understand why.[2] The channel is cut for 'the bright stream' but the channel is dry. The lameness of the poem, apparent in the opening stanzas,

[1] *CPW*, III, 124.

[2] Letter of 1869 to F. T. Palgrave, cited in G. W. E. Russell, *Matthew Arnold*, 1904, 43.

Saint Brandan sails the northern main;
The brotherhoods of saints are glad.
He greets them once, he sails again;
So late!—such storms! The Saint is mad!

He heard, across the howling seas,
Chime convent-bells on wintry nights;
He saw, on spray-swept Hebrides,
Twinkle the monastery-lights . . . ,

contrasts painfully with the unassuming appeal of the little 'song about a song in Heine's manner' (*Poems*, 463),

In Summer, on the headlands,
  The Baltic Sea along,
Sits Neckan with his harp of gold,
  And sings his plaintive song.

Green rolls beneath the headlands,
  Green rolls the Baltic Sea;
And there, below the Neckan's feet,
  His wife and children be.

He sings not of the ocean,
  Its shells and roses pale;
Of earth, of earth the Neckan sings,
  He hath no other tale . . .

'The Neckan', which belongs to the years 1852–3, lies nearer to the hither side of the geological fault than 'Tristram and Iseult' and the less ambitious but closely related 'The Church of Brou'. These poems belong to the unsettled years from 1849 to 1851 and the qualities in them which override their unevenness spring from the same haunted and divisive feelings which found expression in the Merman's lament for his lost Margaret. Both poems again dramatize contrasts of passion and calm. 'Tristram and Iseult' tells of two kinds of love, one magically intense, passionate and doomed, and the other domestically settled and temperate:

> *There were two Iseults who did sway*
> *Each her hour of Tristram's day;*
> *But one possessed his waning time,*
> *The other his resplendent prime . . .*

In 'The Church of Brou' the lovers are first identified with gaiety and movement and then with eternal stillness, although the interplay of these contraries reaches poetic intensity only in the forty or so lines which make up the third and final Part. Arnold's readers have generally passed quickly, though not slightingly, over 'The Church of Brou', but their usually warmer response to 'Tristram and Iseult' is a tribute to a quality of feeling in the poem which triumphs over its various weaknesses, including the uneasy half-dramatic, half-narrative style (a device which Arnold borrowed from Byron's *The Giaour*) and the lamentable tameness of the dialogue between the lovers in Part II. We could say by way of a summary description that this is one of Arnold's hybrid pieces in which the kinds do not run easily into one another and yet in which there is a compelling 'predominant note' which is elegiac.[1]

The mainspring of the poem is the reference to Tristram's lifelong recollection of a lost and irrecoverable love which Arnold encountered during his stay—probably in 1849—in the Swiss town of Thun, the scene of his love affair with, and his parting from, Marguerite. It occurs in a paragraph of Théodore de la Villemarqué's article for the *Revue de Paris* of 1841 on '*Les poèmes gallois et les romans de la Table Ronde*', which recounts how Tristram was sent by his uncle, King Mark of Cornwall, to bring home from Ireland 'La Belle Yseult' to be the King's bride; how he and Iseult drank together the love-potion which made them fall passionately in love; and how though Iseult married Mark and Tristram eventually married another Iseult—Iseult of Brittany—this love remained at the centre of their lives.

For Tristram,

[1] 'The whole tone of "Tristram and Iseult" is elegiac, a chastened review of passion spent and past, not of passion strong and present', 'The Poet of Elegy', *Spectator*, 18 July 1885, repr. *Dawson*, 381. Praise for the poem from, among others, Clough, Froude, J. D. Coleridge, Swinburne and R. H. Hutton appears in *Dawson*, 72–4, 89, 108–9, 164, 226–7.

> *Toutefois c'est en vain qu'il essaie d'oublier son premier amour, c'est en vain qu'il court les aventures périleuses . . .*
>
> (*Poems*, 196)

This is the sentence which captured Arnold. The same source records numerous details which he failed to use, most of them associated with cruelty and deceit—notably the stratagem by which Tristram's disguise as a beggar enables the first Iseult to swear falsely to Mark that she is chaste and the malice of the second Iseult who lyingly tells Tristram that her rival will not visit his sickbed, whereupon he perishes '*de chagrin*'. Arnold's poem is based on this selective use of La Villemarqué with some additional details from Malory and the Vulgate *Merlin* which he consulted after his return to England. The legend was less well known then than now (Wagner's opera appeared thirteen years later in 1865, and the versions in Tennyson and Swinburne are of 1872 and 1882). Arnold's, then, is the first modern English treatment and the unfamiliarity of his story together with his oblique narrative method won him charges of obscurity from his earliest readers. When he added in 1853 some explanatory notes from Dunlop's *History of Fiction* he must have found difficulty in patching together sentences suitable to his own treatment, for he would have found from Dunlop's version that Iseult of Ireland, in order to hide her unchastity from her bridegroom, persuaded her maid to take her place on the wedding night and then had her cruelly punished, and that Iseult of Brittany, still more maliciously than in La Villemarqué, told Tristram on his deathbed that the ship crossing the seas from Ireland carried black sails instead of the white sails signalling her arrival. Arnold would probably not have used such details even had he known them earlier. There is no 'bed-trick' in La Villemarqué, but, as we have seen, he rejected from this source all suggestions of cruelty and dishonour, though he retained Tristram's fidelity to the second Iseult after their marriage, a detail not found in his other sources. Even in the story of Merlin and Vivien, related by his Iseult of Brittany to her children in the poem's third Part, and based on the Vulgate *Merlin*, Vivien is not cruel or vicious (as she is in Tennyson). If Arnold suppresses the one sympathetic touch in his original source, 'oftentimes she regretted what she had done',[1] this is

[1] Southey's translation of the Vulgate *Merlin* in his edition of Malory, 1817.

because he wishes to make her merely bright and indifferent; she enchants Merlin because she is 'passing weary of his love' (did Arnold see Marguerite as bright and enchanting but also 'passing weary of his love'?).

Trickery and sexual stratagem have no place in the world inhabited by Arnold's fated characters. The two women are conventionally contrasted in colouring, the passionate first Iseult being dark and the gentle second Iseult being fair, but the former is not vindictive and the latter is beyond jealousy—her look 'is like a sad embrace', she has

The gaze of one who can divine
A grief and sympathise . . . ,

and she is faithful to Tristram as he is to her in his 'exiled loneliness' and 'stately deep distress'. The history of these elevated figures is related in Parts I and II ('Tristram' and 'Iseult of Ireland') from the perspective of Tristram's deathbed and in Part III ('Iseult of Brittany') from the point of view of the widowed Iseult. In Part I, Tristram, attended by his wife and a page (and, so to speak, by the unseen Breton bard who is present with his interpolated passages of narrative throughout the poem), 'on this wild December night' lies feverishly awaiting the first Iseult's return, sometimes falling into fitful dreams about the spring and summer of their passionate youth. In Part II she arrives, they speak of their separated lives and their unquenched love and accomplish their final reunion in death, the narrator coming in after the *Liebestod* with his closing epitaph. In Part III the narrator tells how the widowed Iseult, 'dying in a mask of youth', tends her children through the long hours and 'one bright winter's day' relates to them the story of Merlin and Vivien.

By closing with this additional record of fatal love Arnold manages to comment obliquely on his main story; and by using his narrator uninterruptedly throughout this last Part he rediscovers a consistent distancing technique for his themes of loneliness, separation and the destructiveness of passion. He gains furthermore the added advantage of consolidating his portrait of Iseult of Brittany. This second Iseult is not permitted to relate the story of Merlin in her own words, nor indeed to speak in her own person anywhere in the poem, but she remains the most sharply individualized and the most sympathetic of the poem's three characters. Her prominence has much to do with

Arnold's current inner 'history', as we shall see, but there is also a formal stylistic reason for his success with her. She is represented—apart from some sympathetic but perfunctory glances in her direction from Tristram—through the eyes of the mediating Breton bard, whose octosyllabics in Parts I and II and measured blank verse in Part III are more assured than the blank verse assigned to Tristram in Part I and the 'stychomythia' of the exchanges between Tristram and the first Iseult in Part II. Arnold is not at ease with the 'stage' devices of soliloquy and dialogue through which these figures carry on the dual task of relating their personal history and expressing their passion. Tristram's blank verse speeches must convey his present feverish sickness, his recollections of the past and his continual pain and grief, and under the strain they tend to collapse into sputtering rhetoric in the manner of 'Saint Brendan'. The true voice of feeling is heard at intervals when Tristram recalls the irrecoverable intensity of youthful feeling: early summer in 'the sweet green fields of Wales'; the chilliness of 'the pleasaunce walks' where he parted from Iseult;[1] and, with a hallucinatory sharpness of vision, the night of chill and fever, moonlight and shadow, when he bathed his 'hot brow' in the 'cold spring' and seemed to see her face looking up at him from the moonlit water (II, ll. 276–87). The incident is Arnold's invention and the use of natural imagery, with the moon once more seeking to mitigate a morbid and feverish intensity, is individual.

This native imaginative bent explains his quickened response to that interplay of warmth and cold found in Keats's 'The Eve of St. Agnes', a love story which exercises considerable influence on his own romantic narrative. We know now—it is a recent addition to our knowledge about him—that Arnold was familiar with Keats at this time not only from Milnes's *Life, Letters and Literary Remains* of 1848 but also from the 1851 Moxon edition of the *Poems* of which he possessed a copy and in which he wrote out the 'Bright Star!' sonnet (the poem, unaccountably, was omitted from the edition).[2] Echoes of Keats play in and out of 'Tristram and Iseult' and Part III of 'The Church of Brou', in both cases most influentially from 'The Eve of St. Agnes', though there is also some flavour from 'The Eve of St. Mark', especially in the

[1] Perhaps a personal reminiscence (see *Poems*, 202 n).

[2] We are indebted for this new information to Mrs. Mary Moorman, who has generously made a gift to me of Arnold's copy of this edition.

Breton bard's octosyllabics and in the medieval atmosphere and furnishing, together with a certain affinity—possibly unconscious—with the 'Ode on a Grecian Urn'. The principal Keatsian echoes have already been recorded in detail, notably those from the lines on the stained glass window in 'The Eve of St Agnes' which affect Arnold's descriptions of the arras over Tristram's deathbed and the window over the lovers' tomb in 'The Church of Brou'; and the certainly conscious parallel between the Breton bard in 'Tristram and Iseult' reminding us that the 'marble' lovers are now

> *Cold, cold as those who loved and lived*
> *A thousand years ago . . . ,*

and Keats's deliberate distancing of his romantic lovers at the end of 'The Eve of St. Agnes',

> *And they are gone; ay, ages long ago*
> *These lovers fled away into the storm*
>
> *The Beadsman, after thousand aves told,*
> *For aye unsought for, slept among his ashes cold . . .*
> (*Poems*, 213–14, 215)

'Tristram and Iseult' and 'The Church of Brou' have further in common the situating of a 'marble repose' against the passion and stir of life, a juxtaposition which releases ambiguous feelings not unlike the mixed emotions with which Keats views his Grecian Urn. 'Calm's not life's crown, though calm is well . . .' is the burden of 'Youth and Calm', which, it is generally agreed, forms part of a passage originally designed to describe the death of Iseult of Ireland (*Poems*, 224), and the line could serve as a motto for 'The Church of Brou'. Arnold's revision of 'Tristram and Iseult' in the autumn of 1852 falls within the period of his composing 'The Church of Brou' and helps to explain the resemblances between the two poems, in particular the parallels already noticed between the second part of the one and the third part of the other, though 'The Church of Brou' took its first inspiration from Edgar Quinet's '*Des Arts de la Renaissance et de l'Eglise de Brou*' of 1839, in which the Church is seen as a monument not only to the Duke and

Duchess of Savoy but to conceptions of faith, eternal love and unbroken union beyond the grave which belong to a vanished age (*Poems*, 294). Arnold opens the story of the 'princely Pair' in the ballad style of Part I, The Castle, which relates somewhat briskly the hunting tragedy which abruptly severs them, the Duchess's decision to rebuild the Church of Brou and place in it a tomb for herself and her husband, and her death as soon as the work is finished. He continues with the five stanzas of Part II, The Church, in which the metrical gesture towards 'The Lady of Shalott' draws attention to his setting up a similar contrast between, on the one hand, sunlit green fields and the everyday bustle of life and, on the other, the substitution for life of one kind of artistic creativity—here represented by the remote, richly decorated mountain church in whose vicinity 'the woods and fields are dumb'. He closes with the rhymed pentameter couplets of Part III, The Tomb, in which the sculptured 'marble Pair' are first seen against the 'chequer work' of brilliant colour cast on them by sunlight shining through the stained glass window and then in intermittent rays of the moon on an autumn night of wind and rain, when, if they lift their heads from their 'cold white marble beds', they will hear

> *. . . on the lichen-crusted leads above*
> *The rustle of the eternal rain of love.*

Whatever Arnold's incidental indebtedness in these two poems to other poets, the working out of the ambiguities surrounding the oppositions of life and art, passion and calm, is peculiarly his own. 'I will write historically, as I can write naturally in no other way.' Through 'Tristram and Iseult' and 'The Church of Brou' can be traced a part of that inner history which led from the conception of 'calm' and

> *Hours, if not of ecstasy,*
> *From violent anguish surely free! . . .*
>
> (I, 232–3; *Poems*, 204)

to the search for a poetic subject first (and abortively) in the character of Lucretius and then in that of the Stoic poet-philosopher Empedocles, who—as Arnold portrays him—forces himself to contemplate with disciplined calm 'the pale cold star of Truth' (*Poems*, 288) and knows that with the struggling feelings thus left behind he has also left behind his source of poetic creativity. The Arnold of 'Tristram and Iseult' has not yet travelled so far, though in Iseult of Brittany he has perhaps arrived at 'a pale contented sort of discontent' (Keats's description of Lamia when the enchantment is nearly at an end); in Part III what is grey, still, and solitary can still find injections of vitality from the natural world and from magic and legend. 'Joy has not found her yet, nor ever will', says the Breton bard of this Iseult whose 'historical' importance for Arnold at this time now begins to be clear. But she is placed in a setting where the grassy hollow, the 'white-gleaming quartz', the red holly berries and her children's screams of pleasure at their play enliven the 'stern' grey castle turrets and 'this iron coast'. In Iseult's magic story Merlin is enchanted on an April day bright with green boughs and golden sunshine, and Vivien as she rides her white palfrey (Arnold's favourite combination of white, green and gold is, as we have already seen, associated with a sense of magical enchantment) has 'the morning's fresh grace' as she leads her 'stately prize' to his imprisonment.

We have already learned from the narrator in Part I that Tristram, too, was 'stately' in his 'exiled loneliness' and 'deep distress'. He and Merlin are both victims of 'this fool passion' which is

> *. . . but a diseased unrest,*
> *And an unnatural overheat at best . . .*

These lines occur in the passage (III, ll. 133–50) which has been described as 'a Stoic sermon on restlessness'[1] and forms part of the longer sequence (III, ll. 2–50), later omitted perhaps because too explicitly autobiographical, in which Arnold, through his bard, seeks to define the cause and consequence of the 'fever'. Passionate love, though, is not alone to blame. It may be 'the eternal furnace of the world'—what Arnold elsewhere calls 'the eternal tumult of the world mingling, breaking in upon, hurrying away all'; or it may be 'some tyrannous single thought, some fit/ Of passion which subdues our souls to it . . .' (*Poems*, 220 n, 221). Either way, the outcome is the erosion of the power to feel without loss of the 'fierce necessity' to do so. The complex of feeling which brings together the sorrowful Iseult with 'her features so

[1] W. D. Anderson, *Matthew Arnold and the Classical Tradition*, 1965, 138; see also his 'Arnold and the Classics', p. 279 below.

fatigued, her eyes, though sweet/ So sunk' (III, ll. 70–1), the Stoic 'sermon on restlessness' and the linking of this restlessness with depression and ennui, is related to the melancholy inspiring 'Empedocles on Etna', the 'dramatic poem', again composed during the crucial period between 1849 and 1852, which finally crowded out of the way Arnold's projected Lucretian tragedy.

We have learned from the careful disentangling of the philosophical and literary sources of 'Empedocles on Etna' that whatever Arnold may have taken for his portrait of Empedocles from his reading of Karsten's *Philosophorum Graecorum Veterum* . . . (1838), the influences most deeply affecting the central thought and feeling in the poem—and which were therefore at work at some level of his mind when he was writing 'Tristram and Iseult' and 'The Church of Brou'—derive from his response to Lucretius, Marcus Aurelius and Epictetus among the ancients, Spinoza among later writers, and Carlyle among his contemporaries, together with strong injections of Romantic melancholy from nineteenth-century writers ranging from Byron to George Sand and from Foscolo to the Senancour of *Obermann*.[1] The poem's importance in his intellectual and emotional development was recognized by readers even at the time, in spite of the criticisms which it provoked, and more than one reviewer welcomed its restoration to his collections after 1867. It has been taken by many if not all of Arnold's critics in our own day to be among the few important longer poems of the Victorian period, satisfying both in its intellectual and poetic musculature. It can certainly be regarded as the culmination of Arnold's earlier poetry, his most complex achievement and the most 'subjective' of his longer poems, in other words the one in which his attempt to understand himself and the world is most intimately projected through his fable. It may be seen as a flawed, bitter and ill-balanced work if it is judged by the incongruous length of Empedocles's philosophical rhapsody in Act I, but it has poetic vitality, not only in the songs of Callicles but throughout Act II in the urgency with which Arnold attempts to 'unite matter' in his dissecting of the Romantic temperament and Romantic world-sorrow. Paradoxically, his engagement with the loss of poetic creativity and with the complexities surrounding this loss, which his new subject

[1] See Kenneth Allott's 'A Background for "Empedocles on Etna"' (cited p. 77 n. 2) and *Poems*, 148–9.

matter now enables him to explore, becomes the most important single source of the poem's imaginative life.

The tripartite structure used in 'Tristram and Iseult' and 'The Church of Brou', and to be used again in 'Balder Dead', now appears in disguise as three scenes in a 'drama' made up of two 'Acts'. This 'dramatic poem' improves on its model, Byron's *Manfred*, in developing a coherent symbolic structure. The scenes—two of them occur in the first Act—are set on the slopes of Etna and move from the lower rich forest region of the first scene to the 'glen on the highest skirts of the woody region' of the second scene; the third scene, which comprises Act II, is the bare charred summit of the volcano. The movement of Empedocles through these scenes represents the movement from youth to middle age, and from contentment to near despair. The emphasis on the passage of time begins with the Greek motto, 'Time is wisest for it discovers everything', which turns out to be a bitter truth. Callicles, whose joyful singing contrasts with the austere utterances of the melancholy middle-aged philosopher who dislikes the age he lives in, is the happy instinctive poet. He is beloved of Empedocles as a kind of 'self when young' before he had plunged too deeply into the philosophical problems which have undone his content. Empedocles speaks of youth with Wordsworthian nostalgia:

> *And yet what days were those, Parmenides!*
> *When we were young, when we could number friends*
> *In all the Italian cities like ourselves,*
> *When with elated hearts we joined your train,*
> *Ye Sun-born Virgins! on the road of truth.*
> *Then we could still enjoy, then neither thought*
> *Nor outward things were closed and dead to us;*
> *But we received the shock of mighty thoughts*
> *On simple minds with a pure natural joy . . .*
>
> (II, 235–43; *Poems*, 185)

Arnold wrote in January 1851 to the sister whom he addresses as Fausta in 'Resignation',

> The aimless and unsettled, but also open and liberal state of our youth we *must* perhaps all leave and take refuge in our morality and character; but with most of us it is a melancholy passage from

> which we emerge shorn of so many beams that we are almost tempted to quarrel with the law of nature which imposes it upon us . . .[1]

Callicles, we may then say, is 'the aimless and unsettled but also open and liberal state of our youth', and Empedocles's climb up Etna is away from youth and towards 'morality and character'. This process of growing older, of mastering oneself, of thinking and interpreting life is seemingly '*almost* quarrelled with', for Empedocles leaps into the crater, while Callicles remains to sing the beauty of the world. The difficulty with this reading is that in the second scene, on the outskirts of the fertile wooded region, Empedocles in his long philosophical monologue teaches Pausanias—the friend who admires but does not understand him—how to live and what to believe, yet in the following Act himself commits suicide. The quarrel with the 'law of nature' seems final. Empedocles's 'lesson' emphasizes the indifference of nature, who

> *. . . with equal mind,*
> *Sees all her sons at play;*
> *Sees man control the wind,*
> *The wind sweep man away;*
> *Allows the proudly-riding and the foundering bark . . . ;*
>
> (I, ii, 257–61; *Poems*, 167)

the necessity for man to see things in their true state—

> *. . . for those who know*
> *Themselves, who wisely take*
> *Their way through life, and how*
> *To what they cannot break,*
> *Why should I say that life need yield but* moderate *bliss?—*
>
> (I, ii, 387–91; *Poems*, 171)

and his need to be satisfied with 'moderate desire':

> *Nurse no extravagant hope;*
> *Because thou must not dream, thou need'st not then despair!*
>
> (I, ii, 425–6; *Poems*, 172)

[1] *Letters*, I, 14.

Yet there can still be delight:

> *Is it so small a thing*
> *To have enjoyed the sun,*
> *To have lived light in the Spring,*
> *To have loved, to have thought, to have done;*
> *To have advanced true friends and beat down baffling foes?*
> (I, ii, 397–401; *Poems*, 172)

Arnold's teaching here follows Carlyle's teaching of 'Lower your denominator', don't ask too much of life, work at what is in front of you. It is good advice for the ordinary man. But Empedocles is no ordinary man, as Callicles with his own endowment of poetic insight is quick to see:

> *'Tis not the times, 'tis not the sophists vex him;*
> *There is some root of suffering in himself,*
> *Some secret and unfollowed vein of woe . . .*
> (I, i, 150–3; *Poems*, 155)

He is, in effect, a poet, another Obermann, as he shows himself to be in the next Act (which belongs to Senancour, not Carlyle): isolated and suffering in isolation, he is true to the Romantic idea of the poet as an outlaw and as one who suffers for his penetration. This special condition of being a poet puts a strain on him which is too great for his advice to Pausanias to avail. The ordinary man can take refuge in morality and character because it will improve him to do so, but for the poet this can only be achieved at the expense of the openness and flexibility that makes him what he is. 'Empedocles on Etna', then, projects the journey towards truth as a journey towards a lifeless desert—the 'blackened melancholy waste' of Act II—and to endure this, stoicism is necessary. This may be well enough for the ordinary man but it is death to the artist. Empedocles's suicide is Arnold's recognition that to see the truth and not yield to despair requires a disciplining of his whole nature which would cause him to die as a poet. Empedocles does not die in despair, but in order to avoid this he must die as a poet to become a mere moralist. Only in youth—as in Callicles—is it possible to achieve that balance between feeling and thinking which ensures poetic freedom and flexibility.

The quarrel with the 'law of nature', then, is not irreparable for the 'man of morality and character', though it may seem to be so for the poet as he moves to the outskirts of the 'fertile region'. To put it another way, the 'impetuous heart' in Arnold is still sufficiently strong in its contention with the 'contriving head' for his poem to receive animation from his struggle to express the conflict between them. We have noticed already that the conflict is dramatically heightened by metrical variations which are served by a considerable degree of poetic resourcefulness, especially in distinguishing the philosopher-poet's long formal monologues from the irregular chanting of Callicles's happy songs in celebration of a world which is not 'sick or sorry': a world where 'One sees one's footprints crushed in the wet grass', the 'sea-side air is/ Buoyant and fresh' for Cadmus and Harmonia as they 'Bask in the glens or on the warm sea-shore' and the 'leaping stream' throws on to mossed roots its 'Eternal showers of spray'.[1] For Empedocles the 'spring of hope is dried', but—as with Coleridge in his 'Dejection, an Ode'—the sombre feeling becomes in turn a source of inspiration, in this case sometimes heightening the poetic temperature even of the lengthy monologue in hexameters in Act I. Images released under the pressure of intimate feeling lend distinction to particular passages, as in this reflection on the destructiveness of time where the metaphor in the last line has the effect of transfiguring the entire stanza:

We see in blank dismay
Year posting after year,
Sense after sense decay;
Our shivering heart is mined by secret discontent . . .

(I, ii, 363–6; *Poems*, 170)

More than once the struggle with contradiction disciplines the progress throughout a stanza of a particular image, conducting it with considerable syntactical confidence to culminate in a firm hexameter, for example in this case, where the idea of immutable process is made to combine with notions of development and growth:

. . . man grows
Forth from his parents' stem,

[1] I, i, 14–20; I, ii, 432–3; I, ii, 46–7; *Poems*, 150, 173, 157.

And blends their bloods, as those
Of theirs are blent in them;
So each new man strikes roots into a far fore-time . . .
(I, ii, 187–91; *Poems*, 164)

It is in effect the renewal in the poem of Arnold's inveterate preoccupation with the erosions of time which is chiefly responsible for the fresh variations which he introduces into his characteristic imagery, whether drawn from the sense of stifling, suffocation and 'congestion of the brain' ('The numbing cloud/ Mounts off my soul', says Empedocles at the end),[1] or from the sense of the vastness and complexity of existence, for which his favourite image is the sea—variously at one moment in his poetry the sundering sea of life and at another the tranquil sea of eternity. In 'Empedocles on Etna' the sea appears as a metaphor for experience, its attributes changing with the passage from youth to middle age. In youth, poignantly, the world,

. . . a rolling flood
Of newness and delight
Draws in the enamoured gazer to its shining breast . . . ,

but the years gradually annihilate distinctive feelings, distinctive ideas, the hoped-for clarity of settled belief; instead of the shining flood magically enticing the 'enamoured gazer',

Experience, like a sea, soaks all-effacing in . . .
(I, ii, 355–6, 201; *Poems*, 170, 165)

Arnold, as everyone knows, dropped 'Empedocles on Etna' from his 1853 collection (though he retained Callicles's fine lyric on Cadmus and Harmonia) because it presented, as he said in the 1853 Preface, 'a situation in which a continuous state of mental distress is prolonged, unrelieved by incident, hope, or resistance; in which there is everything to be endured and nothing to be done'—this startlingly resembles the 'airless atmosphere of reflection unventilated by action' in which

[1] '. . . Yes—*congestion of the brain* is what we suffer from—I always feel it and say it—and cry for air like my own Empedocles', Letter of 12–13 February 1853, *Letters to Clough*, 130.

Kierkegaard lived his life from the 1840s onwards (one might add that Empedocles could be said to have died not 'with deliberation but from deliberation', as Kierkegaard said of the suicide). Arnold's business as a poet must now be to 'animate' and 'rejoice' the reader with 'excellent actions' which 'powerfully appeal to the great primary human affections', thus preventing the indulgence of 'morbid' subjectivity and—though he does not say so in the Preface—the exhaustion which, he explained to his sister in the September of 1858, attends poetic creation when 'you . . . descend into yourself and produce the best of your thought and feeling naturally'.[1] But the drawing up of this programme could not in itself at once, or indeed at any time, finally subdue subjectivity. If Arnold as a thinker cannot 'decerebrate' himself, although this means that poetry for intellectual honesty's sake must eventually be sacrificed, a plight which in his distress he projects on to his own Empedocles, the detachment which prevents him from being unsettlingly 'penetrated' by his material has its lapses even in his latest and most frigid narrative and dramatic verse. This is not to exclude either *Merope*, his fastidiously chiselled and finally unsuccessful attempt at a tragedy, or his other honourable failure, 'Balder Dead', a poem by which he set much store and whose cool reception greatly disappointed him. As to 'Sohrab and Rustum', which replaced 'Empedocles on Etna' in the 1853 volume, and which is not yet quite 'three parts iced over' (as its author ruefully described himself at the age of thirty-one),[2] it is now a critical commonplace that towards the close of his story his personal involvement with his subject momentarily frees him from constraint and makes of the last fifty or so lines one part of his poetry which 'we all almost knew by heart'.

Arnold's undiminished craftsman's skill in selecting and reworking his material is placed in these three late works at the service of what is clearly taken to be a 'public' rather than a 'private' need, but his conception of such need is still affected by that strain of melancholy and the necessity to resist it to which we must once more return. Even in the preface to *Merope* (written in 1857), the temperamental habit gives a special resonance to passages in which he applauds the formal disciplines of Greek tragedy for endowing the human spirit with a sense of mastery 'over its own stormiest agitations' and for conducting it—the italics are

[1] *Letters*, I, 63.
[2] *Letters to Clough*, 128.

Arnold's—to '*a sentiment of sublime acquiescence in the course of fate and the dispensations of human life*'. The cherished prize of this Stoical acquiescence is calm ('a sentiment of *repose*'). Goethe, it is argued, is not at fault because he seeks 'repose' in tragedy, but because he achieves it by eliminating 'agitating matter' and the 'domain . . . of the passions', in other words everything which makes the desire for repose both urgent and intelligible.[1]

'Sohrab and Rustum' and 'Balder Dead' are alike in aiming at this 'noble' rising above anguish and each looks to classical models for aid, though the first retells a Persian tale from Firdousi and the second a Norse legend from the Prose Edda. Arnold first found his 'very noble and excellent story' of Sohrab's death in John Malcolm's *History of Persia* (1815), but it was Saint-Beuve's account of Firdousi which fastened on him, with its references to the story of Sohrab as '*une belle et touchante histoire*', to Firdousi as '*L'Homère de son pays*' and to the calming self-forgetfulness induced by taking such imaginative journeys: '*Les jours où l'on est trop entêté de soi-même et de son importance je ne sais rien de plus calmant que de lire un voyage en Perse ou en Chine*'.[2] But Arnold, after all, had his appointment in Samarra. He worked lovingly at the poem from the end of 1852 to the spring of 1853, putting together the stages of his story with admirable narrative carpentry, 'orientalizing' his Homeric similes by drawing on Malcolm, Burnes's familiar *Travels into Bokhara* (especially for the description of the Oxus) and J. A. Atkinson's translation (1832) of Firdousi's *Sháhnáma*, and attempting throughout to keep strictly to the principles of 1853: 'the all-importance of the choice of subject; the necessity of accurate construction; and the subordinate character of expression'. But few readers have warmed to the earlier phases of his story, or to his polished Homeric similes and studied repetitions of words and phrases in the manner of his classical models. On the other hand many readers have sensed the quickened feeling at the climax of this story about 'a strong son . . . slain by a mightier father'. Sainte-Beuve in rendering another part of Firdousi's poem has the line, '*O Roi! pense à l'instabilité de la vie qui doit passer sur nous comme le vent*'.[3] Arnold's Sohrab, near to death, tells the father who has mortally wounded him,

[1] *CPW*, I, 59.

[2] Sainte-Beuve, *Causeries du lundi*, I, 332, 343, 342.

[3] *Loc. cit.* 342.

. . . like the lightning to this field
I came, and like the wind I go away—
Sudden and swift, and like a passing wind . . .

(*Poems*, 326)

Something more than 'a shadowy personal significance'[1] begins to make itself felt at this moment: there is a good case for those who argue that the father killing the son unwittingly is a re-enactment of the sacrificial destruction of the poetic life in 'Empedocles on Etna'; the situation once again is the death of youth—the poetic imagination—at the hand of middle age—'morality and character'. Some detect in this the dead hand of the great moral teacher Dr. Arnold reaching out to control his son whom he had thought (in 'Matt's' days of self-protective dandyism at Oxford and in London) too light-hearted and irresponsible. Certainly the imagery of the closing passages is nourished by themes of separation, loss and sacrifice:

Unwillingly the spirit fled away
Regretting the warm mansion which it left
And youth and bloom, and this delightful world . . . ,

and our feeling that Sohrab sheds '*le sang d'un poète*'—

. . . all down his cold white side
The crimson torrent ran, dim now and soiled,
Like the soiled tissue of white violets
Left freshly gathered, on their native bank . . .— (*Poems*, 329)

takes strength from '. . . youth and bloom and this delightful world' recalling, through association with Arnold's emotionally-charged favourite word 'bloom' (which carries connotations of both ripeness and evanescence), his earlier lament for the dead poet in 'The Youth of Nature' who became

. . . a priest to us all
Of the wonder and bloom of the world . . . (*Poems*, 247)

[1] Lionel Trilling, *Matthew Arnold*, 134.

The Oxus coda, with its imagery of the moonlight, the steadfast stars and the river, freed at last from its 'foiled and circuitous wanderings' and finally flowing at ease into the tranquil sea (the river of life flowing into eternity), is the finest of Arnold's many invocations of calm.

This poetic level is beyond his reach in 'Balder Dead', which was composed during the next year (1853–4) as the last and most ambitious of his major narrative poems. Though not 'unique and unapproached' as W. E. Henley saw it, neither is it the 'complete and frigid failure' which John Middleton Murry took it to be.[1] Arnold considered 'Balder Dead' superior to 'Sohrab and Rustum' and felt that it had 'not had justice done to it', especially since it sustained a 'natural *propriety* of diction and rhythm which is what we all prize in our Virgil' (his comment seems at odds with his non-Virgilian decision to relate the story through a series of discrete episodes).[2] His studied obedience to the style of classical epic, with borrowings from Homer as well as Virgil (the poem 'is noble in the Homeric not the Eddic way', as C. H. Herford put it in 1919)[3] and his choice of an 'excellent action' are indications of his single-minded desire to sustain his 1853 programme. His 'propriety' of diction and rhythm and his sensitive re-structuring of the materials which he took from Mallet's *Northern Antiquities* (via translations by I. A. Blackwell and Bishop Percy) command respect, but the winning preoccupations in the poem are not Virgilian or Homeric or Nordic but Arnoldian. The traditional story of Balder's death in any case suggests, at least to a modern sensibility, a melancholy in keeping with Arnold's own in that it sets forward through the figures of Loki and the blind Hoder, the one a willing and the other an unwilling destroyer of the beloved god, a 'something that infects the world' from which not even the best and the most cherished can be saved. So Empedocles grieves:

Yet, even when man forsakes
All sin—is just, is pure,

[1] W. E. Henley, *Atheneaum*, 22 August 1885, repr. *Dawson*, 289; J. M. Murry, 'Matthew Arnold the Poet', *Discoveries: Essays in Criticism*, 1924, 207.
[2] The subtitle in 1855, 'An Episode', which is the subtitle of 'Sohrab and Rustum', was dropped in the 1869 volume; see further *Poems*, 351.
[3] *Commentary*, 91.

Abandons all which makes
His welfare insecure—
Other existences there are, that clash with ours . . .
(I, ii, 242–6; *Poems*, 166)

Arnold's additions to the story are in keeping with this pathos. He opens his narrative after Balder's death (he thought later of adding 'a first book with an account of the circumstances of the death of Balder himself')[1] and in Part I, The Sending, which relates how Hermod sets out on his journey to the underworld to plead for Balder's return, he introduces his own story of the blind Hoder's lonely sorrow and remorse, his suicide and his 'Later lonely appearance in the land of the dead', together with Balder's equally sorrowful appearance after his death to his wife Nanna. In Part II, Journey to the Dead, it is to Arnold that we owe Balder's melancholy prediction that no one can save him. In Part III, Funeral (the funeral takes place before the journey in the *Edda*), Arnold's inventions are the lamentation of the gods over the funeral pyre, the council of the Aesir and the last poignant meeting between the brothers Hermod and Hoder.

. . . Si vis me flere, dolendum est
Primum ipsi tibi . . .

The presentation of the suffering Hoder throughout the poem suggests that the poet has himself 'felt pain first'. Towards the close of the poem the flavour of the author's earlier poetic idiom faintly revives in Balder's farewell to his kingdom, a kingdom which here has less to do with Valhalla than with Arnold's personal world where, 'In action's dizzying eddy whirled', men grow weary and despondent and long for calm:

Mine eyes are dizzy with the arrowy hail;
Mine ears are stunned with blows and sick for calm . . .
(III, 507–8; *Poems*, 387)

But the resemblance in the poem to this earlier poetic landscape are rare. In this speech, for example, Arnold, now returning to his source

[1] *Poems*, 351.

in Percy's translation of Mallet, continues with a quasi-apocalyptic vision of the second Asgard,

> *. . . we shall see emerge*
> *From the bright Ocean at our feet an earth*
> *More fresh, more verdant, than the last, with fruits*
> *Self-springing, and a seed of man preserved,*
> *Who then shall live in peace, as now in war . . .*
>
> (III, 527–31; *Poems*, 388)

a passage which partly foreshadows the millennial vision which, some ten years or so later, appears in 'Obermann once More', the poem in which Arnold took his final leave of Senancour.

Between 'Balder Dead' and 'Obermann once More' lies *Merope. A Tragedy*, which was worked on from the autumn of 1865 to the autumn of 1857 and published at the beginning of 1858. 'Far more than "Sohrab" or "Balder"', say the authors of the *Commentary*, '*Merope* really illustrates the *architectonicè* and the strictures against "fine writing" laid down in the Preface of 1853.' They add that it has 'in its own way' arresting qualities: 'fine Sophoclean irony, some noble and lofty rhetoric, a certain pathos and humanity given to Merope's own character, an atmosphere of old ancestral crime that Aristotle might have understood, Arnold's usual talent for resounding proper names and local colour—these are effective. The defect in the poem is Arnold's failure to adhere to Aristotle's favoured "single unhappy issue"' (*Commentary*, 284). But one might well reply that the 'defect' is in fact associated with what is still alive in a work which, as a sedulous piecing together of the *disjecta membra* of a bygone age, has much in common with George Eliot's attempt in *Romola* to reconstruct Savonarola's Florence. Arnold's admiration for the formal peculiarities of Greek tragedy owes much, as we have seen, to his recognition of their disciplined containment of powerful feeling: 'The agitation becomes overwhelming . . . the torrent of feeling flows for a space without check: this disorder and the general order produce a powerful effect; but the balance is restored before the tragedy closes' (*CPW*, I, 59). There is no 'torrent of feeling' in *Merope*.

> If the suppression of Empedocles was an act of poetic castration, a punishment of the mobile poetic self, then *Merope* is the work of

> one who had made himself a poetic eunuch, whether or not it was for the kingdom of heaven's sake. . . . It is a cardboard imitation of Sophocles's *Electra*, which ironically utterly fails to give us, as Arnold hoped it would do, 'a specimen of the world created by the Greek imagination'. If Polyphontes bleeds (off-stage), he bleeds sawdust; the stateliness has something false about it like the solemn hush of an undertaker's parlour. It is not unreadable—indeed it contains some tolerable blank verse—but it is dead. Nothing in fact really connects Arnold's two dramatic poems but the fact that they were written by the same man at different times of his poetic career. If 'Empedocles on Etna' is the most 'subjective' of the longer poems, *Merope* is the most 'objective', that is to say the least personal of them, the kind of poetry that supervenes when a poet transfers his 'operations to a region where form is empty' or, to put it differently, the kind of poetry that may be written at half pressure 'without knocking yourself to pieces'.[1]

The gestures towards Sophocles in the numerous borrowings and parallels fail to bring *Merope* even distantly within sight of the power, austerity and heroism of Sophoclean tragedy, where, as Arnold saw it, the function of the chorus was to provide lyrical relief for intense emotion: 'To combine, to harmonize, to deepen for the spectator the feelings naturally excited in him by the sight of what was passing upon the stage. . . . After tragic situations of the greatest intensity, a desire for relief and relaxation is natural . . .' (*CPW*, I, 61). The songs of Callicles interrupting and relieving Empedocles's despondent monologues come closer than the low-temperatured choric passages in *Merope* to reaching this ideal harmony and balance. Arnold's so-called 'Greek tragedy' is, in effect, the product of an accomplished craftsman who has substituted the 'fascination of what's [technically] difficult', for what Henry James calls 'felt life' (James too has been charged often enough with effecting this kind of substitution in some of his later work).

All the same, *Merope* sets before us a new turn in Arnold's thinking at the same time that it reminds us—in spite of his efforts to subdue it—of an old obsession. Aepytus, the avenger of his father's slayer Polyphontes, has been seen as the first of Arnold's characters who

[1] Kenneth Allott, unpublished notes on Arnold.

cannot be identified with any form of quietism nor yet described as the prophet of a new dawn. 'He is the first of Arnold's heroes who actively imposes his will upon the world. With him "Exit Hamlet, enter Fortinbras"', says one critic, adding, 'the publication of *Merope* preceded by just one year Arnold's own entrance into the world in the pamphlet *England and the Italian Question*, a work which Arnold connected "with a new sense of identification with his father's spirit" ("I have often thought, since I published this on the Italian question, about dear papa's pamphlets. Whatever talent I had in this direction I certainly inherited from him").'[1] As another Arnoldian has it, 'The "missionary" side of Arnold as a poet grew with the years and when very strong it suppressed poetry altogether', so that 'Arnold as a "missionary" exists mainly in prose'.[2] The fluctuating movements of this 'missionary' impulse can be felt as Arnold travels from 'Sohrab and Rustum', where the man of 'morality and character' is victorious, but sorrowfully so, through 'Balder Dead', where action is violent and deplorable but may yield to a better age, and on to *Merope*, where Aepytus acts according to plan, yet in doing so slays a usurper who is portrayed as a troubled figure for whom force is a regrettable necessity. Arnold argues in his Preface against the handling of Polyphontes by Maffei and Voltaire, the two out of his many predecessors in adapting the story who most interested him. They did not in his view make Polyphontes 'tragic' nor his relationship with Merope sufficiently intelligible. In his own treatment, Polyphontes and the situation centred on him are refracted through an entirely un-Greek modern sensibility, which is concerned with the movements of a modern moral consciousness and the battle between absolutism and pragmatism (the twentieth-century French dramatist, Jean Anouilh, explores this conflict when portraying Creon in his version of the *Antigone*).

Such public themes signpost the beginning of the end of Arnold's poetic life. But in the expression of them is still felt intermittently and with a gradually decreasing strength the pulse of the loneliness, uncertainty and dissatisfaction which first brought that life into being. Polyphontes longs like Balder for calm—'Peace, peace is what I seek,

[1] Dwight Culler, *Imaginative Reason*, New Haven and London 1966, 228; *Letters*, I, 125.

[2] Kenneth Allott, unpublished lecture.

and public calm'—and he mourns like Empedocles the destructiveness of time:

> *O Merope, how many noble thoughts*
> *How many precious feelings of man's heart,*
> *How many loves, how many gratitudes,*
> *Do twenty years wear out, and see expire!*
> *Shall they not wear one hatred out as well?* (*Poems*, 406)

What is more, Arnold cannot even now disengage Aepytus, supposedly his 'man of action', from the youthful figures in his earlier poems, who virtually by definition are poets and singers celebrating their delight in the physical world. Merope thinks of Aepytus in his absence as 'A gladsome hunter of deer', who 'Basks in his morning of youth', and

> *. . . with a light uncareworn spirit, turns*
> *Quick from distressful thought, and floats in joy . . .* (*Poems*, 415)

Aepytus speaks of himself in much the same way when, as the plot requires, he deceives the court with the story of his own death while hunting in the Arcadian hills. The tempo of his narrative quickens with the remembered exhilaration of the chase. It has been said with some truth that the passage 'almost alone in the drama, is vital and alive because in it Arnold is returning to the source of his true poetic feeling'.[1] But the service intended to Arnold in this particular critical commentary is damaged by the suggestion that the strength of Aepytus's story depends on its being an allegory of rebirth from youthful idleness to responsible maturity, and the setting of the hunt being a reworking of a characteristically Arnoldian 'symbolic' landscape. The quickened imaginative activity—which necessarily eludes this kind of schematism—has nothing to do with moral disapproval of youthful idleness and everything to do with a momentary poignant recapturing of a sense of unreflecting delight in the natural world, poignant because for Arnold the sense is at best fleeting and is associated with the short-lived creativity of the youthful poet in whom, as in Callicles, 'the brave impetuous heart' has not yet yielded to the 'subtle contriving head'. But with *Merope*—it was not

[1] Dwight Culler, *op. cit.*, 227.

yet so with 'Empedocles on Etna'—the battle is lost and won, the days of Callicles are past, and Empedocles's course is now set towards his second career as 'an excellent and indispensable master of prose and reason'.[1]

[1] *CPW*, IX, Kenneth Allott's preparatory notes for this chapter include the following passage: 'The rejection of "Empedocles on Etna", defended in the 1853 preface, is as I have said elsewhere, "like the crisis of a long and punishing illness from which the patient recovers to lead a diminished life" ['A Background for "Empedocles on Etna"', see n 2, page 77]. That diminution is ended in *Merope* and in the years of prose-work which however important it may be in the eyes of those who severally value highly the literary criticism, the social criticism or the theological writings, was, I am sure, to Arnold a *pis-aller*, no more than "comparatively journeyman-work, to be done well and estimably rather than ill and discreditably, and with precious rewards of its own, besides, in exercising the faculties and in keeping off ennui; but still work of an inferior order" (*CPW*, V, 305)'.

4: *Arnold and Literary Criticism: (i) Critical Ideas*

DAVID J. DELAURA

'IN A SOCIETY IN WHICH the arts were seriously studied, in which the art of writing was respected, Arnold might have become a critic,' T. S. Eliot once said.[1] That is, Arnold might have been a more exclusively 'literary' critic, after the pattern of a Sainte-Beuve, not only if he had not spent most of his life inspecting schools, but also if he had not had to belecture a perverse generation in elementary principles about the critical habit of mind—not to speak of related matters in education, religion, and social policy. This fact accounts in part for what Chesterton called Arnold's 'smile of heart-broken forbearance, as of a teacher in an idiot school, that was enormously insulting'.[2]

But some countervailing points need to be recalled, too. First, Arnold was a shrewd judge of literature, and looked at a good deal of it closely, especially in the Homer and Celtic lectures. Arnold's particular literary judgements and attitudes are surveyed in Chapter 5 of this volume by R. H. Super. Moreover, even those who do not concede importance or originality to Arnold as a critic—and there are a surprising number of them even today—recognize a sure instinct for literary 'rightness' even in the touchstones, so easily dismissed. Also, despite that frequently irritating tone of superior taste and knowledge, Arnold is never an esoteric thinker. In this he contrasts sharply with the PRB, his 'disciple' Pater, and the succeeding Aesthetes. All of Arnold's interests converge in his growing sense of his public role as a promoter of qualities necessary, at this special moment in history, for the improvement of the quality of English life generally. He had his eye

[1] Introduction to *The Sacred Wood*, 1920; rpt. London and New York 1960, xiii.

[2] G. K. Chesterton, *The Victorian Age in Literature*, New York n.d., 78.

especially on a growing class of literate and sensitive men and women who were detached from the older political and religious orthodoxies but who were by no means either indifferent to the claims of the past or receptive to the more radical attempts to 'reconceive' human life in the late nineteenth century. More literarily, when we say (often accusingly) that Arnold was preoccupied with the 'moral' effect of poetry, we are to a large extent saying that he was concerned with its public as well as its private consequences. And this was a concern that all critics, from the Greeks right up to and including the English Romantics, had assumed to be a matter of central importance for poets and readers alike.

What we still lack is a view of the unity and continuity of Arnold's critical attitudes. This chapter attempts such a view by showing the interconnections among Arnold's concerns, as they develop in response to the needs of his own career and to his growing perception of the cultural crisis of his times.

I

There is a rich if inchoate body of literary theory and opinion in Arnold's early poetry and his letters to Clough, culminating in the Preface to the *Poems* of 1853. The letters, which have never been 'read' definitively or set into the full context of Arnold's and Clough's early poetry, show Arnold for the most part detaching himself from the various possible positions of the day. And (as other readers have noted) it should not be forgotten that what Arnold condemns in Clough is often a part of himself he is struggling with. A reading has become standard, with some justice, that the early Arnold of *The Strayed Reveller* (1849) is highly 'aesthetic' in attitude, that the poems of *Empedocles on Etna* (1852) show the pose of detachment getting unravelled, and that by 1853 he has worked out a 'moral' aesthetic first fully displayed in 'Sohrab and Rustum'.[1] But the particulars suggest a good deal more ambiguity. The 'high' poet of the 'Shakespeare' sonnet (1844), 'To a Friend', and 'Resignation' is in fact austere and enduring to the point of anaesthetic impassibility. He sheds tears as he hears from

[1] A pioneering discussion of Arnold's early poetry appears in A. Dwight Culler, *Imaginative Reason: The Poetry of Matthew Arnold*, New Haven and London 1966.

a distance the Wordsworthian still, sad music of humanity ('Resignation', ll. 186ff.), but his focus is on 'That general life, which does not cease,/ Whose secret is not joy, but peace.' The ideal is Goethean, but the claim of being superior to experience ('Blame thou not . . . him who dares/ Judge vain beforehand human cares') inevitably suggests an intolerance of confusion and a distaste for ordinary human contact—a frequent note in Arnold's most intimate work.[1]

From the first, Arnold is so far from the merely 'aesthetic' mood of the century as to reject with scorn 'Tennyson's dawdling with [the] painted shell' of the universe or Keats the mere 'style and form seeker' (*Letters to Clough*, 63, 100). His championing of a 'very plain direct and severe' poetry against the 'exuberance of expression' and 'richness of images' of both the Elizabethans and the Romantics is as complete in the 1840s as it is in 1852–3 (*Letters to Clough*, 124, 63, 65, 101). 'The Strayed Reveller' is (after the early and not very coherent 'The New Sirens') Arnold's fullest exploration of the Romantic poet's 'plunge' into experience and the consequences for his creativity. Some modern readers see it as Arnold's most authentic anatomy of true 'classicism' too, before the more frozen and Apollonian pseudo-classicism of 1853 and later. Still, though we have no agreed-upon reading of the poem, there is good evidence that even here Arnold was critical of the 'strayed' poet giving himself up to a kaleidoscopic and almost psychedelic swirl of visions—and curiously exempt from the 'pain' which the reveller himself says a poet must undergo.[2]

The letters back up this suspicion: as early as 1848 or 1849 Arnold insists that a poet, unlike Keats or Browning, 'must begin with an Idea of the world in order not to be prevailed over by the world's multitudinousness' (*Letters to Clough*, 97). This is not, he is quick to

[1] On Arnold's unsuccessful struggle to come to terms with a 'Shakespearean' ideal of impersonality and tolerance, see my 'A Background to Arnold's "Shakespeare"', in *Nineteenth-Century Literary Perspectives*, ed. C. de L. Ryals, Durham, N.C., 1974, 129–48.

[2] W. A. Madden offers a reading of this difficult poem in an earlier chapter of this book. Two of the best earlier discussions are Warren D. Anderson, *Matthew Arnold and the Classical Tradition*, Ann Arbor, Michigan 1965, 24–31, and Alan Roper, *Arnold's Poetic Landscapes*, Baltimore 1969, 99–107.

explain, at all the same as Clough's attempt 'to *solve* the Universe'.[1] Arnold regularly permits himself a rather wounding contempt for Clough's 'apostrophes to duty', and even his praise for Clough's 'sincerity' and his 'striving evidently to get breast to breast with reality' (*Letters to Clough*, 63, 86) is undercut by his own reluctance to write a poetry directly engaging ethical and metaphysical problems. Arnold's own poetic 'Idea of the world' involves the attempt not to '*solve*' but to '*re-construct* the Universe'—though he admits that this Shakespearean ideal, which is part of 'the poetic office in general', is for himself somehow baffling and unsatisfactory (*Letters to Clough*, 63). He insists that to give pleasure and to preserve poetry's essential 'sensuousness', and not merely to excite 'curiosity and reflexion', one must avoid both 'trying to go into and to the bottom of an object' as well as 'mere painting'. The aim will be that of 'grouping *objects*', and he quotes his own 'Resignation': 'Not deep the Poet sees, but wide' (*Letters to Clough*, 99).

But by September 1849, in the midst of writing his *Sturm und Drang* poems, a marked change is evident. He is 'snuffing after a moral atmosphere'; he insists, 'ye must be born again'; he still resists a Clough-like 'craving . . . for profound thoughts, mighty spiritual workings', but insists that conscious self-mastery and 'a distinct seeing of my way' must *precede* action (*Letters to Clough*, 109–110). Something was going very wrong with that earlier impassive ideal. He seems aware of severe losses. Certainly the disturbed confessional poems of the 1852 volume were far from the ideal of 'grouping objects', though he defends the necessity of his desolating analysis of 'the modern situation in its true *blankness* and *barrenness*, and *unpoetrylessness*' (*Letters to Clough*, 126). His own autobiographical Empedocles, not unlike Hamlet, experiences the disintegration of the 'balance' of faculties, of inward and outward, of thought and feeling.[2] At the age of thirty, Arnold felt 'three parts iced over' (*Letters to Clough*, 128).

[1] The phrase seems to be Goethean in origin. See the entry for 12 October 1825, in Eckermann's *Conversations with Goethe*, tr. John Oxenford, Everyman's Library, London 1930, 120: 'Man is born, not to solve the problems of the universe, but to find out where the problem applies, and then to restrain himself within the limits of the comprehensible.'

[2] That Coleridge's Hamlet criticism may have influenced Arnold's portrait of Empedocles, is the argument of my 'Coleridge, Hamlet, and Arnold's Empedocles', *Papers on Language and Literature*, 8, Supplement, Fall 1972, 17–25.

The distress caused by this exploration of himself and the modern situation was part of the complex set of decisions about himself and his poetry reflected in the Preface to the 1853 *Poems*.[1] Kenneth Allott refers to the Preface as 'Arnold's quarrel with himself about "subjectivity" in poetry' (*Poems*, 590). For a document usually described as both 'moral' and insistent on the importance of action and structure, it is a very curious business. The Preface, dated 1 October 1853, explains the suppression of 'Empedocles' by declaring that a poem 'in which there is everything to be endured, nothing to be done', can give no pleasure: it is 'morbid' and 'monotonous'. In contrast, he speaks of 'the eternal objects of poetry' as 'human actions; possessing an inherent interest in themselves', thereby almost implying that 'poetic' subjects exist apart from treatment. But when he turns later to defend the subjects of classical tragedy, he is strangely silent about the 'terrible old mythic story', 'the situation of Orestes, or Merope, or Alcmaeon', and *why* it forms a more 'grand, detached, or self-subsistent object for a tragic poem' than the subjects he dismisses in the works of Goethe, Byron, Lamartine, and Wordsworth—except, implicitly and negatively, because the Greek stories avoid precisely 'the problems of modern life, moral, intellectual, and social' (*CPW*, I, 2–7). Arnold's real concern is with a rather mysterious Goethean 'Architectonicè': 'that power of execution, which creates, forms, and constitutes' (*CPW*, I, 9). The modern poet may learn from the ancients three things: 'the all-importance of the choice of a subject; the necessity of accurate construction; and the subordinate character of expression' (*CPW*, I, 12). Here, 'execution' or 'construction' emerges as a power in itself, almost independent of 'content'; what is important is 'the moral impression left by a great action treated as a whole'. Hovering between a Winckelmannian classicism and a pre-Freudian therapeutic effect, Arnold finds in the classics 'intense significance, . . . noble simplicity, . . . calm pathos' (*CPW*, I, 12). What the classics confer, finally, on the poet (the *reader*, in 1853, is pretty much delivered over to the 'spiritual

[1] The document, and its place in Arnold's career, are best explored in Ch. 9 of Alba H. Warren, Jr., *English Poetic Theory, 1825–1865*, 1950; rpt. New York 1960; Sidney M. B. Coulling, 'Matthew Arnold's 1853 Preface: Its Origin and Aftermath', *VS*, 7, March 1964, 233–63; and Kenneth Allott, 'A Background for "Empedocles on Etna"', *Essays and Studies 1968*, London 1968, 80–100.

discomfort' of the age) is 'a steadying and composing effect', a stern, stoic, and resistant demeanour in face of 'the false pretensions of his age' (*CPW*, I, 13–14). Every reader senses how autobiographical all this is: Arnold is defending his own choice of historical subjects and exotic settings, as well as his refusal to take up the task of 'interpreting' the age to itself. But the figure that emerges, proud and consciously isolated, bears himself 'nobly' by an intense act of will. The poet will not even attack

> the false pretensions of the age; he will content himself with not being overwhelmed by them. He will esteem himself fortunate if he can succeed in banishing from his mind all feelings of contradiction, and irritation, and impatience; in order to delight himself with the contemplation of some noble action of a heroic time, and to enable others, through his representation of it, to delight in it also (*CPW*, I, 14).

The 'Hamlet'-Arnold is still very close to the surface here: a man nearly overwhelmed by 'the bewildering confusion of our times' (*ibid.*), who has by a severe resolve adopted a pose of dispassionate calm. The costs seem very great.

The showcase for this new poetic is the dubious 'Sohrab and Rustum', with its fine elevated conclusion, written in the late spring of 1853. Interestingly, 'The Scholar-Gipsy', almost Arnold's last fling as an openly alienated and suffering poet,[1] was written later, in the summer. There, the action is divided between the almost sexless title-figure—innocent and exempt from modern dissociation, a kind of 'idiot' version of the poet-figure in 'Resignation'—and a railing denunciation of the age, of the sort threaded through the 1852 volume. Clough liked 'The Scholar-Gipsy'. But the reformed Arnold responded, rather depressingly: '. . . what does it *do* for you? Homer *animates*—Shakespeare *animates*—in its poor way I think Sohrab and Rustum *animates*—the Gipsy Scholar at best awakens a pleasing melancholy. But this is not what we want' (*Letters to Clough*, 146).

'What we want' became slightly clearer in Arnold's Inaugural Lecture as Professor of Poetry at Oxford in 1857, 'The Modern

[1] 'Stanzas from the Grande Chartreuse', published in 1855, may have been begun as early as 1851; see *Poems*, 285.

Element in Literature', not published until 1869. In his defence of the culture of fifth-century B.C. Athens for its ideal of 'human nature . . . in its completest and most harmonious development', Arnold still speaks of Sophocles's 'noble serenity', but now associates this with energy, maturity, freedom, and intelligent observation. 'Modern' thought and 'modern' feeling—leading to depression, *ennui*, lassitude, and 'incurable tedium'—are now seen as recurring syndromes throughout history, plaguing the highest civilizations. Poetry, the right Sophoclean sort of poetry, emerges as a chief counteragent against modern disenchantment and gloom. And poets can be ranked now by the extent to which they fall short of Sophocles's 'serious cheerfulness': Virgil's 'ineffable melancholy' and Lucretius's 'rigid, . . . moody gloom' deprive them of the highest rank. Poetry is to be 'interpretative and fortifying' (*CPW*, I, 28, 32, 35–6).

The effects of the best literature are spelled out a bit further in the Preface to *Merope* (1858), Arnold's inert specimen of classical tragedy. 'Severe form' is again a means for achieving a '*profound moral impression*' (*CPW*, I, 59, 60).

> This sense of emphatic distinctness in our impressions rises, as the thought and emotion swell higher and higher without overflowing their boundaries, to a lofty sense of the mastery of the human spirit over its own stormiest agitations; and this . . . conducts us to a state of feeling which it is the highest aim of tragedy to produce, to *a sentiment of sublime acquiescence in the course of fate, and in the dispensations of human life* (*CPW*, 58–9).

Psychologically, this is an interesting interplay of 'mastery' and 'acquiescence'; substantively, for the first time an austerely 'religious' note of submission to an obscure fate.

II

All of the foregoing represents Arnold's varied though sustained attempt to clarify his notion of poetry before his public career was fairly begun in the sixties. It contains the seeds of much of his later literary thought; but it should be remembered that in its general direction his struggles of the forties and fifties led towards the extinction of his own best poetry. To understand the underlying unity of Arnold's literary concerns, we need to look at a series of statements in which Arnold began to spell out his religious position and to see how deeply this latter affected his conception of poetry. An entry in the Yale MS., perhaps dating from the late forties and written almost in the voice of his own Empedocles, explains why Arnold was never to become, on the one hand, a mere 'aesthete', or on the other, a rationalist intellectual. 'I cannot conceal from myself the objection which really wounds and perplexes me from the religious side is that the service of reason is freezing to feeling, chilling to the religious mood. And feeling and the religious mood are eternally the deepest being of man, the ground of all joy and greatness for him' (*Poems*, 262). But religion, in the breakdown of metaphysics and theology, needs a new *kind* of embodiment. He writes to Clough in May 1850: 'He [the despised F. W. Newman] bepaws the religious sentiment so much that he quite effaces it to me. This sentiment now, I think, is best not regarded alone, but considered in conjunction with the grandeur of the world, love of kindred, love, gratitude etc. etc.' (*Letters to Clough*, 115). The literary implications are even clearer in a remark of October 1852. As against the 'exquisite bits and images' of a Shelley or a Keats, he argues,

> modern poetry can only subsist by its *contents*: by becoming a complete magister vitae as the poetry of the ancients did: by including, as theirs did, religion with poetry, instead of existing as poetry only, and leaving religious wants to be supplied by the Christian religion, as a power existing independent of the poetical power. But the language, style and general proceedings of a poetry which has such an immense task to perform must be very plain direct and severe: it must not lose itself in parts and episodes or ornamental work, but must press forwards to the whole (*Letters to Clough*, 124).

This is virtually a sketch for Arnold's later poetics, especially his discussion of the 'religious' future of poetry in his writings around 1880. But though Arnold obviously from the first saw Christian dogma as outmoded and irrelevant to true religion, I think it misleading to say, as some have done,[1] that this foundation stone of Arnold's poetics is simply predictive of the 'Aestheticism' or art for art's sake of the later nineteenth century. The point will have to be taken up later. There was to be, however, one significant change. Here, in 1852, Arnold is still struggling to produce an adequate 'modern' poetry; after the early sixties he virtually abandons all post-Wordsworthian poetry, including his own, and concentrates in effect on making his special anthology of Western poetry that will act, almost liturgically, as a *magister vitae.* These early statements are capped by a remark of September 1853, virtually simultaneous with the Preface:

> If one loved what was beautiful and interesting in itself *passionately* enough, one would produce what was excellent without troubling oneself with religious dogmas at all. As it is, we are *warm* only when dealing with these last—and what is frigid is always bad. I would have others—most others stick to the old religious dogmas because I sincerely feel that this *warmth* is the great blessing, and this frigidity the great curse—and on the old religious road they have still the best chance of getting the one and avoiding the other (*Letters to Clough*, 143).

There are some alarming implications here for Arnold's later theory, indeed for all later poetic theory, in the suggestion that truth and poetry are incompatible, that our deepest emotional need for a high and 'religious' poetry is necessarily founded on a metaphysical illusion.

III

Arnold has been repeatedly disparaged as a 'didactic' and 'moral' critic for his statements in the early sixties that 'the most essential part of poetic greatness' lies in 'the noble and profound application of ideas to life', or that poetry is '*a criticism of life*' (*CPW*, I, 211–12; III, 209). Though he incautiously repeated these notions, he fortunately qualified the first statement in 1879 by adding, 'under the conditions immutably

[1] See Warren, *loc. cit.*, 155; E. D. H. Johnson, *The Alien Vision of Victorian Poetry*, 1952; rpt. Hamden, Conn. 1963, 163, 165, 200, 218–19; and William A. Madden, *Matthew Arnold: A Study of the Aesthetic Temperament*, Bloomington and London 1967.

fixed by the laws of poetic beauty and poetic truth' (*CPW*, IX, 44; see also 163). Arnold repeatedly and convincingly denies that he is calling for either the work of 'modern philosophical poets and philosophical moralists' or 'doctrine such as we hear in church, . . . religious and philosophic doctrine' (*Works*, IV, 341; *CPW*, IX, 49). Still, the *contents* of poetry as a '*magister vitae*', the nature of the 'ideas' he would 'apply' to life, and his conception of 'poetic truth' are central to his view of poetry and its functions. I think the 'contents' can be identified to some extent, and that in them several of Arnold's most familiar critical doctrines take on new meaning as they reveal themselves to be mutually supportive.

A decisive step in clarifying Arnold's views of poetry was taken in 'Maurice de Guérin' (1863), one of the most important essays on poetry in the nineteenth century. In it, he distinguishes two kinds of 'interpretative power': the first expresses 'with magical felicity the physiognomy and movement of the outward world', the second interprets, 'with inspired conviction, the ideas and laws of the inward world of man's moral and spiritual nature' (*CPW*, III, 12, 33). In very broad terms, Arnold's categories correspond to Keats's 'chameleon poet' and the Wordsworthian Egotistical Sublime. The most original aspect of the essay is Arnold's definition of the 'peculiar temperament, an extraordinary delicacy of organisation and susceptibility to impressions', that belongs to the poet of 'natural magic', a Keats or a Guérin. In 'a great degree passive', 'he aspires to be a sort of human Aeolian harp, catching and rendering every rustle of Nature':

> he resists being riveted and held stationary by any single impression. . . . He goes into religion and out of religion, into society and out of society, not from the motives which impel men in general, but to feel what it is all like; he is thus hardly a moral agent. . . . He hovers over the tumult of life, but does not really put his hand to it (*CPW*, III, 30–1).

This is Keats's ego-less poet, with touches of Arnold's Scholar-Gipsy, in one stage of his transformation into Pater's ideal aesthetic-observer.[1] What is most remarkable is that Arnold here, for a moment, seems to

[1] See my *Hebrew and Hellene in Victorian England: Newman, Arnold, and Pater*, Austin and London 1969, Ch. 15.

revert to a 'poetic' side of himself that he had, in Auden's phrase, 'thrust . . . in prison' in 1853. Of course he holds that the 'great poets', like Aeschylus and Shakespeare, unite the two kinds of interpretation, 'the naturalistic and the moral'. But, Arnold points out, even Shakespeare's 'expression tends to become too little sensuous and simple, too much intellectualised' (*CPW*, III, 33). Thus Arnold is not merely concerned to do justice to this almost 'morbid' expressiveness and felicity; he virtually identifies poetry itself (sensuous and simple) with this 'magical' kind of interpretation. He had said something similar (and equally surprising) in February 1849, when he told the intellectualizing and moralizing Clough that 'an absolute propriety—of form' is 'the sole *necessary* of Poetry as such: whereas the greatest wealth and depth of matter is merely a superfluity in the Poet *as such*' (*Letters to Clough*, 98–9).

But that the essay of 1863 is a kind of aberration in the inexorable course of Arnold's poetic thinking is evident in his treatment of the very same notions in the Celtic lectures (1865–6), where the 'Celtic' temperament, filled with 'passionate, penetrating melancholy', is presented in terms very close to those earlier applied to the 'hovering' poet—and is finally rejected. Again, Arnold virtually identifies 'poetry' with the Celt's magic, beauty, and grace, and assigns to it genius, sentiment, emotion, impressions, passions, 'technic', elaboration, skill. We are not surprised, however, to hear that the Greek poets are superior in their combining 'steadiness, patience, sanity' with this 'perceptive, emotional temperament': they are marked by reason, measure, harmony, sanity, and '*architectonicè*'. This last is associated with 'a steady, deep-searching survey, a firm conception of the facts of human life', whereas 'in the contents of [the Celt's] poetry you have only so much interpretation of the world as the first dash of a quick, strong perception, and then sentiment, infinite sentiment, can bring you' (*CPW*, III, 343–6). This 'Greek' balance is of course central to Arnold's emerging view of life and poetry in the 1860's, and is precisely the point of the well-known conclusion to 'Pagan and Mediaeval Religious Sentiment' (1863). There, after seeming to award the palm to medieval Christianity as the religion of 'the heart and imagination', over later Greek paganism and its exaltation of 'the senses and understanding', he had abruptly upended this scale of values in favour of 'imaginative reason', 'the element by which the modern spirit, if it would live right, has chiefly to live'. The balance this represents, later expressed as a balance between 'the thinking power' ('the senses' have been quietly put aside) and 'the religious sense', is illustrated in a quotation from the *Oedipus Tyrannos* that piously invokes 'holy innocence', 'august laws', heaven, everlasting laws, and the unageing 'power of God' (*CPW*, III, 230–1). It is hard to see how even 'the thinking-power' is involved here in any special way. How far—by 1866—the balance could tip *away* from heart and imagination and 'natural magic', and towards the thinking-power, is evident in a later passage of the Celtic lectures discussing the task of the archetypal 'modern' poet, Goethe. A Dante could assume 'the basis of spiritual life'; a Shakespeare could allow the 'spectacle of human life . . . to bear its own significance': neither had to question 'the traditional religion, reformed or unreformed, of Christendom'.

> But when Goethe came, Europe had lost her basis of spiritual life; she had to find it again; Goethe's task was,—the inevitable task for the modern poet henceforth is,—as it was for the Greek poet in the days of Pericles, not to preach a sublime sermon on a given text like Dante, not to exhibit all the kingdoms of human life and the glory of them like Shakespeare, but to interpret human life afresh and to supply a new spiritual basis to it. This is not only a work for style, eloquence, charm, poetry; it is a work for science. . . . (*CPW*, III, 381)

This complicated passage needs explication. Goethe's Spinozism and 'denial of final causes' (*CPW*, III, 176–9)—his 'imperturbable naturalism'—were indeed playing a vital role in the formation of Arnold's own 'natural' Christianity and, above all, in the function of criticism and culture in the new order. But neither Goethe nor any other 'enlightened' modern poet was finally judged to have *produced* poetry 'adequate' for the deepest spiritual-aesthetic needs of the men and women Arnold conceived himself to be addressing. As we shall see, the highest kinds of poetry singled out by Arnold, culminating in the touchstones of 1880, studiously avoid any hint of a modern or post-theological 'reinterpretation' of life. Arnold had already, in 1863, advised: 'And who has not rejoiced to be able, between the old idea [such as special Providence, or divine wrath], tenable no longer, which once connected itself with certain religious words, and the new idea [presumably Arnold's "reconstructed" spiritualized Christianity], which has not yet connected itself with them, to rest for awhile in the healing virtue and beauty of the words themselves?' (*CPW*, III, 81). In fact, that 'while' was to continue indefinitely; and the 'beauty' of the old words became central to Arnold's programme for the present and future of poetry. The phrase about 'the Greek poet in the days of Pericles' refers to Arnold's growing interest in an historical scheme in which, just as in Arnold's generation, higher religious and spiritual ideals were maintained by certain poets and philosophers while the traditional religion itself was falling into desuetude.[1] But of course the passages Arnold gives from Pindar or Sophocles (*CPW*, I, 191; III, 231) are in themselves indistinguishable from the poetry of traditional religion and myth.

IV

Most, then, of Arnold's later views of poetry and its functions had been developed in scattered contexts by the early and mid-sixties. Equally important in this period was Arnold's working out of a doctrine of style that would be the proper vehicle for his elevated 'new idea'. In the 1853 Preface he had associated the simplicity and restraint of the '*grand style*' of the ancients with 'action' and 'the pregnancy of the matter which it conveys', and opposed it precisely to 'expression' in the sense of incidental and scattered felicities of thought and image (*CPW*, I, 5, 12). But even earlier, in March 1849, Arnold had explained to Clough the relationship of style and character, and seemed to attribute an independent and mysterious moral effect to the sustained and elevated style of a Milton or a Sophocles:

> . . . there are two offices of Poetry—one to add to one's store of thoughts and feelings—another to compose and elevate the mind by a sustained tone, numerous allusions, and a grand style. What other process is Milton's than this last, in Comus for instance. There is no fruitful analysis of character: but a great effect is produced. What is Keats? A style and form seeker, and this with an impetuosity that heightens the effect of his style almost painfully. Nay in Sophocles what is valuable is not so much his contributions to

[1] Arnold's thinking about the parallels between Greek culture and the modern European situation was stimulated by his reading of Ernst Curtius's *History of Greece*. His five notices (1868–76), recently discovered, are gathered in *CPW*, V, 257–94.

> psychology and the anatomy of sentiment, as the grand moral effects produced by *style*. For the style is the expression of the nobility of the poet's character, as the matter is the expression of the richness of his mind: but on men character produces as great an effect as mind (*Letters to Clough*, 100–1).

This is generally taken to be the scope of Arnold's sometimes deplored theory of the grand style. This view would seem to be sustained in the elaboration of the doctrine in the Homer lectures. Arnold approves of Homer's plainness and (as a kind of concession) the 'inversion and pregnant conciseness of Milton or Dante'—and only *Paradise Lost* and the *Divine Comedy* qualify among 'modern' literatures for inclusion as works in the grand style (*CPW*, I, 102, 112, 144). The list is, and tends to remain, disconcertingly select: Homer, Pindar, Sophocles, Dante, Milton—but not Goethe, Calderon, Corneille, Schiller, or even Shakespeare. Arnold tries to distinguish the effects of the grand style, which is more than 'touching and stirring; it can form the character, it is edifying'. The 'few ancients in the grand style . . . can refine the raw natural man, they can transmute him' (*CPW*, I, 138–9). The only explicit reason for this effect that Arnold suggests is that Homer's nobleness or Milton's austerity of style communicate their own parallel moral qualities to the reader. This is implicit in Arnold's very Victorian[1] final definition: 'the grand style arises in poetry, *when a noble nature, poetically gifted, treats with simplicity or severity a serious subject*' (*CPW*, I, 188).

Now 'subject' is here quite explicitly made a *sine qua non*; the grand style cannot effect its work of 'transmutation' and 'edification' by simply bombinating in the void. Saintsbury, like most readers, interprets Arnold's emphasis on the 'Poetic Subject' to mean 'a demand for a subject of magnitude, elaborate disposition, a maintained and intense attitude'.[2] But as the whole scope of Arnold's succeeding criticism shows, not *any* serious and sustained subject will fill the bill. For Arnold's

[1] Ruskin, as recently as 1856 in *Modern Painters* III, Part IV, Ch. I ('Of the Received Opinions Touching the "Grand Style"'), had defined poetry as 'the suggestion by the imagination, of noble grounds for the noble emotions'.

[2] George Saintsbury, *A History of Criticism and Literary Taste in Europe*, Edinburgh and London 1904, III, 533.

continuous use of touchstones, beginning in the Homer lectures, suggests the rather narrow range of specific attitudes and emotions which qualify for inclusion in Arnold's select anthology. In the language of the letter of 1849, the 'office' of poetry 'to compose and elevate the mind by a sustained tone, numerous allusions, and a grand style' will not operate except within a special class of 'thoughts and feelings' (*Letters to Clough*, 100). John S. Eells has written a valuable study of Arnold's well-known touchstones in 'The Study of Poetry' (1880), showing that the bulk of them express these states of mind: 'the abiding pathos of young death; the manifold sorrow of man; the pathetic vicissitudes of man; the inward petrifaction caused by grief too deep for tears; the pain of living; the grandeur and majesty of a noble personality brought to ruin by a tragic flaw; the sense of loss of something beloved'.[1] Eight of the eleven, Eells notes, express varying degrees of melancholy and strong pathos, and seem to reveal that 'the chief control under which Arnold brought his personal preference was . . . a contemplacion, profoundly earnest, of the grimness and darkness of the human adventure'.[2] Eells is no doubt correct in objecting, as many others have, that the full meaning of each quotation is not clear when thus deprived of its original context.[3] But although he shows that these attitudes pervade Arnold's poetry and prose, and that some of the touchstones occur as early as the Homer lectures, he fails to relate these attitudes to Arnold's general theory of poetry or to his emerging views in other areas, especially religion.

There are two classes of touchstones proper, and in connection with one of the classes an overlooked comparative method. Eells correctly notes that the bulk of the eleven touchstones of 1880 express Arnold's specially favoured emotions of loss, pain, grief, death, the transience of both glory and happiness. He sees a new 'class' of emotions in numbers 5, 6 and 7, which he calls 'the need for peace' series—especially in the two from Dante, which express, first, gratitude to God for exempting the dead from human misery, and second, the supreme religious attitude of joy in submission to the divine will, the 'In la sua voluntade è nostra pace' that Eliot was to make much of years later. Inexplicably, however, Eells seems unaware that these two touchstones are intimately connected with the 'Christianization' of Arnold's thought

[1] *The Touchstones of Matthew Arnold*, New Haven, Conn. n.d., 203.
[2] *Ibid.*, 242, 222.
[3] *Ibid.*, 208.

over the preceding years. Scattered through the Homer lectures were 'specimens of the grand style' from Homer, Virgil, Dante, and Pindar, expressive of the most familiar touchstone emotions (*CPW*, I, 115, 125 n, 136–7, 188, 191). Later (*CPW*, I, 212), Arnold provides his more concentrated collection of touchstones from Homer, Dante, and Milton—two of which were to reappear in 1880. (The *Iliad* is almost invariably in Arnold's career quarried for the sense of lost and irrecoverable happiness, and *Paradise Lost* for the sense of lost and irreclaimable glory.) This may be called the continuing 'secular' component of Arnold's apprehension of the human condition: for him, it represents—against Victorian activism, complacency, and liberal progressivism—an honest facing of the permanent and irreducible contingency, opacity, and pain of human life. The attitude is, potentially, sub- or pre-theological in character, though Arnold, especially in the earlier stages of his public career, contemptuously rejects the modern or Ruskinian attempt to sentimentally 'console' oneself for the sadness of life by reading a 'tender pantheism' into Homer. He offers in its place Goethe's reading of Homer: 'in our life here above ground we have, properly speaking, to enact Hell'. Arnold finds *this* attitude genuinely 'tonic and fortifying' (*CPW*, I, 102, 108, 149). The bulk of Arnold's supreme touchstones are 'formative' and 'transforming' for human character because, in an un-Victorian and surprisingly 'existential' mood, they repudiate precisely the easier sorts of nineteenth-century consolation, whether religious or rationalistic. The touchstones have frequently been dismissed as simply further examples of Tennysonian or Virgilian melancholy and self-pity; they are, instead, *challenges* to the softer kinds of palliation. Any authentically 'religious' view of human possibility, Arnold is saying implicitly, must make its way against such a view and, in a sense, can never simply cancel this perception of the quality of human life, faced unflinchingly.

Touchstones expressive of the growing 'religious' component of Arnold's views begin to appear, more tentatively, shortly thereafter. We have already noted the favourite quotation from Sophocles (*CPW*, III, 231); but even earlier, in the Maurice de Guérin essay, Arnold had offered as examples of 'moral interpretation' a passage from Aeschylus on divine justice, and Hamlet's 'There's a divinity that shapes our ends' (*CPW*, III, 33). It is worth noting that for the rest of his career, the bulk of Arnold's 'tonic' and 'fortifying' touchstones—whether of the secular or the religious variety—that will do the work of religion are in effect examples of 'moral profundity'. The felicity and magic of 'naturalistic interpretation', except incidentally, largely drop out of Arnold's central views of poetry: this is undoubtedly a measure of his repudiation of some central aspects of Romanticism, and indeed of his own personality, as well as an indication of the rapid movement towards the setting out of his view of poetry as a 'complete magister vitae'.

The related 'comparative' method begins to appear very shortly thereafter; it is a key agent in defining Arnold's now more favourable attitude towards Christianity. 'Marcus Aurelius' (1863) is Arnold's first developed statement of his changing religious views. He insists on the need for inspiration and joy 'to make moral action perfect'. 'The paramount virtue of religion is, that is has *lighted up* morality, that it has supplied the emotion and inspiration needed for carrying the sage along the narrow way perfectly, for carrying the ordinary man along it at all' (*CPW*, III, 134). This is essentially Arnold's definition of religion in the next decade, too: '*morality touched by emotion*' (*CPW*, VI, 176). Characteristically, Arnold defines by examples. The elevated morality of a Seneca, an Epictetus, or a Marcus Aurelius is, in varying degrees, cold and inadequate. Against them, Arnold holds up quotations from both the Old and the New Testament: they convey gladness, elation, joy (*CPW*, III, 135, 149). Also characteristically, he refuses to rehearse the contents of his scriptural citations, which in fact deal with Providence, future happiness, God's blessing, and spiritual regeneration—even though Arnold goes out of his way in the essay to chide Marcus Aurelius for the 'scientifically' unsound view that 'the whole course of the universe . . . has a providential reference to man's welfare' (*CPW*, III, 155)! This same comparative method is employed in an important passage in *Literature and Dogma*, for the same purpose and with the same evasions (*CPW*, VI, 177–8). Again, classical moralists, enjoining conduct, are played off against Biblical citations, where 'feeling' has been 'added' to conduct. Though Arnold again refuses to explain, this 'feeling' obviously has a specific *content*: the sober self-interest of the moralists lacks the motivation of exalted love and self-surrender conveyed in the scriptural quotations. The novelty here is that Arnold's favourite citation from Sophocles is added to the others; in general, he prefers, in both literary and religious contexts, to separate Scripture and such expressions of 'purely religious sentiment' as the *Dies Irae* and the *Imitation of Christ*, from the works of the freely inventing 'imaginative reason' (*CPW*, III, 369), where even a Christian like Dante can take his place alongside Sophocles. This of course suits Arnold's purposes in his campaign to 'include' religion with poetry. Strictly devotional writings, even of the best scriptural variety, will fall short, however honourably, of that highest combinative working of the thinking-power and the religious sense.

But the increasingly 'devout' mood of Arnold's later career made him less finical, less 'Greek', in this matter, and in 'Literature and Science' (1882), the final and most complete statement of his later humanism, he uses not the largely 'secular' touchstones of 'The Study of Poetry' (1880) but the more strictly religious ones of 'Marcus Aurelius' and *Literature and Dogma*—and in the process finds Jesus as pat to his purpose as Homer. Arguing precisely for the power of 'humane letters' to 'engage the emotions'—in the never very clearly explained task of 'relating the modern results of natural science to man's instinct for conduct, his instinct for beauty'—it becomes evident in Arnold's examples that the needed emotions are explicitly of the religious class. Using the comparative method, Arnold points out the inadequacy of even Spinoza's morality when compared with Jesus's 'What is a man advantaged, if he gain the whole world, and lose himself, forfeit himself' (in Arnold's tendentious recasting), and Homer's 'for an enduring heart have the destinies appointed to the children of men'—the latter having the benefit of *combining* the 'grim' Homeric view of life with an acknowledgement of a larger providential framework (*CPW*, x, 67–8).

V

This movement of Arnold's literary thought can be better understood by tracing Arnold's widely-misunderstood notion of 'culture' and its involvement in the shifting entanglement of religion, poetry and intellect in Arnold's thinking. Part of the confusion comes from Arnold, for whom culture once or twice came close to being all things to at least a select class of men. Even more confusion has proceeded from a still influential attack by T. S. Eliot, who has it that 'literature, or Culture, tended with Arnold to usurp the place of Religion'—in short, that Arnold fathered 'the view of life of Walter Pater'.[1] It is worth showing, briefly, that culture and literature (in its most obvious sense) are generally not simply identified in Arnold, and, more importantly, that culture by no means simply swamps or engorges religion—even Arnold's residual and spiritualized religion of morality touched by emotion.

Arnold attempts different formulations of the problem, and a solution, at several stages in his career. Eliot is roughly correct that Arnold's religious writings affirm 'that the emotions of Christianity can and must be preserved without the belief' and that 'The effect of Arnold's religious campaign is to divorce Religion from thought'.[2] But the nature of 'thought' or 'intellect' or 'ideas' tends to shift meaning in Arnold's formulas. In 1863 it is 'new thought'—in the sense of the emerging nineteenth-century naturalistic view of reality—that Arnold is concerned with, and which he admits cannot 'yet' be harmonized with 'the religious life'—though his lifelong, and finally unsuccessful, attempt is precisely to make 'new intellectual ideas', 'truth of science', somehow available to 'truth of religion'. His temporary, and unstable, solution, as we saw, is 'to rest for awhile' in the beauty of scriptural texts *until* 'the new idea'—which may be both Arnold's still embryonic 'natural' religion, as well as its larger anti-metaphysical background—succeeds in 'connecting' itself with those powerful words. At any rate, 'Religious life resides not in an incessant movement of ideas, but in a feeling which attaches itself to certain fixed objects' (*CPW*, III, 65–82).

This is the very period of Arnold's explorations of the 'kinds' of poetry in the Guérin essay and his assertion of the holistic idea of 'imaginative reason' in 'Pagan and Mediaeval Religious Sentiment'. But although Arnold speaks of the power of Scripture to effect a truce between religion and 'new thought', poetry in a more general sense had not yet taken on 'the immense work' as 'a healing and reconciling influence' between religion and physical science which, by 1870, Arnold was to begin to assign to it and to himself.[3] What intervened was the rise and partial fall of Arnold's doctrine of culture. For the

[1] *Selected Essays*, 3rd edn, London 1951, 434.
[2] *Ibid.*
[3] *Letters*, II, 35–6.

more continuous line of Arnold's thought in the sixties was the definition and sponsorship of an intellectual ideal which would be the adequate agent of Arnold's reforms in the social, political, and educational arenas. It begins, in 'The Function of Criticism at the Present Time' and elsewhere, as the rather intellectualist ideal of 'criticism'—involving Goethe's 'profound, imperturbable naturalism', the notion of 'the free play of the mind upon all subjects' as 'a pleasure in itself', and of course the characteristic stance of distance-with-concern that he called 'disinterestedness' (*CPW*, III, 110, 268, 270). But by the time of the farewell lecture at Oxford in 1867, criticism's successor, 'culture', though retaining this essentially intellectual character, is said to have 'its origin in the love of perfection' and to be like religion in being an inward condition, 'Not a having and a resting, but a growing and a becoming'. Religion ('that voice of the deepest human experience') is patronized and somewhat submerged in this most confidently secular and 'Greek' statement of Arnold's career, since culture draws upon '*all* the voices of human experience', including that of religion (*CPW*, V, 91–4). The closest Arnold comes simply to merging religion into culture-as-poetry ('religion and poetry are one' in the 'best art and poetry of the Greeks') is in the statement that

> the idea of beauty and of a human nature perfect on all sides, which is the dominant idea of poetry, is a true and invaluable idea, though it has not yet had the success that the idea of conquering the obvious faults of our animality, and of a human nature perfect on the moral side,—which is the dominant idea of religion,—has been enabled to have; and it is destined, adding to itself the religious idea of a devout energy, to transform and govern the other (*CPW*, V, 99–100).

Here 'poetry', as it tended to do with the German Idealists, takes on its widest extension in Arnold's writings: it is nothing less than a cover-term for *all* of human perfection, in all its high aspects. The rest of Arnold's career is a drawing back from such a confident, and complacent, view of human possibility, though he never ceases to assert its desirability and even, in some indefinite future, its achievability.

Partly in response to telling rebuttals,[1] Arnold retreats and later in *Culture and Anarchy* calls for a 'spiritual balance' between culture's avatar, Hellenism, whose bent is 'to see things as they are, and by seeing them as they are to see them in their beauty', and Hebraism, which emphasizes 'the following not our individual will, but the will of God, *obedience*' (*CPW*, V, 165–7). Certain particulars in these familiar passages bear pointing out. First, although Arnold used for Hellenism the borrowed phrase 'sweetness and light', presumably meaning a close union of beauty and intellect, in fact both art and 'poetry' are much less to the fore in these later chapters, and Hellenism remains largely the intellectualist ideal of 'Greek intelligence', whose essence is 'the instinct for what Plato calls the true, firm, intelligible law of things' (*CPW*, V, 178). 'Greece and Greek art' are now simply patterns for this intellectual ideal, for the 'serenity which comes from having made order among ideas and harmonized them', and because 'Greek art, . . . [and] Greek beauty, have their root in the same impulse to see things as they really are' (*CPW*, V, 125, 178). The stinging accusations against Arnold's would-be 'religion of culture' (*CPW*, V, 115) seem indeed to have caused him to rethink his position somewhat, and in the succeeding years culture becomes a highly refined mode of knowing and discrimination, a form of intellectual and spiritual 'tact', and conduct and religion emerge and remain a distinct and generally *superior* area of experience (the 'three-fourths . . . of human life': *CPW*, VI, 173). In other words, although culture, as a high ideal of percipience, continues to *sponsor* an ideal of balance and harmony of faculties, Arnold now and hereafter draws back from implying (as Pater already was doing) that, in John Morley's words, 'aesthetic interest' should be raised 'to the throne lately filled by religion',[2] and from treating religion and religious art simply as the most highly refined material for the aesthetic sense, newly enfranchised from all substantive issues of theology and philosophy. Pater unerringly and

[1] For an excellent account of the immediate controversial matrix of *Culture and Anarchy*, see Sidney M. B. Coulling, 'The Evolution of *Culture and Anarchy*', *Studies in Philology*, 60 (October 1963), 637–68. On the metamorphosis and promotion of criticism into culture, see my *Hebrew and Hellene*, 70–9.

[2] See John Morley's penetrating review of Pater's *Renaissance*, in the *Fortnightly Review*, n.s. 13, April 1873, 476.

boldly selected from *Culture and Anarchy* elements for the new Aestheticism that Arnold had broached only tentatively and had almost at once reissued in a tamer form—mostly as a result of his deepening insight into the religious crisis of his time. In short, Arnold here, as everywhere, is a doubtful godfather of Aestheticism—almost, it will appear, a Dutch uncle.

The progress of culture and 'literature', even within *Literature and Dogma* (1873), is complex. Culture and religion are certainly not identified; culture indeed is largely stripped of the enormous and quasi-religious claims made for it in 1867. Culture or 'letters' is again a form of 'criticism' exhibited in 'justness of perception', 'tact', and a 'sense' of history—in short, the right method or instrument for reading religious documents (*CPW*, VI, 158, 160, 153, 162). In this usage 'letters' and literature become simply the most refined and adequate (Montaigne's '*ondoyant et divers*': *CPW*, I, 174) working of the modern critical intellect freely playing with the most delicate and complex data. On the other hand, 'poetry' and its associated terms—'imagination', 'emotion', 'intuition'—are linked with religion itself, or at least with that blameless tendency of the religious man who 'helps himself in his conduct by taking an object of hope and presentiment [e.g., immortality] as if it were an object of certainty' (*CPW*, VI, 232). From this point on in Arnold's religion of morality lit up by emotion, 'poetry' is increasingly identified as virtually this intense 'extra-belief' needed if a man is to live out the fullness of the moral life. In other words, poetry—the poetry that now absorbs Arnold's most serious attention—is a body of work expressive of the 'necessary' illusion that enables us to survive as integral human beings. Though Arnold insisted that as against the older supernaturalism his new religion was both 'natural' and 'verifiable' after the manner of science, he increasingly rebuffed the pretensions of the new scientism as firmly as those of the new Aestheticism.[1] The problem is that, despite Arnold's continued insistence on a fairly naturalistic harmony of all human impulses—the 'four powers' of conduct, intellect, beauty, and manners—the most deeply felt passages in his later writings imply that the maintenance of

[1] For Arnold's stiffening attitude towards science, see Fred A. Dudley, 'Matthew Arnold and Science', *PMLA*, 57, March 1942, 275–94. Arnold deplores the influence of both Swinburne and Huxley in a letter of November 1870: *Letters*, II, 43–4.

the most precious human qualities depends upon an untruth: the fullness of 'religion', which Arnold hopes to sustain, and the special class of poetry that conveys its attitudes best, imply a providentialism negated (in Arnold's own view) by the injunctions of the modern intellect.

But where do these special uses of 'poetry' leave mere poems— and poets—in the far more ordinary sense of those terms? The answer throws a good deal of light on Arnold's allegedly hyper-aesthetic understanding of 'culture'. For all his greater suavity, his unquestionably wider acquaintance with the literatures of the world, and his greater interest in the texture of poetry, Arnold was usually as contemptuous as Carlyle of the world of literary and artistic salons, the life of connoisseurship as well as the *vie de Bohème*—in short, one fears, of the actual and inevitable world of productive poets and artists, and even critics. His real scale of values is clear when he says in 1873: 'Compare some simple and pious monk, at Rome, with one of those frivolous men of taste whom we have all seen there!—each knows nothing of what interests the other; but which is the more vital concern for man: conduct, or arts and antiquities?' (*CPW*, VI, 314). Three years later, he complains that 'An Italian is always apt to count literary and artistic achievements as all in all in a nation's life . . . and to forget what has been [Italy's] curse—a relaxed moral fibre' (*CPW*, VIII, 8). For his generation's most common version of 'harmonious' self-development—'the life of the free, confident, harmonious development of the senses, all round', triumphant in modern Paris as 'the ideal life'—Arnold is especially full of scorn. Modern French drama, he says in 1879, 'represents the life of the senses developing themselves all round without misgiving; a life confident, fair and free, with fireworks of fine emotions, grand passions, and devotedness,—or rather, perhaps, *dévouement*,—lighting it up when necessary' (*CPW*, IX, 78). Not to understand the chasm between Arnold's notion of culture and the 'life confident, fair and free' which, one supposes, is for a good many succeeding 'literary' people unquestioningly assumed to be the essence of a modern and liberated life, is to miss utterly the tone and intent of Arnold's mature humanism. It is also to miss the finally rather narrow basis of his severe judgement of almost all nineteenth-century literature—though fortunately an unrepented youthful preference could sometimes break through at the end: if not quite

Byron, at least George Sand. All of this explains why only Wordsworth (and even he 'cut himself off from the modern spirit': *CPW*, III, 121), and no one after him, qualifies for high honours, and why in the last twenty-five years of his life Arnold gave up searching for the adequate modern poet whose 'inevitable task' is 'to interpret human life afresh, and to supply a new spiritual basis for it' (*CPW*, III, 381).

VI

The preceding may serve as background to one of Arnold's most important, often quoted, and baffling statements—his prediction concerning the religious future of poetry in 'The Study of Poetry' (1880). The words bear repeating:

> The future of poetry is immense, because in poetry, where it is worthy of its high destinies, our race, as time goes on, will find an ever surer and surer stay. There is not a creed which is not shaken, not an accredited dogma which is not shown to be questionable, not a received tradition which does not threaten to dissolve. Our religion has materialised itself in the fact, in the supposed fact; it has attached its emotion to the fact, and now the fact is failing it. But for poetry the idea is everything; the rest is a world of illusion, of divine illusion. Poetry attaches its emotion to the idea; the idea *is* the fact. The strongest part of our religion to-day is its unconscious poetry (*CPW*, IX, 161).

The 'higher uses' and 'higher destinies' Arnold assigns to poetry come from this fact: 'More and more mankind will discover that we have to turn to poetry to interpret life for us, to console us, to sustain us. Without poetry, our science will appear incomplete; and most of what now passes with us for religion and philosophy will be replaced by poetry' (*CPW*, IX, 161–2). Almost every term has a special Arnoldian sense and can be connected with the complex development of both his religious and his literary thinking. What is clear, first, is that the two classes of touchstones given later constitute the range of permissible 'ideas' endorsed here: that grim perception of human life as a tapestry of loss and pain, with the attendant need for endurance, and latterly, a suggestion of the possibility of divine illumination and the joy of submission to the divine will. This second range of emotions, though derived from the 'divine illusion' of Dante's 'materialised' supernaturalism, is adaptable—as Arnold had for several years been saying about Scripture and the Christian liturgy—to the permanent 'facts' of Arnold's spiritualized version of Christianity.

Poetry, which 'gives us the idea, but . . . gives it touched with beauty, heightened by emotion' (*CPW*, IX, 62) is virtually identified with Arnold's religion that is a set of moral ideas 'heightened, enkindled, lit up by feeling' and '*touched by emotion*' (*CPW*, VI, 176), and to this extent Arnold is open to Eliot's charge of a confusion of categories. Still, further discriminations are essential. Historically, dogmatic Christians, like Plato before them, had characteristically rejected poetry as either falling short of an assumed metaphysical norm or as constituting a positive temptation ensnaring men through the 'imagination', or they had admitted poetry as a 'handmaiden' of religion, stimulating the reader's imagination in the direct service of morality and faith. The suspicion of imaginative literature on the part of Christians, especially the Evangelicals, persisted well into the nineteenth century.[1] At the same time, a 'high' metaphysical claim for poetry's nature and power had developed in the Renaissance—in England, in figures like Sidney and Spenser—and, though diminished in force, it still cast some glow over the speculations of Christians in the nineteenth century. Even a John Henry Newman, at the height of the Oxford Movement, could make the rather mysterious and suggestive remark:

> How, then, in our age are those wants and feelings of our common nature satisfied, which were formerly supplied by symbols, now that symbolical language and symbolical rites have almost perished? Were we disposed to theorize, we might perhaps say, that the taste for poetry of a religious kind has in modern times in a certain sense taken the place of the deep contemplative spirit of the early Church. . . . Poetry then is our mysticism; and so far as any two characters of mind tend to penetrate below the

[1] John Foster's powerful polemic, 'On Some of the Causes by which Evangelical Religion has been Rendered Unacceptable to Persons of Cultivated Taste', 1802–4, in *Essays in a Series of Letters to a Friend*, went through numerous English and American editions throughout the century.

> surface of things, and to draw men away from the material to the invisible world, so far they may certainly be said to answer the same end; and that too a religious one.[1]

Another line of speculation had developed in Germany in the eighteenth century, especially in Schiller and Goethe, and to an important extent derived from Kant, emphasizing the autonomy of poetry. This is the remote background of art for art's sake and French and English Aestheticism, and to some extent of Symbolism—all of which, though in varying degrees, stressed the uniqueness of poetry and its special virtue as an independent instrument for revealing truth. In England, unsurprisingly, these important (and still not fully chronicled) attempts in Germany and France to 'liberate' poetry from its traditional metaphysical and moral moorings were met by men of various allegiances with a mixture of fascination and fear. Carlyle's is the most instructive case, and his moderate statement in 'Characteristics' (1831) was well-known and anticipatory of Arnold's position: 'Literature is but a branch of Religion, and always participates in its character: however, in our time, it is the only branch that shows any greenness; and, as some think, must one day become the main stream.'[2] This neatly sums up the older view while not quite endorsing the new hope for poetry as a 'religious' vehicle in the assumed breakdown of traditional Christianity. That hope, inchoate and not easily formulated, was somehow, everywhere, in the air; as even the very unmystical Walter Bagehot put it in 1864: 'All about and around us a *faith* in poetry struggles to be extricated. Some day, at the touch of the true word, the whole confusion will by magic cease; the broken and shapeless notions cohere and crystallise into a bright and true theory. But this cannot be yet.'[3]

Aestheticism, both as a loose cloak to cover this long-term nineteenth-century line of thought and as a more specific gathering of

[1] *Essays Critical and Historical*, London 1897, I, 290–1. For the possible connection with Arnold's views, see my *Hebrew and Hellene*, pp. 139–40.
[2] *The Works of Thomas Carlyle*, Centenary Edition, ed H. D. Traill, New York 1897–1901, XXVIII, 23.
[3] Walter Bagehot, 'Wordsworth, Tennyson, and Browning; or, Pure, Ornate, and Grotesque Art in English Poetry', 1864, in *Literary Studies*, Everyman's Library, London and New York 1911, II, 307.

forces after mid-century in France and England, could take at least two forms. It could claim that art, accountable only 'to itself', has no ulterior responsibilities to the moral or social order, and hence could avoid the question of poetry's metaphysical status and its claims to speak the 'truth'. More ambitiously, Aestheticism could claim that 'aesthetic experience', whether in the artist or in the observer, is the highest form of consciousness open to man, and that even in a post-metaphysical universe, it is not only an independent source and discoverer of truth, but can claim the supreme and authoritative position once arrogated by dogmatic religion.

Although Arnold's claims for poetry, from the earliest years and culminating in the statement of 1880, have been interpreted as precisely a Paterian call for the liberation of poetry from its traditional subordination to theology, metaphysics, and morals and for the elevation of aesthetic experience to the point where it passes over into 'religious worship',[1] the facts are more complex, and Arnold's boldness less clear. Pater's early mixture of aesthetics and religion takes a special form: first, aesthetic perception (always more in the observer than in the artist) is man's supreme mode of consciousness, but the most apt *material* for this highest range of experience is precisely the 'religious graces' of the older culture, now relieved from any metaphysical content or claims.[2] Arnold's affirmation, by contrast, is more like Carlyle's cautious prediction. A special and even narrow class of 'high' and 'serious' poetry is to perform for man much the same function of 'interpreting' life—'to animate, to console, to rejoice—in one word, to *strengthen*' (*CPW*, VIII, 1)—that the churches once performed but cannot now that their historical and metaphysical claims can no longer be sustained. Arnold's 'religion' is grievously defective by the orthodox Christian standards of his day; but the function of poetry in his prediction is, precisely, 'religious' and not simply 'aesthetic': it concerns the older religious art and poetry as it is experienced by a man who rejects its literal belief-content but not its perennial 'spiritual' content. This high sort of poetry is neither something for the aesthetic sense to play with, choice morsels upon which to feed itself, nor is it

[1] Madden, p. 176; and see his 'The Divided Tradition of English Criticism', *PMLA*, 73, March 1958, 69–80.

[2] See my *Hebrew and Hellene*, Ch. 13.

quite a new and independent form of 'salvation', as Madden alleges.[1] For although in Arnold's view poetry is independent of the older metaphysical theology, it is by no means independent of Christian worship or of Christian experience, and it is not so wholly autonomous or merely psychologistic as an I. A. Richards would have it.[2] This is true, partly, because Arnold's religion, however scanty in doctrine its two essential points—'*Salvation by Righteousness* and *Righteousness by Jesus Christ*' (*CPW*, VIII, 133)—and agnostic as to assertions about God, is not so simply pragmatic as some have claimed and even wished.[3] Whether Arnold's prophecy has been fulfilled, or even accurately understood, remains an open question.[4]

Undoubtedly, Arnold, though repelled by the actual world of art and artists around him, was strongly and indelibly marked by nineteenth-century Aestheticism. But again, not unlike Carlyle, he continued to assert an ideal balance of art, intellect, and religion,[5] and although this is indeed a challenge to traditional Christianity's insistence on the supremacy of the spiritual, it is next to impossible to find contexts in Arnold's writings where the 'purely' aesthetic is

[1] See Madden, 'Divided Tradition', 72, 79.

[2] An interesting attempt to read Arnold's poetics as a more than Ricardian mode of radical subjectivity is made by Epifanio San Juan, Jr., in 'Matthew Arnold and the Poetics of Belief', *Harvard Theological Review*, 57, April 1964, 97–118. The attempt forces the author, however, into smoothing out a host of complications and hesitations on Arnold's part.

[3] William Robbins, *The Ethical Idealism of Matthew Arnold*, London 1959, the best book on Arnold's religious views, acknowledges (while deploring as 'illogical' and inconsistent) the frequency of the transcendental reference in Arnold's religious writings.

[4] David Daiches, in *Some Late Victorian Attitudes*, New York 1969, 87–90, finds the prophecy erroneous; F. W. Bateson, in 'the Function of Criticism at the Present Time', *Essays in Criticism*, 3, January 1953, 21, quite the opposite. See also Richard Foster, *The New Romantics: A Reappraisal of the New Criticism*, Bloomington, Indiana 1962.

[5] E.g., *CPW*, VI, 409. But see VIII, 162 (1877), where a Platonic unification of the 'moral' and 'intellectual' is called for, and beauty quietly forgotten. The completest survey of Carlyle's views on art and poetry is now A. Abbott Ikeler's *Puritan Temper and Transcendental Faith*, Columbus, Ohio 1972.

isolated from the ensemble and elevated into some sort of autonomy as the very pattern for all the other activities of life.

VII

How does all of this rather theoretical matter affect the kind of judgements Arnold makes about particular authors and works? Again, 'The Study of Poetry' is more of an epitome of Arnold's thinking on the matter than has usually been perceived, since the often attacked criterion of 'high seriousness' follows directly from the apparently detached prophecy that opens the essay. This is clearest in his treatment of Chaucer, which has distressed so many readers. Chaucer is granted a great deal. In 'substance', he offers 'a large, free, sound representation of things'; in 'style and manner', 'divine liquidness of diction, . . . divine fluidity of movement'. But whatever his 'poetic truth of substance', Chaucer lacks 'high poetic seriousness', which Arnold proceeds characteristically to define obliquely by offering two touchstones. These are a quotation from Villon involving the themes of loss, regret, the memory of past happiness, and the transiency of life, and Dante's '*In la sua voluntade é nostra pace*'— in short, both the secular and the sacred components of Arnold's religious-aesthetic ideal, the first present from the time of the Homer lectures, the second more clearly evident from the period of the religious writings (*CPW*, IX, 174–7). However narrow and exclusive this dual range of attitudes has seemed to later readers, it explains Arnold's judgements of a large gallery of sages and literary figures, both ancient and modern.

The criteria emerge from that lifelong attempt of Arnold's to 'analyse the modern situation in its true *blankness* and *barrenness*, and *unpoetrylessness*' (*Letters to Clough*, 126; Dec. 1852), an attempt of obviously the greatest autobiographical significance. Arnold's best early poetry—in figures like the poet of 'Resignation', Empedocles, and the Scholar-Gipsy—had shown an affinity for the withdrawn and excessively introspective personality associated with suffering sages like Obermann, Hamlet, Faust, 'Werter[,] Réné[,] and such like' (*CPW*, I, 1; *Letters to Clough*, 126). In the reconstruction of his values and of his personality symbolized by the Preface of 1853, Arnold bids a half-reluctant farewell to the 'air of languor, cold, and death' that broods over Obermann's soul (*Poems*, 131), and enforces hereafter in both poetry and prose the 'moral lesson' that Goethe learned from Spinoza, 'not of mere resigned acquiescence, not of melancholy quietism, but of joyful activity within the limits of man's true sphere' (*CPW*, III, 177). There is a very long catalogue of 'modern' attitudes regularly condemned by the mature Arnold: melancholy, disgust, regret, isolation, gloom, disappointment, morbidity, impatience, inquietude, lassitude, ennui, irritability, jealousy, severity, forlornness, dejection, weariness, constraint, 'ineffectuality', languor, and depression. By this standard, some of the most congenial and attractive personalities Arnold presents are judged finally to fall short, in varying degrees, of serving as adequate models for sensitive men and women who remain nevertheless fully aware of the spiritual barrenness of the modern situation. Classical and stoic moralists—Lucretius, Virgil, Marcus Aurelius, Epictetus—are judged deficient, in varying degrees, as are modern figures like Gray, Joubert, the Guérins, Senancour, Leopardi, Amiel, for not having undergone a 'moral deliverance' from self-involvement, and the indulgence of a sense of the 'emptiness and nothingness' of life, leading to inanition and spiritual death. They represent the deepest attraction and temptation of Arnold's early career.

More specifically literary figures like Burns fail to pass muster, if even their 'piercing' sense of the pathos of life, their 'profound and passionate melancholy', is not balanced and relieved by a more 'fortifying' and 'interpretative' view of life (*CPW*, IX, 185–7). The chief criterion of spiritual soundness is, increasingly, a religious 'joy'. To serve, the poet and the sage must not only exhibit 'inwardness' and a fully developed sense of the pathos of life in a world given over to the blind optimism of progress and activism, but they must '*animate* and *ennoble*', 'inspirit and rejoice' the reader too (*Letters to Clough*, 146; (*CPW*, I, 2). Joy involves warmth, emotion, sincerity, and is revealed in sweetness and serenity of temper, a sense of struggle overcome, and increasingly in 'deep religious feeling' and 'happy self-sacrifice'. Not surprisingly, very few literary and spiritual figures, except Jesus, seem to have undergone the transformation, and then only imperfectly: Homer, Sophocles, Dante, Shakespeare (intermittently), Milton, Spinoza, Pascal, St. Francis of Sales, Goethe (arguably), and Wordsworth. On a more practical and secular level, the ideal comes down to a kind of cheerfulness of social demeanour, a brave and civilized readiness for action, maintained alongside a never quite eradicated withdrawal and alienation from the chilling spiritual conditions of modern life.

Arnold sought, throughout his career, to identify a range of works, ancient and modern, which would conduce to the formation of a certain set of intellectual and moral characteristics adequate for the needs of Arnold's most sensitive and alert contemporaries. These attitudes resist either moral categories or systematic formulation: the touchstones, instead, embody a set of supremely valuable feelings, attitudes, and experiences, conveyed in one or another variety of the 'grand style' that is both their vehicle and their authentication. Poetry has an immense task because it is the most effective means of recovering and fostering a *kind* of consciousness under grave threat in the modern world, at a time when the older institutions have faltered in their task. What poetry is and does implies, for Arnold and a good many of his successors, nothing less than what it is to be fully 'human'. This is not precisely Aestheticism, but it is, in a special sense, 'a *faith* in poetry'.

5: *Arnold and Literary Criticism: (ii) Critical Practice*

R. H. SUPER

A VERSATILE AND ACCOMPLISHED FRIEND of Socrates once charged him with going around saying the same things year after year. 'What's worse,' replied Socrates good-naturedly, 'they're always on the same subject.' And he engaged his friend in one more discourse upon justice.[1] With Arnold too there is a good deal of movement back and forth over the same ground, not only in his love of catchwords like 'sweetness and light' or 'the best that is known and thought in the world' (Arnold tried various forms of this expression), but in his basic propositions, even in his illustrations of his views.[2]

And as 'justice' for Socrates led easily to discussion not only of ethics and politics, but of literature and the arts, of education, of science and philosophy, and of the immortality of the soul, so Arnold early embraced the widest range of knowledge under the single term of *criticism*: 'Of [the literatures of France and Germany], as of the intellect of Europe in general, the main effort, for now many years, has been a *critical* effort; the endeavour, in all branches of knowledge,—theology, philosophy, history, art, science,—to see the object as in itself it really is'

[1] Xenophon, *Memorabilia* IV, iv, 6.

[2] Arnold ironically described himself in 1882 as 'a nearly worn-out man of letters, . . . with a frippery of phrases about sweetness and light, seeing things as they really are, knowing the best that has been thought and said in the world, which never had very much solid meaning, and have now quite lost the gloss and charm of novelty' (*CPW*, X, 74). In the same way T. S. Eliot remarked that any student was certain to pass an examination on his criticism 'if he alludes to the "dissociation of sensibility" and the "objective correlative"'.—Preface to the second edition of *The Use of Poetry and the Use of Criticism*, London 1964, 9.

(*CPW*, I, 140). Characteristically, he drew the expression 'to see the object as it really is', whether consciously or unconsciously, not from literary criticism but from a theologian, from Joseph Butler,[1] a writer who dearly loved another of Arnold's favourite expressions, 'disinterestedness'.

Amiel, remarked Arnold, is masterly in 'criticism of society, politics, national character, religion'.[2] But Amiel's true vocation, Arnold felt, was that of literary critic. It is perhaps Arnold's fault as well as his virtue that his own range of interest was as wide as it was, that though one of the most influential of nineteenth-century literary critics he was not exclusively, not even primarily, a literary man. He once wistfully remarked, when called upon to respond to a toast to literature, 'Whatever I may have once wished or intended, my life is not that of a man of letters, but of an Inspector of Schools' (*CWP*, VIII, 374). The gently ironic modesty was deliberately assumed for the occasion, of course, and it drew the appropriate laughter from its audience; nevertheless his life, if much more than that of an inspector of schools, was not at all the life of most literary critics we know.[3] He intruded at great length upon religious questions. Very early in his career, as 'a voice from the world of literature' (*CPW*, III, 82), he ridiculed Bishop Colenso's mechanical and unimaginative approach to the problem of Biblical inspiration. *Literature and Dogma* is an essay in the literary criticism of Scripture, and *God and the Bible* is in large measure a discussion of the misuse of criticism in the interpretation of a great book. When at last he turned overtly away from religious writing 'to literature, more strictly so-called', he felt he was 'returning, after all, to a field where work of the most important kind has now to be done, though indirectly, for religion' (*CPW*, VIII, 148). Moreover, Arnold too was masterly in 'criticism of society, politics, national character'. His lectures from the chair of poetry at Oxford, lectures published as *Essays in Criticism*, were often political and social in substance; 'The Function of Criticism at the Present Time' is perhaps best remembered for the sentence 'Wragg is in custody'. *Culture and Anarchy* is 'an essay

[1] 'A mind which sees things as they really are' (Sermon XV, ¶ 4).

[2] *Works*, IV, 232.

[3] See H. W. Garrod, 'Unless I mistake, it is precisely the interest which he had in education, politics, and religion which makes his criticism original' —*Poetry and the Criticism of Life*, Cambridge, Mass. 1931, 74.

in political and social criticism', and its first chapter was the final lecture from the chair of poetry. One of the most sensitive of Arnold's works of literary criticism, *On the Study of Celtic Literature*, gives over its Introduction to discussion of 'England's difficulty in governing Ireland' (*CPW*, III, 392). And so Arnold's remarks on his fellow critics and poets often stress aspects not narrowly literary: 'Goethe is the greatest poet of modern times, not because he is one of the half-dozen human beings who in the history of our race have shown the most signal gift for poetry, but because, having a very considerable gift for poetry, he was at the same time, in the width, depth, and richness of his criticism of life, by far our greatest modern man. . . . His preciousness and importance as a clear and profound modern spirit, as a master-critic of modern life, must communicate a worth of their own to his poetry, and may well make it erroneously seem to have a positive value and perfectness as poetry, more than it has.' And therefore, curiously, 'it is by no means as the greatest of poets that Goethe deserves the pride and praise of his German countrymen. It is as the clearest, the largest, the most helpful thinker of modern times. It is not principally in his published works, it is in the immense Goethe-literature of letter, journal, and conversation . . . that the elements for an impression of the truly great, the truly significant Goethe are to be found' (*CPW*, VIII, 274–5).

'Whoever seriously occupies himself with literature will soon perceive its vital connection with other agencies', Arnold remarked as he tried to show the unity of a collection published in 1879 which he accurately named *Mixed Essays* (*CPW*, VIII, 370). 'Literature is . . . indisputably . . . a powerful agency for benefiting the world and for civilising it, . . . [but] there are many obstacles preventing what is salutary in literature from gaining general admission, and from producing due effect. . . . Literature is a part of civilisation; it is not the whole. . . . [Civilisation] is really so complex and vast a matter that a great spiritual power, like literature, is a part of it, and a part only. Civilisation is the humanisation of man in society.' The overlapping of Arnold's terms is remarkable. Just as 'criticism' has as its aim seeing the object as in itself it really is, so too has 'culture'—'a desire after the things of the mind simply for their own sakes and for the pleasure of seeing them as they are'; yet culture is also 'a study of perfection'. It has 'its origin in the love of perfection; . . . it moves by the force, not merely or primarily of the scientific passion for pure knowledge, but also of the moral and social passion for doing good' (*CPW*, V, 91). And if criticism is the means of seeing things as they are, if culture is that and more, if civilization is another word for culture, 'the end and aim of all literature, if one considers it attentively, is . . . *a criticism of life*' (*CPW*, III, 209). But such 'criticism of life', such literature, includes, as he says in *Discourses in America* (1885), 'all knowledge that reaches us through books'[1]—includes, therefore, the works of scientists and all other kinds of writers, not merely poets and practitioners of *belles lettres*. However scientific the ideal of criticism may be, we clearly are not here dealing with the logical preciseness of mathematical terminology.

Arnold returned to 'literature, more strictly so-called' from his excursion into religion armed with one other sentence of Joseph Butler's that thereafter became axiomatic with him: 'Things and actions are what they are, and the consequences of them will be what they will be; why then should we desire to be deceived?' (*CPW*, VIII, 12). It was a somewhat more memorable way of generalizing what he had already said of Goethe in 1863: that his 'profound, imperturbable naturalism is absolutely fatal to all routine thinking; he puts the standard, once for all, inside every man instead of outside him; when he is told, such a thing must be so, there is immense authority and custom in favour of its being so, it has been held to be so for a thousand years, he answers with Olympian politeness, "But *is* it so? is it so to *me*?"' (*CPW*, III, 110). 'Naturalism' was Arnold's word for Sainte-Beuve's central quality also, 'carrying into letters, so often the mere domain of rhetoric and futile amusement, the ideas and methods of scientific inquiry' (*CPW*, V, 306). Elsewhere Arnold called this quality 'positivism'; it was an appeal to the reader's 'practical experience' (*CPW*, VIII, 171, 173).

Nevertheless, although the appeal is made to individual experience, to the conscience of each reader, it is the duty of the individual to make his judgement a responsible judgement. Arnold's view of 'the State'

[1] *CPW*, X, 58. The relation of literature to culture, as well as the formative impact of art upon life, is the subject of David Perkins's essay, 'Arnold and the Function of Literature', *ELH*, XVIII, December 1951, 287–309. Professor Perkins draws upon the whole range of Arnold's prose, not merely the essays in literary criticism.

differed from the Liberal (or 'anarchic', in Arnold's terms) by being not the mere sum of the people in the nation but the collective operation of their best aspect. And so in criticism—the criticism that one applies to one's own writing as well as to others' work—individual aberration must be controlled by the desire for the best: this notion is the sole import of the essay whose title continued to mislead those who did not read it, 'The Literary Influence of Academies' (1864). 'A Frenchman has, to a considerable degree, what one may call a conscience in intellectual matters; he has an active belief that there is a right and a wrong in them, that he is bound to honour and obey the right, that he is disgraced by cleaving to the wrong. All the world has, or professes to have, this conscience in moral matters. . . . A like deference to a standard higher than one's own habitual standard in intellectual matters, a like respectful recognition of a superior ideal, is caused, in the intellectual sphere, by sensitiveness of intelligence' (*CPW*, III, 236–7).[1]

Two of Arnold's first literary essays after he laid aside religious questions were somewhat misleadingly entitled 'A French Critic on Milton' and 'A French Critic on Goethe'. Both, in fact, are essays on the art of literary criticism. Early in the second of these he lists the false approaches critics have used to every great poet, every considerable writer: 'There is the judgment of enthusiasm and admiration, which proceeds from ardent youth, easily fired, eager to find a hero and to worship him. [Is he thinking, perhaps, of Swinburne on Victor Hugo?] There is the judgment of gratitude and sympathy, which proceeds from those who find in an author what helps them, what they want, and who rate him at a very high value accordingly. There is the judgment of ignorance, the judgment of incompatibility, the judgment of envy and jealousy. Finally, there is the systematic judgment, and this

[1] Arnold always conceived that an author must write for an audience of the *best* critics. A translator of Homer must write as if for the approval of Professor Jowett, Professor Thompson, or the Provost of Eton (*CPW*, I, 99). Arnold himself wrote, he once said, in the hope that his tone and style would favourably impress Cardinal Newman. An Academy, in Arnold's view, is not an authoritarian judicial body, but a spur to the conscience of a writer (much as a Christian's conduct may be moulded as if Christ were watching, without any thought of eternal rewards and punishments or a last judgement).

judgment is the most worthless of all. The sharp scrutiny of envy and jealousy may bring real faults to light. The judgments of incompatibility and ignorance are instructive, whether they reveal necessary clefts of separation between the experiences of different sorts of people, or reveal simply the narrowness and bounded view of those who judge. But the systematic judgment is altogether unprofitable. Its author has not really his eye upon the professed object of his criticism at all, but upon something else which he wants to prove by means of that object. He neither really tells us, therefore, anything about the object, nor anything about his own ignorance of the object. He never fairly looks at it, he is looking at something else. Perhaps if he looked at it straight and full, looked at it simply, he might be able to pass a good judgment on it. As it is, all he tells us is that he is no genuine critic, but a man with a system, an advocate' (*CPW*, VIII, 254–5). Arnold delighted to invade the temples of the Philistines; he published this essay in the *Quarterly Review*, a journal he had once used to illustrate his proposition that 'the bane of criticism in this country' was 'that practical considerations cling to it and stifle it. It subserves interests not its own' (*CPW*, III, 270).

'A French Critic on Milton' aims to contrast false critical methods with the true, to contrast the 'rhetorical' approach (Macaulay's), in which the critic's eloquence is the end in itself, not the illumination of the work he pretends to examine; the 'conventional' approach (Addison's), which begins with the assumptions that *Paradise Lost* is a great poem and that a great poem must have, *a priori*, certain characteristics, then simply predicates these qualities of this poem; and finally the 'disinterested' approach (Scherer's). In the end, 'poetical defects, where they are present, subsist, and are what they are. . . . Time and attention bring them to light; and when they are brought to light, it is not good for us, it is obstructing and retarding, to refuse to see them' (*CPW*, VIII, 275). But even the virtue of 'disinterestedness' must not be praised merely out of convention; the English critic Arnold seems most to love is Dr. Johnson, with his 'straightforward remarks, on Milton and his works, of a very acute and robust mind'. 'At many points bounded, at many points warped, . . . neither sufficiently disinterested, nor sufficiently flexible, nor sufficiently receptive, to be a satisfying critic of a poet like Milton,' Johnson could write the 'terrible sentence, "Surely no man could have fancied that he read Lycidas with pleasure had he not known the author!'—terrible for revealing the deficiencies of the critic who utters it—yet Johnson's simple description of Milton in old age touches us more than anything in Scherer's balanced critique' (*CPW*, VIII, 174, 182).

Arnold was fully aware that works of art and literature were embedded in a climate, in the conventions and circumstances that produced them. Such a perception is at least as old as Aristotle, who is Arnold's support for the statement that 'Greek tragic forms were not chosen as being, in the nature of things, the best tragic forms; such would be a wholly false conception of them. They are an adaptation to dramatic purposes, under certain theatrical conditions, of forms previously existing for other purposes; that adaptation at which the Greeks, after several stages of improvement, finally rested. The laws of Greek tragic art, therefore, are not exclusive; they are for Greek dramatic art itself, but they do not pronounce other modes of dramatic art unlawful. . . . Travelling in a certain path, the spirit of man arrived at Greek tragedy; travelling in other paths, it may arrive at other kinds of tragedy' (*CPW*, I, 58). Sometimes the spirit of man arrived at a form eminently unsuitable for its purpose—the Alexandrines of French tragic and heroic verse, for example, 'that [indefensible] metre, faulty not so much because it is disagreeable in itself, as because it has in it something which is essentially unsuited to perfect tragedy' (*CPW*, I, 50). England after the Restoration desperately needed a style 'favourable to the qualities of regularity, uniformity, precision, balance', found such a measure in the French Alexandrine, and adapted it into the ten-syllable couplet; by adopting this form, England re-enforced the virtues of its new prose style. 'This may have been of no great service to English poetry, although to say that it has been of no service at all, to say that the eighteenth century has in no respect changed the conditions for English poetical style, or that it has changed them for the worse, would be untrue. But it was undeniably of signal service to that which was the great want and work of the hour, English prose' (*CPW*, VIII, 317). And as with forms, so with ideas: 'Intellectual ideas, which the majority of men take from the age in which they live, are the dominion of [the] Time-Spirit', and insensibly the Time-Spirit brings to men's minds an awareness that ideas have undergone a development, a change' (*CPW*, III, 77).

From the outset, therefore, Arnold was convinced that truly great literature must spring from the union of two powers, 'the power of the man and the power of the moment, and the man is not enough without the moment; the creative power has, for its happy exercise, appointed elements, and those elements are not in its own control' (*CPW*, III, 261). The ways of thinking and the substance of thought varied from era to era, and so too did the idiom available to the writer. Arnold's inaugural lecture 'On the Modern Element in Literature' attempts to deal with the various conjunctions of these elements: the age of Pericles, in which the pattern of thought was like our own, the religious impulses were those eternally true ones to which mankind will always return from whatever its long periods of aberration, and the idiom was responsive to the needs of the writers; the age of Augustus, in which the practical and material problems of life were solved much as we should solve them, but which lacked insight into the spiritual depths; and the age of Elizabeth I, which like the beginning of the nineteenth century was an age of excitement but which in nearly every aspect of life was simply barbarous, and which altogether lacked an appropriate language for a literary man to find expression in. Into the happy conjunction of the age of Pericles fell writers of a splendid genius, Pindar, Aeschylus, Sophocles, Aristophanes; but even the greatest writers of the age of Augustus were injured by the spiritual alienation of their day and their poetry suffered accordingly; whereas in the age of Elizabeth I, the supreme genius of all time found himself without an appropriate idiom, he lacked a cultivated and exacting audience, and despite his magnificent triumphs his work is irregular and uncertain. There was, indeed, in Arnold's view a relation between the idiom and national success: Germany, a new nation, lacked 'a great national life, with its practical discipline, its ever-active traditions; its literature, for centuries past, powerful and incessant', and hence had never forged a national style and continued to print in its black-letter type the insufferably clumsy sentences Arnold never ceased to marvel at; Italy, for the same reason, despite the advantage of a Latin tongue, produced a modern prose of much the same circuitousness and slowness; but France and England, with 'a long-continued national life, a long-continued literary activity, such as no other modern nation has had', inevitably developed 'a turn for directness and clearness of speech, a dislike for futility and fumbling', such as one will rarely find general in a nation that lacks a great national life (*CPW*, VIII, 256–7). Even Goethe was betrayed into the solemn inanity of 'symbol, hieroglyphic, mystification', 'on which a man of Goethe's powers could never have wasted his time, but for his lot having been cast in a nation which has never lived' (*CPW*, VIII, 274).

It will be seen that Arnold did indeed try to take history firmly into account in his literary evaluations. He may have failed to sense the true history of nations; he may sometimes have equated success with virtue, or looked in the wrong direction in evaluating success, but he never repudiated the method. When he criticized it, it was for its misuse, for its faddism, for the sense of its practitioners that it provided a formula that could be applied mechanically. 'The advice to study the character of an author and the circumstances in which he has lived, in order to account to oneself for his work, is excellent. But it is a perilous doctrine, that from such a study the right understanding of his work will "spontaneously issue." . . . Let us not confound the method with the result intended by the method—right judgments. The critic who rightly appreciates a great man or a great work, and who can tell us faithfully—life being short, and art long, and false information very plentiful—what we may expect from their study and what they can do for us; he is the critic we want, by whatever methods, intuitive or historical, he may have managed to get his knowledge' (*CPW*, VIII, 175–6).[1]

Form and style, however, are highly individual even within the context of the spirit of the age. 'The magic of Heine's poetical form is incomparable; he chiefly uses a form of old German popular poetry, a ballad-form which has more rapidity and grace than any ballad-form of ours; he employs this form with the most exquisite lightness and ease, and yet it has at the same time the inborn fulness, pathos, and old-world charm of all true forms of popular poetry.' And because it is so individual, style is what most easily disappears in translation: 'To feel it, one must read him; he gives [his characteristic impression] in his

[1] The fallacy of the 'historic estimate' against which Arnold warns in 'The Study of Poetry' is, as we shall see, something a little different—it is setting a high value upon a work of art because of its place in the historical development of the art, or indeed sometimes because of its place in the historical development of a nation, rather than because of its intrinsic merit. It is the fault of the literary historian, rather than of the historical critic.

form as well as in his contents, and by translation I can only reproduce it so far as his contents give it' (*CPW*, III, 124). The great stylist in English poetry is of course Milton. 'Milton has always the sure, strong touch of the master. His power both of diction and of rhythm is unsurpassable, and it is characterised by being always present—not depending on an access of emotion, not intermittent, but, like the grace of Raphael, working in its possessor as a constant gift of nature. Milton's style, moreover, has the same propriety and soundness in presenting plain matters, as in the comparatively smooth task for a poet of presenting grand ones. . . . Shakespeare himself, divine as are his gifts, has not, of the marks of the master, this one: perfect sureness of hand in his style. Alone of English poets, alone in English art, Milton has it; he is our great artist in style, our one first-rate master in the grand style' (*CPW*, VIII, 183). Whether in the man or the *milieu*, moreover, style is a mark of morality. In a letter to Clough early in 1849 Arnold spoke of 'the grand moral effects produced by *style*. For the style is the expression of the nobility of the poet's character, as the matter is the expression of the richness of his mind: but on men character produces as great an effect as mind.'[1] And so with Milton: 'As a man, too, not less than as a poet, Milton has a side of unsurpassable grandeur,' despite the surliness and cantankerousness he caught from his Puritanism. 'Some moral qualities seem to be connected in a man with his power of style. Milton's power of style, for instance, has for its great character *elevation*; and Milton's elevation clearly comes, in the main, from a moral quality in him,—his pureness' (*CPW*, VIII, 184). Almost the only thing Arnold accepts from Francis Newman is the proposition that Homer's style can be defined in terms of 'moral qualities' (*CPW*, I, 125)—but that those moral qualities are the qualities of the English ballad he firmly denies: 'quaintness' and 'garrulity' may indeed be among the moral qualities of the ballad; they are not those of Homer (*CPW*, I, 128). As for the 'grand style', Arnold's definition of it ('when a noble nature, poetically gifted, treats with simplicity or with severity a serious subject' [*CPW*, I, 188]) need not be taken altogether seriously; there is a touch of irony in the discussion of it, a side glance at Ruskin's solemnity. Arnold had used the expression for years without defining it, and as so often with him, he thought the thing better known by intuition than by definition.

[1] *Letters to Clough*, 101.

There is, moreover, a 'beneficent law,' which, in the region of grave and serious composition, connects bad poetry with false moral sentiments. Good rhetoric may consist, in this region, with false moral sentiments, but good poetry, poetry which satisfies, never' (*CPW*, VII, 10). Arnold can hardly be said to have applied this concept very satisfactorily to individuals, still less, as in the last passage cited, to a nation: it may seem plausible to perceive in the inadequacies of Victor Hugo's style (or François Coppée's) the same moral failure that led to France's defeat in 1870, but the proposition will not bear close examination.

One aspect of style Arnold was especially sensitive to, both in his own poetry ('Tristram and Iseult', 'Philomela', 'The Scholar-Gipsy') and in the poetry of others—what he called 'natural magic'. He was inclined to attribute the trait to the Celtic influence, to find it pre-eminent in works like the *Mabinogion*. It was a significant aspect of poetry, if only to make clear how poetry might work to bring about change in the character of the reader. If the highest poetry embodied the quality of 'imaginative reason' (*CPW*, III, 230), the imaginative aspect was the more enticing; the natural magic of a poet like Keats, or Wordsworth, or Shakespeare demonstrated, though it did not explain, how poetry engaged man's emotions 'so as to exert an influence upon [his] sense for conduct, his sense for beauty' (*CPW*, X, 67). 'The grand power of poetry is its interpretative power; by which I mean, not a power of drawing out in black and white an explanation of the mystery of the universe, but the power of so dealing with things as to awaken in us a wonderfully full, new, and intimate sense of them, and of our relations with them. When this sense is awakened in us, as to objects without us, we feel ourselves to be in contact with the essential nature of those objects, to be no longer bewildered and oppressed by them, but to have their secret, and to be in harmony with them; and this feeling calms and satisfies us as no other can. . . . To make magically near and real the life of that Nature, and man's life only so far as it is a part of Nature, was [Guérin's] faculty; a faculty of naturalistic, not of moral interpretation. This faculty always has for its basis a peculiar temperament, an extraordinary delicacy of organisation and susceptibility to impressions' (*CPW*, III, 12–13, 30). 'Magic of style is creative: its possessor himself creates, and he inspires and enables his reader in some sort to create after him. And creation gives the sense of life and joy; hence its extraordinary value.'[1] There are, Arnold says, many ways of handling nature: among these, the conventional way, the faithful way, the Greek way, and the magical way. 'In all these three last the eye is on the object, but with a difference; in the faithful way of handling nature, the eye is on the object, and that is all you can say; in the Greek, the eye is on the object, but lightness and brightness are added; in the magical, the eye is on the object, but charm and magic are added' (*CPW*, III, 377). The great merit of Keats, who is certainly one of Arnold's favourite poets, is his genius for passing at will from the Greek way to the magical way, from 'What little town, by river or seashore' to 'magic casements, opening on the foam / Of perilous seas, in fairy lands forlorn' (*CPW*, III, 378).

Arnold's range of critical approach seems so wide that perhaps it would be well to indicate briefly some methods of criticism fashionable with us that he expressly or by implication repudiated. The poet is a man, and the character of the man passes from his life into his work; hence a critic may properly deal with a poet's character, as Arnold treats Gray and Keats. And 'let no one suppose that a want of humour and a self-delusion such as Shelley's have no effect upon a man's poetry'.[2] But biography may be misused: it may be irrelevant, or—still worse—it may be inferred from the works, then circularly used to explain the works. Theodore Martin's biographical sketch of Dante, prefaced to a translation of the *Vita Nuova*, 'has, as applied to real personages, the grave defect of being entirely of Mr. Martin's own imagining. But it has a still graver defect, I think, as applied to Dante, in being so singularly inappropriate to its object. The grand, impracticable Solitary, with keen senses and ardent passions, . . . but with an irresistible bent to the inward life, the life of imagination, vision, and ecstacy; . . . this Dante is transformed, in Mr. Martin's hands, into the hero of a sentimental, but strictly virtuous, novel!' (*CPW*, III, 8–9). Secondly, he repudiated a special critical vocabulary. He praised Joubert's admonition to 'distrust . . . words which have not been able to get currency in the world, and are only calculated to form a special language', as well as his caution against employing common words in a special sense (*CPW*, III, 194). Thirdly, he was no 'new critic'. There are few more devastating attacks anywhere on a self-

[1] *Works*, IV, 225.

[2] *Works*, IV, 185.

contained, insulated approach to literature than Arnold's discussion of Baur and his fellow-interpreters of the Bible. And finally, 'It seems lost labour to inquire what a poet's *aim* may have been' (*CPW*, VIII, 274).

The critic, then, must keep his eye on the object, and he must be 'sincere, simple, flexible, ardent, ever widening [his] knowledge' (*CPW*, III, 285). Sainte-Beuve, the critic *par excellence*, is 'well-informed, intelligent, disinterested, open-minded, sympathetic', blessed with 'elasticity and cheerfulness, . . . that gaiety, that radiancy, as of a man discharging with delight the very office for which he was born', delicate, felicitous of touch, crisp in style, charming in effect, firm and sure in judgment (*CPW*, VIII, 174–5). 'The great art of criticism is to get oneself out of the way' (*CPW*, III, 227). 'The true critic is he who can best disengage [the] real significance' of the matter he discusses (*CPW*, III, 327). 'To ascertain the master-current in the literature of an epoch, and to distinguish this from all minor currents, is one of the critic's highest functions; in discharging it he shows how far he possesses the most indispensable quality of his office—justness of spirit' (*CPW*, III, 107). A critic also needs occupation: Amiel's inferiority to Sainte-Beuve was not a want of true vocation for the task, but quite simply of the 'toils and limits [of] composition' to 'make his fragments into wholes, to fit them for coming before the public', instead of leaving them mere jottings in his diary.[1] Arnold early described his own qualifications in criticism as neither time nor knowledge; not talent, genius nor learning: 'nothing but a passion for the great Masters, and an effort to study them without fancifulness' (*CPW*, I, 64).

Again and again he acknowledged his debt to Sainte-Beuve. His early views of romanticism clearly echoed his French master. A good deal of what he knew about French literature came first from the *Portraits contemporains* and the *Causeries du lundi* (why else would *Jocelyn* appear in the 1853 Preface?) and some at least of his taste was formed from them; Saint-Beuve's influence on his judgments provided a principal ground for Swinburne's critical attacks on Arnold. Sainte-Beuve is the parent of the *Essays in Criticism*, and through him Arnold found himself as a literary critic. Though he intended his Oxford course of lectures 'On the Modern Element in Literature' for publication, only the first of the series of eight saw print, and that nearly a dozen years after its delivery. The lively controversial nature

[1] *Works*, IV, 235.

of the four lectures *On Translating Homer* gave them some public when they appeared as small books. But only with the lecture on 'Maurice de Guérin', with its acknowledged debt to 'the first of living critics' (*CPW*, III, 12), did Arnold find the kind of subject out of which he made the *Essays in Criticism*. (No doubt the determination to publish the lectures in a magazine rather than a book was significant to their success also.) Four of the first series ('Maurice de Guérin', 'Eugénie de Guérin', 'Joubert', and 'The Literary Influence of Academies') drew their subjects from Sainte-Beuve. After Arnold's return to literary criticism in 1877, there were essays on George Sand and Joseph de Maistre, both subjects of *Causeries*; 'A Genevese Judge' (on a grandson of Mallet du Pan) drew on Sainte-Beuve and so did the discussion of Bonstetten in the essay on Gray. Of the subjects on which he planned to write but did not, three at least ('St. Martin', 'Alexandre Vinet', and 'Vauvenargues') were from Sainte-Beuve; the last was planned for 1888, the year of his death. And yet Arnold's essays were markedly different from, and richer than, Sainte-Beuve's, both because he tried to make illuminating parallels between Continental subjects and the English writers his audience would know and because he was dominated by his thesis of the main course of nineteenth-century social, religious, and intellectual development.[1]

Wide as his range of subjects was, Arnold's principal focus was the Europe of his own century, and for that Europe the principal fact for Arnold was the final break-up of the last vestiges of the Middle Age. The dissolution that began with the Reformation was completed with the Revolution of 1789. Never again could monarch and aristocracy dominate the scene, even though it was the English aristocracy, in its last great moment, that defeated the evangelist of the Revolution at Waterloo. The present belonged to the middle class, the future to the masses. Never again could a Christian church assert its authority by the mere force of its dogma. The ideas of 'Obermann Once More', 'Dover Beach', and 'Stanzas from the Grande Chartreuse' dominate Arnold's critical essays. 'Dante's task was to set forth the lesson of the world from the point of view of mediaeval Catholicism; the basis of spiritual life was given, Dante had not to make this anew. Shakespeare's task

[1] Arnold's use of the stratagem of comparison is well illustrated in Robert A. Donovan's perceptive essay, 'The Method of Arnold's *Essays in Criticism*', *PMLA*, LXXI, December 1956, 922–31.

was to set forth the spectacle of the world when man's spirit re-awoke to the possession of the world at the Renaissance. The spectacle of human life, left to bear its own significance and tell its own story, but shown in all its fulness, variety, and power, is at that moment the great matter; but, if we are to press deeper, the basis of spiritual life is still at that time the traditional religion, reformed or unreformed, of Christendom, and Shakespeare has not to supply a new basis. But when Goethe came, Europe had lost her basis of spiritual life; she had to find it again; Goethe's task was,—the inevitable task for the modern poet henceforth is,—as it was for the Greek poet in the days of Pericles, not to preach a sublime sermon on a given text like Dante, not to exhibit all the kingdoms of human life and the glory of them like Shakespeare, but to interpret human life afresh, and to supply a new spiritual basis to it' (*CPW*, III, 381). The test of any poet of the nineteenth century, for Arnold, was his perception of this problem and his fruitful response to it. And the value of any poet of an earlier age was likely to be the extent to which he helped the man of the nineteenth century live in the modern world. 'All intellectual pursuits our age judges according to their power of helping to satisfy [our demand for an intellectual deliverance]; of all studies it asks, above all, the question, how far they can contribute to this deliverance' (*CPW*, I, 19). The critic is the synthesizer: 'I hate all over-preponderance of single elements, and all my efforts are directed to enlarge and complete us by bringing in as much as possible of Greek, Latin, Celtic culture. More and more I see hopes of fruit by steadily working in this direction,' he told his mother as he worked at his Oxford lectures (*CPW*, III, 492). And even more, the critic provides the materials with which the poet works, and the climate in which he prospers: criticism 'tends, at last, to make an intellectual situation of which the creative power can profitably avail itself. It tends to establish an order of ideas, if not absolutely true, yet true by comparison with that which it displaces; to make the best ideas prevail. Presently these new ideas reach society, the touch of truth is the touch of life, and there is a stir and growth everywhere; out of this stir and growth come the creative epochs of literature' (*CPW*, III, 261).

'The present has to make its own poetry, and not even Sophocles and his compeers, any more than Dante and Shakespeare, are enough for it,' though they may help 'show to the poetry of the present the way it must take' (*CPW*, III, 231). On the other hand, 'no man can trust himself to speak of his own time and his own contemporaries with the same sureness of judgment and the same proportion as of times and men gone by' (*CPW*, VIII, 248). That Arnold did make such judgements—indeed, was obliged to make them—is nevertheless evident enough. As we read what he said of his contemporaries, we must have our historical wits about us, and a firm grasp of dates. Tennyson, he said, 'dawdled with the painted shell of the Universe'[1]—Tennyson, that is, before *In Memoriam* (about which Arnold had quite other grounds for complaint), the Tennyson of 1832 and 1842; it was no bad description of the former volume at least. Browning was 'a man with a moderate gift passionately desiring movement and fulness, and obtaining but a confused multitudinousness',[2] on the basis of *Paracelsus* and *Sordello* but before more than a handful of the poems we now read had been published. Our historical sense can sometimes illuminate other judgements he makes; especially of the poets who wrote at the beginning of the nineteenth century, we must not assume that opinions almost axiomatic with us had already crystallized when Arnold wrote. He did not deliberately choose an inferior poem to denigrate Keats in the 1853 Preface;[3] he was far from unique in stressing in his selection the Promethean and the Faustian aspects of Byron rather than the Aristophanic.

The understanding of Arnold's criticism must also take into account the various audiences to which it was directed. (In the same way, Sainte-Beuve's having written his *Causeries* as a weekly feature for the readers of a daily newspaper does much to account for their tone, even their thinness.) The Prefaces of 1853 and 1854 stand almost by themselves (though most closely linked to the ruminations of the letters to Clough) as the work of a poet addressing an audience of readers and critics in defence of his own work, and with an eye on the contemporary reviewers: like Wordsworth, having launched his poems naked to the world in a first edition, he buttressed them on their

[1] *Letters to Clough*, 63.

[2] *Letters to Clough*, 97.

[3] 'Isabella' is the one poem Shelley alludes to explicitly in *Adonais*. It gave the subject for the first paintings which Millais, Holman Hunt and Rossetti proposed to undertake as the Pre-Raphaelite Brotherhood in 1848–9 (only Millais's was completed).

second appearance with a statement of the theory upon which they had been composed. The lectures from the chair of poetry at Oxford—'On the Modern Element in Literature', *On Translating Homer*, most of the first series of *Essays in Criticism*, *On the Study of Celtic Literature*, and the opening chapter of *Culture and Anarchy*—were serious discourses aimed at a university community; their author might not count on specialist or esoteric knowledge in the audience (indeed, he often aimed at introducing new knowledge, an acquaintance with unfamiliar literary currents or figures), but he could assume a reasonably high level of intellectual interest in his subject. In general these lectures set the tone for Arnold's subsequent critical essays, those published in the magazines and reviews. There is, incidentally, a marked improvement in stylistic ease between the earlier lectures and those printed in *Essays in Criticism*, but in very few instances can one perceive a stylistic difference between what was written as a lecture and what was written as an essay.[1]

In a few of his best known essays, however, Arnold addressed a much less sophisticated audience and adapted his tone and substance accordingly, as in (obviously) 'A Speech at Eton' and (I should say) 'A Guide to English Literature'. The most notable instances are the prefaces he wrote in the latter part of his life to introduce to a wider audience authors in whom he had an especial interest—Isaiah, Johnson, Wordsworth, Gray, Keats, Byron (the Burke selection was more polemical, directed to the Irish question).[2] The most familiar of all, 'The Study of Poetry', aimed at helping the purchaser of a new anthology of English poets to understand and judge what he had bought. These introductory essays, in many ways the most delightful Arnold ever wrote, are somewhat evangelical in their aim. They bear the mark of the expert teacher who must engage his audience because he cannot count upon its prior interest and experience: the essays may be solidly based, but they cannot be conspicuously profound. When

[1] Occasionally, it should be added, Arnold wrote principally to call favourable attention to the work of someone he wished to befriend—the Irish poet Charles P. O'Conor, for example. He wrote a series of articles on his cousin's translation of Curtius' *History of Greece* and one article on his niece's translation of Amiel.

[2] Arnold planned other books of the same sort but never completed them. A collection of Greek poetry with a prefatory essay is perhaps the one we miss most.

one reads the letters between Arnold and his niece's husband, Humphry Ward, one perceives by what a narrow margin we have 'The Study of Poetry', 'Gray', and 'Keats' at all: Arnold was far too busy to undertake them, he thought, and had it not been for the kinship and for a debt of gratitude he owed Ward for intervention on Dick Arnold's behalf at Oxford, the essays might not have been written.

As he composed 'The Study of Poetry' Arnold clearly had in his mind his own criticisms of Stopford Brooke's brief popular history of English literature only two years earlier, and he had perhaps some wish to emulate Brooke in miniature. (A contemporary is said to have remarked that Arnold's review told Brooke 'he had written a most charming book, only unfortunately he had said nothing in it which he ought to say, and put in everything he ought to have left out' [*CPW*, VIII, 441].) The historian of literature must not only avoid dullness in itself, he must avoid pretending that a dull book is a good one merely because it is representative of a period or movement in literature. Hence Arnold's warning against the fallacy of judging historically. 'It is not difficult', he said of one page of Brooke's book, 'to be dull in speaking of Layamon's *Brut*, or even in quoting from it' (*CPW*, VIII, 242). It is perfectly natural that 'the study of the history and development of a poetry may incline a man to pause over reputations and works once conspicuous but now obscure, and to quarrel with a careless public for skipping, in obedience to mere tradition and habit, from one famous name or work in its national poetry to another, ignorant of what it misses, and of the reason for keeping what it keeps, and of the whole process of growth in its poetry'. 'The course of development of a nation's language, thought, and poetry, is profoundly interesting; and by regarding a poet's work as a stage in this course of development we may easily bring ourselves to make it of more importance as poetry than in itself it really is, we may come to use a language of quite exaggerated praise in criticising it; in short, to overrate it' (*CPW*, IX, 163–4).[1] The caution is valid, and is needed

[1] René Wellek points out in his *A History of Modern Criticism: The Age of Transition* how often Sainte-Beuve also warns against the historical estimate: 'He protests against . . . comparisons of [French medieval mysteries] to Racine and Sophocles. . . . "Anybody who had read Sophocles in the original would have been preserved from these eclipses or aberrations of taste"' (New Haven and London 1965, III, 54). It might

nowhere so much as in our schools of literature. The extent to which Arnold's position precludes the revaluation of past literatures is not clear, however. It must strike any twentieth-century reader with amazement that Arnold's sketch of the course of English poetry does not mention Donne; but then Ward's four-volume anthology finds place for only five of Donne's poems, and Brooke's *Primer* gives Donne but three sentences that emphasize his wanton obscurity. Arnold seems never to have mentioned Blake. Occasionally, indeed, he is even willing to seek transcendental support for accidents that control our present scale of values, as when 'the instinct of self-preservation in humanity' (*CPW*, I, 29) is credited with the survival of some eleven of Aristophanes' comedies while Menander's were (he thought) all lost. Since the motive for writing critical essays—for writing on Joubert or the Guérins—is to make some claim for a revaluation of the past, we should perhaps interpret Arnold to mean that only the recent past can be significantly revalued. In that case he is certainly wrong. In the highly civilized world of Victorian England the denial of burial to Polyneices was an outmoded and impossible vengeance, and an action 'which turns upon the conflict between the heroine's duty to her brother's corpse and that to the laws of her country, is no longer one in which it is possible that we should feel a deep interest' (*CPW*, I, 12). In the renewed barbarism of the mid-twentieth century, the central figure of Sophocles's play is seen to be Creon, not Antigone, and the central problem, that of the corrupting influence upon him of power, is vital indeed. Perhaps, however, Arnold's last word on Creon is the character of Polyphontes in his *Merope*.

The second fallacy which may impair critical judgment, the 'personal estimate', is not unlike some of the grounds of misjudgment which Arnold listed in 'A French Critic on Goethe'. 'Our personal affinities, likings, and circumstances, have great power to sway our estimate of this or that poet's work, and to make us attach more importance to it as poetry than in itself it really possesses, because to us it is, or has been, of high importance' (*CPW*, IX, 164). 'The historic estimate is likely in especial to affect our judgment and our language when we are dealing with ancient poets; the personal estimate when

be added that when Professor Wellek writes on Arnold as critic, he writes as one of the very few who seem to have read *all* of Arnold.

we are dealing with poets our contemporaries, or at any rate modern' (*CPW*, IX, 166).

Both fallacies lead us astray from the 'real' estimate, as Arnold calls it, 'a sense for the best, the really excellent', the formulation of which is the principal use of a poetical collection such as that he was introducing (*CPW*, IX, 163). Arnold, to be sure, cautions against too much reverence even for the greatest of poets: 'We must read our classic with open eyes, and not with eyes blinded with superstition; we must perceive when his work comes short, when it drops out of the class of the very best, and we must rate it, in such cases, at its proper value' (*CPW*, IX, 165). Nevertheless, he does seem to be dealing in absolutes: there are 'real classics' as there are eternal verities. No doubt he could hardly avoid this position, given his audience: the first thing any neophyte in the appreciation of the arts wants to be told is 'What *are* the great works of art?' and the second, 'What's great about them?' But it looks very much as though Arnold tended to believe his proposition. 'Any one who can . . . [establish] in any quarter a single sound rule of criticism, a single rule which clearly marks what is right as right, and what is wrong as wrong, does a good deed. . . . Somewhere or other, in the literary opinion of Europe, if not in the literary opinion of one nation, in fifty years, if not in five, there is a final judgment on these matters, and the critic's work will at last stand or fall by its true merits' (*CPW*, I, 172). In a more flexible mood or with a more sophisticated audience he might have admitted that even the greatest classics appeal, or fail to appeal, for personal reasons, reasons that may change as one's experience changes, just as we might hope he would confess that different eras of criticism reorder their pantheons markedly.[1]

Greatness in poetry, he said, is a matter of substance and a matter of style. Neither can easily be handled by definition or analysis. 'It is much better simply to have recourse to concrete examples;—to take specimens of poetry of the high, the very highest quality, and to say: The characters of a high quality of poetry are what is expressed *there*. They are far better recognised by being felt in the verse of the master, than by being perused in the prose of the critic' (*CPW*, IX, 170–1). He

[1] The passages Arnold selects as touchstones of the very greatest poetry have a relatively few themes and it is hard to avoid the sense that their appeal to him is very personal indeed.

had already shown the futility of Addison's attempt to win readers for *Paradise Lost* by argument on its substance. And though stylistic analysis has made genuine advances in the century since Arnold wrote, it still can hardly tell us why one style pleases and another does not. Therefore Arnold returned to a technique he had used in his lectures *On Translating Homer*, where by the nature of the subject style was the only matter of debate: he referred matters of judgment directly to the personal experience of the reader by quoting characteristic passages. 'There can be no more useful help for discovering what poetry belongs to the class of the truly excellent, and can therefore do us most good, than to have always in one's mind lines and expressions of the great masters, and to apply them as a touchstone to other poetry. . . . If we have any tact we shall find them, when we have lodged them well in our minds, an infallible touchstone for detecting the presence or absence of high poetic quality, and also the degree of this quality, in all other poetry which we may place beside them' (*CPW*, IX, 168). For style alone, the touchstone technique serves brilliantly not only in the Homer lectures but in the illustrations of 'natural magic' in 'Maurice de Guérin' and *On the Study of Celtic Literature*. But if substance as well as style is to be illustrated, the reader imperatively requires a knowledge of the context of each passage. The 'simple, but perfect, single line, "In la sua volontade è nostra pace"' (*CPW*, IX, 169) is nothing unless it calls up, first the interview between Dante and Piccarda, who utters it, and then the entire conceptual structure of the *Divine Comedy*. Given some knowledge of the context, the touchstone method makes its appeal, as Arnold intended, to intuition, not to an argument; in any case, it is hard to escape the spell of the passages Arnold quotes.

The guided tour of the high spots of English poetry with which Arnold completes his essay has been more a battleground than a joyous field full of folk to its readers. (Strictly speaking, it is not meant as a historical sketch, but as a selective illustration of the kinds of questions the critical judgment must deal with and the principal errors into which it may fall.) For modern taste it is dominated too much by the notion that 'high seriousness' (he uses Aristotle's word) is necessary for the greatest poetry; devotees of Chaucer who would not themselves place Chaucer on a level with Dante nevertheless are indignant that Arnold finds him lacking the tone and texture of Piccarda's speech. Undoubtedly Arnold chose the wrong tale to quote from; his favourite is not everyone's favourite, and the Prioress's Tale is not in fact printed among the selections from Chaucer in the Ward anthology. Still, his praise of Chaucer's substance and style is high enough to please anyone, had he only forborne to express the limitation. Chaucerians should be grateful for the deftness with which he demonstrates that Chaucer must be read in his own language, not in a modern version.

The partisans of Dryden and Pope cannot tolerate the proposition that they 'are not classics of our poetry, they are classics of our prose' (*CPW*, IX, 181). 'If Pope be not a poet, where is poetry to be found?' was Dr. Johnson's way of answering the question Arnold might not have attempted to deal with if Johnson had not raised it. Arnold's position is often enough expressed in his writings, as we have seen. 'Though Pope's genius for didactic poetry was not less than that of Horace, while his satirical power was certainly greater, still one's taste receives, I cannot but think, a certain satisfaction when one reads the Epistles and Satires of Horace, which it fails to receive when one reads the Satires and Epistles of Pope. Of such avail is the superior adequacy of the vehicle used to compensate even an inferiority of genius in the user! In the same way Pope is at a disadvantage as compared with Addison. The best of Addison's composition . . . wears better than the best of Pope's, because Addison has in his prose an intrinsically better vehicle for his genius than Pope in his couplet' (*CPW*, III, 15). Calling attention to Joubert's statement that 'Boileau is a powerful poet, but only in the world of half poetry', Arnold comments, 'How true is that of Pope also!' (*CPW*, III, 204–5). Even Goethe's is 'the style of prose as much as of poetry; it is lucid, harmonious, earnest, eloquent, but it has not received that peculiar kneading, heightening, and recasting which is observable in the style of . . . Milton,—a style which seems to have for its cause a certain pressure of emotion, and an ever-surging, yet bridled, excitement in the poet, giving a special intensity to his way of delivering himself' (*CPW*, III, 362).

If the only quarrel were one of terminology, it would not be worth pursuing; Pope's poetry and Dryden's are certainly very different from Shakespeare's and Milton's on the one hand, Wordsworth's and Keats's on the other, and if a critic wishes to point that difference by using different terms, he may do so, just as modern taxonomists mean no disparagement to a rabbit when they no longer classify him with the rodents. But the admirers of Dryden and Pope cannot believe there is no disparagement in Arnold's terminology, and there are grounds for their conviction. 'Poetry, no doubt, is more excellent in itself than prose. In poetry man finds the highest and most beautiful expression of that which is in him. We had far better poetry than the poetry of the eighteenth century before that century arrived, we have had better since it departed. . . . We do well to place our pride in the Elizabethan age and Shakespeare, as the Greeks placed theirs in Homer. We did well to return in the present century to the poetry of that older age for illumination and inspiration, and to put aside, in a great measure, the poetry and poets intervening between Milton and Wordsworth' (*CPW*, VIII, 315–16). An age of prose called forth 'in general men's powers of understanding, wit and cleverness, rather than their deepest powers of mind and soul' (*CPW*, IX, 200). The poetry of Dryden, Pope, and all their school 'is conceived and composed in their wits, genuine poetry is conceived and composed in the soul' (*CPW*, IX, 202).

Perhaps the most unexpected part of Arnold's very useful essay is his long discussion of Burns. In fact, the writing of the essay forced Arnold to make some new literary acquaintances: 'I have been reading Chaucer a great deal, the early French poets a great deal, and Burns a great deal', he told his sister. 'Burns is a beast, with splendid gleams, and the medium in which he lived, Scotch peasants, Scotch Presbyterianism, and Scotch drink, is repulsive. Chaucer, on the other hand, pleases me more and more, and his medium is infinitely superior. But I shall finish with Shakespeare's *King Lear* before I finally write my Introduction, in order to have a proper taste in my mind while I am at work' (*CPW*, IX, 379).

The two other essays Arnold wrote for Ward's *English Poets*, those on Gray and Keats, attempt not so much direct critical interpretation of the poetry as an illumination of the poetry primarily through the poet's letters. Both essays suffer when they are removed from their function as introductions to selected poems. The Keats essay is especially significant for its perception of Keats's critical talent. The famous pontification, 'He is; he is with Shakespeare' (*CPW*, IX, 215), was not meant merely to canonize by a lofty comparison, it was meant (as its context makes clear) to seize upon a pre-eminent quality of Keats's work. As we have seen, Arnold believed that one of the greatest problems facing the poets of the beginning of his century was the forging of an adequate poetic language; Keats, 'a style and form seeker',[1] turned for his model to Shakespeare, and was indeed 'the very chief among those who seem to have been formed in the school of Shakespeare: . . . one whose exquisite genius and pathetic death render him for ever interesting'[2] (*CPW*, I, 10). Arnold's earlier references to Keats, as in 'Maurice de Guérin', are generally more affectionate and engaging than this essay.

Wherever one turns, in the figures Arnold chooses and in the associations between them he makes, one perceives that his greatest interest lies in the writers who most influenced his own generation, who had the greatest impact on his own youth.[3] The volumes of selections from Wordsworth and Byron were foretold as early as the 'Memorial Verses' of 1850, a poem which, as I have elsewhere pointed out,[4] owed much to Carlyle's early critical essays. The Wordsworth volume is still in print at the original publisher's after nearly a century, and its introductory essay has become the cornerstone of Wordsworth's reputation; however it may be debated and criticized, it must be

[1] *Letters to Clough*, 101.

[2] In one sentence on Keats, Arnold appears to make early death a moral defect: 'Keats passionately gave himself up to a sensuous genius, to his faculty for interpreting nature; and he died of consumption at twenty-five' (*CPW*, III, 122). In fact, Arnold did believe that Keats's early death might be attributed to his temperament: 'The temperament is *devouring*; it uses vital power too hard and too fast, paying the penalty in long hours of unutterable exhaustion and in premature death' (*CPW*, III, 32).

[3] As a passage in his essay on Obermann reveals, his essays were in some measure giving the intellectual background of his own creative work: 'Of the letters of Obermann, the writer's profound inwardness, his austere and sad sincerity, and his delicate feeling for nature, are . . . the distinguishing characteristics. His constant inwardness, his unremitting occupation with that question which haunted St. Bernard—*Bernarde, ad quid venisti?*—distinguish him from Goethe and Wordsworth, whose study of this question is relieved by the thousand distractions of a poetic interest in nature and in man. His severe sincerity distinguishes him from Rousseau, Chateaubriand, or Byron, who in their dealing with this question are so often attitudinising and thinking of the effect of what they say on the public' (*CPW*, V, 296). Four of these six names appear in 'Stanzas in Memory of the Author of *Obermann*', 'Memorial Verses', or 'Stanzas from the Grande Chartreuse'.

[4] *The Time-Spirit of Matthew Arnold*, Ann Arbor, Michigan 1970, 8–10.

reckoned with. If Wordsworth joins Shakespeare and Milton as the greatest of English poets from the age of Queen Elizabeth I to the middle of the nineteenth century—and those who are fond of ranking their poets seldom omit him from the sphere of the fixed stars—he is there not by the power of merit alone, but because Arnold placed him there. Arnold's express distaste for discussion of Wordsworth's 'philosophy' springs from his conviction that poetry, unlike ethics, produces its effect not by persuasion of reason but by its impact upon the whole of man. And in this belief, of course, he is a Wordsworthian himself: the impulse from the vernal wood, transmitted through the mind and tongue of the poet, may teach us more of moral evil and of good than all the sages can. The essay is written with the warmth of personal affection Arnold always felt for Wordsworth, whom he had known as a family friend for the greater part of his early life. It is a pity that he was not more fond of *The Prelude*, but it was published too late: by the end of 1850 Arnold was twenty-eight and his image of Wordsworth had already been crystallized. He re-read the poem in 1884, but wrote no more about it.

The Byron of Arnold's selections was primarily 'the Pilgrim of Eternity', the poet of *Childe Harold* and of poems like *Manfred* that echoed *Childe Harold*.

> *What helps it now, that Byron bore,*
> *With haughty scorn which mock'd the smart,*
> *Through Europe to the Ætolian shore*
> *The pageant of his bleeding heart?*
> *That thousands counted every groan,*
> *And Europe made his woe her own?*[1]

And yet his introductory essay, with its clear echoes of the earlier essay on Heine (where Arnold had coupled the two poets [*CPW*, III, 121–2]), lays greatest stress on Byron's passionate revolt on the one hand against medievalism in church and state, against George III, Castlereagh, Wellington, and Southey, and on the other against the power of Philistinism which had supplanted it: he 'found our nation, after its long and victorious struggle with revolutionary France, fixed in a system of established facts and dominant ideas which revolted him.

[1] 'Stanzas from the Grande Chartreuse', ll. 133–8.

The mental bondage of the most powerful part of our nation, of its strong middle class, to a narrow and false system of this kind, is what we call British Philistinism' (*CPW*, IX, 232). Shelley he was somehow unable to see in the same light.

> *What boots it, Shelley! that the breeze*
> *Carried thy lovely wail away,*
> *Musical through Italian trees*
> *Which fringe thy soft blue Spezzian bay?*
> *Inheritors of thy distress*
> *Have restless hearts one throb the less?*[1]

'For the votary misled by a personal estimate of Shelley, as so many of us have been, are, and will be,—of that beautiful spirit building his many coloured haze of words and images

> *"Pinnacled dim in the intense inane"*—

no contact can be wholesomer than the contact with Burns at his archest and soundest' (*CPW*, IX, 187). Arnold noted 'Shelley's poetry' in his pocket diary for 1888 as one of the subjects he wished to write upon, but death intervened, and so his last word upon Shelley is unfortunately his review of Dowden's biography.[2]

One of the most interesting of the essays in which Arnold deals with the formative influences upon his young manhood is the discourse on Emerson he composed for his lecture tour in America the year after Emerson's death. Arnold disliked nationalistic fervour as much as any other false ground for judgement: '[Theodore] Parker, born an American, is as a preacher and writer a genuine American voice, not an echo of English pulpits and books; that is much. In the same way, Mr. Walt Whitman, born an American, is as a poet a genuine American voice, not an echo of English poetry; that, too, is much. But the admirers of Theodore Parker or of Mr. Walt Whitman easily make

[1] 'Stanzas', ll. 139–44.

[2] Dowden once wistfully remarked after Arnold's death that nothing he wrote ever seemed to please Arnold. He never faced up to the implication of that remark, for Arnold was not really hard to please. See Dowden's review of *Letters, Saturday Review*, 7 December 1895, 758.

more of it than it is worth. At this time of day it is not enough to be an American voice, or an English voice, or a French voice; for a real spiritual lead it is necessary to be a European voice. When American intellect has not only broken, as it is breaking, the leading strings of England, but has also learnt to assimilate independently the intellect of France and Germany and the ancient world as well as of England, then, and not till then, may the spiritual construction of an American be "a many-gated temple, with a dome wide and lofty enough to include all earnest minds"' (*CPW*, V, 81). Though Arnold admitted that it was becoming less and less true that American authors were 'English authors of more or less merit, whose birth has happened to be in America, but who are fed on English books, follow the literary movement of England, and reproduce English thought', he remained convinced that 'the basis of [the American's] nature is indeed still that of the Englishman's nature, the Englishman of the middle class, the English Puritan' (*CPW*, V, 79). And so he saw resemblances the American critic was not likely to see, or to admit: 'the Quinionian humour of Mr. Mark Twain', for example (Arnold had just been reading *David Copperfield* to his daughter and was much struck by the Philistinism of Quinion and Murdstone). But Emerson came with the high accreditation of Arnold's youthful enthusiasm, a personal acquaintance through Clough, and a continued relationship of mutual esteem. The lecture on Emerson, then, embraced warm tributes to Carlyle, Goethe and Newman, with precisely the praise of Emerson himself that we now perceive to be most accurate—not a great poet, not a great writer, not a great philosopher, but 'the friend and aider of those who would live in the spirit'. 'As Wordsworth's poetry is, in my judgment, the most important work done in verse, in our language, during the present century' (and Arnold was speaking near the end of it), 'so Emerson's *Essays* are, I think, the most important work done in prose'. He could 'break through the hard and fast barrier of narrow, fixed ideas which he found confronting him, and win an entrance for new ideas'; he did 'the right work to be done, at the hour when he appeared' (*CPW*, X, 14, 177, 182, 180).

The central core of Arnold's criticism is, then, his sense of a writer's value in supplying the spiritual and intellectual needs of the nineteenth century. To the extent that we may believe he misjudged those needs, or to the extent that those needs are no longer ours, his criticism is diminished in its significance. He firmly believed that literature made things happen, that it changed people; it was 'the noble and profound application of ideas to life' (*CPW*, I, 211). It changed them by working upon all their powers—not intellectual merely, but aesthetic, moral, and social. And because it changed them, it was, if one thought about it, not unlike religion.[1] We cannot forget that Arnold was the son of a clergyman and a schoolmaster. It may seem strange to us that one whose social ideals looked beyond the dominance of the Philistines to a reign of equality and the masses should so concern himself with the civilizing power of art; without debating the point, one may merely remark that the very editors of journals for the working men, like W. J. Linton and Thomas Cooper, also conceived their mission to be in part raising the taste of their readers to an appreciation of *Paradise Lost.*[2]

Finally, Arnold had genuine delight in and enthusiasm for literature, though it is seldom so explicit as in the essays on Wordsworth and Emerson. Dryden and Dr. Johnson could write sentences such as: 'I admire [Ben Jonson], but I love Shakespeare', and 'If the reader should suspect me, as I suspect myself, of some partial fondness for the memory of Dryden, let him not too hastily condemn me; for meditation and enquiry may, perhaps, shew him the reasonableness of my determination.' But despite the personal anecdotes that occur more frequently in his essays than one may suppose, Arnold only reluctantly wrote in the manner of his well-known sentence, 'I am a Wordsworthian myself' (*CPW*, IX, 55). 'Even in speaking of authors dear to me', he tells us, 'I would try to avoid' the 'personal sort of

[1] Arnold tries to express this combination of effects in 'Literature and Science': 'Why should it be one thing, in its effect upon the emotions, to say, "Patience is a virtue", and quite another thing, in its effect upon the emotions, to say with Homer, "for an enduring heart have the destinies appointed to the children of men"? Why should it be one thing, in its effect upon the emotions, to say with the philosopher Spinoza, "Man's happiness consists in his being able to preserve his own essence", and quite another thing, in its effect upon the emotions, to say with the Gospel, "What is a man advantaged, if he gain the whole world, and lose himself, forfeit himself"? How does this difference of effect arise? I cannot tell, and I am not much concerned to know; the important thing is that it does arise, and that we can profit by it' (*CPW*, X, 67–8).

[2] I am indebted for this significant point to my colleague Professor Steven Weiland.

estimate' (*CPW*, X, 169). The magisterial manner, 'as communing with Time and Nature' (*CPW*, X, 169),[1] belies the fact of genial personality, of taste, of strong sense for style as well as substance. He is most illuminating, not because of his dogmas but because he did indeed with some success aim at flexibility, at disinterestedness, at keeping his eye on the object. 'Surely the critic who does most for his author is the critic who gains readers for his author himself, not for any lucubrations on his author;—gains more readers for him, and enables those readers to read him with more admiration' (*CPW*, IX, 235). 'Things and actions are what they are, and the consequences of them will be what they will be; why then should we desire to be deceived?'

[1] 'In Matthew Arnold the pose of impersonality is carried with such art that it would be absurd to withhold our admiration. If he passes judgment, it is not he that does it, but the *orbis terrarum*, the whole congregation of saints' (Garrod, *op. cit.*, 158).

6: *Arnold and Clough*

JAMES BERTRAM

Ye, too, marvellous Twain, that erect on the Monte Cavallo
Stand by your rearing steeds in the grace of your
motionless movement . . . (*Amours de Voyage*, I, 186–7)

ON THE WALL OF RUGBY CHAPEL—not the modest oak-panelled building in which Dr. Arnold preached on Sunday evenings, but that more Byzantine and 'most unlovable of school chapels' reared by Butterfield in the later nineteenth century[1]—there is a memorial to three poets. It takes the form of a marble triptych with carved portrait medallions: an Olympian Matthew Arnold in striking three-quarter pose holds the centre, flanked by the crisper, more businesslike profiles of Landor and Clough.[2] Lines of verse are incised beneath each portrait. For Landor—perhaps inevitably, but with special appropriateness for an unruly pupil who was asked to leave the school for writing bawdy Latin poems—his own swelling epitaph, 'I strove with none, for none was worth my strife . . .' For Clough, that legendary goal-keeper and paragon of the School House who needed two fags to help carry off his books at his last prize giving,[3] an unassuming couplet from 'Come, Poet, come!':

[1] See T. S. R. Boase, *English Art 1800–1870*, Oxford 1959, 244.
[2] The Librarian, Mr. N. C. Kittermaster, tells me the memorial portraits were put up about 1902, the origin being a donation sent to the Headmaster by an American admirer of Clough; the medallion of Landor was made to match the other two at a later date. The sculptor was Miss Lilian Morris.
[3] See Katharine Chorley, *Arthur Hugh Clough: The Uncommitted Mind*, Oxford 1962, 25. The author of the unsigned article in the *Spectator* of 23 November 1861 was *not* Tom Hughes, but R. H. Hutton.

Young children gather as their own
The harvest that the dead had sown—

(with the implied final line, for anyone likely to remember it, 'The dead forgotten and unknown'). For Arnold, with a touch of irony he would certainly not have missed, the last four lines of 'Thyrsis':

Why faintest thou? I wandered till I died.
  Roam on! The light we sought is shining still.
  Dost thou ask proof? Our tree yet crowns the hill,
Our Scholar travels yet the loved hill-side.

'Why faintest thou?' In the poem, Clough (or Clough's ghost) says it consolingly or reproachfully to an Arnold only too conscious that for him the spring of poetry was drying up. Yet this was just what Arnold had been saying to Clough, with damnable iteration over the years since 1848 when he first began to suspect his friend of aimless drifting. And Clough, too, had said something like it to Arnold in life when he called his verse *'mollis et exspes'*, mocked 'the dismal cycle of his rehabilitated Hindoo-Greek theosophy', and linked it with the 'over-educated weakness of purpose in Western Europe'.[1] With Clough and Arnold—two complex men who knew each other's strengths and limitations very well indeed—a complex and affectionate irony is never far away. If we are ever tempted to read their high Victorian story in terms of Hamlet and Fortinbras, of scrupulous uncertainty and cool compelled resolution, the poetry is always there to remind us how often the resolute Arnold was on the defensive, the doubting Clough resolute through all his doubts. It is not just a matter of setting 'Dover Beach' against 'Say not the struggle nought availeth', or the *élan* of *The Bothie* against the barely controlled despair of 'Empedocles'. These are extreme

[1] 'Recent English Poetry', review article by Clough in the *North American Review*, LXXVII, July 1853, 1–30; reprinted in *Poems and Prose Remains of Arthur Hugh Clough* (2 vol ed Mrs. Arthur Hugh Clough (1869); hereafter referred to as *PPR)*, I, 359–83, and Buckner B. Trawick, *Selected Prose Works*, Alabama 1964, 143–71, *passim*. Arnold wrote from Fox How in August 1853: 'They think here that your article on me is obscure and peu favorable—but I do not myself think either of these things' (*Letters to Clough*, 140).

examples; what we have to do is to establish how much these two friends had in common, before we can distinguish with any accuracy their marked differences in outlook and literary practice.

The documentation—despite some notable gaps—is remarkably complete. It owes much to the excellent Rugby and Balliol habit of keeping notebooks, and most to the vast mass of 'Clough papers' religiously preserved by his family and finally deposited in the Bodleian after the death of the daughter Clough never saw. The use made of this material since the 1930s has significantly altered our view of both poets. Arnold was the first to benefit with H. F. Lowry's admirable edition of his letters to Clough: though this correspondence, thanks to Arnold's *penchant* for destroying private papers,[1] remains regrettably one-sided, it is clear these youthful letters could not have been so lively unless they had been meeting pretty robust opposition. Clough's turn came next, with the first major Oxford edition of the *Poems* in a reasonably full critical text (1951), and F. L. Mulhauser's two volumes of selected *Correspondence* (1957). Lowry, in reviewing the evidence, set a rare example of benevolent neutrality; subsequent critical studies have showed a clear tendency to take sides. Lionel Trilling in his influential *Matthew Arnold* (1939) selectively used *Letters to Clough* to make the young Arnold more interesting at Clough's expense. Biographers and editors with fuller access to Clough's correspondence and occasional prose writings have since been able to reconstruct with more confidence his side of the debate, and have understandably attempted to redress the balance. Especially important here is the work of W. E. Houghton in *The Poetry of Clough* (1963), Buckner B. Trawick's faulty but useful edition of the *Selected Prose Works* (1964), and Evelyn Barish Greenberger's *Arthur Hugh Clough: The Growth of a Poet's Mind* (1970). Concurrently we have had some spirited attempts, in selections from Clough's verse edited by John Purkis (1967) and Michael Thorpe (1969), to stake out a much higher claim for his poetry at its best, and promote against a humourless self-conscious Arnold the more engaging figure of 'the shrewd, witty, delightful Clough'.

Yet we have surely by now passed the stage when it is necessary to take

[1] Arnold, through reticence or inspectorial habit, destroyed letters; Clough, more donnish and scholarly, kept them. The other chief offender in this context was Theodore Walrond, who seems to have ordered the destruction of many letters from both Arnold and Clough.

sides, and score up points for one man at the other's expense. What really matters is that over the last ten years, while Arnold has certainly not been neglected, we have heard a good deal less of Clough's 'failure', a lot more of his positive and distinctive achievement both as man and poet. We have had three full-scale biographies, Lady Chorley's closely documented and (apart from its last chapter) highly persuasive *Clough: The Uncommitted Mind* (1962), Paul Veyriras's more formal and encyclopaedic *Arthur Hugh Clough* (1964), and the very sympathetic *Arthur Hugh Clough: towards a reconsideration* (1972) of Robindra Kumar Biswas. Briefer and brisker studies by Isobel Armstrong, Michael Timko, Wendell V. Harris, David Williams, and Mrs. Greenberger (1962–70) are all evidence of fresh appreciation and a renewed critical interest in a poet who had been, at least within our own century, consistently undervalued. Clough's poetry is now readily available in the *Oxford Standard Authors*, and in the new enlarged second edition of *Poems* (1974), edited by F. L. Mulhauser. Since 1967 students have had the valuable tool of a *Descriptive Catalogue* of Clough poetry, prose, biography, and criticism; recent detailed work on Clough has been scrupulously summarized by Michael Timko in the second edition of F. E. Faverty's *The Victorian Poets* (1968); and in the following year Isobel Armstrong's collection of *The Major Victorian Poets* (1969) contained a beautifully sensitive evaluation of Clough's lyrical technique by Barbara Hardy. In short, Clough need no longer be seen as 'a half-hewn Matthew Arnold, left lying in the quarry' (F. L. Lucas, 1930), nor as a mere attendant satellite, but rather—in the phrase of his sole surviving letter to Arnold from Rome in 1849—as one of 'two serene undeviating stars' that may on equal terms 'salute each other once again for a moment amid the infinite spaces'.[1]

If then it is possible to discuss the relationship between Arnold and Clough—certainly the most intimate if not always the most harmonious between any two English poets—with reasonable objectivity, we might begin with biography, and move on to some consideration of their poetic views and practice.

In the general shape of their lives, the superficial parallels are almost uncanny. Both were Dr. Arnold's pupils, both Balliol scholars; both took second classes in the schools (Clough surprisingly, Arnold chiefly thanks to Clough's coaching); both won fellowships at Oriel. Both lost

[1] Letter of 23 June 1849, *Letters to Clough*, 107–9.

their fathers early and incurred heavy family responsibilities; both had strong-minded slow-developing sisters in whom they confided, and whose lives they helped to form. Sharing the Fox How passion for hill walks and clear water, both seem to have been vulnerable to the attraction of young women in a mountain setting, yet both in the end made conventional middle-class marriages at some cost to their youthful dreams. If Arnold seemed for a time to be seeking a career in diplomacy and 'the great world', practical needs soon drove him back to the true Arnold calling of education. Clough never knew any other: after his brave revolt against Oxford conformity, the blind alley of University Hall, his brief 'consideration of the Antipodes', and his bold but ill-judged sortie to America, he ended up in a lowlier billet in the same Education Office to which his friend had preceded him. The general similarity in pattern is unmistakable, and in one sense the lines were predetermined: though Arnold 'submitted' earlier and with a better grace, neither record, in a material way, is at all commensurate with the talents of either man. As Arnold so wryly but accurately observed in 1852: 'Au reste, a great career is hardly possible any longer—can hardly now be purchased even by the sacrifice of repose dignity and inward clearness—so I call no man unfortunate. I am more and more convinced that the world tends to become more comfortable for the mass, and more uncomfortable for those of any natural gift or distinction—and it is as well perhaps that it should be so . . .' (*Letters to Clough*, 122).

It is in particular phases, rather than in the general pattern, that the most striking differences are seen. Clough and Arnold barely overlapped at Rugby, and reacted very differently to the pressures of the place. Clough, the model Rugbeian who received from his headmaster that unprecedented school report of 'eight years without a fault', had been clay in the potter's hand. He was to spend most of the next eight years painfully extricating himself from the Rugby mould. Matthew, by contrast, was a very dubious Rugbeian: with his brother Tom he had already spent a year at Winchester, achieved a precocious air of insouciance, and in manner at least remained a Wykehamist for life. At Rugby he was the headmaster's son, an invidious distinction for a schoolboy (as Graham Greene's *A Sort of Life* has recently reminded us); and though he won his prizes and scholarships and obviously worked a good deal harder than he was prepared to admit, he carefully and even ostentatiously refrained from taking 'the higher line' for which Clough and his particular Rugby friends were conspicuous. In later years, the pupil who had most earnestly and fervently submitted himself to the full power of Dr. Arnold's influence was to sketch, in the Epilogue to 'Dipsychus', the most incisive deflation of that influence on the tender conscience of the young. Even more devastating, because more judicial, was his earlier estimate of Dr. Arnold in his 'Review of Mr. Newman's *The Soul*' (*PPR*, I, 294): 'There are men—such was Arnold—too intensely, fervidly practical to be literally, accurately, consistently theoretical; too eager to be observant, too royal to be philosophical, too fit to head armies and rule kingdoms to succeed in weighing words and analysing emotions; *born to do, they know not what they do*' (my emphasis). The Arnold son who at school had mocked or seemed indifferent was in fact the true-born disciple destined to reassert, revindicate in verse and prose, and ultimately most effectively continue his father's reforming mission.

As at Rugby, so at Balliol, there was only the briefest overlap between a harassed, ascetic, still desperately earnest Clough in his final year, and the carefree new Balliol scholar who affected a greater enthusiasm for field sports than for his books. But by 1842, when Clough had recouped his comparative failure in the schools by his election to a fellowship at Oriel, when the shock of Dr. Arnold's sudden death had drawn him again into the role of responsible elder brother to the Arnold boys, and when the younger Tom Arnold and Theodore Walrond had both arrived at Oxford from Rugby, at last a real intimacy could begin. Then was gathered the 'little interior company' of Clough, the two Arnolds, and 'Todo' Walrond: they breakfasted regularly in Clough's rooms at Oriel, shared their Sunday walks, responded eagerly to new voices in the air (Carlyle and Goethe, Emerson and George Sand), thrashed out new ideas in long evening discussions in that select debating society known as 'The Decade'. All four of them were to recall the next five years with increasing gratitude, and this inner ring of what Tom Arnold later called 'the Clougho-Matthean circle' is so representative of the second generation of Arnoldian Rugbeians and of the problems they faced in settling upon a career and a life style, that it is worth dwelling upon the very different ways in which they tackled it.

The two younger members can be regarded as representing the extremes of impetuousness and moderation. Both took excellent degrees, both if they had conformed might have looked forward to distinguished 'establishment' careers. Walrond, the intelligent, athletic, 'naturally good' all-rounder, was not unprepared to subscribe: no doubt he would have reasoned, with Clough's forthright older friend J. P. Gell, that 'after all, you must sign something'. In August 1847 Walrond wrote a disarmingly modest letter to Clough asking his advice as to whether he should take Orders or alternatively seek to enter public life; in the upshot he taught for three years at Rugby, later became a very successful fellow at Balliol, and finally entered the Civil Service, ending up as one of the three Commissioners.[1] In 1869 he was a favoured candidate for the headmastership of Rugby in succession to Frederick Temple, but was passed over because he was still a layman—a reverse which Matthew Arnold never forgave the Governors of his old school. 'This for our wisest . . .'.

Tom Arnold, the quiet sensitive stammering young man on whom Dr. Arnold had pinned his highest hopes, was in fact the first of the four to rebel. Swinging, even as an undergraduate, between extremes of evangelical piety and radical agnosticism, he scornfully rejected fellowships, abjured the law as 'a hardening worldly profession', threw away without regret a very promising career in the Colonial Office, and by November 1847 was already embarked on the *John Wickliffe* for the distant colony of New Zealand, determined to work with his hands in a new unspoilt democratic community.[2] From near the Line, in the 'Equator Letters' he sent back to friends in England to explain his apparently rash action, he wrote an eloquent apologia on his motives which was to prove a remarkably accurate forecast of Clough's own dilemma when he too, in the course of the same year, was to take the same decisive step of cutting adrift from Oxford and a clerically-dominated establishment:

> Take but one step in submission, and all the rest is easy: persuade yourself that your reluctance to subscribe to Articles which you

[1] See the excellent article by John Curgenven, 'Theodore Walrond: Friend of Arnold and Clough', *Durham University Journal*, n.s. XIII, No. 2, March 1952.

[2] See J. Bertram, *New Zealand Letters of Thomas Arnold the Younger*, Oxford and Wellington 1966, introduction and *passim*; also K. Allott, 'Thomas Arnold the Younger, New Zealand, and the "Old Democratic Fervour"', *Landfall*, XV, No. 3, September 1961, 208–25.

> do not believe is a foolish scruple, and then you may go to the Bar, and become distinguished, and perhaps in the end sway the counsels of the State; prove to yourself, by the soundest arguments which political economy can furnish, that you may lawfully keep several hundred men, women and children at work for twelve hours a day in your unwholesome factory, and then you may become wealthy and influential, and erect public baths and patronize artists. All this is open to you; while if you refuse to tamper in a single point with the integrity of your conscience, isolation awaits you, and unhappy love, and the contempt of men; and amidst the general bustle and movement of the world you will be stricken with a kind of impotence, and your arm will seem to be paralysed, and there will be moments when you will almost doubt whether truth indeed exists, or, at least, whether it is fitted for man. Yet in your loneliness you will be visited by consolations which the world knows not of; and you will feel that, if renunciation has separated you from the men of your own generation, it has united you to the great company of just men throughout all past time; nay, that even now there is a little band of Renunciants scattered over the world, of whom you are one, whose you are, and who are yours for ever. (*NZ Letters*, 215–16).

In the same 'Equator Letters', Tom Arnold raised the problem of marriage for any young man of his unorthodox opinions: '. . . in the age in which we live, and in the society in which we move, there is a curse on love and marriage for those who will not bow the knee to the world's laws; those who have resolved to put away illusions, and to live for truth, be it at the risk of all that is held precious here below, rest, happiness, nay, of love itself, which is the very life of life . . .' (*NZ Letters*, 217).

The relevance of this to his own circumstances is apparent: not long before, Tom Arnold had been turned down by Henrietta Whately, the dutiful daughter of his father's old friend the Archbishop of Dublin. But the comment is also relevant to that first 'disappointment in love' (perhaps with Agnes Walrond) that Thackeray detected in Clough in 1848;[1] and to the exactly contemporary involvement of his brother

[1] See Chorley, 93 and note. On a possible identification of the lady, see Bertram, *NZ Letters*, Appendix C ('Clough and Agnes Walrond'); and compare Clough's *Epithalamium* (*Poems*, 445ff.), especially lines 45–52: the poem was certainly written for Agnes Walrond's wedding in 1849.

Matthew with both the French Marguerite and the 'Cruel Invisible', Mary Claude.[1] Tom Arnold's later career was to provide an astonishing series of plunges and reversals: two points of particular interest may be noted here. First, when he crossed from New Zealand to Van Diemen's Land in 1850, met at a dance in Hobart a 'wild colonial girl' with a distinctly scandalous reputation, and swept her off in a whirlwind courtship, he became one Arnold who *did* marry his Marguerite. Second, years later, when he parted company with Newman and the Birmingham Oratory School (over the old Arnold issue of liberalism in religion as in politics) he was able to break back into the closed world of academic Oxford—something that Clough, unlike Matthew Arnold, was never able to do.

When Matthew Arnold won his fellowship at Oriel in 1845, he and Clough seemed at last to have closed the gaps between them and to be facing the future on equal terms. Yet their styles remained very different—Arnold's Mecca was Paris, for aesthetic rather than political reasons; Clough was following a humbler path of aid to his fellow men by working patiently for the Oxford Mendicity Society in the slums of St. Ebbe's. In politics Clough was decidedly the more radical, active, and sanguine of results, though he retained a coolly objective view of human limitation in moments of economic and revolutionary stress; Arnold was frankly sceptical about political action, and found 'Citoyen Clough' rather an amusing object. Neither, it is clear, was really reconciled to the privileged life of an Oxford don. Clough was already in 1845 angling for a professorship in 'one of the new Irish Colleges'; Arnold never intended to try for an Oxford tutorship, and by May 1846 Clough was already telling his sister Anne that 'Matt's inspectorship will not be decided for an age'.[2] In the light of this comment, an inspectorship of schools must have been thoroughly canvassed well before Arnold accepted his appointment as Lord Lansdowne's private secretary the following year.

In other words, over the Oriel period Clough was vigorously seeking employment where 'no oaths' would be required, and Arnold—who had had reservations about subscription when he first

[1] See *NZ Letters*, 119 and note; also K. Allott, 'Matthew Arnold and Mary Claude', *NQ* n.s. XVI, June 1969, 209–11.

[2] *MS. Bodl. eng. lett. d. 175*, letter of 3 May 1846, reproduced in part in Mulhauser, 170.

came up to Oxford, and regarded his fellowship merely as a stepping-stone to secular work of some kind—was already looking outwards from dreaming spires to a wider world.

We can see then, as we approach the year of European revolution that was also the great divide for this little band of Oxford men, that Tom Arnold—the 'emotee', in his brother's phrase, the enthusiast who lacked 'a still considerate mind'—had led the way with a dramatic flourish, and fully earned his place as the volatile hero of Clough's parting salute to the Oxford years, *The Bothie of Toper-na-Fuosich*. Matthew, while keeping open the Oriel option, more coolly followed him into the more civilized sanctuary of Lansdowne House. By 1848 Walrond had gone to teach at Rugby, and Clough was at last ready to make his move and resign both tutorship and fellowship. Towards the end of this year of decision, Clough suddenly and quite without warning brought out his first major poem, *The Bothie*. And unconsciously precipitated thereby the first major rift with Matthew Arnold. But at this point, we must turn from their lives to their writing.

Both Clough and Arnold had written verses, almost as a matter of course, from their schooldays. If it seems risky to lean on juvenilia and 'prize poems' for early evidence of literary interests and inclinations, yet some clues of real significance may be gathered. From the first, Arnold is more concerned with the form of a poem, with the construction of a cadenced stanza to an elegiac mood. Clough is more concerned with content and a vigorous if rough statement of it: he shows an early fondness for ballad measures. Clough is at his best with light verse on a topical subject: 'The Effusions of a School Patriarch' is good clean boyish writing. Arnold is at his best with an exotic subject like 'Constantinople' or 'Alaric at Rome', treated in the sounding manner of Byron's *Childe Harold*. Arnold's university poem on *Cromwell* which won the Newdigate is certainly a more eloquent piece, with more memorable single lines, than either of Clough's two unsuccessful entries for the same prize some four years earlier. Only in the very incongruous tribute to an English woodland inserted at the end of 'Salsette and Elephanta' does that dry exercise quicken into some semblance of life. 'The Judgement of Brutus', a severely moral subject, claims interest less for its own sake than for the spirit and the direct images of Dr. Arnold that inform it:

O Heart prepared and Strong! as on thee burst
The sudden, clear conviction of the worst,
Without one change, one strain of self controul
Thy purpose on thee came and filled thy soul:
As who on some broad hill's extended wild
With turfy heights successive still beguiled,
At some swift turn, at once, at last descries
The bold bare Peak—the crowning rocks arise
Thence doth afar a cloudy chart unrolled
Of Steeps on Steeps, and Vale on Vale behold,
And seems no more those meaner tops to know
Now stretched, a tost and tumbling sea, below;—
So thou thenceforth mid visions of thine own
Dwellst oer the rest exalted and alone.

. . . .

'Off, idle doubts, thou double heart away,
'Arise, shrunk arm, ye, wearied limbs obey,
'In His high name, who with this temporal bound
'Of stern probation girt our being round
'Who set the strife and bade the race be run
'The deed shall be, the duty shall be done'!
Spirit of Valour mighty een in death,
Of Courage, Patience, Constancy and Faith,
If yet thou live, and live thou dost indeed
Come, raise us, nerve us, aid us in our need!

(Greenberger, 213–14, 218)

Anne Clough noted in her journal of July 1840, '. . . Reading Arthur's poem on Brutus, disappointed rather in it; it is too rough . . .'; she was certainly right, but the reaching out towards Dr. Arnold's example in the two passages quoted above is surely a genuine *cri de cœur* from Clough's unheated Balliol rooms.

By contrast, in the early pieces Matthew Arnold wrote in his Oxford years from 1843 onwards (these include 'To a Gipsy Child by the Sea-shore', 'Mycerinus', 'The New Sirens', 'The Voice', and the sonnet on Shakespeare) he reaches at a stride a complete poetic style and an assured resonance of phrasing, with single lines as fine as any he ever wrote ('Glooms that enhance and glorify this earth'; 'Sweep in the sounding stillness of the night'; 'Mixed with the murmur of the moving Nile'; 'O unforgotten voice, thy accents come,/ Like wanderers from the world's extremity,/ Unto their ancient home!'; 'Others abide our question. Thou art free.'). Clough's poetry of the Balliol period is intensely subjective and confessional (most notably in the 'Blank Misgivings' sequence) and for the most part tentative and awkward in manner. Only in two short early pieces, 'In a Lecture Room' and 'Duty—that's to say complying . . .', does he reach either the objectivity or satiric bite that were later to become his special strength; and both these Arnold clearly failed to appreciate (*Letters to Clough*, 61, 63). The Oriel period is different: Clough had come out of his dark tunnel, and from 1844 onwards with renewed confidence could command his own exact tone, as in concentrated short poems such as '*Sic Itur*' and '*Qua Cursum Ventus*', or the gay 'Commemoration Sonnets', or such a fine piece of sustained and moral rhetoric as '*Qui Laborat, Orat*'—the first of Clough's poems to which Arnold gave unstinted praise (*Letters to Clough*, 99).

It is unlikely that Clough and Arnold exchanged or discussed their own poems much before 1847, for up to this time Clough's main literary confidant and correspondent had been a man who was anathema to Arnold and to many of Clough's other friends. 'Sweet Thomas Burbidge', the improbable Victorian clergyman with the Elizabethan name, had been both a delight and a temptation to Clough from his Rugby years. At this distance, it is not easy to see why so many people disapproved of Burbidge and his 'freedom of speech' (once more, the sturdy Anne Clough, who knew him, took a more favourable and common-sense view). He was obviously effusive, emotional, theatrical in a manner not unknown in some Anglican curates of a later day; perhaps he was also a bit silly, which would have been enough for Matthew Arnold—'young, but intolerably severe'—to damn him out of hand. Clough found him excellent company and a stimulating, unexacting companion; his letters to Burbidge are more relaxed and spontaneous than those to any other early associate; and though he did not keep Burbidge's letters—'they are too often over-flippant to be pleasant for second readings' (*Correspondence*, ed. Mulhauser, 54)—he maintained the friendship intact, despite the opposition of Stanley, Lake, Ward and Arnold, up to the joint publication of his poems with those of Burbidge in

Ambarvalia in 1849. By this time Burbidge was serving abroad as a British chaplain at Trieste and had with characteristic bravura married a young Italian girl: though he returned to England in 1851 to become headmaster of Leamington College (and involved a reluctant Clough in a lecture on Wordsworth to the Mechanics' Institute there as late as 1852), it is clear the friendship did not survive joint publication. Burbidge as poet did: in 1851 he published his third volume of poems, *Hours and Days*, with a preface that is clearly a kind of poetic manifesto.[1] This may justify some consideration, since (lacking his letters to Clough) we have only his verses and this document to go on, to hint at the nature of his influence on the younger man.

Hours and Days was an avowed experiment to test whether poetry could really reach the people in the same way that music and pictorial art, through cheap concerts and exhibitions and cheap reproductions, had already begun to do. Burbidge is anxious to make poetry accessible 'as the principal and most potent instrument of the higher culture of the highest part of man's nature (for even of religion the best parts are those which are taught thus, and appeal to the affections and imagination) . . .'. He believes that the poet, bearing the peculiar stamp of his own generation, 'can speak to his living contemporaries with greater force than to any future time . . .'. 'The present publication, then', he continues, 'is an attempt to bring the Poet into the same freedom of communication with his contemporary Public which is at present enjoyed by the prose writer, and towards which artists in other kinds are daily advancing.' So the book is published in paperback, at cost price, and if successful is to be followed by 'two other similar *livraisons*' to bind up with it 'like the numbers of a serial work' of fiction. 'My chief endeavour', Burbidge concludes, 'has been to enlarge the domain of Religious Poetry, by representing the ordinary subjects of poetical treatment under the light in which they naturally appear to my own mind.' There is much here of Wordsworth in phrasing, and of Browning in publishing practice; it is clear that Burbidge was attempting something like a more popular development of *Bells and Pomegranates*. Whatever his reservations about the nature of Burbidge's performance, Arnold could have had little quarrel with his estimate of the power and potential of poetry to educate and inform public taste.

[1] Thomas Burbidge, *Hours and Days*, Edinburgh 1851.

What is especially interesting is to meet here, in Burbidge's preface of 1851, ideas about the scope and function of modern poetry that Clough was to unlimber against Arnold's first two volumes of verse in his essay on 'Recent English Poetry' in the *North American Review* (see above, p. 179). Clough makes Burbidge's main point in a more exact and particular manner: 'Poems after classical models, poems from Oriental sources, and the like, have undoubtedly a great literary value. Yet there is no question, it is plain and patent enough, that people much prefer Vanity Fair and Bleak House.' No doubt he is following Burbidge as well as Wordsworth when he argues for a poetry that 'should deal more than at present it usually does with general wants, ordinary feelings, the obvious rather than the rare facts of human nature . . .', should take in 'the actual, palable things with which our everyday life is concerned . . .'; should seek also 'to deal with what *is* here'.

Burbidge's practice, of course, was another matter. It is disastrously obvious to anyone who seeks out his work—not least, in the verses he published together with Clough in *Ambarvalia*—that he is often tepid, over-inflated, egotisical, and capable of appalling bathos. But he is in his own way daring and frank, he has strong liberal sympathies in religion as in politics, and he is not afraid to lift, however gently, the Victorian curtain on some intimacies of human conduct. In 'Lilie. A Myth' he can write.

> *I was a coarse and vulgar man,*
> *I vile and vulgar things had done;*
> *And I, as Nature's instincts ran,*
> *Was wont to let them run . . .* (*Ambarvalia*, 78)

These lines have a clear affinity with the strange 'lyrical ballad' titled '*Homo sum, nihil humani—*' which Clough cancelled from the proof sheets of his part of *Ambarvalia:*[1]

[1] P. G. Scott, in a most useful bibliographical study, 'The Publication of Clough's *Ambarvalia* poems', *The Book Collector*, 19, No. 2, Summer 1970, has demonstrated that only one setting of type was made for the printing of *Ambarvalia* and subsequent 'reissues'. Sheets from this in two distinct bindings were distributed by Clough to friends who wished to have his part only of the collection; the cancellation of *Homo sum* occurs in a third (probably pre-publication) binding of proof-sheets.

She had a coarse and common grace
As ever beggar showed,
It was a coarse but living face,
I kissed upon the road.

But why have aught to do with her,
And what could be the good?
I kissed her, O my questioner,
Because I knew I could!

The situation is very close to that in '*Ho Theos meta sou*', and is not developed further; the female vagrant is dismissed, after a single piercing look of the kind for which Clough in feminine company was celebrated, with a high-handed benediction, 'God give you of his grace!' But the implications (as in '*Ho Theos*', and *The Bothie*, and '*Les Vaches*', and 'Dipsychus' have been fully faced: this was a manner of 'striving evidently to get breast to breast with reality' that Matthew Arnold would *not* have approved, any more than Mrs. Clough could ever reconcile herself to the delightful '*Natura Naturans*'. A franker and more realistic treatment of sex in everyday life—something for which Clough is remarkable in the high Victorian prime, between Byron and Hardy—he may in part have learnt from Burbidge, and for such influence we can only be grateful. Clough at least was never prone to such lapses in taste as this of Burbidge, in 'The Question':

O Minnie, which are thy true charms?
Now heavenly, now human,
Say, shall I fold thee in my arms
An Angel or a Woman?

. . . .

I heard; my heart began to melt,
And further inquest urging
My eyes—that dared not see it—felt
The bosom of the Virgin. (*Ambarvalia*, 126–7)

Here at least one can appreciate the justice of some of Arnold's more devastating comments on Burbidge, as when he conjectures that

Clough's pieces 'will stand very grandly, with Burbidge's "barbaric ruins" *smirking around them*' (*Letters to Clough*, 61; my emphasis).

On the whole, Arnold approved of 'the great precision and force you have attained in those inward ways' which formed the substance of Clough's contribution to *Ambarvalia*. It was far otherwise with *The Bothie*. And since *The Bothie* had come out first, to be greeted in Oxford at least with some youthful enthusiasm, Arnold's immediately hostile reaction to that poem (which seems to us to mark an enormous advance in freedom, scope and freshness of treatment upon anything in *Ambarvalia*) remains mysterious, and must surely be referred to a personal as well as to a literary context. The key passage occurs in a letter of November 1848, when Arnold was just back from Switzerland after his first meeting with Marguerite, was seeing something of Mary Claude, and was obviously in a state of private turmoil about the 'question of women' that occupies so central a place in Clough's 'Long Vacation Pastoral'.

> —I have been at Oxford the last two days and hearing Sellar and the rest of that clique who know neither life nor themselves rave about your poem gave me a strong almost bitter feeling with respect to them, the age, the poem, even you. Yes I said to myself something tells me I can, if need be, at last dispense with them all, even with him: better that, than be sucked for an hour even into the Time Stream in which they and he plunge and bellow. I became calm in spirit, but uncompromising, almost stern. More English than European, I said finally, more American than English: and took up Obermann, and refuged myself with him in his forest against your Zeit Geist (*Letters to Clough*, 95).

This begins with humorous exaggeration but ends *au sérieux*, and the strength of feeling is obviously in excess of any mere literary judgment. Five years later, at a time when the friendship came under a longer period of strain, Arnold expanded on this earlier moment of instinctive revulsion:

> There was one time indeed—shortly after you had published the Bothie—that I felt a strong disposition to intellectual seclusion, and to the barring out all influences that I felt troubled without advancing me: but I soon found that it was needless to secure

> myself against a danger from which my own weakness even more than my strength—my coldness and want of intellectual robustness—sufficiently exempted me—and besides your company and mode of being always had a charm and a salutary effect for me, and I could not have foregone these on a mere theory of intellectual dietetics (*Letters to Clough*, 129).

We are brought very close, in these two passages, to the innermost conflict of Arnold's years of *Sturm und Drang*: the struggle to maintain equilibrium and a poetic as well as personal identity at a time when 'this strange disease of modern life' was further enfevered for him by 'the fury and the mire of human veins'. It is the highest tribute to Arnold's mature self-mastery that the friendship survived unimpaired, and that he could continue to write, after the second passage just quoted, 'In short, my dear Clough, I cannot say more than that I really have clung to you in spirit more than to any other man—and have never been seriously estranged from you at any time' (*Letters to Clough*, 129).

The friendship survived: but nothing in it is odder than the disconcerting blind spots that show up in judgements about each other's poetry—especially about major works. Arnold was later to praise *The Bothie* in general terms of broad appreciation that have not been surpassed. He was even moved to revise, however slightly, his early indifference to *Amours de Voyage*: 'Dipsychus' he never seems to have read in Clough's lifetime, and never commented on later. Clough was early moved by 'The Strayed Reveller' (we must assume, the poem not the volume), but thought 'The Gulistan is much better'.[1] He was cool about 'Empedocles', and—rightly, we must think—preferred 'The Scholar-Gipsy' to 'Sohrab and Rustum'. Of course these preferences can be referred to what we know of both men's general literary taste: apart from the classics, Dante, Goethe and Schiller, on which they agreed, it is obvious that Clough thought much more highly than Arnold of Chaucer, of Cowley and Dryden and Restoration writers generally, of Burns and of Crabbe—a significant list. Without going overmuch into 'the theory of it' (for, as the uncle insists in the Epilogue to 'Dipsychus', 'If you're wrong in it, it makes bad

[1] Letter of January 1852, *Correspondence*, I, 301. The *Gulistan* (1258), i.e., 'The Rose Garden' by the Persian poet Musli-Uddin Sâdi; was edited by A. Sprenger in 1851 and an English translation appeared in 1852.

worse; if you're right, you may be a critic, but you can't be a poet'), I think we can locate the core of their disagreement in Clough's deliberate choice and defence of the modern subject, of an inclusive poetry of earthy and often colloquial treatment, against Arnold's lifelong preference for a poetry that was to be properly exclusive and dignified, both in choice of subject, and in form and style.

As early as 1839, Clough had written in a Balliol essay on 'The Moral Effect of Works of Satire':

> Nor is it hard to see how one employed so continuously in strife after immediate objects as of necessity is the case of the orator, is likely thereby to disqualify his nature for the use of a medium so contemplative, so careless of the present, so impatient in its love for the end of the anxieties and struggles of the pursuit as it would seem Poetry must generally be. Midway between the two [i.e., Oratory and Poetry] in its Moral character and effects stands Satire, in many ways genuine poetry, yet in its angry indignant spirit giving indications numerous and evident of a position among the jarring and discordant elements of what is technically termed Life (Trawick, 64).

The last phrase is pure Clough; and it is not difficult to find here both a definition of Arnold's kind of poetry that he might have thoroughly approved, and a hint of the rougher and homelier verse texture (to which the general label 'satirical' could not unfairly be applied) which Clough himself was to come to prefer, and to excel in.

A few illustrations may bring out this difference of approach. In Arnold's love poetry (if we except, perhaps, 'A Modern Sappho') the setting is staged picturesquely, distanced, often heightened by some classical or historical reference; the feeling is filtered through a romantic screen. Arnold can at times do this very well; when Clough attempts something in the same manner (as in '*Selene*,' or '*Epi Latmo*') he is frigid and even incoherent. In Clough's better love poems, from 'When the dews are earliest falling' through '*Ho Theos*' and '*Natura Naturans*' and '*Les Vaches*' to the unemphatic little 'Songs in Absence', we usually have an everyday setting, a plainer language, and a much closer concentration on the object—in short, on a woman of flesh and blood and a human and unhistrionic lover. Clough's best love poetry, of course, is to be found in his lyrical narratives: it is given to Philip and Elspie in *The Bothie*, to Claude and Mary Trevellyn in the *Amours*, where following his earlier precept of the desirability of 'the dramaticisation of private feelings in poetry' he succeeds in convincing us that he knows very well what it means to be in love, for a man or a woman. Neither Clough nor Arnold is exactly a great lover, in life or in verse; but I think we must grant that of the two, Clough had the wider and less self-centred sympathy for the lover's state.

'Women', Arnold told Clough in 1848 with a not altogether convincing attempt at worldliness, 'We know beforehand all they can teach us: yet we are obliged to learn it directly from them' (*Letters to Clough*, 93). It has not been remarked, I think, how much more closely these words fit Clough—the man who imagined in advance a frustrated love relationship between a lonely intellectual and a shy but '*douce et paisible*' young Victorian miss, gave this exact and delicate expression in the exchanges of *Amours de Voyage*, and then within a year found himself writing out—surely with some sense of *déjà-vu*—almost exactly the same scrupulous reservations and dubieties to Miss Blanche Smith. Palgrave said of Clough that 'he rather lived than wrote his poem':[1] in the case of Blanche Smith he certainly lived his poem over again, and if she had been a less determined young lady with a less wealthy father behind her, it is likely enough that Clough like Claude might have made his escape. '*Les natures profondement bonnes sont toujours indécises*', Stevie Smith liked to say: nowhere does this show itself more clearly than in Clough's daily correspondence to his fiancée from University Hall.[2] Only Clough, perhaps, could have written to the young woman he had asked to marry him: 'The single life, according to the doctrine of compensation, has some superiorities, as, for example, that of being more *painful*, which, in a state of things that offers but little opportunity for elevated *action*, may be considered a temptation to the aspiring temper. . . . What I looked forward to originally, in case of not going to Sydney, was unmarried poverty and literary work' (*PPR*, I, 172).

[1] *Poems by Arthur Hugh Clough*, ed F. T. Palgrave, Cambridge and London 1862, xxi. Though the text and introduction are idiosyncratic, this little book remains one of the pleasantest in which to read Clough as his own age came to know him: the arrangement of the shorter poems is masterly.

[1] See Chorley, Ch. IX, *passim*.

Clough wrote this in 1852, with three major poems—*The Bothie*, *Amours de Voyage*, and 'Dipsychus'—already behind him, though only the first had been published, and the other two were lying in notebooks that passed only to a very few friends. It is doubtful if anyone besides Blanche (against his wishes) and his young American friend Charles Eliot Norton ever saw 'Dipsychus'. All were vacation poems, though written in very different moods. *The Bothie* had come in a very few weeks of the autumn of 1848, written—with a frank enjoyment his sister always remembered—in an upper room of the little house in Vine Street, Liverpool, that has now been levelled to make room for an expanding university. It was a sign of Clough's buoyant response to the clean break he had made with Oxford that this distillation of so much in Oxford life he recalled with affection should have been sent post-haste to the printer, to be in university common rooms within two months of its happy first inspiration. Tom Arnold is here, downstage, as the impetuous hero Philip Hewson; and Walrond, as 'Arthur, the bather of bathers *par excellence*, Audley by surname'. Clough himself figures twice, under one aspect of the portly Hobbes—'Mute and exuberant by turns, a fountain at intervals playing'; and under another of the Tutor, the grave man Adam. There is no recognizable portrait of Matthew Arnold—unless, indeed, we may glimpse somewhere by the wings the eyeglass of Lord Lansdowne's secretary in 'the Attaché detecting his Honour' (*The Bothie*, I, *passim*).

Amours de Voyage, that ironic tragi-comedy of human frustration which surely we must now regard as Clough's masterpiece, was almost surprising in the speed of its drafting and composition: crammed into three months of a desperately crowded late spring and early summer at Rome, at a time when its author was dashing from political interviews to art galleries to direct observation from several chosen vantage points of the progress of the siege of the city, while maintaining an heroic correspondence to his family and friends at home. 'But, (so finish thy tale)', he wrote at the end of his original envoy to the poem,

> *But, (so finish thy tale,) I was writ in a Roman Chamber*
> *While from Janiculan heights thundered the Gallican guns.*

Was it with one of Arnold's strictures on his Homeric translations freshly in mind that he later altered the final line? '"Gerenian horseman'' is a bad *style* of thing—', that implacable critic had told him just before he left England for Italy: 'Put articles—The horseman of Gerenia, I should say, to avoid obscurity' (*Letters to Clough*, 105). So when J. R. Lowell, nine years later, prevailed on Clough to release his 'Roman poem' for publication in *The Atlantic Monthly*, the envoy was made to read:

> *'But,' so finish the word, 'I was writ in a Roman chamber,*
> *When from Janiculan heights thundered the cannon of France.'*

However that may be, it is hard not to see at least the spectre of Matthew Arnold behind a poem about the brief abortive love affair of an Englishman abroad, in which the two hesitant lovers are named Mary and Claude. Clough knew about Marguerite; he knew too about Mary Claude, since his sister Anne had been on intimate terms with her in Liverpool, and later visited her when she was staying in the Lake district. There is clear evidence that Matthew Arnold, in the months following his first encounter with Marguerite at Thun, was also stirred by the 'pale and pensive' Mary Claude.[1] It is likely enough that Clough, in choosing the key names for his Roman comedy, was having a dig at his friend's recent emotional entanglements: their correspondence of this year 1849 may have been filled on both sides (as it certainly was on Arnold's) with private jokes of this Auden-Isherwood kind.

The *Amours*, unfortunately, did not suit Matthew Arnold any better than *The Bothie* had done, though it did not 'offend' as markedly as the first draft of 'Adam and Eve', Clough's deliberately modernized

[1] Park Honan, in his lively 'A Note on Matthew Arnold in Love', *VN* No. 39, Spring, 1971, 11–15, does his best to suggest that Mary Claude and Marguerite were one and the same; but he is building bricks without straw. The romantic relation with Mary Claude may indeed antedate Marguerite: in a letter of 9 November 1845 (*MS. Bodl. eng. lett. d. 175*) Clough wrote to his sister, in a context of discussion of her friends the Wotherspoons and the Claudes in Liverpool: 'And I hope Matt will not burn his fingers again in the opportunity for so doing which is beginning to present itself. But he is a wary dog, and has been well scalded once.' This may, however, refer to Matt. Harrison, who is 'going to be married' in the continuation of this letter, dated 15 November.

treatment of *The Mystery of the Fall* (*Letters to Clough*, 86, 87). So a year later to 'Dipsychus', that Venetian 'dialogue of the mind with itself' that once again got roughed down on paper in a few weeks of hurried vacation from the 'Sadducees' of University Hall in the early autumn of 1850. One must insist again on the swift drafting of these three major narratives in which so much of the strongest of Clough's work is contained, all written around '*l'an de mon trentiesme age, / Que toutes mes hontes j'eus beues*'. Clough, when the mood was on him and a burning subject presented itself, could lose himself in it and write almost at the pace of a Byron or a Balzac. And this, perhaps, was one of the things Arnold most distrusted about his composition.

For if any Victorian poet is distinguished, where his most serious work is concerned, by 'long choosing and beginning late', it is Matthew Arnold. Professor Super has lately showed (*The Time-Spirit of Matthew Arnold*, 14–17) how the early jottings of the 'Yale Manuscript' all tend in the same direction and 'are recognisably the foundation of some of Arnold's most important poems': 'one of them is almost a summary of "Obermann Once More", a poem that cannot have been begun earlier than 1865'. There is something splendidly Miltonic in this deliberate choice of subjects, prolonged meditation about them, and steady progress with composition when the time was ripe and occasion, or Her Majesty's Inspectorate, served. Yet the product inevitably must be, like Milton's, a highly artificial kind of poetry. We are especially conscious of this with such works as 'Sohrab and Rustum' and 'Balder Dead', where 'Form of Conception', like an architect's master plan, imposes its own rigidity on both structure and decoration. To observe the process on a smaller scale, we have only to think of one of Arnold's extended similes from 'Sohrab', and compare it with one of Clough's in *The Bothie* or the *Amours*. Both are ostensibly 'Homeric', but where Arnold is chiefly pictorial and striving to observe an almost heraldic decorum, Clough is abrupt, functional, and determined to exploit rawly modern subjects and effects.

'Empedocles', in Arnold's total *œuvre*, is the great exception. Here if anywhere one feels the poet's sinews cracking in the effort to unify matter: one sees how in the end he has managed to do it, but the force of the struggle has almost torn him apart. As Kenneth Allott has perceptively remarked, '"Empedocles on Etna" is not what the Arnold who sought an "intellectual deliverance" wanted to say, but what the truth-telling poet was unable not to say . . .' ('A Background for "Empedocles on Etna"', *Essays and Studies*, 1968). It left the poet *sehr zerrissen,* and determined never to risk such volcanic fires again. Clough's equivalent work is 'Dipsychus': if this equally searching poem strikes us now as a good deal more relaxed and human, more genially in touch (thanks to the Spirit) with the real world, that is surely one result of trusting more to spontaneity and the impulse of the moment than to 'form of conception'. There was room in 'Empedocles' for fine stoical speeches in which the modern author could unpack his mind, and for the superbly cadenced lyrics of Callicles by which he might seek to console it. In the baggy monster that is 'Dipsychus' there was room for the resounding rhetoric of 'Easter Day' *and* for '"There is no God," the wicked saith'; for the gondola song and 'As I sat at the café, I said to myself'; for the glimpse of 'the room of an Italian *fille*':

> *The chamber* où vous faites votre affaire
> *Stand(s) nicely fitted up for prayer;*
> *While dim you trace along one end*
> *The Sacred Supper's length extend.*
> *The calm Madonna o'er your head*
> *Smiles,* col bambino, *on the bed*
> *Where—but your chaste ears I must spare—*
> *Where, as we said,* vous faites votre affaire.
>
> ('Dipsychus', IIA, 107–14)

We need only remember the tone of 'The Terrace at Berne', to guess what Arnold would have made of such writing as this.

Yet it is only to Clough that Arnold can write with complete freedom and assurance, with the certainty of not being mentally censored, that lets him slip in such a schoolboy phrase as, 'Goly what a Shite's oracle!' That marvellously Arnoldian early poem 'Resignation' which he was so fond of quoting to Clough—'"Not deep the Poet sees, but wide":—think of this as you gaze from the Cumnor Hill toward Cirencester and Cheltenham' (*Letters to Clough*; 99)—drew from Clough in Rome the deliberately irreverent rejoinder, 'Resignation—to Faustus' ('Now you shall have some sweet pretty verses, in *your* style'):

O Land of Empire, art and love!
What is it that you show me?
A sky for Gods to tread above,
A soil for pigs below me!

The Pantheon—a favourite haunt of Clough's, with its swarm of beggars on the porch and its Christian altars so incongruously ranged under the great open pagan dome—is drawn on for details of all too human Italian habits:

Though priest from prayer stop short to spit
Beside the altar solemn
Must therefore boys turn up to ——
By this Corinthian column?

But having made his point about 'angelic limbs' and 'bestial-filthy function', Clough goes on to write in all seriousness:

So is it: in all ages so,
And in all places man can know,
From homely roots unseen below
In forest-shade in woodland bower
The stem that bears the ethereal flower
Derives that emanative power;
From mixtures fetid foul and sour
Draws juices that those petals fill.

And the conclusion is a fair enough riposte to the poet's lofty stance and distant view Arnold had recommended:

. . . *With resignation fair and meet*
The dirt and refuse of thy street
My philosophic foot shall greet,
So leave but perfect to my eye
Thy columns set against thy sky!
(Poems, 66ff.; Bodleian MS.)

One can see why Arnold reproached Clough for 'the deficiency of the *beautiful'* in his poems: by Arnold's standards, this was a true lack. What is harder to accept is his charge that Clough's poems in general 'are not *natural*' (*Letters to Clough* 66, 98). For this surely—at least between the weaker parts of *Ambarvalia* and the final gathering of simplified, deliberately flattened narrative in '*Mari Magno*'—is just what they so remarkably are. If we can accept the terms 'natural' and 'artificial' as neutral labels indicating two different kinds of poetry, Clough in his middle period is pre-eminently a natural poet, Arnold an artificial one—until, in his mellowest years, he learnt to write naturally (and altogether charmingly) about dogs and cats.

It would be unprofitable to develop any comparison of the work of Arnold and Clough in prose, for here Arnold became a master where Clough remained a mere apprentice. After his struggle to control a persuasive medium for argument in the 1853 Preface, Arnold rapidly developed into one of the most flexible, readable, and consistently entertaining of Victorian prose-writers. Clough's critical prose seldom moves freely; it is too often constrained and self-consciously donnish, though it can at times command a bleak objectivity of statement. Yet where he is inventing a fable, or dramatizing attitudes in dialogue, the qualities of well-bred ease he admired in Restoration writers (and that made him one of the true English masters of light verse) reassert themselves, and he can write with enviable directness and limpidity. Examples may be found in the early 'Conversations of the Earth with the Universe' (Greenberger, Appendix B, 191–6), in 'The Young Cur' (*ibid.*, 146), and in the Epilogue to 'Dipsychus'. Some of the Letters of Parepidemus written in America have the same zest and freshness.

To return to the poetry, and the friendship. Here were two gifted men, thrown together in the first place by shared institutions but also by a strong affinity of mind and feeling, with 'the common quality, now rare, of being unambitious' (*Letters to Clough*, 76). In the Oxford years when they were closest, Clough was 'in great force', splendidly abundant, and probably had more to offer the younger man: we must always remember that at this time Clough seemed established for life and was relatively well off, while Arnold still had his way to make. After 1848 the positions were reversed: Arnold, at whatever cost to his private feelings, made the break with Marguerite and whatever attractions Mary Claude held for him,[1] saw his way clear to a highly

[1] See p. 198 n.

suitable 'Belgravian' marriage and financial independence, and was able to turn immediate loss to gain, both in his public life and in his poetry, by a sheer triumph of will and hard work. Clough, slowly brought to realize that by quitting Oxford he had 'jumped over a ditch, for the fun of the experiment, and would not be disinclined to be once again in a highway with my brethren and companions' (*Correspondence*, I, 290; *NZ Letters*, 202), should have found some compensation in the released flow of poetry that came so freely in these difficult years, yet drew such scant appreciation from his closest friends. Daunted but not defeated, he fell back upon silence, domesticity, and Florence Nightingale. It is understandable that those who were unaware of how much striking and original work he had written since *The Bothie* should see the rest of his life as rather painful anti-climax.

Modern readers, less predisposed to see Clough as a failure, will admire rather the dogged persistence with which he maintained his refusal to conform, and the uncomplaining equanimity with which he finally accepted his much reduced *assiette* for life. Arnold had made his own submission to Cosmarchon, 'The Power of this World' ('Dipsychus', XIII, 71), a good deal earlier, when he accepted the high-handed terms of the Wightman family for his marriage to Fanny Lucy. One may suspect it was some resentment at this, as well as some short-lived jealousy of his younger friend's married state, that provoked the second serious rift in the friendship about the time of Clough's departure for America in 1852. We who look back across the years can never regret this temporary misunderstanding, because it provoked so generous and tactful a response, so noble a defence, from the younger and already more successful man. The patience and magnanimity of Arnold's letters to Clough in 1853 are the clearest testimony we have of the true nature of their relationship, and the highest (because most private) tribute to Arnold's essential humanity. On the deep emotion of these letters, 'Thyrsis' is but an elegant gloss.

As for the poetry—that, in the end, is a matter of preference. Some people will always prefer plain fare to cake, and it is at least arguable that there is more common daily sustenance in Clough's verse than in Arnold's. What should be possible, now they can be seen not as amateur and professional, but as two considerable Victorian poets fully deserving study in their own right, is an understanding of how admirably they complement each other—the Martha and Mary, poetically speaking, of the industrial age. For Clough *did* succeed in getting into the world as Arnold, for all his travels at home and abroad, did not; did succeed in assimilating elements of Victorian life that no one before Hardy and Meredith could bring into the strict domain of poetry. And Arnold, for his part, succeeded in controlling form and idea, in blending both into a poetry of high seriousness that was genuinely a criticism of life, in a manner which makes Browning seem fussy and Tennyson flaccid. '*Honorate l'altissimo poeta*' can be said of Arnold, as it can never be said of Clough; for him a line of his own is the best commentary: 'Bread is it, if not angels' food.'

On sober consideration, 'Empedocles' is decidedly Arnold's most impressive poem, containing more of the whole man than any other. For Clough, *Amours de Voyage*—that ironic and delicately-shaded modern comedy—is the nearest he came to a complete and self-sufficient work of art, where execution most closely matches conception. For all their looseness of form. *The Bothie* and 'Dipsychus' seem to me more interesting poems than 'Sohrab' or 'Balder': it is only in the middle range of the *paysage moralisé* or lyrical meditation ('The Scholar-Gipsy', 'Thyrsis', 'The Strayed Reveller') that Arnold can claim a clear superiority, even over such telling pieces as 'Easter Day' and 'The Shadow'. In pure or elegiac lyric over a narrow range Arnold has probably more short poems that are completely satisfying; but for pungency and bite, apart from 'Growing Old' he has little to match 'The Latest Decalogue', 'In the Great Metropolis', or '*In Stratis Viarum*'. In lighter satirical verse, of course, Clough is *hors concours*: only the sparkling *Friendship's Garland* rivals him in this kind.

Which brings us—inevitably and inadequately—to 'Thyrsis'. I am sure this is more properly regarded as a continuation of 'The Scholar-Gipsy'—Arnold's most perfect poem—than as an independent tribute to a friend; and Clough, who had fully appreciated the earlier poem, would have been as happy, one must suppose, to admire its companion-piece. 'No Thyrsis he,' J. C. Shairp stoutly affirmed of its ostensible subject, when he paid his own over-sentimental tribute to Clough:

No Thyrsis thou, for old Idyllic lays,
But a broad-bowed, deep-souled, much suffering man,
Within whose veins, thrilled by these latter days,
The ruddy life blood ran.

Warm throbbing from a heart as hero's brave,
Yet sensitive and tender as a child's;
Stirred with all human passion glad or grave,
By shores and mountain wilds . . .[1]

No Thyrsis indeed, within the terms of Arnold's poem—*The Bothie* alone is sufficient answer to that. But in terms of the quest, of the signal-tree (that may have been Dr. Arnold's oak or elm; and Clough—who quietly corrected Macaulay on the elms of Magdalen—would have seen to it that Arnold got the genus right),[2] the poem gravely and beautifully celebrates the high hopes and longings of those earlier Oxford years, and the sober aftermath to which they had come. Elsewhere in public Arnold had paid eloquent tribute to the quality of Clough's life; here he could hymn with nostalgia the things they had once most cared for, and never entirely given up. And if Thyrsis is only brought back into the poem at the end by 'a kind of confidence trick', as Michael Thorpe puts it (*Matthew Arnold*, 1969, 85), at least the monody gave Clough one sort of immortality through the lean years when his reputation was at lowest ebb. Not the least gain of the new attention Clough has secured in this last phase, is that it is now possible for his admirers to read 'Thyrsis' straight, without undue resentment at some of its factual distortions and unintended slurs.

Graves and their location, as Professor Culler has admirably demonstrated (*Imaginative Reason*, Chap. 8), had a special significance for Matthew Arnold: they were part of his symbolic landscape. Of the three poets commemorated in that marble panel in Rugby Chapel, Clough—against every expectation—died first, and is buried not far from Landor (who followed him three years later) in the tree-shaded Protestant cemetery in Florence, islanded in the Piazza Donatello outside the old Porta a Pinti.[3] This *Camposanto degli Inglesi*—where lie also Elizabeth Barrett Browning and Holman Hunt's wife and the mother of Anthony Trollope—had been declared a burial-ground for foreign heretics as early as 1827; for Clough it would be some

[1] Quoted in William Knight, *Principal Shairp and his Friends*, 1888.
[2] See Sir Francis Wylie's delightful essay on 'The Scholar-Gipsy Country', *Commentary*, 357.
[3] See Enrico Barfucci, *Il Camposanto degli Inglesi*, Firenze 1951.

consolation to know that, on Swiss property, there was less risk of the kind of nuisance he had wryly deplored on other sacred Italian ground. Arnold lived on to find wider fame in the world and wave of men, and at the last a quiet grave at Laleham in the Thames valley he so loved. These two friends were divided in death, but in life they were not divided: and either might have welcomed on his tombstone those lines to commemorate all intrepid doubters:

> *It fortifies my soul to know*
> *That, though I perish, Truth is so . . .*

Neither man, in the long run, had 'traduced his friends, nor flattered his enemies, nor disparaged what he admired, nor praised what he despised'. And with this clear assurance, we may leave them.

7: *Arnold's Social and Political Thought*

P. J. KEATING

'The majority are bad,' said one of the wise men of Greece: but he was a pagan. *Discourses in America*

I

IN HIS THOUGHTFUL and sympathetic essay 'Matthew Arnold and the Educationists', John Dover Wilson argued that the popularity of *Culture and Anarchy* has created a misleading impression of Arnold's true stature as a political thinker: written during a period of intense political excitement it placed a greater reliance on, 'the State as a centre of authority and on the necessity of a firm executive than in any other of his political writings before or after', and this has tended to obscure his passionate belief in social equality. Dover Wilson was himself writing at a time of heightened political feelings and his reasoning was influenced by the need to save Arnold from those twentieth-century critics who would have relegated him, along with Carlyle, to a dark footnote in history as one of the intellectual founding fathers of totalitarianism. We are offered instead a Liberal Civil Servant Arnold who was strongly critical of excessive centralization, and for whom State authority (apart from the need to keep order during times of crisis) was that 'which is accorded by the best in us to our guiding ideals and principles'. The essay closes with an eloquent tribute to R. H. Tawney as representing the true type of Arnold's heirs.[1]

Much of what Dover Wilson was saying needed, and still needs to be said, but he was certainly over-reacting, and to over-react to Arnold

[1] 'Matthew Arnold and the Educationists', *The Social and Political Ideas of Some Representative Thinkers of the Victorian Age*, ed F. J. C. Hearnshaw, 1933, 165–93.

is to lose sight of him almost entirely, for elusiveness is his most characteristic quality. It is one of the tantalizing, and important, ironies of Arnold's continuing influence that the man who was so proud of his ability to graft instantly memorable labels onto social groups and individuals of the Victorian period, should consistently elude the attempts by others to classify his own social and political beliefs. We do not get very far by calling him an authoritarian, but we get little further by seeing him as a Liberal Civil Servant. The position is complicated by Arnold's own habit of fixing labels to himself which he either immediately qualified or which he intended as ironic. He is a Liberal, but 'a Liberal of the future'; he can write that, 'on the reasonableness of the Conservative party our best hope at present depends' and also 'I should never myself vote for a Tory'; he will proclaim, as a cardinal doctrine, that 'the critic must keep out of the region of immediate practice in the political, social, humanitarian sphere',[1] and yet argue for very specific reforms in his essays on Ireland, local government and education. Many of his letters to the press he signed pseudonymously as 'A Lover of Light' which may sometimes be intended seriously, sometimes ironically. And throughout much of his most attractive work, there is certainly an undercurrent of authoritarianism, a feeling that, if pushed far enough, the lover of light really *would* hurl the enemies of reason from the Tarpeian Rock.

There is clearly much in this that seems contradictory and helps justify the charge made by his Victorian critics that Arnold was an unsystematic and confused thinker. Yet Arnold has survived as a living classic in a way that has been denied to Frederic Harrison or James Fitzjames Stephen, and, it is reasonably safe to conjecture, is more widely read today than, say, John Stuart Mill or Walter Bagehot, neither of whom could be criticized as unsystematic or confused. Arnold's survival is a recognition of his representative nature: his centrality, as it seems looking back over the space of a hundred years, is more a matter of what he stands for than of any achieved body of social analysis. As F. R. Leavis has pointed out, to say that Arnold cannot be

[1] 'The Future of Liberalism', *CPW*, IX, 138; 'The Nadir of Liberalism', *Essays, Letters and Reviews by Matthew Arnold*, ed Fraser Neiman (referred to below as *Neiman*), 261, 278; *Letters*, II, 304; 'The Function of Criticism at the Present Time', *CPW*, III, 275.

summarized is to indicate not his weaknesses and inconsistencies as a thinker, but his essential strength.[1]

It is for this reason that it is misleading to try to draw attention away from *Culture and Anarchy*, and by concentrating on Arnold's more practical proposals turn him into a Liberal Civil Servant. For *Culture and Anarchy* considered, as it should always be, together with 'My Countrymen' and *Friendship's Garland*, did not suffer from being the product of the threatened turmoil of the 1860s: on the contrary, it draws its real force from these circumstances. The main points being made in these books had certainly already been developed by Arnold in a more rational manner in his earlier essays, and the existence of this work (the fact that the argument is already familiar to the reading public he is concerned with) is an important underlying assumption on Arnold's part which allows him a freedom to exploit his irony to the full, something he could not otherwise have done. In addition, the Fenian outrages and Hyde Park 'riots' coming at a time when Arnold was fully engaged in a debate with his critics over *Essays in Criticism* (1865), and more specifically 'The Function of Criticism at the Present Time', forced upon him a challenge he could not avoid without seeming to backtrack and thereby surrendering any claim to seriousness as a thinker and social critic. His considered response is to be found in 'My Countrymen', *Culture and Anarchy*, and *Friendship's Garland*, which were published in serial form as parts of a running debate between February 1866 and November 1870. If there is less sustained reasoning than in his previous essays on education and society, there is a more passionate sense of involvement in central issues, and, with his discovery of a characteristic mode of expression, a different kind of clarity which he employs to goad his critics and then to soar above the ensuing debate. Even today readers of those polemical works of the 1860s feel the irritation which Arnold's method was meant deliberately to provoke, and may be tempted by Dover Wilson's advice to seek a more comfortable Arnold in the educational reports and political articles. But the comfort is illusory. *Culture and Anarchy* and *Friendship's Garland* are no less representative than, say, 'Equality' or 'The Future of Liberalism'; nor do the later works offer a view of society significantly different from that to be found in the earlier. In 1882 Arnold made this point himself: 'I wish I could promise to change my old phrases for

[1] Introduction to *Mill on Bentham and Coleridge*, 1950, 36.

new ones, and to pass from my one practical suggestion to some other. . . . But I fear there is no chance of this happening. What has been the burden of my song hitherto, will probably have, so far as I can at present see, to be the burden of it till the end.'[1]

II

The criticism that Arnold's views were divorced from real life, the product of a dilettantish aesthetic rather than a man tested by the pressures of everyday events, angered him more than any other. Time and again he returns to it:

> That Alcibiades, the editor of the *Morning Star*, taunts me . . . with living out of the world and knowing nothing of life and men. That great austere toiler, the editor of the *Daily Telegraph*, upbraids me,—but kindly, and more in sorrow than in anger,—for trifling with aesthetics and poetical fancies, while he himself, in that arsenal of his in Fleet Street, is bearing the burden and heat of the day. . . . While, finally, Mr Frederic Harrison . . . gets moved to an almost stern moral impatience, to behold, as he says, 'Death, sin, cruelty stalk among us, filling their maws with innocence and youth,' and me, in the midst of the general tribulation, handing out my pouncet-box.[2]

The same objection recurs in his later work, though now the constant need to defend himself has bred a tone of weariness: 'I think I hear people saying: *There! he has got on his old hobby again!* Really, people ought rather to commend the strictly and humbly practical character of my writings.'[3] And Arnold is not being ironic here: he did see himself as a practical man, and his criticisms of Victorian society as fundamental. It is not difficult to abstract from his writings a large number of specific reforms which he either advocated or supported, and to point to moments in his life when he took practical steps to help publicize or bring about those reforms. He supported the enfranchisement of agricultural labourers in 1884 on the grounds that it was better for them to be their own spokesmen than to rely on others;

[1] *CPW*, X, 75.
[2] *Culture and Anarchy*, *CPW*, V, 115–16.
[3] 'The Incompatibles', *CPW*, IX, 283.

argued passionately for the establishment of Catholic schools and universities in Ireland, and the expropriation of bad landlords; attacked the Real Estate Intestacy Bill as perpetuating that social inequality which he saw as the cause of so much misery and discontent in England;[1] and, in the face of considerable hostility and derision, proclaimed throughout his life the need for a central State authority which would transcend class divisions and partisan self-seeking.

On educational matters above all others he demonstrated an intense concern which ranged from broad statements of general policy to minute criticisms of school syllabuses. For thirty-five years he earned his living as an Inspector of Schools, and was on several occasions commissioned to examine and report upon educational systems in European countries. These experiences provided him with the detailed knowledge of conditions in English schools and the confidence in making comparative judgements which distinguish not only the books which resulted from his journeys abroad, *The Popular Education of France* (1861), *A French Eton* (1864), and *Schools and Universities on the Continent* (1868), but his writings as a whole. He can be plain to the point of boredom on the required changes in English education:

> What is really needed is to follow the precedent of the Elementary Education Act, by requiring the provision throughout the country of a proper supply of secondary schools, with proper buildings and accommodations, at a proper fee, and with proper guarantees given by the teachers in the shape either of a university degree or of a special certificate for secondary instruction. An inquiry, as under that Act, would have to be made as to the fulfilment of the necessary conditions by the actual schools now professing to meet the demand for secondary instruction, and as to the correspondence of the supply of schools fulfilling those conditions with the supply fixed after due calculation as requisite. The existing resources for secondary instruction, if judiciously co-ordered and utilised, would prove to be immense; but undoubtedly gaps would have to be filled, an annual State grant and municipal grants would be necessary.[2]

[1] *CPW*, IX, 140; 'Irish Catholicism and British Liberalism', *CPW*, VIII, 321–47; 'The Incompatibles', *CPW*, IX, 252; 'Equality', *CPW*, VIII, 277–305 (*passim*) and *CPW*, V, 200–5.

[2] 'Porro Unum Est Necessarium', *CPW*, VIII, 365–6.

Nor was he content to remain simply a theorist, but took every opportunity to propagate his views. He played an active part in opposing Robert Lowe's plans to allot government grants to schools according to the numbers of their students capable of passing an examination set by the School Inspectors—the 'Payment by Results' controversy as it came to be called—and he both reviewed and edited text books for use in secondary schools. Letters by him criticizing educational policy were frequently published in newspapers and periodicals, and his books were, as he told his mother, directed at an audience of influential people.[1] They were directed at selected members of that audience in a more obvious manner as well. Gladstone frequently received copies of Arnold's books ('Pray do not think of troubling yourself to acknowledge it—but if you could find time to give a glance at the introduction, and at one or two of the later chapters, I should be very glad'), and when T. H. Huxley was appointed a member of The Royal Commission on Scientific Instruction and the Advancement of Science, Arnold immediately sent him a copy of his *Popular Education of France*. Cobden received a copy of *A French Eton* and on replying that he was more interested in the condition of the lower classes, was given a stern lecture by Arnold on middle class education and the superiority of the French over the English peasant.[2] As Arnold's views rarely coincided with those held by the government department for which he worked, he had good cause to say on his retirement: 'Our Government here in England takes a large and liberal view of what it considers a man's private affairs, and so I have been enabled to survive as an inspector for 35 years; and to the Government I at least owe this—to have been allowed to survive for 35 years.'[3]

It is not, then, difficult to make out a case for a practical Arnold, or even to see him as a man with a programme, but to do so would be grotesquely inadequate. Indeed, it is upon such men that Arnold directs his most scathing criticism, finding their adherence to and propagation of any given programme or set of political beliefs, a denial of what he

[1] *Letters*, I, 158.

[2] W. H. G. Armytage, 'Matthew Arnold and W. E. Gladstone: Some New Letters', UTQ, XVIII, April 1849, 219; 'Matthew Arnold and T. H. Huxley: Some New Letters', *RES*, XXV, July 1949, 251.

[3] 'Arnold's Speech on his Retirement', *Neiman*, 307.

himself felt to be the most urgent need of the nineteenth century—disinterestedness, or, as he defined it in *On Translating Homer*, 'the endeavour, in all branches of knowledge,—theology, philosophy, history, art, science—to see the object as in itself it really is'.[1] In so far as Arnold may be said to have a programme at all, it is summed up in the one word 'disinterestedness'. The reforms he supports are justified as being those in which the disinterested observer can believe, and his essays are almost always attempts to illustrate the methods he advocated in others, and this includes, though indirectly and sometimes very indirectly, those fiercely rhetorical pieces where total involvement is employed in the name of disinterestedness. Even when talking on a subject in which he could be expected to have a strong personal involvement, for example the Copyright question, he claims to be speaking for neither authors nor publishers but as 'one whose sole wish is to let things appear to him fairly and naturally, and as they really are'.[2] This, in Arnold's view, is to be truly practical, and it is both the most important single informing quality in his work, and the criterion he employs to judge the beliefs and actions of others. The marked changes in tone, moving from the restrained and balanced reasoning of *England and the Italian Question* and 'Democracy', through the manipulated complexities of *Culture and Anarchy* and the defiant bravado of *Friendship's Garland*, to the more staid *Irish Essays*, rarely represent any kind of significant shift in Arnold's intellectual position, but rather reflect the changing nature of his relationship with readers and critics, and a growing awareness of the difficulty of his self-appointed task.

His analysis of English society relies for its justification almost entirely upon his own insight and reasoning power, and allows no influence of political party or religious doctrine. Like the young Carlyle, from whom he learnt so much, his main concern is to awaken public consciousness to 'the signs of the times', or to use one of Arnold's many similar phrases 'the way the world is going'. Again like Carlyle, the study of the past performs a central function in this kind of analysis because it is only through what is felt as the ever changing pattern of history that the determining forces can be perceived and influenced. Arnold's use of the term '*Zeitgeist*' or 'time spirit' to

[1] 'On Translating Homer', *CPW*, I, 140.

[2] *CPW*, IX, 117.

describe this process of change has provoked a great deal of hostile comment. In a thorough study of the concept Fraser Neiman has demonstrated how Arnold's use of it fluctuates: in his earlier work it can be taken to mean, 'the temper of the times, with the additional idea that time is a local, changeable phenomenon opposing eternal values', while in the later work, 'Zeitgeist is an aspect of the eternal, promoting change as a manifestation of its own being.'[1] Of these two definitions, it is the first which Arnold intends in writing of social and political issues. He employs it to illustrate the enormous changes taking place in Western society during the nineteenth century, and to inculcate ideals which will serve to modify, and to some extent harness, those changes for the benefit of mankind. That sense of divine intervention which is so obviously present in much of Arnold's poetry, is held largely in abeyance in his social criticism where human responsibility must in no way be weakened or undermined. The role of the disinterested observer is to distinguish the forces making for change in society *and* to convince others of the truth of his interpretation.

In 'My Countrymen' Arnold describes history as being a 'series of waves, coming gradually to a head and then breaking . . . as the successive waves come up, one nation is seen at the top of this wave, and then another of the next',[2] and this image, with its connotations of naturalness and inevitability, expresses clearly enough Arnold's sense of an historical process at work. It is the continuous nature of this process that Arnold most wishes to convey, and his social criticism gains much of its emotive strength from the use of two contrasting groups of images, those of stasis, blind stability, and stagnancy on the one hand, and those of growth, development, movement, on the other; the former always carry Arnold's disapproval, the latter his approval, the sole but important qualification being that any growth, development or movement must be governed by reason. The pace and radical nature of social change in the nineteenth century has given, Arnold argues, a greater sense of urgency than ever before to the disinterested contemplation of the historical process, the need to 'find a true point of view', and the man who can discover this (and Arnold never doubted he had done so) becomes the potential prophet of nineteenth-century society:

[1] 'The Zeitgeist of Matthew Arnold', *PMLA*, LXXII, 1957, 978–9.
[2] *CPW*, V, 30.

> He who has found that point of view, he who adequately comprehends this spectacle, has risen to the comprehension of his age: he who communicates that point of view to his age, he who interprets to it that spectacle, is one of his age's intellectual deliverers.[1]

For Arnold the principal transforming force at work in Western society is the movement towards democracy, and the nation most fitted to ride the nineteenth-century wave of history is France who has recognized this fact and tried to communicate its truth to other countries. In his first published essay on a political topic, *England and the Italian Question* (1859), he describes the time as one 'when the masses of the European populations begin more and more to make their voice heard respecting their country's affairs . . . when sovereigns and statesmen must more and more listen to this voice, can less and less act without taking it into account'; and in 'Democracy', the introductory essay to *The Popular Education of France*, he describes this 'movement of democracy' as being 'like other operations of nature' which 'merits properly neither blame nor praise'.[2] It is both natural and inevitable, and to stand against it is to defy the lessons offered by history, in this case particularly the French Revolution which inspired the 'work of making human life, hampered by a past which it has outgrown, natural and rational'.[3] There, as always in Arnold, is the conviction that social structures only ever possess a relative significance: they reflect a society's dominant needs, and must change as those needs change: 'There arrive periods, when, the circumstances and conditions of government having changed, the guiding maxims of government ought to change also.'[4] It is simply not true, as is so often charged against him, that Arnold admired everything French to the detriment of everything English; the whole direction of his criticism points away from this view, and there are many specific disavowals, such as his reply to a French correspondent that he doesn't want the English to be 'café-haunting, dominoes-playing Frenchmen, but rather some third thing, neither the Frenchmen nor their present selves'.[5] But in their

[1] 'On the Modern Element in Literature', *CPW*, I, 20.

[2] *CPW*, I, 81; II, 7.

[3] 'My Countrymen', *CPW*, V, 15.

[4] 'Democracy', *CPW*, II, 3.

[5] 'A Courteous Explanation', *CPW*, V, 34.

acceptance of the democratic spirit the French have much to teach the English, and, as we have seen, it is a lesson too crucial to be avoided. Louis Napoleon is praised for possessing '*largely and deeply interwoven in his constitution, the popular fibre*'; France for being 'the country in Europe where *the people* is most alive'; and the French educational system is hailed as one which is founded on the principle of the state as a unifying and egalitarian corporate body of right reason.[1] As the chorus of Arnold's foreign friends put it in 'My Countrymen': 'What is the modern problem? to make human life, the life of society, all through, more natural and rational; to have the greatest possible number of one's nation happy. Here is the standard by which we are to try ourselves and one another now, as national grandeur, in the old regal and aristocratical conception of it, was the standard formerly.'[2] In Arnold's view, this problem the French have recognized and tried to solve while the English have scarcely begun even to understand it.

The main obstacle preventing England from following the example of France is a social structure based upon a rigid system of classes and dominated by an aristocracy who, whatever their good qualities, are quite incapable of seeing 'how the world is going':

> Members of an aristocracy, forming more or less a caste, and living in a society of their own, have little personal experience of the effect of ideas upon the masses of the people. They run little chance of catching the influence of these ideas by contact. On the other hand, an aristocracy has naturally a great respect for the established order of things, for the *fait accompli*. It is itself a *fait accompli*, it is satisfied with things as they are, it is, above everything, prudent. Exactly the reverse of the masses, who regard themselves as in a state of transition, who are by no means satisfied with things as they are, who are, above everything, adventurous.[3]

Here once again is the conflict between rigidity and stasis, the refusal or inability to change, and the movement and growth implied by 'a state of transition' and the 'adventurous' nature of the masses. Arnold's historicism does not allow these contrasting qualities only to classes of

[1] *CPW*, I, 81; III, 265; II *passim*.
[2] *CPW*, V, 18.
[3] *England and the Italian Question*, *CPW*, I, 83.

people—periods of time are defined in similar terms. In a period of concentration, such as England experienced in the eighteenth century, the aristocracy in speaking for the few spoke also for the many and epitomized the spirit of the age; but in a period of expansion, the nineteenth century, different qualities are demanded and there is no virtue in being a *fait accompli*. Aristocratic England had won its greatest victory at Waterloo, but it was incapable of understanding that its military opponents had already won an even greater victory, that of the 'idea-moved masses'. Nor did the military triumph have any chance of stopping democracy from spreading throughout the Western world, from holding back the waves of history. Instead of acknowledging the inevitability of democratic change, the English aristocracy offered those qualities appropriate only to an age of concentration, with the result that, 'At the very moment when democracy becomes less and less disposed to follow and to admire, aristocracy becomes less and less qualified to command and to captivate.'[1] In *Culture and Anarchy*, Arnold's most sustained assault on the imperviousness of the English to the natural and inevitable movement of social change, the aristocracy are labelled the 'Barbarians', men isolated on their country estates, dispensing 'sweetness' without 'light', and providing for other classes a social model which lacks intelligence, morality, and responsibility; in *Friendship's Garland*, they are reduced to the representative figure of Lord Lumpington whose name alone sufficiently indicates his uselessness in an epoch 'when new ideas are powerfully fermenting in a society'.[2]

With the working class and the poor Arnold was notably less at ease. His contact with them had been primarily in his role as a school inspector, and for a man who placed such emphasis on light, intelligence, or '*Geist*', this meant that they were irrevocably associated in his mind with ignorance and illiteracy. They were, to use one of his own favourite words in this context, raw, and rawness was even more dangerous than aristocratic barbarianism and middle class philistinism because—and Arnold never wavered in this belief—the future belonged to the mass, which is to say the majority or democracy, not the workers. He feared the fact that the working class was becoming a

[1] 'Democracy', *CPW*, II, 15.

[2] *Ibid.*, *CPW*, II, 12.

powerful and well-organized force in society, and he deplored the support this movement was given by a handful of middle class intellectuals. 'Sir, I tell you confidentially that I saw the other day with my own eyes that powerful young publicist, Mr Frederic Harrison, in full evening dress, furbishing up a guillotine.'[1] He also tended to equate working class agitation with destructive anarchy: as Raymond Williams has neatly put it: 'The Hyde Park railings were down, and it was not Arnold's best self which rose at the sight of them.'[2] More surprisingly, he attached far less importance to working class education than might have been expected, even going so far as to tell an audience of working men in Ipswich that he would talk to them of 'public schools for the middle classes' because, 'Even so long as twenty years ago, popular education was already launched.'[3] But while Arnold in some cases underestimated, and in others over-reacted to, the working class, the same is true of his response to the middle and upper classes as well. To place one's faith in any single class was to go against the spirit of the age, to perpetuate the social divisions which Arnold saw as destined to evaporate with the growth of mass democracy.

In one of his most important lectures, given at about the same time as the lecture to the Ipswich working men, Arnold mocked the 'religion of inequality' propounded, in the name of the English nation, by Froude, Lowe, and Gladstone. He argues against this that 'inequality' is actually the root cause of England's social ills, and attacks the assumption that 'our signal inequality of classes and property is expedient for our civilisation and welfare'. As always he is urging recognition of the facts of social change, and the urgency of adapting to them: 'Our present organisation has been an appointed stage in our growth; it has been of good use, and has enabled us to do great things. But the use is at an end, and the stage is over. . . . Certainly equality will never of itself alone give us a perfect civilisation. But, with such inequality as ours, a perfect civilisation is impossible.'[4]

One aspect of English society tolerated by the 'religion of inequality' is the squalid poverty which 'brutalises' the working class. Arnold may have underestimated working class respectability and over-reacted to

[1] *Friendship's Garland*, *CPW*, V, 76.

[2] *Culture and Society*, 1958, 133.

[3] 'Ecce, Convertimur Ad Gentes', *CPW*, IX, 7.

[4] 'Equality', *CPW*, VIII, 285, 304.

working class militancy, but he demonstrates a Johnsonian contempt for any cant about working class poverty. In the Royal Institution lecture, he counters Gladstone's claim that the English love inequality, with a brief vignette of the social structure of Scotland; at the summit 'a landed aristocracy fills the scene' squeezing back and effacing the other classes, while at the base, 'the hardly human horror, the abjection and uncivilisedness of Glasgow'. In *Friendship's Garland*, Arminius is made ironically to express Arnold's own view of the condition of the London poor in the dreadful winter of 1866–7: 'About the state of the streets he was bad enough, but about the poor frozen-out working men who went singing without let or hindrance before our houses, he quite made my blood creep. "The dirge of a society *qui s'en va*," he used to call their pathetic songs.' And most memorably there is the fierce debunking of Robert Buchanan's theories of 'divine philoprogentiveness' in *Culture and Anarchy*.[1]

Concentration by critics on Arnold's mockery of the English obsession with individual freedom, with 'doing as one likes', has tended to obscure what is in fact one of the most attractive and fundamental aspects of his social philosophy—the conviction that reforms can and should be effected, that the ills of society can be cured. The spirit of the age, the *Zeitgeist*, is merely a metaphor which expresses dominant trends, in this case the movement towards mass democracy. The changes indicated are natural and inevitable, but the form those changes take is not in any sense predetermined; this is a human responsibility made possible only by an understanding of the spirit of the age. To try to bring about reforms without dispassionate comprehension is simply to contribute to the 'chaos of false tendencies, wasted efforts, impotent conclusions' which typifies the nineteenth century.[2] Poverty and ignorance have no part in the civilization which Arnold wants established, but at such a time they can be dealt with only in relation to root causes and ultimate aims, and it is these Arnold is concerned to reveal in his analysis of the English class system. In his tri-partite division, the past belonged to the aristocracy, the future to democracy, while the present belongs firmly to the middle class, 'the heart of the English nation'.[3]

[1] *Ibid.*, *CPW*, VIII, 303; *CPW*, V, 65, 214–15.

[2] *On Translating Homer: Last Words*, *CPW*, I, 172.

[3] 'My Countrymen', *CPW*, V, 4.

It is because Arnold truly believes the middle class to be 'the heart of the English nation' (the ironic use of the phrase in *Friendship's Garland* is directed to reinforcing a firm belief) that he concentrates so much upon it. The first of his characteristic works of social analysis, 'Democracy', is a measured, unironic, plea to the middle classes to see themselves as they really are (in effect, as always, to accept themselves as Arnold sees they really are):

> No one esteems them more than I do; but those who esteem them most, and who most believe in their capabilities, can render them no better service than by pointing out in what they underrate their deficiencies, and how their deficiencies, if unremedied, may impair their future. They want culture and dignity, they want ideas. Aristocracy has culture and dignity; democracy has readiness for new ideas, and ardour for what ideas it possesses. Of these, our middle class has the last only; ardour for the ideas it already possesses.[1]

In compensation Arnold praises the middle classes for their industriousness in business matters, and their firm belief in individual liberty, virtues which are vitiated by an unwillingness to open their minds to a fresh climate of opinion. The danger is that like the aristocracy they will rest contented with their achievements and declare themselves a *fait accompli*. So far as the aristocracy are concerned this scarcely matters, for their day is over, but nineteenth-century industrial society, based economically on free-trade and politically on Liberalism, is, for Arnold, the creation of the middle classes, and to rest content is to surrender the next great step—the transformation of a wealthy society into a civilized society. Ardour for what one 'already possesses' or what one already is, leads to smugness and self-satisfaction, to, as Arnold was to spend the greater part of his life proclaiming, a faith in mere machinery. Most seriously of all, it denies the possibility of life as growth or development, even in effect denies that life is or should be concerned with any such thing.

As it became clear to Arnold that the middle classes were not going to listen to him, his exhortations gave way to angry, very often bitter, portraits of them; still, certainly, ready enough to allow that, 'Their love of industry, trade, and wealth, is certainly prodigious; and their

[1] *CPW*, II, 23.

example has done us a great deal of good,' but now rejecting balance in a relentless forcing home of the narrowness and stultifying meanness of middle class life:

> Drugged with business, your middle class seems to have its sense blunted for any stimulus . . . except religion; it has a religion, narrow, unintelligent, repulsive. All sincere religion does something for the spirit, raises a man out of the bondage of his merely bestial part, and saves him; but the religion of your middle class is the very lowest form of intelligential life which one can imagine as saving. What other enjoyments have they? The newspapers, a sort of eating and drinking which are not to our taste, a literature of books almost entirely religious or semi-religious, books utterly unreadable by an educated class anywhere, but which your middle class consumes, they say, by the hundred thousand; and in their evenings, for a great treat, a lecture on teetotalism or nunneries. Can any life be imagined more hideous, more dismal, more unenviable?[1]

It is a destructive, if often very amusing, technique, and has provoked the frequent charge that it is not merely a reaction to vulgarity, but 'is surely vulgar in itself . . . a kind of witty and malicious observation better suited to minor fiction',[2] and it is not difficult to see the justice of such a criticism. But Arnold survives it, and has survived it for a hundred years, with a force that renders weak the comparison with minor fiction. At its most bitter or 'vulgar' his work displays a concentrated vigour which directs us back time and again to his central concerns. It is the technique of a propagandist whose social analysis is allowed to go only so far as those concerns dictate, and satire and irony are his natural weapons. In this he belongs properly with social critics of the nineteenth century such as Cobbett, Carlyle, Ruskin and Morris, rather than with Newman or Mill, with whom—on the grounds of his own emphasis on objectivity and culture—one might be tempted to place him.

In urging the acceptance of State action by the middle classes, especially in the field of education, Arnold was asking them to modify their belief in laissez faire politics (on which their wealth and assertion of personal liberty depended), and to give up their identity as 'the heart

[1] *CPW*, V, 19.

[2] Raymond Williams, *Culture and Society, ed. cit.*, 116.

of the English nation', in order to work in concert with 'that impulse which drives society as a whole,—no longer individuals and limited classes only, but the mass of a community—to develop itself with the utmost possible fulness and freedom'.[1] It was a great deal to ask, and, as Arnold recognized, the force of the historical past, if not the spirit of the age, was against him. His mockery of the religion of Nonconformity and the gradual accumulative process of parliamentary reforms (of which, for Arnold, the Deceased Wife's Sister Bill, was the type), amounted to an attack on the most cherished traditions of middle class life. When his middle class readers were slow to respond, he asked them to admit that not only were they narrow-minded, ugly, intolerant, and ignorant, but that their cherished traditions were responsible for their condition. It was not an attractive proposition, and when the awaited response did come it caricatured Arnold as the languid and unpractical aesthete.

The rather bland assumption by Arnold that the middle classes should be willing to discard their past appears curious, coming as it does from someone whose approach is largely historicist, but it does not really involve a contradiction. Indeed it provides a further neat illustration of Arnold's extreme selectivity and consistency in such matters. The past in itself has no attraction for him; it is only in so far as the past illuminates, guides, or acts in any way as a model for the present, that he speaks with approval of its study, as he does variously in 'On the Modern Element', 'The Function of Criticism at the Present Time', and chapter 4 of *Culture and Anarchy*. When the past is invoked against or appears in conflict with the spirit of the age (as, for example, in the widespread Victorian concern with the Middle Ages, the 'great frippery shop' as Arnold calls them;[2] or the lingering influence of Hebraism, strictness of conscience, which is no longer needed, as against the much needed Hellenism, spontaneity of consciousness)—then it must be rejected—the *Zeitgeist* demands it. As modern government should be concerned pre-eminently with the problems created by the establishment of mass-democracy, class divisions are seen as an anachronism, and the defining qualities they encourage as severe hindrances to the rational solution of social problems.

[1] 'Democracy', *CPW*, II, 8.

[2] 'Civilisation in the United States', *Five Uncollected Essays, ed. cit.*, 51.

Arnold's answer to this difficulty is the State, defined in Burke's words as, 'the nation in its collective and corporate character', and in Arnold's gloss as 'the representative acting-power of the nation'.[1] In serving this representative function the State surmounts the limitations of the individual classes, drawing what is best from each and acting on behalf of the whole. It also provides a centre of excellence thus destroying the hierarchical nature of English society, in which each class, incapable of recognizing and correcting its own deficiencies, apes the manners of the class above. The Populace are in training as Philistines, the Philistines envy the Aristocracy, and the Aristocracy are content to accept their surface culture as the real thing. This argument, implicit in *Culture and Anarchy*, was later polished into one of Arnold's eye-catching sentences and used repeatedly by him: 'Our inequality materialises our upper class, vulgarises our middle class, brutalises our lower.'[2]

III

With all this said—the practical nature of many of his proposals acknowledged and his analysis of English society milked for as much consistency as it can offer—it remains to be stressed once again that Arnold's ultimate significance lies elsewhere. The charges made against him by his critics, or 'enemies' as Arnold preferred to call them, carry too much weight to be easily dismissed. Arnold *is* grotesquely selective in the qualities he allots to the different classes; the terms he uses *are* often vaguely defined and calculated to avoid rational debate; he *was* viciously unfair to his opponents, so much and so brilliantly so that students of the Victorian period need to be warned against accepting Arnold's portraits of, say, Frederic Harrison, Cobden, Bright and Lowe, as the final or even the first word. It is futile to attempt to defend Arnold too rigorously against these charges, but it is equally futile to believe that such charges obliterate Arnold's claim to survival; he was aware of this himself: 'And here I think I see my enemies waiting for me with a hungry joy in their eyes. But I shall elude them.'[3] And elude them he still does. Two twentieth-century critics

[1] 'Democracy', *CPW*, II, 26.
[2] 'Equality', *CPW*, VIII, 302.
[3] *Culture and Anarchy*, *CPW*, V, 124.

who have clearly learnt much from Arnold have offered suggestive lines of approach. F. R. Leavis writes that Arnold 'has been judged by inappropriate criteria, as if he offered what he doesn't, and as if a critic who fails of logical rigour and strictness of definition is left with no respectable function of intelligence that he might be performing'. And T. S. Eliot claimed that Arnold is less a critic than a propagandist for criticism.[1]

If we allow that Eliot's two terms are not mutually exclusive, this does seem to provide a right way of looking at Arnold. Throughout his work there is a constant reiteration that what most typifies nineteenth-century society is its chaotic nature. The aggressive differentiation of class divisions is symptomatic of a widespread uncertainty and lack of direction; each class encouraging further fragmentation in listening only to what it wants to hear, reading the newspapers which are produced for its exclusive consumption, attending to those ideas which reinforce its present position and ignoring all criticism. The traditional centres of authority no longer seem to function as stabilizing forces: aristocratic government is defunct, the church is subjected to the same flurry of contradictory ideas that characterizes social organization as a whole, and Parliament is itself becoming rigidly divided on party lines, contributing to the fragmentation, not rising above it. Arnold's description of Parliament as a 'Thyesteän banquet of clap-trap' carries brilliantly his sense of political disillusion; just as Thyestes fed unknowingly upon the flesh of his own children, so Parliament devours the 'clap-trap' it breeds, ignorance will not save parliamentary government anymore than it saved the house of Atreus.[2] If democracy is allowed to emerge haphazardly in a country unprepared for it, then even greater chaos will follow. Middle-class Liberalism, with its belief in the free and full play of economic and social forces, will not serve as a model for a mass democracy:

> The difficulty for democracy is, how to find and keep high ideals. The individuals who compose it are, the bulk of them, persons who need to follow an ideal, not to set one; and one ideal of greatness, high feeling, and fine culture, which an aristocracy

[1] Leavis, *Mill on Bentham and Coleridge*, 38; Eliot, 'The Perfect Critic', *The Sacred Wood* (1920), 1.
[2] *Culture and Anarchy*, *CPW*, V, 227.

> once supplied to them, they lose by the very fact of ceasing to be a lower order and becoming a democracy. Nations are not truly great solely because the individuals composing them are numerous, free, and active; but they are great when these numbers, this freedom, and this activity are employed in the service of an ideal higher than that of an ordinary man, taken by himself. Our society is probably destined to become much more democratic; who or what will give a high tone to the nation then? That is the grave question.[1]

Arnold's answer to this 'grave question' is culture defined variously as, 'a disinterested endeavour to learn and propagate the best that is known and thought in the world', 'a study of perfection' and 'a harmonious perfection . . . which unites sweetness and light'.[2] Arnold never means culture to be taken as an established body of knowledge, though he does sometimes tend to give this impression; more often he equates the study or possession of culture with that open-minded objectivity which makes it possible to see things as they really are. It is more a frame of mind than a programme of action, and represents disinterestedness, reason, intelligence, and *Geist*—those qualities which will be needed above all others in a mass democratic society. Education is the crucial issue because in such a society the schools must be the main civilizing agents. Most important of all, Arnold's view of culture is entirely non-static; the only interest it claims to serve is that of reasoned impartiality:

> The culture which is supposed to plume itself on a smattering of Greek and Latin is a culture which is begotten by nothing so intellectual as curiosity; it is valued either out of sheer vanity and ignorance or else as an engine of social and class distinction, separating its holder, like a badge or title, from other people who have not got it. No serious man would call this culture, or attach any value to it, as culture, at all.[3]

True culture, like the historical process itself, reflects the relativity of

[1] 'Democracy', *CPW*, II, 17–18.

[2] 'The Function of Criticism at the Present Time', *CPW*, III, 283; *Culture and Anarchy*, *CPW*, V, 91–9.

[3] *Culture and Anarchy*, *CPW*, V, 90.

life, and while striving always for the best and trying to make it prevail, can never itself become a *fait accompli*, for it is marked by continuous growth, change and development: 'Not a having and a resting, but a growing and a becoming.' Culture 'begets a dissatisfaction'.[1]

To persuade others that the disinterested contemplation of events was an active not a passive process was the most difficult, and certainly the least successful, aspect of Arnold's campaign on behalf of culture. His constant criticism of actions which were not governed by reason and of the misdirected energy of the middle classes, simply rebounded upon him. The only possible solution was to demonstrate in his own work both a reaching after perfection and the kind of dissatisfaction that Culture begets. The most spectacular example comes in 'The Function of Criticism' where the 'Wragg is in Custody' news-cutting is juxtaposed against the complacency of Roebuck and Adderley, the two then being fused together by the disinterested mind; but the same purpose informs the greater part of Arnold's work, ranging from the ironic examination of Liberal approaches to the Deceased Wife's Sister Bill in *Culture and Anarchy*, through the establishing of distinctions between 'excellent and inferior, sound and unsound or only half-sound' in the critical essays, to the relatively straightforward application of reason to the Irish Question which one finds in the later essays.

It follows naturally from this that the men Arnold most admired were those who had demonstrated their ability to analyse society from a position of intelligent detachment while avoiding the blandishments of party factions. The images he uses to praise such men are significantly those of coolness or calmness, usually set against contrasting images of frenzied movement or blind energy. Sending an article of Carlyle's to his mother, he writes: 'How deeply restful it comes upon one, amidst the hot dizzy trash one reads about these changes everywhere.'[2] In this case disillusionment soon set in and Carlyle becomes a 'moral desperado', and his *Latter-Day Pamphlets* 'a furious raid' into the 'region of immediate practice'.[3] Later still Carlyle's disembodied voice, 'so sorely strained, over-used, and misused', is employed to heighten the superior lasting memory of

[1] *Culture and Anarchy*, *CPW*, V, 94–8.

[2] *Letters*, I, 3–4.

[3] *Letters to Clough*, 111; 'The Function of Criticism . . .', *CPW*, III, 275.

Newman as a 'spiritual apparition, gliding in the dim afternoon light through the aisles of St. Mary's'.[1] Arnold's most striking use of this technique comes in his description of Burke's 'return upon himself' in 'The Function of Criticism at the Present Time':

> This is what I call living by ideas: when one side of a question has long had your earnest support, when all your feelings are engaged, when you hear all around you no language but one, when your party talks this language like a steam-engine and can imagine no other,—still to be able to think, still to be irresistibly carried, if so it be, by the current of thought to the opposite side of the question, and, like Balaam, to be unable to speak anything *but what the Lord has put in your mouth*. I know nothing more striking, and I must add that I know nothing more un-English.[2]

Here the calmness is equated firmly with activity, with 'living by ideas' and 'thinking', with being 'irresistibly carried, if so it be, by the current of thought'—all of this in the midst of the mechanical clatter of the party 'steam-engine'. Burke was not one of the four men from whom Arnold claimed he was 'conscious of having learnt',[3] but he might well have been, for he provided Arnold with a model of the finely practical man. In one of his many subsequent references to Burke, Arnold described him as 'the greatest of English statesmen' because 'he is the only one who traces the reason of things in politics, and who enables us to trace it too'.[4] It is especially in the essays on Ireland that the memory of Burke is evoked, partly because of his deep association with that country, but also because his example puts to shame Gladstone's handling of the Home Rule issue (a policy which Arnold opposed) and the party manipulation of parliament which it encouraged:

> Long ago the country had made up its mind that to pretend 'discussion' to be the object of such debates as those which have gone on in the House of Commons during the last few years was an absurdity; a conspicuous instance of that inveterate trick of parliamentary insincerity of which one is inclined to ask with Figaro, 'Who is being taken in by it?' It matters not what party it

[1] 'Emerson', *CPW*, X, 165.

[2] *CPW*, III, 267–8.

[3] Letter to Newman, 28 May 1872, *Unpublished Letters*, 65.

[4] 'The Incompatibles', *CPW*, IX, 246.

> is which may seek to profit by such 'discussion', whether Conservatives, or Radicals, or Parnellites: it should be made impossible. The state of the House of Commons, since such 'discussion' grew to prevail there, had become a scandal and a danger. Mr. Gladstone seems now doomed to live, move, and have his being in that atmosphere of rhetorical and parliamentary insincerity of which I have spoken.[1]

Arnold's hope for the future rests almost entirely on the ability of certain individuals to develop within themselves the qualities which he admired in Burke—high reason and detached objectivity placed at the service of the nation as a whole. In *Culture and Anarchy* these individuals are called the 'Aliens', men who have remained uncorrupted by the class faults and 'stock notions' of the Barbarians, Philistines, and Populace: in developing their 'best selves' and working for the State, as opposed to others working for their class or party, they become the 'best self' of the nation. The term 'Alien' is not one of Arnold's more inspired labels, suggesting as it does a chillingly isolated condition for the finest men England is capable of producing, and it is probable that Arnold realized this. But although the term is not pursued in his later essays the idea is, though now with less emphasis placed on individual isolation and more on the corporate strength of such people. In 'The Incompatibles' he makes a direct appeal to those 'insignificant people, detached from classes and parties and their great movements, people unclassed and unconsidered'; and in 'Up to Easter' makes a similar appeal to those 'plain reasonable people' not to be duped by the 'insincerity . . . fiction, and claptrap' of politics, and adds: 'There are happily thousands of such people in this country, and they are the greater force here in England because to their plain reasonableness, which is a thing common enough where men have not interest to bind them, they add courage. . . . To them, as one to whom some of them are not ill-disposed to listen, I speak; as one of themselves, as one who wants nothing for himself through politics.' In the American lectures the people to whom he appeals become 'the remnant'.[2]

From none of this would it be possible to construct any kind of valid

[1] 'Up to Easter,' *Neiman*, 339.
[2] 'The Incompatibles', *CPW*, IX, 240–1; 'Up to Easter', *loc. cit.*; 'Numbers; or The Majority and the Remnant', *CPW*, X, 143–64.

political programme, and there is no point in trying to do so. Arnold himself was very clear on this point:

> Now for my part I do not wish to see men of culture asking to be entrusted with power; and, indeed, I have freely said, that in my opinion the speech most proper, at present, for a man of culture to make to a body of his fellow-countrymen who get him into a committee-room, is Socrates's: *Know thyself!* and this is not a speech to be made by men wanting to be entrusted with power.[1]

What he advocates is, as we have seen, the development of a frame of mind which is well characterized by the Socratic advice to 'Know thyself!' But in spite of this, it is foolish to deny that however far removed from the realities of nineteenth-century government Arnold may seem to be, the driving force behind much of his work is profoundly and deeply political. In any immediately practical sense Arnold is obviously sincere in saying that he does not wish to see 'men of culture' being 'entrusted with power', but the whole drift of his argument is that men of culture—taking Arnold's not his critics' use of the term—are the only ones truly fitted to be entrusted with power, considering the 'way the world is going'. And Arnold's vision of a future classless democracy run by a State authority which incorporates and represents the finest elements of that democracy is a political vision, and not made any the less so by the assertion that it rises above politics. Nor is Arnold's claim that, 'It is in its effects upon *civilisation* that equality interests me,' with its supporting definition of civilization as 'the humanisation of men in society',[2] as non-political as he intends it to be, for it is made increasingly clear in his work that he regards the lack of standards of any worthwhile kind in a democracy to be the greatest bar to the attainment of an egalitarian civilization. The disinterested nature of Arnold's propaganda on behalf of culture and his analysis of the faults and weaknesses of Victorian society in terms of its dissociation from the spirit of the age, are convincing so long as his own reason can allow the *Zeitgeist* if necessary to prove him wrong, but this he is never willing to do. The logic of his inevitable and natural democracy is that standards will be not those appropriate to an

[1] *Culture and Anarchy*, *CPW*, V, 88.
[2] 'Equality', *CPW*, VIII, 284–6.

aristocratic or middle class society, but of an entirely different kind, determined by and for the mass. Arnold rejects entirely this possibility and speaks always in the name of the few and of making their standards 'prevail' in a society which is to be governed ostensibly by the many.[1] Here again such a position is concerned as much with political as with 'cultural' or 'humanising' issues, and Arnold could hardly have been unaware of the fact. It is noticeable that the Socratic advice which men of culture are told to offer their fellow-countrymen is appropriate only 'at present' and not for all time; Arnold was too much of a relativist to believe otherwise, and too much of a realist to believe that should this advice prove ineffectual then the *Zeitgeist* would come to his rescue. The time might well arrive when quite other advice could be necessary, when the many would be urged to know not themselves but the few, those 'plain reasonable people' whom Arnold addresses in his later work. The great need so obviously felt by Arnold in the 1880s to move from a position of isolated detachment to one of affiliation with a larger group of like-minded people, was prompted by his thoughts on two countries—America and Ireland.

J. H. Raleigh has noted that, 'Arnold began his career talking about the French, but he concluded it by talking about the Americans',[2] and this is clearly a change of emphasis which represents a cultural shift of outstanding significance. As always with Arnold it is easy to demonstrate that subjects which obsessed him late in life were present in his mind many years earlier. Writing to his mother in 1848 he referred to 'the intolerable *laideur* of the well-fed American masses',[3] and this could be taken to epitomize his attitude to the Americans on his lecture tours nearly forty years later: he is more urbane, if not more polite, but his sentiments are little different. What has changed radically is the seriousness with which he now handles the subject. In 1848 he could be flippant about America because he had the 'idea-moved masses' of France to offer as an ideal contrast, but by the 1880s he was far less sure about the stability of France, and in America he saw

[1] Some of the implications of Arnold's distinction between the few and the many, are explored in a valuable article by Sidney M. B. Coulling, 'The Background of "The Function of Criticism at the Present Time"', *PQ*, XIII, October 1963.

[2] *Matthew Arnold and American Culture*, Berkeley 1961, 38.

[3] *Letters*, I, 6.

created the mass democracy which he had spent much of his life proclaiming was inevitable and natural. He did not like what he saw, and whereas he had once worried that England would be insufficiently influenced by France, he was now terrified that England would be too much influenced by America. The dangers of the American way of life he had typified in 'Democracy' as those 'which come from the multitude being in power, with no adequate ideal to elevate or guide the multitude',[1] and this remains his message in the later essays. There is even an amazing resurgence of his old satirical methods, with the target now being American not English Philistinism:

> 'Ours is the elect nation,' preaches this reformer of American faults—'ours is the elect nation for the age to come. We are the chosen people.' Already, says he, we are taller and heavier than other men, longer lived than other men, richer and more energetic than other men, above all, 'of finer nervous organisation' than other men. Yes, this people, who endure to have the American newspaper for their daily reading, and to have their habitation in Briggsville, Jacksonville, and Marcellus—this people is of finer, more delicate nervous organisation than other nations! It is Colonel Higginson's 'drop more of nervous fluid' over again.[2]

Here, on a bigger scale than even Arnold had feared, Philistinism had become a *fait accompli*, and employing his most circuitous mode of address, he told the Americans that this was the case. He warns them not to rely on 'numbers' but on 'the remnant' and draws on Newman, Plato, Isaiah and the New Testament, to support his conviction that, 'The majority are bad.'[3] America has attained social equality 'before there has been any . . . high standard of social life and manners formed'; it is a country that has adopted a democratic norm and that, for Arnold, is insufficient: 'The *average man* is too much a religion there; his performance is unduly magnified, his shortcomings are not duly seen and admitted.'[4]

While America offered a warning of the probable future development of Western democracy, Ireland provided a test case for

[1] *CPW*, II, 18.
[2] 'Civilisation in the United States', *Five Uncollected Essays, ed. cit.*, 61–2.
[3] 'Numbers', *CPW*, X, 144.
[4] 'Equality', *CPW*, VIII, 288; 'Milton', *Works*, IV, 43.

efficient government. It also tested Arnold's social and political views, for the Irish question embodied in an even more strikingly dramatic manner than the working class agitation of the 1860s, all of the issues Arnold had examined in *Culture and Anarchy*—vast inequality, a large poverty-stricken population, an artificial educational system, conflict based upon unyielding political and religious beliefs, and the threat of violence as a means of solving the problem once and for all. Arnold, as always, called for a period of calm so that the Irish question could be seen 'as in itself it really is', and the required reforms instituted. Gladstone's conversion to Home Rule struck Arnold as a betrayal not only because he regarded this as the wrong solution, but because it confirmed his fears that English politicians had lost the will to govern:

> Let us take the present state of the House of Commons. Can anything be more confused, more unnatural? . . . The members of the House themselves may find entertainment in the personal incidents which such a state of confusion is sure to bring forth abundantly, and excitement in the opportunities thus often afforded for the display of Mr. Gladstone's wonderful powers. But to any judicious Englishman outside the House the spectacle is simply an afflicting and humiliating one; the sense aroused by it is not a sense of delight at Mr. Gladstone's tireless powers, it is rather a sense of disgust at their having to be so exercised. Every day the House of Commons does not sit judicious people feel relief, every day that it sits they are oppressed with apprehension.[1]

Instead of guiding and governing the newly enfranchised 'populace', politicians are inflaming 'the feather-brained democracy' with 'clap-trap and insincerities!'[2] Public opinion in this emergent democratic society is a power which is totally irrational and unreliable: '"All sorts of opinions grow out of the air, from hearsays and talk behind people's backs; opinions with little or no foundation in fact, but which get spread abroad through newspapers, popular meetings, and talk, and get themselves established and are ineradicable. People talk themselves into believing the thing that is not; consider it a duty and obligation to adhere to their belief, and excite themselves about prejudices and

[1] 'A Word More about America', *CPW*, X, 204.
[2] 'From Easter to August', *Neiman*, 60.

absurdities." Who does not recognise the truth of this account of *public opinion*?'[1] The manipulation of people's minds which Arnold had attacked so forcibly in his analysis of the three classes, is now seen to have reached a new and less tangible stage, and politicians are more concerned with learning how to manipulate these new forces than with creating a centre of excellence which would provide the ideals which a mass democratic society needs.

Arnold's solution to this problem, as to all others, remained constant throughout his life—the development of a frame of mind which could bring reason to bear on all aspects of life, and this is to be achieved through the civilizing power of education. But the question remains, what happens to those people who do not believe that this is what is needed, who continue to speak or fight for sectional interest? And here again Arnold's answer remained constant—if they are the enemies of reason then they must be repressed. Arnold has often been criticized for his authoritarianism, and as often defended for it. The most surprising recent defence is R. H. Super's reported belief that the notorious Tarpeian Rock passage in *Culture and Anarchy* was intended as a joke.[2] If this was simply an isolated instance of Arnold resorting to force as a solution then it might be possible to share Professor Super's sanguinity, but it is not. Similar examples are to be found everywhere in his work. In *Culture and Anarchy*, not only are rioters to be flung from the Tarpeian Rock, but the young lions of the *Daily Telegraph*, and Mr. Beales and Mr. Bradlaugh are to 'be sacrificed', and we are also told that one of the benefits of culture is that is provides, 'a much wanted principle, a principle of authority, to counteract the tendency to anarchy which seems to be threatening us'. Arnold's letters written about the same events express a similar discontent with the government's feeble handling of the Hyde Park riots: 'What the State has to do is to put down *all* rioting with a strong hand, or it is sure to drift into trouble'; and to his sister he confided his belief that increasing

[1] 'The Future of Liberalism', *CPW*, IX, 148.

[2] Fred G. Walcott, *The Origins of Culture and Anarchy*, 1970, 130. Dover Wilson also found Arnold's deletion of the Tarpeian Rock passage an 'amusing example' of the way he toned down subsequent editions of *Culture and Anarchy*, 'Matthew Arnold and the Educationists', *The Social and Political Ideas of Some Representative Thinkers of the Victorian Age*, ed F. J. C. Hearnshaw, 1933, 167.

the number of special constables in London was no way to deal with 'an enemy who is not likely to come in force into the streets'—what is needed is 'a good secret police to track his operations'. And in his essays on Ireland Arnold makes his position on this issue as clear as it is possible to be: 'Who does not admire the fine qualities of Lord Spencer?—and I, for my part, am quite ready to admit that he may require for a given period not only the present Crimes Act, but even yet more stringent powers of repression. For a given period, yes!'[1] That final qualifying phrase is characteristic, but it can never be totally reassuring for those who are determined to allow the authoritarian element in Arnold's work to obscure the greatness of his achievement.

Yet it is hard to see how he could have argued otherwise, and it is misleading to attach too much importance to his authoritarianism. To have spoken so strongly for culture without wishing to make it prevail would have been to become the aesthetic trifler his critics tried to see him as; and to make culture prevail through an educational system which encourages people to formulate independent judgement by studying 'the best that is known and thought in the world' is hardly a policy which any true authoritarian would care to try. Nor, of course, was Arnold ever actually in a position to repress anyone. The power he sought was one of persuading others to believe as he did, and his occasional support of repressive measures reflects a fear that he will be somehow prohibited from exercising that power; as Lionel Trilling has said, 'Arnold . . . believed so firmly in reason that he was certain it justified the use of its antithesis, force, without which it was powerless'.[2] For the twentieth-century reader such a position carries too many grim connotations to be easily accepted, but one cannot assume that because Arnold contained within him authoritarian elements he was himself an authoritarian; the whole intellectual and emotional force of his work directs one to a quite contrary conclusion. In so far as Arnold's political beliefs can be expressed in political terms, he is a Liberal, 'a man of movement and change', opposed to the Conservative whose 'business is to procure stability and prominence for that which already exists'.[3] And because he is capable of recognizing

[1] *Culture and Anarchy*, *CPW*, V, 105, 123; *Letters*, I, 377–9; 'A Word More about America', *CPW*, X, 206.

[2] *Matthew Arnold*, 1970 edn, [first edn 1939], 260.

[3] 'The Nadir of Liberalism', *Neiman*, 269.

the nature of nineteenth-century 'movement and change' he must devote himself to preparing others for the advent of democracy—he is a Liberal of the future. However much he distrusts the values and standards of a mass society, such a society will eventually come about. All he can hope is that the 'remnant', those 'judicious' or 'plain reasonable people' will share his vision:

> Many people will tell us that . . . the multitude, by whose votes the elections are now decided, is ignorant and capricious and unstable, and gets tired of those who have been managing its affairs for some time and likes a change to something new, and then gets tired of this also, and changes back again; and that so we may expect to go on changing from a Conservative government to a Liberal, and from a Liberal government to a Conservative, backwards and forwards for ever. But this is not so. Instinctively, however slowly, the human spirit struggles towards the light; and the adoptions and rejections of its agents by the multitude are never wholly blind and capricious, but have a meaning. And the Liberals of the future are those who preserve themselves from distractions and keep their heads as clear and their tempers as calm as they can, in order that they may discern this meaning.[1]

[1] 'The Future of Liberalism', *CPW*, IX, 141.

8: *Arnold and Religion*

BASIL WILLEY

'Professed ardent enemies of the Church have assured me that I am really . . . one of the worst enemies that the Church has,—a much worse enemy than themselves. Perhaps that opinion is shared by some of those who now hear me. I make bold to say that it is totally erroneous' (Arnold at Sion College, 1876).

'Matt is a good Christian at bottom' (Mrs. Matthew Arnold).

I

IF JOHN HENRY NEWMAN had asked about Matthew the famous question he once asked about Dr. Thomas Arnold: 'but is *he* a Christian?'—what answer could have been given? What answer could be given today? It would depend, of course, upon the view of Christianity held by whoever answered. Some, like the late C. S. Lewis, holding that Christianity is nothing if not supernatural and miraculous, would dismiss Arnold's religious writings as futile attempts to water down 'unacceptable' dogmas and to replace orthodoxy by a non-miraculous, minimal religion based on moral precepts. Others, professed Christians whose 'modernism' far exceeds Arnold's, might acknowledge him as a forerunner if they could bring themselves to admit that he had anticipated so much of their own teaching. The great majority, who care for none of these things, will evade the issue by regarding Arnold as poet and critic only, and ignoring his religious books altogether. Religion being for them a dead thing, they will despise Arnold—or at best pity him—for trying to resuscitate what the time-spirit had killed. In a sense this was indeed Arnold's aim, but with one important difference: he did not think religion was dead, or that men could live without it. The *Zeitgeist* had touched it with a finger of death, but what it had killed was only excrescence, not the inward life.

To make this clear to his generation, and to encourage the tree by stripping off its incrustations, was Arnold's purpose in all his religious writings. Let us take a closer look at what he was and what he did.

Of the various influences which built up the Arnold that we know, that of his father was by far the most powerful. The great headmaster and his Rugby provided the soil, the air and the climate in which Matthew was nurtured, and his deepest certainties were thence derived. It is well known that in his youth, and long after, Matthew assumed, in reaction from his father's high seriousness, a foppish and *insouciant* style of talk and dress, so that (as Lionel Trilling says) 'all who saw the boy and the youth, even his intimate friends, perhaps even himself, thought the son was the very antithesis of the father'.[1] Charlotte Brontë, who met him in 1850, wrote of him: 'Striking and prepossessing in appearance, his manner displeases from its seeming foppery. I own it caused me at first to regard him with regretful surprise: the shade of Dr. Arnold seemed to me to frown on his young representative.' Miss Brontë admitted that this impression was superficial and soon wore off; but as late as 1880 Mrs. E. M. Sellar spoke of his 'grand manner . . . which, though it savoured of affectation, was really natural to him, and . . . was neither repellent nor did it put you off your ease'.[2] Nevertheless, in spite of Matthew's outward manner, and his rejection of 'that severe, that earnest air'; and in spite of his father's own opinion (in 1841) that his son was 'not apt to fix', there is no doubt that Matthew was steadied and animated throughout his life by the thought of his father, and felt that in all his own educational and religious work he was continuing in his father's footsteps, and doing what he would have approved of. All his later references to his father confirm this, especially his letters to his mother, which abound in them. Take a few examples:

> *Dec. 17, 1862.* [papa] is the last free speaker of the Church of England clergy who speaks without being shackled, and without being obviously aware that he is so, and that he is in a false position in consequence; and the moment a writer feels this his

[1] Lionel Trilling, *Matthew Arnold*, 1939 edn, 76.

[2] Charlotte Brontë, Letter of 15 January 1851, *The Brontës: Their Lives, Friendships and Correspondence*, ed T. J. Wise and J. A. Symington, III, 1932, 199–200; E. M. Sellar, *Recollections and Impressions*, 1908, 151–2.

power is gone. . . . The best of them (Jowett, for example) obviously do feel it, and I am quite sure papa would have felt it had he been living now. . . . Not that he would have been less a Christian, or less zealous for a national Church, but his attention would have been painfully awake to the truth that to profess to see Christianity through the spectacles of a number of second or third-rate men who lived in Queen Elizabeth's time . . . is an intolerable absurdity, and that it is time to put the formularies of the Church of England on a solider basis.

Nov. 18, 1865 . . . papa's greatness consists in his bringing such a torrent of freshness into English religion by placing history and politics in connexion with it.

Feb. 20, 1869 . . . my one feeling . . . is of papa's immense superiority to all the set, mainly because, owing to his historic sense, he was so wonderfully, for his nation, time, and profession, European, and thus so got himself out of the narrow medium in which, after all, his English friends lived.

Nov. 13, 1869 [after his mother had read parts of *St. Paul and Protestantism*] In papa's time the exploding of the old notions of literal inspiration in Scripture, and the introducing of a truer method of interpretation, were the changes for which, here in England, the moment had come. Stiff people could not receive this change, and my dear old Methodist friend, Mr. Scott, used to say . . . that papa and Coleridge might be excellent men, but that they had found and shown the rat-hole in the temple.

June 13, 1868 The nearer I get to accomplishing the term of years which was papa's, the more I am struck with admiration at what he did in them . . . I think of the main part of what I have done, and am doing, as work which he would have approved and seen to be indispensable.[1]

We may say, then, that Arnold inherited from his father his religion—his certainty that its essential truths were unassailable, however much creeds and dogmas might be shaken. He also inherited from him his 'liberalism', taking that word to mean all that Newman

[1] *Letters*, I, 177–8, 311; II, 4, 20; I, 391–2.

most passionately opposed; above all, readiness to trim one's sails to meet new winds of doctrine. Remembering Arnold's many ironic phrases about 'our Liberal practitioners' and 'our philosophical liberal friends' one might hesitate to call him a liberal. And indeed in politics and social philosophy ('in my notions about the State I am quite papa's son, and his continuator') he was no liberal in the usual sense, and certainly no democrat. He believed in rule by a cultured *élite*, and his 'State', as the organ of the collective 'best self', would have been very much like Rugby School writ large. But in religion he was indeed a liberal, and was so regarded by all except those who wanted to see Christianity abolished altogether. To these last he appeared a dangerous reactionary.

That Arnold could appear to anybody a conservative in religion is an important thing to remember, because the seeming paradox indicates the two-sidedness of his nature. Unlike most of the 'advanced' thinkers of his time (or our own time) he was a poet as well as a rationalizer. He could feel as well as think—indeed some would say that his 'thinking' was mostly disguised feeling. And feeling, with him, took the form of love for all that was beautiful, noble and moving in tradition, all that had acquired a hold over men's hearts through hallowed and tender association. Consequently, modernist and demythologizer though he was in doctrine, he loved the historical Church, its Prayer-Book, its liturgy and architecture, even its 'legends'—loved them as the 'poetry' of religion. And this, for anyone holding Arnold's exalted ideas about poetry, meant that he loved them as being at the very heart of religion, and indispensable to its life. In religion, then, he was destroyer and preserver both; like a good surgeon, he destroyed only for preservation's sake. Let us remember here, and keep in mind throughout as a motto, one of his best-known and oft-quoted aphorisms (it is in the Preface to the 'popular edition' of *God and the Bible*, 1884):

> At the present moment two things about the Christian religion must surely be clear to anybody with eyes in his head. One is, that men cannot do without it; the other, that they cannot do with it as it is (*CPW*, VII, 378).

If I were trying to enumerate all the influences that moulded Arnold's mind I should have to mention at least Senancour ('Obermann'), George Sand, Spinoza, Goethe, Wordsworth, Newman, Renan and Sainte-Beuve: 'Obermann' who nourished his youthful *Weltschmerz*; George Sand into whose pastoral, impassioned and pantheistic world he escaped awhile from the stresses of home and Tractarian Oxford; Spinoza, who taught him how to approach the Bible, and whose majestic philosophy and personal character—at once reverent, righteous and unorthodox—befriended him through life like a neighbouring mountain; Goethe, whom he saluted as the master-mind of the modern world; Wordsworth, under whose wing he had been nurtured, both geographically and spiritually; Newman in whom, despite paternal antagonism, he had at Oxford recognized the beauty of holiness; Renan, whose theological studies seemed so central and European compared with our own provincial efforts; and Sainte-Beuve, the ideal critic, who possessed in the highest degree what every modern critic (whether of poetry, religion or society) should have: 'the finest tact, the nicest moderation, the most free, flexible, and elastic spirit imaginable', and who really was the '*ondoyant et divers* . . . being of Montaigne' (*CPW*, I, 174).

But I am writing of 'Arnold and Religion', and therefore I ought, perhaps, to refer only to influences that affected him directly in this sphere—such as Bishop Butler, Bishop Wilson, Thomas à Kempis, the Cambridge Platonists, and above all the Bible? Well, I shall perforce keep mainly to this track. But let nobody think of Arnold's religious work as a side-line, or something which can be disregarded in any total estimate of him. On the contrary, it was quite central; religion, which he called 'the most lovable of things', was to him the culmination, crown and sanction of all his dearest aims—culture, criticism, sweetness and light, the 'promotion of goodness'. When, in the seventies, he turned from Homer, Celtic literature, literary criticism and the condition of England, to devote his energies directly to the religious books which are the subject of this chapter, he was not deviating from his true and original line. He was confronting what had been his main concern from the beginning: 'the question how to live'. But confronting it, not as a metaphysician or theologian, equipped with 'a system of philosophy based on principles interdependent, subordinate and coherent', but as a man of literary experience, 'thrown upon reading this and that', and possessed therefore of some knowledge of man, and especially of how, over the centuries, the human spirit has evolved in its beliefs and its use of words.

II

From the very beginning, even when most directly concerned with education, culture and the function of criticism, Arnold had seen that there was no dividing line between these matters and religion, and that religious writings could not escape the kind of critique he wished to establish in mid-Victorian England. Already, in a letter to Clough written 28 October 1852, he had laid hold upon one of his ruling ideas: that modern poetry must not subsist by producing 'exquisite bits and images', but by

> becoming a complete magister vitae as the poetry of the ancients did: by including, as theirs did, religion with poetry, instead of existing as poetry only, and leaving religious wants to be supplied by the Christian religion, as a power existing independently of the poetical power (*Letters to Clough*, 124).

On the second point—the duty of 'criticism' (in the enlarged sense he gave it) to include religious books in its purview—his early comments on Colenso and Spinoza may serve as an example. John William Colenso, Bishop of Natal, had in 1862 published the first part of his book *The Pentateuch and Book of Joshua Critically Examined*. The Bishop was an expert arithmetician, and his line was to offer (in Arnold's words) 'a series of problems in this his favourite science, the solution to each of which is to be the *reductio ad absurdum* of that Book of the Pentateuch which supplied its terms'—e.g., 'Allowing 10 persons to each tent . . . , how many tents would 2,000,000 [Israelites] require?' or 'If three priests have to eat 264 pigeons a day, how many must each priest eat?' Colenso's aim was to explode the doctrine of verbal inspiration by showing that the Bible narratives would not stand up to this kind of analysis, and that therefore it was impossible to regard 'the Mosaic story as a true narrative of actual historical matters of fact'. Why should 'literary criticism' concern itself with this kind of thing? Because, Arnold replies, 'religious books come within the jurisdiction of literary criticism so far as they affect general culture'[1] and Colenso's

[1] *The Bishop and the Philosopher*, 1863, *CPW*, III, 41.

book could only have a lowering and provincializing effect upon this. Arnold was fully alive to the seeming paradox that he would appear, in criticizing Colenso, to be 'a liberal attacking a liberal'. Readers of 'The Function of Criticism at the Present Time' (printed 1864) will remember the passage:

> It is really the strongest possible proof of the low ebb at which, in England, the critical spirit is, that while the critical hit in the religious literature of Germany is Dr. Strauss's book, in that of France M. Renan's book, the book of Bishop Colenso is the critical hit in the religious literature of England (*CPW*, III, 278).

But what? Do I want, says Arnold, 'to encourage to the attack of a brother liberal his, and [my own], implacable enemies . . . the High Church rhinoceros and the Evangelical hyaena?' Of course not! The point is, however, that in these days the critical spirit demands, not crude arithmetical destruction of the biblical narratives, but a deeper understanding of their religious import, 'the putting a new construction upon them', setting them in the light of new knowledge and interpreting them by an enlarged spiritual discernment. The 'instructed' already knew that there were contradictions in the Pentateuch and elsewhere in Scripture; but Colenso proceeds as though this were a new and vital discovery, and fails to answer the question 'what then?' Spinoza, who had known all that Colenso could teach and much more, had set out three hundred years ago to 'inform the instructed', and warned the uninstructed not to read him. Colenso, writing for the uninstructed, fails in the main duty of such a writer today, especially when the writer is a Churchman, that of *edifying* them—building up where the *Zeitgeist* seemed to be destructive. That task, layman though he was—but son of a clergyman, and no ordinary clergyman either—, was what Arnold attempted in the books which we must now examine.

III

> . . . an attempt conservative, and an attempt religious (Preface to *God and the Bible*).

That was how Arnold hoped posterity might regard his books on religion, and that—he felt—was what distinguished him from such a man as Colenso and from most of the writers in *Essays and Reviews*. He shared their 'liberal' views on verbal inspiration, and indeed had probably rejected as 'unsound' far more of the traditional Christian doctrines than they had. He differed in being zealous above all to show that the enduring truths of religion subsisted despite the onslaughts of the modern spirit, and that at its heart lay a 'joy whose grounds are true'. Many free-thinkers, from Carlyle onwards, would and did say the same; Arnold differed from them in being eager, with Coleridge, to bless the Established Church and its liturgy with an *esto perpetua*.

St. Paul and Protestantism (1870) appeared the year after *Culture and Anarchy*. This is significant, for a good deal of its argument is foreshadowed in the earlier book. Having there defined 'Culture' as a study of perfection, aspiring 'to make reason and the will of God prevail', he had gone on to recognize religion as 'the greatest and most important of the efforts by which the human race has manifested its impulse to perfect itself'. Religion, 'that voice of the deepest human experience', aims, like Culture, at 'inwardness', seeing the character of perfection not in 'a having and a resting' but in 'a growing and a becoming'. In making 'sweetness and light' characters of perfection, culture is 'of like spirit with poetry'. But religion is an even 'more important manifestation of human nature than poetry' because, its dominant ideas being the 'conquering the obvious faults of our animality', and 'human nature perfect on the moral side', its sphere of influence has been so much wider (see *CPW*, V, 93–4).

But *Culture and Anarchy* also looks forward to the later books in its polemic against the Philistines, particularly as philistinism appears in the ethos of Puritanism: the 'Dissidence of Dissent', non-conformist chapels, tea-meetings, and excessive concentration upon Holy Writ as reading matter. 'No man, who knows nothing else, knows even his Bible'. No doubt there is a touch of cultural and social snobbery in Arnold's satire when he asks what Shakespeare or Virgil would have thought of the Pilgrim Fathers, or when he laughs at Mr. Murphy, the Rev. W. Cattle, or the Rev. Mr. Willey (the present writer's grandfather). But his critique is sound enough when he calls the puritan ideal an 'incomplete perfection', and when he follows Coleridge (perhaps unconsciously) in seeing that often the Puritan, 'in virtue of having conquered a limited part of himself', i.e., his 'animality', 'feels free to give unchecked swing to the remainder'—that is, to his worldly and acquisitive impulses, and his 'spirit of watchful jealousy' of the Establishment (see *CPW*, V, 101–4).

Culture and Anarchy foreshadows *St. Paul and Protestantism* especially in its hint that Puritanism, above all in its classical phase, Calvinism, has perverted the language of religion by turning it into a technical jargon; and especially has misused the impassioned imagery of St. Paul by treating it as fixed, mechanical and 'talismanic'. It is in interpreting St. Paul, then, that Arnold first displays his faith in the literary, as opposed to the dogmatic, approach to the Bible: in applying to it, that is, that free, flexible spirit, *ondoyant et divers*, which is the choicest product of literary culture.

Renan had proclaimed that St. Paul was coming to the end of his long reign as the Doctor of Protestantism, and that he had sophisticated the 'simple religion of the heart' taught in the Gospels. But it is Protestantism itself, and its organized denominations, that are now 'touched with the finger of death'; the reign of the true St. Paul, 'disengaged' from misunderstandings, is only just beginning. What in him 'is figure and belongs to the sphere of feeling, Protestantism has transported into the sphere of intellect and made formula'. Arnold is thinking here of the scheme of redemption set forth typically in the Westminster Confession, with its legalistic clauses about justification, vicarious sacrifice and atonement, its 'parties-contractors' and imputed righteousness, and its unbridled 'licence of affirmation about God and his proceedings'. Such a formulation, based on a 'scientific' and mechanical misuse of Paul's emotive phrases, treats God as though he were 'a man in the next street', a 'magnified and non-natural man', whose designs could be perfectly known and described, in terms of an agreement drawn up between himself and his son, and offered to man as the condition for salvation. Such doctrine could have proceeded, says Arnold, 'from no one but the born Anglo-Saxon man of business' (*CPW*, VI, 63, 14).

It is beside such crude and rigid anthropomorphisms as these that Arnold's own notions about God, vague and unsatisfactory as they may seem to many, should be set—if their power and attractiveness is to be felt. He preferred to leave the infinite much more to the imagination and the feelings, disclaiming all precise and pseudo-scientific knowledge of God and his ways. 'Lifted by the stream of modern ideas', ideas which seemed to him unassailable, he invites us to think of

God rather as 'the fountain of all goodness', and as 'that stream of tendency by which all things strive to fulfil the law of their being' (*CPW*, VI, 10, 169). Unsatisfying, no doubt, to the devout who seek a 'personal' Object for their devotion, and to the theologians who seek a more precise formulation. And, no doubt too, all first- or second-generation refugees from orthodoxy have fallen back on such 'emancipated' notions, under the impression that they were getting nearer the truth. But in his day Arnold's work provided a salutary solvent of fossilized religious imagery, and provided it for those who needed it most—the would-be believers unsettled by honest doubt.

Throughout his writings, and notably in *St. Paul and Protestantism*, Arnold's use of the words 'science' and 'scientific' needs special attention. Arnold was sufficiently a child of his own time to revere 'science' as knowledge which could be *verified*. 'Scientific' language is language referring to a verifiable state of affairs. Religious language is, like poetry, emotive language (he does not use the word 'emotive', but he was a forerunner of I. A. Richards in marking the distinction)—that is, language used not to refer to any alleged state of things, but as an incitement to attitudes. It is language (as he says in *Literature and Dogma*) 'thrown out, so to speak, at a not fully grasped object of the speaker's consciousness' (see *CPW*, VI, 187, 189)—literary language, in short. Now Arnold's objection to the Westminster Confession, and to much else in traditional Christian doctrine, is that it uses the scientific type of language to describe what no man can see, hear, know or conceive—uses it just as if we could verify its statements. But the modern mind, imbued with the spirit of science, rightly demands verification in all things, and will accept no allegedly factual statement on authority alone. In religion, however, statements about the ineffable, about God, are by their nature unverifiable, but may be of the highest service if they are recognized to be emotive, to be poetry. In morality, that is to say in the practical conduct of life, the 'scientific' value of language returns, since the central moral precepts, those which have been accepted *semper, ubique et ab omnibus, are* verifiable in age-long and day-by-day experience. Thus the language of morality, and of religion too as long as it speaks of what can be experienced, is truly 'scientific'; whereas that of creeds and theologies is only pseudo-scientific, having the form and prosaic tone of science without any verifiable object of reference.

Arnold will be found, then, often to use 'science' and 'scientific' as equivalent to 'truth' and 'true' according to his own presuppositions and those of his time. Thus Paul, in whom Arnold finds the 'desire for righteousness' to be the master-impulse, whose starting-point was the 'conscience void of offence', and who never tires of exalting the fruits of the spirit and urging transformation by the renewal of mind and spirit, has a firm hold of things which are sure, and has therefore 'an immense *scientific* superiority [my italics]. We begin to see why Arnold, to whom statements like 'righteousness tendeth to life' and 'the wages of sin is death' were truly scientific, while those like 'God is a triune Person, the moral and intelligent governor of the universe' were scientific in form only, but unverifiable in experience, was so anxious (like his father before him, and Coleridge too) to build religion firmly upon morality. It was because he thought men could not do without religion, but could only do with a religion 'whose grounds are true'.

But Paul knew, as we all know, that 'to serve God'—which Arnold characteristically glosses as 'to follow that central clue in our moral being which unites us to the eternal order'—is no easy task. There is conflict with that other law, the 'law in my members'. 'In conformity with the will of God, *as we religiously name the moral order* [my italics], is our peace and happiness' (*CPW*, VI, 32)—yes, but how are we to manage this? The evil that I would not, that I do; and the mere commands of the Law only increase my sense of helplessness. We thus need something 'which binds and holds us to the practice of righteousness'—and that something is religion.

Paul found this constraining power in Christ. 'His concern with Christ is as the clue to righteousness, not as the clue to transcendental ontology.' In identifying himself with Christ, being 'in Christ', he found that

> the struggling stream of duty, which had not volume enough to bear him to his goal, was suddenly reinforced by the immense tidal wave of sympathy and emotion (*CPW*, VI, 43).

He became aware of contact with 'an unseen power of goodness', and discovered that the way to overcome his inner conflict was to have *Faith* in that unseen power, to hold fast to it. This Faith meant not accepting the benefit of justification through the imputed righteousness of Christ (Calvinism), nor mystically tasting and feeling God (Wesley); it meant

> *to die with Christ to the law of the flesh, to*
> *live with Christ to the law of the mind.* (*CPW*, VI, 47)

The grandeur of faith in Paul's sense is that it enlists a real saving power, not a merely notional one, with which to reinforce 'our struggling, task'd morality': the power of love—love first for Christ, and then, through faith in him, love also for our fellows. I propose to discuss Arnold's phrase 'religion is morality touched by emotion' in the next section, but here we can see how the idea arose, and it may save us from doing him an injustice if we bear this context in mind.

So far Arnold has not found it difficult to re-shape Paul in his own image. He now approaches the central problem facing anyone who tries to restate the New Testament in terms acceptable to 'modern' presuppositions: the Resurrection of Christ. As we shall see more fully later, Arnold took it for granted as implicitly as any liberal of his day that phenomena of this kind do not occur. 'Miracles do not happen.' But he does not flinch from admitting that Paul undoubtedly did believe in the Resurrection as a physical miracle. Indeed, the confidence, joy and certitude of the early Christian Church sprang from that belief; without it, Christianity would probably not have come into existence. Arnold's main concern, however, is to show that Paul, while believing in the physical event, also grasped its spiritual meaning. Christ 'died' and 'lived again' throughout his earthly existence, and we can do the like by dying to sin and rising with Christ to the life in God:

> The astonishing greatness of Paul is, that, coming when and where and whence he did, he yet grasped the spiritual notion, if not exclusively and fully, yet firmly and predominantly. . . . (*CPW*, VI, 55).

We can never know how far Paul had consciously gone in finding spiritual truths to transcend and supersede signs and wonders, but we can watch and revere his 'incessant effort to spiritualise . . . to make the intellect follow and secure all the workings of the religious perception' (*CPW*, VI, 71).

In this way, Arnold feels, we have arrived at Paul's fundamental ideas without even a glimpse of the Protestant doctrines supposedly based on him. We have arrived, that is, at dying with Christ, rising with Christ, and 'growing into' Christ, without meeting with calling and election, justification, imputed righteousness, predestination, appeasement or sacrifice. Hear Arnold on predestination:

> To say that peace with God through Christ inspires such an abounding sense of gratitude, and of its not being our work, that we can only speak of ourselves as *called* and *chosen* to it is one thing; in so speaking, we are on the ground of personal experience. To say, on the other hand [that God has 'reprobated' some others, quite arbitrarily, to everlasting torment], is to quit the ground of personal experience, and to begin employing the magnified and non-natural man in the next street (*CPW*, VI, 60).

'Atonement', 'appeasement' of a justly offended deity, 'sacrifice', 'resting in the Saviour's finished work'—are not really Pauline ideas at all; they are derived from the unknown author of the Epistle to the Hebrews. The notion of appeasing an offended God by vicarious sacrifice 'will never truly speak to the religious sense, or bear fruit for true religion' (*CPW*, VI, 64–5). All these are notions belonging to 'the ignorant and fear-ridden childhood of humanity'. It is interesting to note how fully this Victorian sage shares his century's sense of safe distance from that 'childhood of the world'. Worship of the primitive for its own sake, as we know it today, had not yet become an established cult. The Pauline-Arnoldian understanding of Christ's sacrifice, on the contrary, is that it means parting with what to most men is most precious: selfish impulse; and suffering for other men's faults, not his own—and for *their* good. How prosaic, some may exclaim—how unmystical, how irreverent, thus to reduce Jesus to the level of a human leader! Not prosaic: poetry and passion are never far below Arnold's urbane surface, and break through openly from time to time. As for the other charges, we must ask ourselves whether it is preferable to go on uncritically using obsolete slogans, or to try—as Arnold and Mark Rutherford did, and as some contemporaries are doing again today as if for the first time—to *substantiate* them, to make them real in terms of our own life, so that we can appropriate them and use them. The righteous leader does, in fact and in history, suffer more than other men, and more than he would if men were better. He has to spend himself in order to drag degenerate man back to right standards.

In the added chapter 'Puritanism and the Church of England' (*CPW*, VI, 72–107), Arnold, working like his father towards the ideal of Christian unity, shows that the dissenting sects are insecurely based on those very slogans I have just mentioned. Insecurely, because the slogans are unsound, and are perishing of cold in the modern climate; and because the sects exist for the sake of these very tenets, which they take to be the real, the only true Christianity. The historical Church has always been much more flexible and ready to free itself from 'stock notions'. Standing as it does for the whole Christian tradition in all its rich complexity, it has known how to trim its sails to the winds of change. It exists, not for the sake of particular opinions—adult baptism, justification by faith alone, various theories of church government, etc.—but for the promotion of goodness through Christ. The sects, on the contrary, lose their *raison d'être* when their special stock notions are dissolved away. They are now having to find new reasons for existing, such as—in particular—the 'wickedness' of a Church-and-State establishment as such; but are finding it still more in their own immemorial jealousy and resentment. The first step towards church re-union in this country is, then, to convince the Puritans that their 'truth', their 'scriptural protestantism', is not the whole truth, not '*the* gospel' *par excellence*. To do this we must 'Hellenise' them, educate and enlighten them, introducing them to that kind of literary culture by which alone, in these days, the Bible can be properly interpreted. We begin to see how the various threads of Arnold's propaganda are woven together. My kind of approach, Arnold says in effect, is 'in the air', 'belongs to the *Zeitgeist*'; all I have done is to give a plain, *unlearned* exposition, in doing which perhaps 'our notions about culture' may have helped.

I will refer later to the chapter 'A Comment on Christmas' (added in the 'popular' edition of 1886), and conclude this section with Arnold's concise summary of the essence of Christianity:

> *Grace and peace by the annulment of our ordinary self through the mildness and sweet reasonableness of Jesus Christ* (*CPW*, VI, 121).

IV

Literature and Dogma (1873)

The title of this once-celebrated book indicates how the argument will develop, and how it is linked with that of the earlier book. The Bible is 'literature'; it is 'want of literary experience' that has ossified it into credal and doctrinal rigidity. 'Terms which with St. Paul are *literary* terms, theologians have employed as if they were *scientific* terms' (*CPW*, VI, 170). Indeed, orthodox divinity is based upon 'an immense literary misapprehension'. And the remedy is 'a wide and familiar acquaintance with the human spirit and its productions, showing how ideas and terms arose'. The word 'God' is itself an emotive (poetic) word—a word 'thrown out, so to speak, at a not fully grasped object of the speaker's consciousness—a literary term, in short', 'a deeply moved way of saying conduct or righteousness' (see *CPW*, VI, 189–93).

Now the object of religion, that is to say its purpose and *raison d'être*, is conduct: to make us 'do what we know very well ought to be done'; to make us 'order our conversation aright', and 'depart from iniquity'. Every race of mankind has acknowledged a divine 'Not-Ourselves' whose creatures we are, but it was Israel's special distinction to grasp that its 'High and Holy One that inhabiteth eternity' was on the side of righteousness, 'made for righteousness', required righteousness of his people. But, all this stress on 'conduct', even if conduct is three parts of life (or more)—is this not to turn religion into mere 'morality'? No, says Arnold; religion is based on morality and aims at it, but it is morality 'touched', lit up, by emotion.

It is often assumed that F. H. Bradley[1] exploded this idea of Arnold's and disposed of it for good and all. But did he? Bradley had the kind of logical expertise which can make nonsense of any statement by a clever manipulation of words—just the kind of skill which, says Arnold, we literary men 'with our known inaptitude for abstruse reasoning', disclaim. '*All* morality', says Bradley, 'is, in one sense or another, "touched by emotion". Most emotions, high or low, can go with and "touch" morality; and the moment we leave our phrase-making, and begin to reflect, we see that all that is meant is that morality "touched" by *religious* emotion is religious; and so, as answer to the question What

[1] In *Ethical Studies*, 1927 edn, 315–16.

is religion? all that we have said is, "It is religion when with morality you have—religion." I do not think we learn a very great deal from this.' No, except perhaps that the 'phrase-making' of an Arnold can be more useful and influential than the 'reflection' of a Bradley. But Bradley has surely missed Arnold's point: it is *morality*, not creed or dogma, which when touched by emotion becomes religion. Nothing is better known—St. Paul knew it all too well, as we all do—that moral precepts, the 'law', do not necessarily constrain our obedience. We need something more to incite and inspire us to *do* what we *know* to be right. We need 'emotion', not just any emotion 'high or low', but the sort that makes duty less painful, and well-doing a joy. Here is the whole difference between 'Law' and 'Gospel', between Christianity which enlists the affections on behalf of righteousness, and other codes which try to extinguish the affections. If Arnold's phrase points to all this, as I think it does, then we do learn 'a very great deal' from it.

Jesus was not the sort of Messiah the Jews were hoping for, but he alone took the way to realizing the true Messianic function, which was 'to bring in everlasting righteousness', the Kingdom of God. He did this by urging greater inwardness and spontaneity of feeling instead of Pharisaic legalism; mercy and humility instead of pride and self-righteousness.

> The very power of religion, as we have seen, lies in its bringing *emotion* to bear on our rules of conduct, and thus making us care for them so much, consider them so deeply and reverentially, that we surmount the great practical difficulty of acting in obedience to them, and follow them heartily and easily (*CPW*, VI, 217).

For the Christian, love supplied that power and that emotion, love for Christ himself first, and then, through faith, love of the brethren. 'The love of Christ constraineth us'. The original Hebrew vision had hardened into legalism, and become overlaid with eschatological dreams ('*Aberglaube*', extra-belief); it was the office of Jesus to revitalize religion by bringing about 'a life-giving change of the inner man'.

We now come to the very heart of Arnold's message: his treatment of the two allegedly most important of the supports of traditional Christianity—prophecy and miracles. Here especially, if we are not to misunderstand him, we must always remember two things: first, he wanted to preserve Christianity ('men cannot do without it'); and second, he believed that these traditional supports had already gone, been swept away by the time-spirit ('they cannot do with it as it is'). The time comes, has already come, when men find that the old 'proofs' no longer convince; 'prophecies' turn out not to refer to Christ as had been assumed, and miracles become fairy tales. Arnold did not have to disprove or discredit miracles; that had been done already. His concern was with those who felt that, with their disappearance, 'the whole certainty of religion seems discredited, and the basis of conduct gone'.

> For it is what we call the Time-spirit that is sapping the proof from miracles . . . the human mind, as its experience widens, is turning away from them. And for this reason: *it sees, as its experience widens, how they arise* (*CPW*, VI, 246).

What then?

> the sanction of Christianity, if Christianity is not to be lost along with its miracles, must be found elsewhere (*CPW*, VI, 257).

Arnold's whole object, as he says later, is

> to save the revelation in the Bible from being made *solidary*, as our Comtist friends say, with miracles (*CPW*, VI, 324).

Miracles are now 'touched by Ithuriel's spear'; and what will happen, as men feel their foothold slipping? 'I write', he says (in the Preface to *God and The Bible*, popular edition), to convince the lover of religion that . . . he need not . . . lose anything' (*CPW*, VII, 393). Many, he fears, and with good reason, will be for throwing away Christianity and the Bible along with the rejected trappings; it was to prevent this that he wrote these books. 'When religion is called in question because of the extravagancies of theology being passed off as religion, one disengages and helps religion by showing their utter delusiveness' (*CPW*, VI, 201). The sanction of Christianity must now be sought—where, then? In its 'natural truth', truth verified by experience.

A great part of *Literature and Dogma* is devoted to showing the 'natural truth' of Christ's teaching—as far as we can discern it behind the accretions. The New Testament, Arnold says,

> contains all that we know of a wonderful spirit, far above the heads of his reporters, still further above the head of our popular theology, which has added its own misunderstanding of the reporters to the reporters' misunderstanding of Jesus (*CPW*, VI, 265).

We come closest, probably, to what Jesus really said in those passages which the narrators report, as it were, in spite of themselves. What is clear is the 'method' and the 'secret' of Jesus. The 'method' is that of 'inwardness', the emphasis upon '*metanoia*'—change of heart, being 'born again'. To realize what the first impact of this new teaching must have been like, to 'get the feel' of it, we must re-translate the Bible terms, into the familiar language of today: thus, for 'repentance unto life' read life-giving change of the inner man; for 'truth', reality; for 'grace', the boon of happiness; for 'Spirit', influence (unseen yet pervasive, like the wind).

The 'secret' means losing one's own life, dying to our ordinary selves, and rising with Christ to our true selves, to what is really 'life' as opposed to mere existence in this world. Many non-Christian sages—Aristotle, Stobaeus, Goethe, etc.—had seen that the suppressing and transcending of our first impulses and current thoughts was the way to real 'life'; but Jesus above all of them saw that it led also to peace and joy—'blessedness' (see *CPW*, VI, 294–6).

Here then is where Arnold found the true sanction for Christianity—here, where all is demonstrably true and verifiable in experience. But how the scene has been transformed, how the centre of gravity has shifted, since the gospel days! '*Aberglaube*' has 're-invaded', and Christianity 'developed more and more its side of miracle and legend; until to believe Jesus Christ to be the Son of God meant to believe the points of the legend' (*CPW*, VI, 340). Hence the Apostles' Creed, 'the popular science of Christianity'; the Nicene, its 'learned science'; and the Athanasian, 'learned science with a strong dash of violent and vindictive temper' (*CPW*, VI, 341–2).

Thus 'religion has been made to stand on its apex instead of its base; righteousness is supported on ecclesiastical dogma instead of ecclesiastical dogma being supported on righteousness' (*CPW*, VI, 350).

In the latter part of *Literature and Dogma*, especially after his raillery about the popular notion of the Trinity as 'the Three Lord Shaftesburys', Arnold becomes anxious to dissociate himself from 'our friends the philosophical Liberals, who believe neither in angel nor spirit but in Mr. Herbert Spencer' (*CPW*, VI, 399). Our new masses are indeed losing the Bible along with the fairy-tales and the Three Lord Shaftesburys, and

> when our philosophical Liberal friends say that by universal suffrage, public meetings, Church-disestablishment, marrying one's deceased wife's sister, secular schools, industrial development, man can very well live; and that if he studies the writings, say, of Mr. Herbert Spencer, into the bargain, he will be perfect, . . . and the Bible is become quite old-fashioned and superfluous for him . . . (*CPW*, VI, 363),

then the masses 'will applaud them to the echo'. Yet the Bible remains 'the great inspirer' of conduct—which is 'more than three-fourths of human life'; and it is from this that the masses are cutting themselves off. The reason for this deplorable fact is, once again, that the Bible has been 'made to depend on a story, or set of asserted facts, which it is impossible to verify; and which hard-headed people, therefore, treat as either an imposture, or a fairy-tale that discredits all that is found in connexion with it' (*CPW*, VI, 363).

In *God and the Bible* (1875) Arnold replies to some of the many criticisms evoked by *Literature and Dogma*. We need not, I think, concern ourselves here with either the objections or the replies. It is enough to note that he re-affirms and elaborates all his main points. The Bible-reader, the man who loves and needs religion, will have to reconcile himself to the loss of miracles, and abandon all attempts to ignore the human fallibility of the scriptures. But, having done this, he must go back to the Bible and use it for his soul's benefit. 'We wrote,' he says, [not for the learned, but] 'to restore the use and enjoyment of the Bible to plain people, who might be in danger of losing it.' And again: 'It was not to discredit miracles that *Literature and Dogma* was written, but because miracles are so widely and deeply discredited already' (*CPW*, VII, 368). An educated Christian may still perhaps manage to retain belief in them, but his children or grandchildren will lose it. It will evaporate, just as the belief in witchcraft did during the eighteenth century. We have to make men see that our religion, from this altered viewpoint, 'does but at last become again that religion which Jesus Christ really endeavoured to found, and of which the truth and grandeur are indestructible' (*CPW*, VII, 370).

V

Last Essays on Church and Religion (1877)

'The present volume', Arnold says in the Preface, 'closes the series of my attempts to deal directly with questions concerning religion and the Church.' He adds, however, that in returning to literature 'more strictly so-called', he is returning to a field where work of the utmost importance has now to be done, though indirectly, for religion. 'I am persuaded', he goes on,

> that the transformation of religion, which is essential for its perpetuance, can be accomplished only by carrying the qualities of flexibility, perceptiveness and judgment, which are the best fruits of letters, to whole classes of the community which now know next to nothing of them, and by procuring the application of those qualities to matters where they are never applied now (*CPW*, VIII, 148).

Arnold is caught, he feels, between two hostile fires: first, from the traditionalists who think him an infidel; and second, from the infidels who think him a reactionary. In England, *Literature and Dogma* was considered revolutionary and anti-religious; in foreign liberal circles it aroused impatience at the sight of religion being re-established on new and solid grounds, when they had hoped it 'was going to ruin as fast as could fairly be expected', and astonishment, that 'any man of liberal tendencies should not agree with them' (*CPW*, VIII, 150). As for the old guard of religious die-hards, they 'do not know, I think, how decisively the whole force of progressive and liberal opinion on the Continent has pronounced against the Christian religion' (*CPW*, VIII, 151). But Christianity will survive, and its survival will be due to its 'natural truth'. As ever, Arnold hopes with heart and soul and mind to be able to show that it need not perish along with its unsound pseudo-supports: miracles that did not happen, and metaphysical 'proofs' which are 'mere words'. Its true base, its natural truth, is in its summons and incentives to righteousness 'through Christ'—that is, by loving Christ and following him.

And this righteousness, what is it? We have already seen that it involves renouncement of self, dying to sin, and rising to new life on the spiritual plane. In this Preface, Arnold reduces it to a yet simpler formula: *kindness* and *pureness*, or charity and chastity (*CPW*, VIII, 156). I think a reader of today, especially if he is under twenty, will especially notice Arnold's sense of security on this subject; he can appeal to an almost unbroken consensus of opinion about what righteousness meant. There might be, and of course there were, the widest divergencies in credal beliefs, but everybody knew perfectly well what was the right thing to do on any occasion, and what was wrong. A man might not do what he knew he ought to do, or he might do what he knew he ought not; but conscience and universal agreement pointed unfailingly in the right direction.

It may be said—and today it probably will be said—that Arnold's conception of righteousness was too narrow and too uncritical: that what he was defending as the essence of Christianity was really the conventional 'virtue' of a middle-class Victorian home. In the fragmented society of today, which admits no allegiance to traditional standards—least of all to any sanctions which can be called 'Christian' in however modernistic a sense—self-denial, kindness and pureness are little regarded. We hear more often about self-expression, 'honesty', and freedom from authoritarian restraints. Arnold's attempts to preserve Christianity by translating it into nineteenth-century bourgeois morality will not seem to matter, because few now appear to want to preserve it in any form, and nineteenth-century morality (or any morality of a traditional kind) commands no respect. The statements that 'this is what Jesus really meant' or 'this is how you should understand Christianity' will be met with a shrug and a contemptuous 'so what?'

Yet it is surprising how many of today's 'in'-virtues are really implied in Arnold's key-words. 'Commitment', 'concern', 'dedication', and 'compassion', concepts much advertised and approved today, are included in self-renunciation and kindness. 'Pureness', of which Arnold (and Jesus Christ, and others) thought so highly, is, on the other hand, understood very differently by many or most nowadays. It is certainly no longer equated with chastity or sexual restraint. 'Reticence' and 'modesty' are considered signs of prurience or hypocrisy, and 'honesty' seems to have replaced them in the popular regard. To Arnold it seemed almost too obvious to be mentioned that 'Christian purity' was one of the great natural truths, asserted in all the spiritual teaching of the centuries, and vindicated again and again in history, which would keep religion alive and influential even in modern times. He had no belief in the 'legend' of the Virgin Birth of Christ, any more than he had in any other 'points of the legend', but he thought that this story was valuable as paying 'homage to what has natural worth and necessity'.

This brings me to the last point I have space to make: Arnold's tenderness towards old language, old imagery, old symbols, liturgies and rituals—everything, in short, which had once been laden with meaning for the devout—and may still be. The old forms of Christian worship, he says, will not be extinguished by the growth of a truer conception of their essential contents. . . . They will survive as poetry. We can receive the whole miraculous story as poetry growing out of, or investing, the natural truths behind it. 'The legend will still be loved'; at Christmas time angels and shepherds will still sing Nowell, and Men—if they are Wise, will still go to Bethlehem.[1]

No 'new religion', such as Comtism, can have the effect upon us produced by Christianity, with which our affections have for so long been 'intertwined'. We therefore, who are products of two thousand years of Christian discipline, teaching, worship and civilization, should not look outside Christianity for guidance—say to other world-religions or ethical systems—but keep to what we have inherited, the poetry as well as the morality; and keep the Church, which is the living mediator and embodiment of it all.

Arnold's view of the Church as 'a great national society for the promotion of goodness' may now seem, to any Catholic, deplorably low and secular; and, to any average agnostic, smug and school-masterish. 'Promotion of goodness?' the latter will say; 'defence of the status quo, *you* mean! And what do you mean by "goodness"? Docility, I suppose: respect for one's elders and betters, not asking awkward questions, not making unreasonable demands' (etc.,—the list can be expanded by any reader according to taste). Any serious reader of Arnold will know how shallow these criticisms are. But it is worth while to remind even them that Arnold was fully alive to what I suppose would now be called the 'sociological implications' of the Church, as well as of his beloved 'Culture'. The men of culture, he had said, are the true apostles of

[1] See 'A Comment on Christmas', included in *St Paul & Protestantism*, *CPW*, X, 231.

equality, since culture denies its own *raison d'être* if it remains the private possession of an *élite* and is not disseminated equally to all. Similarly, he knows that the Church of England is widely supposed to be 'an appendage to the Barbarians', committed to the defence of the existing class structure, and especially to the support of the landed gentry. The working classes, he says, are now looking for a great transformation and renewal, not in some remote hereafter, but on this earth and soon. Well! he replies, such a transformation—they call it the coming of the kingdom of God, and pray for it daily—is also the ideal of Christians, and has been upheld through the centuries by Christian leaders, whatever men like Mr. John Morley may say now. But the clergy must not only *believe* this; they must work for it and *be seen* to believe it. The Church 'cannot stand secure unless it has the sympathy of the popular classes'.[1]

One last word: the 'legends', and the forms and liturgies of Christianity will 'remain as poetry': what does that mean? As something unimportant, trivial and untrue but pleasant and nostalgic? No one who has read Arnold and absorbed his notion of poetry will suppose so for a moment. If these things remain 'as poetry', they remain as that in which, amid the shaking of creeds and the dissolution of dogmas and traditions, our race 'will find an ever surer and surer stay. . . . The strongest part of our religion today is its unconscious poetry.'

[1] See 'The Church of England' in *Last Essays on Church and Religion*, *CPW*, VIII, 78.

9: *Arnold and the Classics*

WARREN ANDERSON

MATTHEW ARNOLD'S RELATIONSHIP to the literature of Greece and Rome was complex, not to be contained within any single frame of reference. The source of a given concept or attitude may include modern writers who commented on this literature or felt its influence; such contributions have been the subject of many individual studies. The present essay is an attempt to deal mainly with the background and the general nature of Arnold's approach to classical writers. It may be said that in certain respects the approach was intensely personal, and with equal justice that no Victorian embodied with greater clearness the existence of social as well as individual impulses. Responding to both, his classicism also reflected intellectual and aesthetic tendencies which had gained prominence since the later decades of the eighteenth century. As the setting for his own concern with antiquity, this larger background may properly be given initial attention.

Throughout Arnold's lifetime, and for more than fifty years before his birth in 1822, the chief centre of classical scholarship was Germany. After the French Revolution neoclassicism had become increasingly less effective in shaping European intellectual life; by the close of the eighteenth century it would give way in Germany to a humanistic evaluation of classical literature and art, taken as the basis for a new approach to aesthetics and poetics. Meanwhile, a number of remarkable speculative and creative writers sought to understand the classical experience. Of these the greatest was Goethe, whose lyrics of the 'Storm and Stress' period reveal a concern with Apollo, the culture-hero Prometheus and the early Greek view of nature. The lasting consequences long remained private; it had been left to lesser men to speak with a public voice.

Johann Joachim Winckelmann opened the great debate by crediting Greek art with noble simplicity and serene grandeur (*edle Einfalt, stille*

Grösse). From his description derives, in some measure, the misconception that Greek literature too is magnificently statuesque; Arnold himself was not exempt from its influence. What provoked a response from Winckelmann's contemporaries, however, was the way in which he revived and made use of the theory which identifies poetry with painting. This early Greek view is best known through a misreading of the well-known statement by Horace beginning *ut pictura, poësis erit,* 'as with painting, so with poetry'. Winckelmann's interpretation came under attack by Gotthold Ephraim Lessing, whose treatise on poetry and the arts, *Laokoön*, won critical acclaim when it appeared in 1766. As Goethe noted, the doctrine of *ut pictura poësis*, so long misunderstood, went into immediate eclipse. Replacing it was Lessing's distinction between the poet's supposed representation of a succession of moments and the painter's limitation to single moments and to spatial relationships. A third contestant, Johann Gottfried von Herder, charged that Lessing had failed to take sculpture into account and had excluded lyric by requiring that poetry should deal with action. To a minor degree Arnold perpetuates the controversy in 'Epilogue to Lessing's "Laokoön"', siding against Winckelmann. He extends Lessing's terms somewhat as Herder had done, adding the art of music. The 1853 Preface might have shown greater balance if he had given thought to Herder's other objection. His Aristotelian emphasis upon action fits only epic and dramatic poetry; lyric is ignored, as he acknowledged in the Preface of 1854.

Like Goethe and Schiller, Herder belonged to the New Humanist group of literary men. The activity of the New Humanists was notable after 1790, but by this time the main currents of intellectual involvement with antiquity had set in a different direction. The nineteenth century was to be an age in which classical studies would be given a systematic basis, together with a statement of ideals justifying their place of honour in the higher schools and universities. For these undertakings the spirit of the New Humanism afforded a tempering influence of the greatest value. It was manifested chiefly through the intellect and sensibilities of a remarkable man, Wilhelm von Humboldt. Arnold praises him as 'one of the most unwearied and successful strivers after human perfection that have ever lived' (*CPW*, II, 312), and his deep concern with *Bildung* ('culture') as secular salvation is reflected in *Culture and Anarchy*. His range of interests enabled him to serve as a link between the New Humanists and the most significant scholar of this transitional period, Friedrich August Wolf.

Wolf's great contribution was to systematize the multitude of approaches to classical learning. In order to describe this unified approach he coined the term *Alterthums-Wissenschaft*, 'the science of antiquity'. Both the theoretical justification and the practical application were quickly realized. In 1807 Wolf defined his ideal—which was also von Humboldt's—of a culture founded upon Greek tradition as a wholly human education, an 'elevation of all the powers of the mind and soul to a beautiful harmony of the inner and outer man'. The translation is Arnold's (*NB*, 40), and the concept appears repeatedly in his essays. Two years later, von Humboldt established in Prussian state education the pattern for the whole of Germany, and in 1810 the University of Berlin was founded. Wolf himself had been bringing new life to classical studies ever since he came to teach at Halle in 1783.[1]

The next half-century was filled with many of the most celebrated names in German classical scholarship. For the most part, they belonged to one of two sharply opposed schools. Gottfried Hermann and his followers cared for little except textual criticism and analysis; the school of August Boeckh, representing Wolf's influence, was devoted to the study of ancient history and more broadly to the study of the institutions, art and archaeology of the classical world. Among the historians were three scholars of the first rank whom Arnold regarded with deep respect: Berthold Georg Niebuhr, Ernst Curtius and Theodor Mommsen. Niebuhr's history of Rome had provided the model for Thomas Arnold's work; its author believed fervently that the great classical poets and historians should be read reverently, with the aim of assimilating their spirit.[2] Curtius and Mommsen were men

[1] The question of the extent to which Arnold's Hellenism derives from German sources requires a more extended examination than it has yet received. See most recently David J. DeLaura, *Hebrew and Hellene in Victorian England: Newman, Arnold, and Pater*, Austin and London 1969, 171–91, and James Simpson, 'Arnold and Goethe', pp. 304–6 below.

[2] Niebuhr's beliefs, set forth in a letter of 1822, became known in England through a translation by Julius Hare; see John E. Sandys, *A History of Classical Scholarship*, 3 vol. repr. New York 1964, III, 80.

of Matthew Arnold's own generation. When an English translation of Curtius's history of Greece appeared, he was prompted to write a series of review articles. The fact that the work dealt also with literature and art probably accounts for much of his interest. Mommsen brought to his massive survey of Roman history a thorough training in Roman law, and the treatment included the whole of Italy.

By the first years of the eighteenth century, the age of giants was already past in England. The textual critics Richard Bentley and Richard Porson had commanded their subject with such authority that later German scholars looked back to them as master teachers. Unfortunately the more recent example of Porson, who lived until 1808, inspired many successors to produce textual annotations of classical works. Although rebellion was inevitable, it came only after the middle of the nineteenth century. The rebel was Frederick Apthorp Paley, Arnold's exact contemporary. He sought above all to capture through his notes the spirit of an author; his success was such that they can still be read with profit by students.

While Paley's attitude represents the main current of feeling in nineteenth-century England, it was more characteristic of the leading public schools than of Oxford or Cambridge—a fact which has importance for any study of Victorian classicism. The new spirit first became manifest in the achievements of Samuel Butler and Benjamin Hall Kennedy, successively headmasters at Shrewsbury, and Rugby's Thomas Arnold. Under these men the study of Greek came into its own, and antiquity was seen as related significantly to the modern world. Of Kennedy it was said that to him the literature of antiquity was a living voice; in the same way, Thomas Arnold described Thucydides' history as a living picture of things present. Both men resemble the New Humanists in Germany, who regarded the study of ancient authors as a necessary preparation for dealing with contemporary literature.

Another link with *Neuhumanismus* was the greatly increased attention given to translation. The virtuosity displayed by Kennedy and by Dr. Arnold in extempore renderings is a matter of record. The latter brought to Rugby from Winchester the practice of translating passages entire, while at other schools the sixteenth-century method of proceeding word by word and phrase by phrase continued to prevail. He also introduced a variation that seems to have been entirely his own, urging that language and phrasing be adapted to the age and the style of the classical author being translated; the first of these criteria referred to stages of culture rather than chronology. The *Iliad* and *Odyssey*, for example, were to be rendered in the simple language of the English ballads. The lectures *On Translating Homer* would make clear how much his son found to accept or reject in these counsels.

During Matthew Arnold's active years the classical scene in England could show many creditable scholars, but few of the first rank. Some did make notable contributions; and here the genuine worth of *haute vulgarisation* deserves to be recognized. Benjamin Jowett, the Master of Balliol, made the whole range of Plato's dialogues accessible through translations, as Friedrich Schleiermacher had done in Germany. The two foremost English historians of Greece, Bishop Connop Thirlwall and George Grote, represented the Church and the world of finance. They wrote as brilliant amateurs, seeking to reach cultured readers who were not professional classicists, and their works gained a wide audience. Both men had their faults, but neither could conceivably be described as amateurish. The same cannot be said of John Stuart Blackie, whom Arnold regarded with mild amusement. In his case the concern of the New Humanists with content rather than style had an extreme parallel; yet they might have commended his broad humane emphasis upon the enduring power of Greek poetry. More than any other single attitude, their view of the classical past as a propaedeutic for the modern world characterizes the treatment of antiquity by nineteenth-century English writers before Swinburne and Pater. Together with the willingness to hear those who were not academicians, it constitutes a central element of the intellectual milieu in relation to classicism, a milieu in which Arnold found it possible to become a leading figure.

His pre-eminence was solidly based. At Winchester, Rugby and Balliol he read and re-read a quantity of classical literature which is impressive by most modern standards, although no one would have thought it remarkable at the time. Like all his brothers and sisters, Matthew first encountered Latin and probably Greek as well in the family school, administered by Dr. Arnold. In 1830, when he was sent to the first of several tutors, he almost certainly had already undergone three years of academic training; and during the next six years he studied, not always with high seriousness, to prepare himself for entrance into a public school. The first of these preparatory years was rendered strangely memorable through an encounter with Virgil. Now, for the first time, the classical past spoke to him with power and meaning. The occasion was his reading of the *Fourth Eclogue*, known as the 'Messianic': its prediction of the dawn of a new age and the birth of a marvellous child made an immediate and lasting impression. 'How true it is', he wrote at the close of his life, 'that one's first master, or the first work of him one apprehends, strikes the note for us; I feel this of the 4th Eclogue of Virgil, which I took into my system at 9 years old, having been flogged through the preceding Eclogues and learnt nothing from them; but "Ultima Cumaei", etc., has been a strong influence with me ever since.'[1] Only in 'Obermann Once More', and perhaps in 'Palladium', does the poem figure obviously and identifiably; how often it may have informed his visions of a future time beyond the iron age of criticism is another question, not easily answered.

His years of tutoring accomplished, Matthew was sent to Winchester. Since he was placed in the next to highest form (Fifth Senior), evidently he was thought to be well along in both Latin and Greek. During the one year at Winchester his 'set books' probably included works of Homer, Sophocles, Virgil and Horace. Several hours were set aside daily for Latin composition, everywhere taught with a numbing lack of imagination. Among the distinctive features of training at Winchester was public recitation, on special occasions during the school year, of literally thousands of lines of Greek or Latin verse; these were said 'without book'. The young Arnold seems to have been sufficiently advanced in the school to escape this requirement. At all events, he was to become the effectual champion of memorizing English poetry as a means of teaching. Like certain other of his recommendations in the annual school reports and elsewhere, it came out of the realization that first-hand knowledge of classical writers would inevitably become a thing of the past for the overwhelming majority of schoolchildren.

No record exists of Matthew Arnold's classical reading during the four years at Rugby, from 1837 to 1841. Arthur Hugh Clough, who had been a student there just before this period, later recorded the

[1] Letter of 26 June 1887 to Sidney Colvin. The text is given by Edward V. Lucas, *The Colvins and Their Friends*, New York 1928, 193.

works he himself had read. He was, of course, much the more industrious and conscientious of the two men. When he left Rugby for Oxford, Clough says, he 'had . . . read all Thucydides, except the sixth and seventh books; the first six books of Herodotus . . . I had read five plays, I think, of Sophocles, four of Aeschylus . . . four, perhaps or five, of Euripides, considerable portions of Aristophanes; nearly all the "Odyssey"; only about a third of the "Iliad", but that several times over; one or two dialogues of Plato . . . not quite all Virgil; all Horace; a good deal of Livy and Tacitus: a considerable portion of Aristotle's "Rhetoric", and two or three books of his "Ethics" . . . besides of course other things.'[1] Plato and Aristotle, Herodotus and Thucydides, Livy and Tacitus: these now figure prominently. At Winchester, so far as one can tell, they had played no part whatever in Arnold's studies. A further difference becomes evident in the greatly increased emphasis upon Greek drama. A place was found even for Aristophanes, although Dr. Arnold was troubled by the grossness of Old Comedy. In spite of this moral rigidity, he was able to visualize and recreate the past with unparalleled vividness, and he had a strong sense of the present as not only reflecting that past but providing the key to its meaning. In the lessons, we are told, 'it was not only the language, but the author and the age which rose before him'. He himself spoke of 'what is miscalled ancient history, the really modern history of Greece and Rome'.[2]

Both the moral and the comparative approaches left their mark upon his son. They constituted the distinctive legacy of Rugby, and they strengthened immeasurably the impression from early childhood of the family evenings when Thomas Arnold would tell fascinating cautionary tales from Herodotus. A particular interest attaches to the comparative aspect as it appears in his belief that the classical past seen in true perspective actually is modern, and that its literature offers guidance when readers are sufficiently aware of their own times to achieve that perspective. A sense of the same paradox was to inform the essay 'On the Modern Element in Literature'. Again, when Dr. Arnold charged his students to translate classical authors in the style of English writers who were contemporary with the originals, the criterion was

[1] *Prose Remains of Arthur Hugh Clough . . .*, edited by his wife (Blanche Smith Clough), London and New York 1888, 399.

[2] Arthur P. Stanley, *Life of Thomas Arnold, D.D., Head-Master of Rugby*, London 1904, 129, 180.

equivalence in the stages of intellectual, emotional and aesthetic development. For Matthew Arnold this way of understanding contemporaneity provided a paradigm of comparative approaches to literature, a safeguard from the uncritical observance of time-boundaries. Taken all in all, the Rugby legacy was not an inconsiderable one.

In the autumn of 1841 Arnold entered Oxford's Honour School of Literae Humaniores as a Scholar of Balliol. 'Humane letters' consisted chiefly of classical works representing moral and political science, history and poetry. The method of study was close textual criticism, continuing the severe tradition of scholarship practised by Porson and his followers more than a generation earlier. In this respect Oxford had failed to move with the spirit of the times, which had animated New Humanist thought in Germany well before the beginning of the nineteenth century. The Oxford experience bore little relation to the forces stirring in English classicism.

Previous inquiries into Matthew Arnold's undergraduate reading in Greek and Latin have necessarily consisted of generalities and conjectures. Now, however, specific evidence has come to light, in Balliol's Examination Register for the years 1841–4.[1] This was kept by Richard Jenkyns, Master of the College. For each of the nine university terms, the works assigned to Arnold appear under four headings: Divinity, Greek, Latin and finally Mathematics and Logic. Two additional columns, headed 'Exercises' and 'Morals', contain judgements of Arnold's English essays ('considerable power and skill', 'written with much ability'), his translations into Latin ('very good') and his behaviour, never regarded with more than qualified approval.

Entries under Latin are few: three plays of Plautus, one book of Cicero's letters and several books each of the histories of Livy and Tacitus. By contrast, the Greek dramatic poets, historians and philosophers are fairly well represented. Arnold was assigned the Orestes trilogy of Aeschylus and three Sophoclean tragedies, together with a play of Aristophanes in lieu of Euripides. Three books of Herodotus and of Thucydides were required. Aristotle alone represents philosophy; the *Nicomachean Ethics* was to be read entire, with at least the first two books of his *Rhetoric*.

[1] This information was made available through the kindness of E. V. Quinn, Librarian of Balliol College.

The quantity of reading may seem less than impressive. What must also be taken into account is the intensity of reading which the system presupposed. Frederick W. Robertson, who went up to Oxford in 1837, spoke to this point: 'Four years are spent in preparing about fourteen books only for examination. . . . These are made text-books, digested, worked, got up, until they become part and parcel of the mind.'[1] But Robertson was always deeply serious, committed to every undertaking. Not so Matthew Arnold: the repeated comments in the Examination Register on his 'desultory [behaviour] in habits of reading' and want of proper 'diligence & attention' confirm other evidence which has long been available, such as the stories of his cramming for the final examinations. In fact, however, this casualness did not greatly matter. The Register lists hardly a single classical work which he had not already read or re-read at Rugby under close supervision, and often to a more extensive degree. In this period it was an acknowledged fact that the change from Rugbeian to Oxonian meant a step backward so far as academic standards were concerned.

Arnold's undergraduate years did not set any distinctive stamp upon his ways of responding to the classical past, nor did they bring him any discovery of special meaning in its writers. The crucial period of his education was the time spent at Rugby. Idle, rebellious and flippant, he had nevertheless taken on a number of his father's attitudes towards antiquity, and under his father's discipline he had come to know the great written memorials of its culture. The rest was to come after the years at Oxford, from his own lifelong discipline of reading.

The poems of Matthew Arnold's early maturity, like his youthful works, attempt in highly diverse ways to find a working relationship with classical literature. The outcome is not predetermined by any deliberately adopted and methodical attitude towards antiquity that one could describe as classicism. Writing during a period marked by questioning of established standards, the unsystematic Arnold had to work out his individual acceptance of the meaning of the past. In his earlier poems the successive attempts to do so invariably fall short. The essential nature of Sappho or Horace, Herodotus or Sophocles, is ignored; the Sirens suffer a profound sea-change; the Muses become

[1] Stopford Brooke, *Life and Letters of Frederick W. Robertson*, 2 vol, London 1865, II, 208.

meaningless decoration. At the same time, later preoccupations begin to emerge: the values and perils of romanticism, the interplay between Hebraic and Hellenic elements and the significance of the individualistic moral philosophies of Stoicism and Epicureanism.

Two poems are outstanding as efforts to arrive at a view of the classical. In 'The Strayed Reveller' Arnold captured a Dionysiac immediacy of experience. He was able also to set forth in serious poetry the rival claims of classicism and romanticism, a task attempted unsuccessfully in 'The New Sirens'. He could not, however, decide between them, partly because he did not grant Dionysus a place in the nature of the classical. The refusal kept him from establishing any vital relationship with the Hellenic past.

'Empedocles on Etna' is a poem of crisis, looking both to what had been and to what was to be. The Dionysiac experience evoked in the reveller's long soliloquy has a place in the world-view of the serene poet-musician Callicles, a view which Arnold chose in preference to the tortured intellectual credo of Empedocles. But Callicles' themes shift, as the poet himself would soon shift, from lyric to epic—from the turbulence and exaltation of Pindaric sources to the calm range of subjects that Homer assigned to the bard. The myth of Apollo's victory over Marsyas may reflect Arnold's decision to turn away from the Dionysiac element and seek Apolline tranquillity and restraint, although in fact his nature would not permit him to follow the Calliclean ideal of taking joy in all things. 'Empedocles' foreshadows the statements of the 1853 Preface; possibly it represents in poetry the making of the decision which was there to be codified in prose.

Having thus established and defended a deliberate attitude, Arnold achieved a doctrine which may fittingly be described as a form of classicism. Henceforth his relations with the literature of antiquity were normally to be external and formal. In 1853 and 1855 he published two long poems in the epic manner, works which had all too evidently been tailored to fit the thesis of the 1853 Preface. 'Sohrab and Rustum' derives its power not from the Homeric or Virgilian externals, but from a pervasive and quintessentially Arnoldian sense of man's struggle as doomed. Clough was right to call the poem pseudo-antique. The same mood of fatalism lends effectiveness to 'Balder Dead', although classical epic is used here in a very different manner.

At its best, 'Sohrab and Rustum' successfully employs classical embellishment as a vehicle for the expression of the poet's intense feeling. The combination was to prove effective for a number of later short poems; 'Palladium', in particular, is a triumph of this new, detached classicism. Among the longer works it had its greatest success in classically derived elegy. Arnold acknowledges that he was 'carried irresistibly into this form' when he began 'Thyrsis'.[1] The term 'form' is significantly apt: Greek elegy had given him a frame within which he could express deep feeling; anything further was excess. Except perhaps for a short passage from Theocritus' seventh *Idyll*, no classical origins can be attributed to the superb descriptions of meadow and garden; they are thoroughly English.

Arnold's last significant poem, 'Westminster Abbey', was meant to be an elegy; it proved to resemble instead the type of English ode known as pindaric. It has noteworthy affinities with the victory odes of Pindar himself: a range far beyond the immediate subject, an unusually strong concern with myth and a recurring symbolic use of light. In other respects 'Westminster Abbey' embodies the classicism which its author, over a period of more than thirty years, had come to take as his own: periphrases, genteel revisions, sonorous Greek names, an eclectic manner, detachment from the Greek past—all are here. Ornate and heavily majestic, the poems bids a last ceremonious farewell to the ancient writers whom Arnold prized so dearly.

The study of Homer was required of every schoolboy in the 1830s; the optional status of the *Iliad* and *Odyssey* at Oxford witnesses to the thorough grounding in both works which had already been imparted. Yet the case had been quite different during the eighteenth century and even the earlier decades of the nineteenth. Latin had maintained its dominance: few were fortunate enough to come, as did Coleridge, under the training of a master who could make clear Homer's supremacy. Thomas Arnold's schoolmates at Winchester thought him mad when he asked that Greek composition be included in the curriculum. As Headmaster of Rugby, he was to be one of the small group of educators chiefly responsible for a shift of interest to Greek studies, and not least to Homer, paralleling the movement begun somewhat earlier among the German New Humanists.

Matthew Arnold's knowledge of Homeric poetry was sound, and his

[1] Letter of 12 April 1866, *Letters*, I, 327.

devotion to the *Iliad*, at least, remained constant throughout his life. The very early sonnet 'To a Friend' refers to Homer as 'clearest-souled of men'; this estimate never wavered. When Homeric figures or motifs occur in the poetry, however, they often seem changed, sometimes even distorted. The Sirens of the *Odyssey*, who make their appeal to the intellect, appear in 'The New Sirens' as fierce and sensual. In 'The Strayed Reveller' Circe undergoes the opposite transformation, becoming almost a maternal figure, and Ulysses lacks inwardness. Neither is much more than a part of the elaborate and conventional classical decor. The poem's successes arise out of other causes, and among these, paradoxically, is the fact that Arnold does not seek here the quality of elevation which he attributed to Homeric epic.

Such an attempt was made with the utmost deliberateness in 'Sohrab and Rustum' and 'Balder Dead', but these works have no essential affinity with Homer. In the similes Virgilian particularizing and Miltonic exoticism assort oddly with the effort to achieve a Homeric simplicity in the basic narrative style; the mood of the poem, taken generally, is one of melancholy. One notes especially the absence of any great and excellent human action such as the 1853 Preface—partly intended to preface this very poem—considered to be an absolute prerequisite for meaningful poetry. 'Balder Dead', the only work in which Arnold draws heavily upon the *Odyssey*, is a cunning mosaic; it embodies the eclectic manner dictated by an artificial classicism. Suggestions of Homeric or Virgilian epic are now diffused, worked into the main fabric with care and skill but without the attainment of any integral result. As before, the mood works against any serious use of Homer.

With Troy itself as the scene, 'Palladium' succeeds in achieving a timeless and universal quality. The principal sources, however, are not Homeric, and once again the values of the early Greek heroic world prove to be at variance with theme and mood. In fact no clash can occur, since the characters and events of the *Iliad* are handled at a safe remove, with an evocative use of names. Controlling with rare skill his use of the past, Arnold delicately balances it against the demands of deep personal feeling. As a poet he will not turn again to Homer; the responses are to come in his essays and above all in the Oxford lectures *On Translating Homer*.

Throughout the greater part of the eighteenth century, the Homeric poems had been thought to lack a due sense of propriety. The earlier decades of the nineteenth century saw them misinterpreted or praised uncritically for much the same manifestation of unembarrassed directness, as disfavour gave way to popularity. Homer's new respectability was part of a general turning towards Greek that had begun in Germany as early as the 1770s. During the following decade Wolf added greatly to its momentum through his humane scholarship; in 1795 he published the *Prolegomena ad Homerum*, in which he characterized the original poet as a primitive natural genius. The error perfectly represents the tendencies of his age, a time when men of the highest learning and poetic genius were taken in by the *faux-naïf* verses of 'Ossian'. In the reaction against neoclassicism, 'primitive' had now become a term of high praise; simplicity and naturalness, attributed especially to Homer, were the reigning values. Among the German New Humanists of the 1790s there was a marked interest in Homeric poetry, as also in questions of translation.

These same concerns inform Arnold's lectures. Translation, however, has less importance than their title suggests. The professed purpose thinly veils the real one: to give Homer his place in world literature. Despite weaknesses and misinterpretations, this end was splendidly achieved. The Oxford lectures constitute a remarkable comparative study of great writers, centred upon the one gigantic figure whose works are the source of our literary tradition. At the heart of what Arnold says is his description of Homer's poetry as rapid in movement, plain in words and style, simple in ideas and noble in manner. Not long after the lectures were delivered he spoke of this view as being 'that hitherto generally received by the best judges'.[1] The remark shows more modesty than accuracy; if the criteria were familiar, their combination was of his own devising and embodied his critical point of view.

Impossible to reject, the four qualities are equally impossible to accept without qualification. Because he was unwilling or unable to recognize this, Arnold sometimes comes off badly. He had a shaky command of prosody, and he had been wrongly taught to read classical hexameters in triple rhythm. The results for his argument concerning rapidity were confusion and contradiction. When he defines this quality as 'directness and flowingness', his approach runs counter to the precise

[1] Letter of 8 February 1861, *Unpublished Letters*, 52.

distinction he had made some years earlier between rapidity and fluidity.[1] His comparison of the Homeric hexameter with the rhymed couplets of Pope and the Miltonic period shows that actually he is concerned not with rapidity but with the steady onward flow of Homer's narrative.[2]

Stylistic plainness was a safe choice. No long narrative poem can afford to have its momentum checked by complexity in the line structure if it is meant to be heard rather than read silently, and the *Iliad* and *Odyssey* appear to come from a period of Greek history when writing was, at best, a very recent development. Moreover, the fact that the oral formulaic elements in them possess great importance has been conclusively demonstrated during the last half-century. To choose plainness in words as a matching criterion, however, brings many problems. Homeric Greek never was spoken; an amalgam of several dialects, it constituted a purely poetic language. The later Greeks themselves found it difficult at times, and even today the meaning of some words remains uncertain. Yet the Homeric dialect does not consist of a series of philological puzzles; for the most part, it can easily be read by a relative beginner. Ignoring this, Arnold instead appealed for support to several well-known classical scholars. His pleas met with little success, not surprisingly. Regrettable as they may seem, they are at any rate consistent with his avoidance of self-contained literary standards and his consequent misconception of translation.

The third criterion, simplicity of ideas, bears a close relationship to the second, and Arnold regularly explains it in terms of this association. He does not, however, say what the ideas are. In his prose writings he tended to use the term 'idea' with greater frequency than precision, and his views on the relation between form and content remained unresolved, although a preoccupation with form was consistently evident. The Oxford lectures give no indication of any interest in the strange and compelling inwardness of Achilles or of any other character in the *Iliad*. Here Arnold's chosen mode proves to be polemic rather than panegyric. He has come not so much to praise Homer as to censure Shakespeare, Chapman, Pope and a scattering of his own

[1] Letter of 30 November [1853], *Letters to Clough*, 146.

[2] The fact that Pope had associated these two qualities in the Introduction to his translation of the *Iliad* (1715) may have been in Arnold's mind.

contemporaries, all for what he sums up as fancifulness. So, at the close of both the 1853 and 1854 Prefaces, he had warned against caprice. The polemic is undeniably incisive: well-chosen examples make clear Tennyson's un-Homeric sophistication, for example, and his own awareness that the admiration Englishmen felt for Homeric poetry was, as it seemed to him, barbarously imperceptive. A quarter-century earlier, Thomas Arnold had commented sadly on the utter lack of any poetical feeling for Homer in most of the boys at Rugby. Now his son was dealing with these boys and their contemporaries grown to manhood. Not much, perhaps, had changed.

When he discusses nobility of manner, Arnold initially takes the extreme position that Homer invests any subject with this quality. A more moderate view appears in his later statement that the great masters of poetry are wholly sound and good as poets, whether or not the immediate region of their subject is an elevated one; although the subject may sink, the poet never does so. The task of refuting Francis Newman's argument to the contrary carries him over a wide range of writers and genres. Having brilliantly traversed the terrain of world literature, he climaxes his journey with a celebrated definition of the grand style as the manifestation in poetry of a noble nature.

Precisely this kind of critical bravura gives *On Translating Homer* what may be its chief and lasting merit for modern readers. On several other counts the work suffers markedly. The choice of 'touchstone' verses, particularly those from Homer, reflects all too clearly Arnold's fondness for the elegiac note. Moreover, he misconceives translation as a form of transposition, a process whereby some objective entity is shifted in place and time. Because he thinks of this entity as verifiable, he feels compelled to have translations of a classical work judged by classical scholars. Who else, he demands, can know how a fifth-century Athenian audience responded to the *Iliad*? Finally, incompleteness results from the decision to ignore the *Odyssey*, a work which may have seemed uncongenial in its affirmation of the life impulse.[1] For some temperaments, Odysseus makes a less comfortable companion than any of the doomed heroes in 'the battle on the plain' that the poet of 'Palladium' saw as perpetually renewed.

[1] Douglas Bush, *Matthew Arnold*, New York and London 1971, 92, suggests that Arnold 'saw in the *Odyssey* only "the most romantic poem of the ancient world"'.

Arnold nevertheless had the qualities of his defects. The 'touchstones' enabled him to voice personal feeling, and many of the practical comments on details of translation are sensible and helpful. Even his exclusive concentration upon the *Iliad* provided a unifying factor in the lectures, where quotations from the text were repeated to a surprising degree. None of these merits, however, is fundamentally important to the success of the work. One comes back inevitably to Arnold's central achievement: he rescued Homer from the cranks and pedants, and made his place secure among the masters of literature. For almost a century, the reception of Homeric poetry among scholars and men of letters had been marked by parochialism of one kind or another. Arnold was able to move beyond all this pettiness. He saw Homer as one of an immortal company—not the supreme figure but among those who, like Sophocles and Dante and Milton, had reached the highest level. The fact that individual supremacy was not in question gives the Oxford lectures a special validity and power. From this position of disinterestedness, Arnold was able to plan and execute a comparative study of literature such as the world of English letters had never before seen. For us, its continuing excellence lies in the fact that it shows us the level of immortal writers, where place and time are no more, and it makes clear the greatness of Homer by the standards of that immortality.

Although Arnold refers only very rarely to Aeschylus or Euripides, he pays Sophocles the utmost attention and respect. Winchester, Rugby and Balliol had trained him well in the text of the seven extant tragedies by the time he first sought to draw upon them for his own poetry. Probably the earliest such attempts, dating from 1847 or perhaps 1848, are the companion poems 'Fragment of an "Antigone"' and 'Fragment of Chorus of a "Dejaneira"'.

In externals the first of these conventionally imitates its original by means of strophic correspondence, variety of line length and intricate syntax. The content, however, differs remarkably. Central Stoic and Epicurean beliefs are first praised, then 'obedience to the primal law' of blood ties. The interpretation of this obedience is unexpected: by imposing the death penalty Creon is 'mightily' vindicating 'august laws'. Evidently the original has been misconstrued as a conflict between individual and state. The mistaken handling may also reflect

Hegel's theory of eventual synthesis resolving the partial error of both Creon and Antigone. The poem closes with an extended meditation on fate which relates, though only in the broadest and most general manner, to three choruses of the *Antigone*. Again one cannot escape the contrasts with the original, as Arnold emphasizes man's helplessness rather than his power and avoids the Sophoclean equation of heroism with suffering.

No attempt at formal correspondence marks 'Fragment of Chorus of a "Dejaneira"'. Throughout the first three stanzas Arnold generalizes, without support from his source except as a point of departure; the *Trachiniae*, or *Women of Trachis*, is a private tragedy. The two final stanzas do have a Sophoclean basis, however, and the themes of old age and early death are clearly Hellenic. This divison within the poem witnesses to the tentative nature of Arnold's classicism during the years just before mid-century, and to the varying success of his experiments.

From the same period comes the sonnet 'To a Friend', which gives the most succinct and comprehensive portrait of Sophocles in all of Arnold's writings. The claim that he 'saw life steadily, and saw it whole' has been much debated. Any explanation must take account of Arnold's belief that poetry is indeed more 'philosophical' than factual narrative, as Aristotle had maintained, because of the poet's ability to see a larger pattern and a higher truth within the limits of his experience. The sonnet also associates mellowness and sweetness with Sophocles; a decade later, 'On the Modern Element in Literature' takes a more forthright stand, proclaiming him a poet of joy grounded in wholeness of understanding. For Arnold this conclusion was a deep necessity, essential to his view of great poetry. The 1853 Preface had incorporated Schiller's doctrine of joy as the highest aim of art, and the influence of Wordsworth had long been significant. Out of this gathering of forces came the conviction that understanding always gives rise to affirmation and joy.

The difficulty in all this is that the Sophocles of Matthew Arnold does not resemble any Sophocles whom we can readily recognize. The three separate plays which tell the 'Theban story'—in order of production the *Antigone, Oedipus Tyrannus* and *Oedipus at Colonus* —serve to illustrate the differences. What happened to the first of these has already been noted; as for the *Oedipus Tyrannus*, Arnold simply ignored it. Although the omission must be thought surprising, the reason is not far to seek. His transformation of the *Antigone* already suggests it; the phrase 'singer of sweet Colonus' in 'To a Friend' gives a further hint. The *Oedipus at Colonus* does contain lyrics of great sweetness, but they are no more than an interlude in the account of the final hours of Oedipus's life. Old age, poverty and blindness have not taken away his fierceness; the very serenity of his sense of destiny is awesome and apocalyptic. The play has little sweetness, though much profound beauty and terror. As for the *Oedipus Tyrannus*, that drama of relentless self-discovery, it will be evident that such work was even less suited to Arnold's purposes. He could not deal with it because it would not fit his conception of Sophocles; within that view, its heroism had no place.

The intractable nature of Sophoclean tragedy received a final demonstration in *Merope*. While it does have clear affinities with Sophocles's *Electra*, Arnold had elected to build on the plot of a lost Euripidean work that apparently contained strong elements of melodrama: this was an invitation to disaster. He sought to meet the difficulty by emphasizing character portrayal, so that the play might have a Sophoclean tone, but his characters lack the inner strength and dedication of their prototypes. The moral dimension of the work, moreover, has no similarity to that of Sophoclean tragedy. As in Goethe's *Iphigenie auf Tauris*, the gods do not matter: individual conscience is all-important. With formal characteristics Arnold had no more success. Believing that the chief value of Sophocles's work resided in the 'grand moral effect' of his style, he leavened the dialogue portions with more than a score of borrowings from the seven tragedies. But neither this device nor the twisted syntax and compound epithets could be of any avail: *Merope* remains a monument to misunderstanding.

Briefly described, the Sophocles of Matthew Arnold is a composite figure. His wholeness and 'even-balanced soul', the combination of moral greatness and artistic genius, represent the ideals which Arnold held up before himself. Much the same may be said concerning the emphasis upon joy. It is true that in 'Dover Beach' Sophocles is credited with a pessimistic view of human existence; yet the presentation of his 'thought' seems for a moment awkward and self-conscious, perhaps as if the poet felt him to be playing an unaccustomed role. The attributions of wholeness, balance and joy had a public dimension as well. In his lecture 'On the Modern Element in Literature', Arnold took the distinguishing feature of Sophoclean poetry to be 'its consummate, its unrivalled *adequacy*', as representative of 'the highly developed human nature of that age'. He goes on to claim that the Athenians as a whole possessed a comparable energy, maturity, freedom and acuteness of observation (*CPW*, I, 28). The assertion forces both the average Athenian and the extraordinary playwright into false positions. The corollary of this error was a belief that stands on quite another level of credibility, namely that a great age produces a great literature and finds its true spokesmen in the leading talents among its writers. No authentic figure could have satisfied all of the demands imposed by Arnold's desires and preconceptions: his Sophocles is impressive but unreal.

Although no other classical authors appear to have held for Arnold a significance comparable to that of Homer or Sophocles, many others figure to some extent in his writing. He had affinities of temperament with Virgil, who had made the earliest impression upon him. Nevertheless, he rejected the *Aeneid* as antiquarian, formally inadequate and suffused with melancholy, in spite of a deep admiration for the personality of its author. His years of reading Horace likewise left little trace. The very early poem 'Horatian Echo' presents a trivial collection of themes, and the prose essays contain only an essential condemnation: the author of the stern *Roman Odes*, who praised Stoic belief, is dismissed as wanting seriousness and 'not interpretative and fortifying' (*CPW*, I, 36).

Cicero appears only once in a meaningful role; Plato makes many appearances, but always as man of letters or moralist. The purpose of Arnold's approach becomes evident in his comments on Aristotle and in the uses which he made of that writer's works. Almost invariably the choice was the *Nicomachean Ethics* or the *Poetics*, which informs the 1853 Preface; the purpose, without exception, was to validate critical or moral positions which Arnold had already taken up. 'Empedocles on Etna' reveals through many substantial borrowings his interest in Lucretius, whose figure merges into that of Empedocles himself. Both prove to be akin to Arnold, sharing with him the common identity of the brilliant and sensitive individual born too late or too soon.

Pindar, finally, receives little attention except in the poetry. The few critical comments, however, are generous and apt. Upon him, 'above all other poets, the power of style seems to have exercised an inspiring and intoxicating effect', we are told (*CPW*, III, 366). At times his presence contributes importantly to portions of the poems, especially 'Empedocles on Etna', where it is the representative of Greek lyric poetry as intensity of feeling. Here one sees the poet's response; as literary critic Arnold continued to be concerned with style. His tendency to interpret even the religious response in stylistic terms moves him to comment that Pindar exemplifies 'the highest art, the art which by its height, depth, and gravity possesses religiousness' (*CPW*, X, 157); it is a typical judgment.

The greatest single influence of ancient thought upon Matthew Arnold was exerted by Stoicism and Epicureanism, post-Hellenic ethical systems whose spokesmen made no significant contribution to literature. His concern with these teachings began when he was an Oxford student; they continued for forty years to shape his writing and the nature of his devotional life.

During the Hellenistic and Graeco-Roman periods, philosophies centred in metaphysical or social issues gave way to those which emphasized the individual conduct of life. The Stoics counselled freedom from the tyranny of passion and willing submission to natural law. For them the world possessed a twofold unity: outwardly and visibly through the oecumenic concept whereby the entire 'inhabited earth' (*hê oikoumenê*) was viewed as a single entity, with no distinctions of rank or condition among the members of its common humanity; inwardly and invisibly through the *logos*, the rational principle penetrating the universe. In this great design the individual's part was to 'follow nature' through obedience to the 'guiding principle' (*to hêgemonikon*) which resides within each man. Epicurus's followers believed the end of all morality to be true pleasure, achieved through the exercise of prudence, honour, justness and frugality and marked by freedom from inward disturbance (*ataraxia*, or ataraxy, Latinized as *securitas*). This ideal attitude was possessed in perfect measure by the gods alone, who accordingly had no concern for man.

Despite their evident separateness, the two systems have important elements in common. To distinguish the occasions of their influence upon Arnold would prove difficult and unprofitable; the influence was often a diffuse one, not necessarily acknowledged or even realized. There is no doubt that he tended to be more strongly attracted towards Stoic doctrines. Originally counsels of perfection, they were later tempered to apply realistically to the average; this flexibility he found useful and attractive. The rigorous ideals of Epicureanism suffered debasement rather than realistic modification, and during a part of the Oxford years Arnold seemed aware only of the debased and popular version. During these same years, however, he had begun to read the Stoic philosopher Epictetus and also Spinoza, whose system includes Stoic concepts of a pantheistic universe and of individual happiness.

The poems of this period, published mainly in the 1849 and 1852 volumes, frequently reflect the two philosophies. 'Horatian Echo' seems to describe a hedonistic Epicurean position; 'To a Gipsy Child by the Sea-shore' shows an uncertain, even romantic response to Stoicism; and the markedly romantic 'Tristram and Iseult' contains a Stoic sermon on restlessness, with a traditional selection of examples. All three works, however, appear to belong to the period before Arnold's reading of Epictetus.

This reading can be assigned, with a high degree of probability, to 1848. In a letter to Clough, written during the late summer of that year, Arnold quotes the lines describing Epictetus as 'he, whose friendship I not long since won', published the following year as part of the sonnet 'To a Friend' (*Letters to Clough*, 90). The Stoic universe now seems to offer no satisfactory foundation for his attempt to realize an adequate idea of the world through poetry; there are signs that he is turning from the metaphysics and cosmology of Stoicism to its ethics. The reading-lists for this period suggest that he found a guiding ethical principle in a Stoic maxim: 'Our desire is to obey nature rather than to have nature obedient to us'.[1] The words are Spinoza's; the voice is that of Epictetus. In 'Quiet Work', where nature is the teacher of man, this same voice can be heard; and central themes of Stoicism give substance (though little charm) to many of the early short poems, particularly 'Self-Dependence' and 'Courage'. 'Fragment of an "Antigone"' seems to draw from Epicureanism as well when the Chorus praise self-concern as a rule of behaviour. They also commend the man who fashions his own life; this Stoic principle reappears in 'The Buried

[1] Kenneth Allott, 'Matthew Arnold's Reading-Lists in Three Early Diaries', *VS*, II, 1959, 265. Arnold cites Spinoza's Latin text.

Life', although the title itself echoes Epicurus's command to 'live a hidden life (*lathe biôsas*)' of ethical self-reliance.

Among the longer poems written by mid-century, in the years before Stoicism had ceased to affect Arnold's poetry, 'Mycerinus' tells of gods who evidently are the unfeeling deities of Epicurus, while the king himself takes the 'measure of his soul' like a Stoic sage. Both systems contribute to the deepest themes of 'Resignation'. The solitary poet comes from the *De rerum natura* of Lucretius, a devout follower of Epicurus. To be sure, his tears and his sense that he is not truly alone are far from Lucretian. They reflect Arnold's awareness that a hidden life does not mean disdaining society, and that the Stoic wise man never was meant to be insensible to emotion. The most celebrated passages in the poem, especially lines 189–98 and 241–8, directly advocate a Stoic acceptance of the universe. This submission to the *logos* is to appear again in the later essays as the 'sentiment of sublime acquiescence'. Less successful is the well-known reference to the poet's 'rapt security' (246): Epicurean *securitas*, absence of inner unrest, will not combine with the Democritean and Platonic idea of the poet as one possessed.

The evidence from other poems that the two great ethical systems could contribute jointly to Arnold's writing is borne out by the success with which he incorporated them into the doctrines of his Empedocles. Making full use of their degree of compatibility, he fashioned so skilful a composite that only a specialist could be aware of the reconciling process. The nature of the component beliefs has long been familiar. From the school of Epicurus, and most directly from Lucretius, come the comments on the power of right reason, the destructive results of excessive desire, the need to live simply and much else besides. At the heart of Empedocles's teaching, however, is the central Stoic doctrine of self-sufficiency.

Arnold, who admired and profited from this master teaching of Epictetus, found it to be less than wholly adequate as he began to turn away from poetry. Stoic thought had ceased to figure in his poems even before the edition of 1853, except for minor instances; it passed over into the 'buried life' of his devotional reading, where it had a continuing importance that is abundantly clear in the note-books. For the next fifteen years, neither Stoic nor Epicurean doctrines made any major contribution to his writing apart from the essay of 1863 on

Marcus Aurelius. Their absence from the literary essays is not surprising, since both systems dismissed belles-lettres with scorn.

After the early 1850s, only one poem, 'Obermann Once More', contains Stoic teaching, and this is not an independent work but a palinode to the Obermann poem of 1849, which had extolled those who remain 'unspotted by the word'; there are indirect references which seem to apply both to Epictetus and to Marcus Aurelius. 'Obermann Once More', written in 1866, goes beyond the narrowness of this cloistered virtue. Now the visionary figure of Obermann urges Arnold to devote himself, in this brighter age, to the great end of '"One common wave of thought and joy"'. The new element is the stress upon community; in order to account for its appearance, some acquaintance with the 'Manual of Pseusophanes' is necessary.

Obermann's creator, Étienne Pivert de Senancour, presents this work as a treatise by the hedonist Aristippus, founder of the Cyrenaic school. Actually it consists of his own summary of Stoic and Epicurean ethics, and apart from the private joke in 'Pseusophanes'[1] the title is meant to recall the original 'Manual'—the *Enchiridion* (Latin *Manuale*) in which Arrian summarized the teachings of his master Epictetus. Senancour's selection is predominantly Stoic, deriving most directly from Marcus Aurelius. The greater part of it may fairly be characterized by the following maxims: 'Consider only the understanding which is the principle of the world's order. . . . When you have served [this] order, . . . you have acted in conformity with your nature. . . . Live in yourself and seek that only which does not perish. . . . Your welfare follows only in conformity to the will of Nature.' Nothing here alters the primacy of Epictetus's command to be self-sufficient. The final portions of Senancour's handbook, however, sound a new note that may seem to come unexpectedly: 'Console, enlighten and sustain your kind. . . . Know and follow after the laws of man, and you will assist others to know and follow them. Contemplate and show forth to them the centre and end of things. . . . Do not isolate yourself from the whole of the world.'[2]

[1] The name is altered from *pseudophanês*, 'shining with false (borrowed) light', a rare epithet applied to the moon. In itself, *pseusô* as a verb form in Greek means 'I shall deceive'.

[2] Étienne Pivert de Senancour, *Obermann*, tr. Arthur E. Waite, New York 1903, 96–9.

The Obermann of the 1849 poem had been torn between two impulses, one driving him to the world and the other to solitude. The palinode witnesses to a decision between them, taken by Arnold long before 1866. It meant that the essentially individualistic ethical systems of late Greek thought required concealment or modification if they were to appear at all in his prose, with its increasing public concern. The single exception, his study of Marcus Aurelius, portrays a late period of Stoicism when the passive virtues of resignation and forbearance had become supreme. Drawn by a likeness of temperament, he presents the melancholy emperor with vividness and charm. The essay reveals an unwarranted tendency to Christianize its subject, but as an introduction to an attractive moralist it remains without a rival.

Arnold acknowledges that, for a version of Stoic ethical doctrine capable of fortifying our character, we must have recourse to Epictetus; the intellectual Seneca and the touchingly emotional Marcus Aurelius will not suffice. He himself came back constantly to this source. The note-books for 1867 are filled with quotations which derive directly or indirectly from it, and in the next year he introduced into *Culture and Anarchy* Epictetus's use of *euphuia* and *aphuia*. These two terms express the presence or absence, respectively, of hereditary excellence in an individual. Their occurrence in the *Discourses* of Epictetus has been seen as indicating an aristocratic bias. For Arnold's purposes, defining virtue as a gift of heredity and granting a privileged place to the vocabulary of aristocracy were alike useless and dangerous; he was not about to give hostages to the Barbarians. He did succeed, however, in making effective use of the terms themselves. Basically this proved to be possible because he, like Plato, had been able to link the individual with the state through culture. In the particular circumstances, he achieved his success partly by turning the attention of his readers to the strong emphasis upon moral progress in the teachings of Epictetus. He incorporates both approaches in the larger argument of *Culture and Anarchy*: 'Culture . . . places human perfection in an *internal* condition. . . . Men are all members of one great whole, and the sympathy which is in human nature will not allow one member to be indifferent to the rest. . . . Individual perfection is impossible so long as the rest of mankind are not perfected along with us' (*CPW*, V, 94, 215).

Although Arnold apparently considered his emphasis upon altruism to be a Christian addition (his examples come from Thomas à Kempis and the inexhaustible Bishop Wilson), the position does have a Stoic basis, clearly shown in Senancour's 'Manual'. There can be no doubt about the conscious derivation from Stoicism of many striking phrases in *Culture and Anarchy*. Examples are 'trying to do violence to nature instead of working along with it', 'the intelligible law of things', 'right reason',[1] a paramount best self', some of these going back originally to Aristotle or Plato. Yet for the Stoics, despite their oecumenical convictions, the rationale and practice of altruism were beset with difficulties, especially those caused by their acceptance of a thorough-going determinism. Broadly speaking, Arnold was merely seeking an inevitable truce with necessity when, in the shift from poetry to prose, he ceased to debate publicly questions of Stoic and Epicurean thought. Except for the idea of the 'hidden life', Epicureanism makes no meaningful contribution to the lectures and essays. While Stoicism does contribute abundantly, the original context and meaning are ignored on more than a few occasions; thus 'the habit of fixing our mind upon the intelligible law of things' (*CPW*, V, 219) becomes the closing definition of Hellenism in *Culture and Anarchy*. Arnold's attitude towards philosophy might best be described as eclecticism: to achieve his syncretistic goal, he took what he required.

Among the later works, *St. Paul and Protestantism, Literature and Dogma* and *God and the Bible* all employ Stoic principles as an occasional means of reinforcing the argument. Arnold did not cease to be eclectic after 1870; the difference lay in the increasing prominence given to liberal Christianity within his system, or lack of system. To see what Stoicism meant to him we must look elsewhere, to the note-books with their multitude of entries from Stoic sources. It would be difficult indeed to set a limit upon the power, for example, of Epictetus's statement that we have a natural fellowship with one another, a fellowship that we must preserve by every possible means. For some readers of Arnold's work in the 1870s, the presence of such doctrines imparted a real strength. He himself walked in their light until the end of his days.

[1] Bush, *Matthew Arnold*, 153–4, gives a detailed examination of 'right reason' in *Culture and Anarchy*; he also notes its importance for the later theological works, 175, 182.

Any attempt to summarize Matthew Arnold's classicism meets at once with the problem of his elusiveness. The term did not enter English literature before 1837, and Arnold pointedly avoids using it.[1] 'Classic' and 'classical' are clearly more promising, and his works yield a few passing attempts at definition. According to 'The Study of Poetry', their 'true and right meaning' is '[of] the class of the very best' (*CPW*, IX, 165); *Last Essays* mentions experience as the only means of proof which 'assures us that . . . the poetry and artistic form of certain epochs has not, in fact, been improved upon, and is, therefore, classical' (*CPW*, VIII, 11–12). Since these are very late sources, an essay of 1864, 'On the Literary Influence of Academies', has particular interest when classical prose such as that of Bossuet is termed 'prose of the centre', meaning the centre of good taste—prose which is free from the 'note of provinciality'—although we profit little from the reference to 'the best and highest' work, which is classical (*CPW*, III, 246–7, 245).

The merit of these definitions varies, but the variation occurs within rather narrow limits; none of them seems adequate. The first is hardly more than etymologizing, the second a negative statement. There is greater promise in the contrast between town and country with regard to refinement of expression, a view that would have been familiar to Arnold from disparaging comments in Aristophanes and Catullus. He was not, however, dealing directly with antiquity here; and he has left poetry out of account. *On Translating Homer* does contain the assertion that classical and romantic 'remain eternally distinct' as modes of representation (*CPW*, I, 135). Nestor, we are told, may actually have resembled the moss-trooping freebooters of Percy's *Reliques*, but the mode of portrayal has made him exist, for us, as utterly unlike them. He is unalterably classical, as they are romantic. While one may regret that this approach was not pursued further, methodical development of a concept was never Arnold's forte.

In any case, his actual use of the classical cannot be derived from an analysis of his remarks concerning its nature. An attempt has been made here to show the successive stages of his classicism, from the tentativeness of the early poetic experiments to the disengaged formalism which characterizes the Preface and contents of the 1853 edition. This personal attitude of aloofness was carried over into the

[1] The term seems to occur only in a minor essay written in 1870, 'A French Elijah'; see *CPW*, VII, 11.

prose; any warmth of feeling, when classical sources were involved, came either from temperamental affinities or from a private devotional use of Stoic thought. Such unity as his classicism possessed was subjective; a truly objective manner of dealing with antiquity did not lie within the range of his abilities.

This lack of objectivity cannot be ascribed simply to a lack of method; an anti-historical attitude entered into it as well. To this extent at least, the Greeks failed to serve him: the many lessons that Herodotus and Thucydides can teach do not include the historical sense. Arnold claimed to think historically, and the classical past did have reality for him. He also idealized it, however, frequently ignoring its historicity in favour of what he saw as its timeless values. He regularly dealt thus with the Hellenic period, especially with the age of Pericles. For him these were the embodiment of the classical, although he acknowledged that his own affinities were with the later classical periods. His acceptance of historicism as suggesting the future through the past was tempered by an insistence upon the need at times to judge historical fact poetically. Once activated by his eclectic method, this combination of attitudes enabled him to move readily between past and present in his criticism. Suspect as scholarship, the results proved to be uncommonly vivid and persuasive.

Undoubtedly Arnold can be criticized for many shortcomings in his dealings with the classical past. The proper rejoinder is not an attempt at denial but a reminder of what Arnold was able to accomplish. In 'Thyrsis' he has given us one of the great English elegies, a work in which he could transform an unremarkable phrase from a minor Greek poet into the exquisite 'morningless and unawakening sleep'. With the possible exception of *The Waste Land*, no other poem of the nineteenth or even the twentieth century captures the isolation of modern man as does 'Dover Beach', with its use of the Thucydidean night battle. The lectures *On Translating Homer* employ comparative method with remarkable success to establish Homer's place as a master of world literature.

For one who was an overworked inspector of schools throughout his mature life, the total achievement is impressive. His dealings with Greece and Rome reveal no sovereign method, nor yet any single master. Matthew Arnold was his own man, and we must accept him as we find him: flawed, but brilliant.

10: *Arnold and Goethe*

JAMES SIMPSON

MATTHEW ARNOLD WAS A MAN of prodigious culture. The scope of his reading was impressively wide, and clearly it would be dangerous to exaggerate the importance to him of one particular author among the many whom he had read. Nevertheless, Arnold claimed that Goethe was one of the few men from whom he had learned 'habits, methods, ruling ideas, which are constantly with me',[1] and my purpose in this essay is to examine the part played by Goethe in Arnold's intellectual background. My thesis is that Arnold's claim is justified but rather misleading, since it obscures the fact that Goethe's importance altered as Arnold grew older. I will try to show that Goethe's influence on the English poet was greatest in the years 1847–57, and that subsequently it declined, for although Arnold continued to read Goethe as assiduously as ever and referred to him constantly in his published writings, Arnold's views were largely formed by 1857 and his leading interests were moving into areas where Goethe's writings could not be of help.

Very little is known for certain about how or when Arnold first came to be interested in Goethe. When Arnold was born in 1822, Goethe was for the second time rising to literary prominence in England. His first success in this country had been achieved with the novel *Die Leiden des jungen Werthers* (1774)—*The Sorrows of Young Werther*. It was translated into English many times before the end of the eighteenth century, but the novel's notoriety did great harm to Goethe's reputation. In the first place *Werther* apparently belonged to a disreputable class of literature—the sensational or sentimental novel—and in the second place it was widely condemned as 'immoral'; the author appeared to countenance suicide and to have too much sympathy with his hero's potentially adulterous passion. For many

[1] Letter to Cardinal Newman, 28 May 1872, *Unpublished Letters*, 65–6.

years Goethe was remembered only as 'the author of *Werther*'. The publication of *Faust: erster Teil* in Germany in 1808 attracted almost no attention in Britain for several years. This was probably due mainly to the political situation at the time of the Napoleonic wars when England was cut off from the rest of the Continent, but the 'freeze' in literary relations ended in 1813 when Madame de Staël's enormously influential *De l'Allemagne* was published by John Murray. Madame de Staël spoke warmly of Goethe and praised *Faust* as a masterpiece. Murray, who was eager to bring out a translation, offered Coleridge £100 to undertake the task, but unfortunately nothing came of the plan. At last, however, a translator was found, and in 1823 Murray published the first of the many English versions of the play to appear between 1820 and 1850.[1] *Faust I* ultimately established Goethe's fame in England, but initially it compounded his reputation as an 'immoral author'. Amazing as it may seem now, the scene entitled *Prolog im Himmel*, in which Mephistopheles chats familiarly with God, was thought blasphemous and even more offensive to good taste than Faust's seduction of Margarethe.

For this reason it is unlikely that Arnold had read *Faust* before going up to Oxford as an undergraduate in 1841. By the standards of his time Dr. Arnold was a liberal father and headmaster, but his liberalism could hardly have extended to plying his children with reading matter which many, himself included, thought to be of dubious morality. On the other hand, even in 1841 the name Goethe would almost certainly have signified more to Arnold than the obscure German poet to whom Byron had dedicated *Werner* and *Sardanapalus.* Wordsworth always spoke disparagingly of Goethe, but other of Dr. Arnold's friends could be relied on to speak of him with enthusiasm and veneration. Henry Crabb Robinson, for example, whom the Doctor met through the Wordsworths and who had actually known the German sage personally, occasionally visited the Arnolds at Fox How, their holiday home, and read Goethe's poems with 'Miss Arnold'[2]—presumably Jane, the eldest of the children and Matthew's favourite. Arnold may well have become acquainted with Goethe, therefore, through Crabb

[1] Lord Francis Leverson Gower, tr., *Faust: a drama by Goethe and Schiller's Song of the Bell*, 1823.

[2] See *Diaries, Reminiscences and Correspondence of Henry Crabb Robinson*, ed T. Sadler, 3rd edn, 2 vol, 1872, II, 214.

Robinson, but his serious reading of Goethe and other European writers probably began only after 1841. By this time Arnold was sufficiently advanced in German to be able to read works in the original language, which he had learned in the Upper School at Rugby.

Once at Oxford Arnold's literary tastes matured. His younger brother, Thomas, recalled in his autobiography that Goethe 'displaced Byron in [Matthew's] poetical allegiance'.[1] Carlyle played an important part in bringing the change about. We have Arnold's word for it that in the early 1840s 'the greatest voice of the century . . . came to us in those youthful years through Carlyle: the voice of Goethe'.[2] Carlyle had translated *Wilhelm Meisters Lehrjahre* in 1824 and it was in this translation that Arnold first read Goethe's novel. Furthermore, Carlyle's writings on Goethe in his *Critical and Miscellaneous Essays* (1839) represented the only good critical appraisal of the German poet available in English until G. H. Lewes's biography *Life of Goethe* appeared in 1855. Carlyle's view of Goethe was certainly a distorted and personal one. He interpreted the poet's life as a passage from 'scepticism' to 'Faith', and he could see in Faust only a pitifully misguided figure lost in the pursuit of happiness. This depiction of a 'Goethe moralisé' is a long way from the truth, but at least it has the merit of being a serious attempt at interpretation—as opposed to the gossip and slander which then often passed for criticism—and for a time Arnold heeded Teufeldröckh's strident appeal: 'Close thy *Byron*; open thy *Goethe*.'[3] In 1847 Arnold purchased the sixty-volume Cotta edition of Goethe's works, the *Ausgabe letzter Hand*, and in the next few years added to it various volumes of Goethe's letters and conversations. Few Englishmen of the time were better equipped than Arnold to understand the work of the German poet and this reading had important consequences for his own development.

No account of Goethe's significance to Arnold would be adequate that ignored the English poet's religious position as it evolved in the years immediately after he left Rugby School. Arnold's first volume of poetry, *The Strayed Reveller and other Poems* (1849), hardly made a secret

[1] T. Arnold, *Passages in a Wandering Life*, 1900, 56–7.

[2] M. Arnold, 'Emerson', *Discourses in America*, 1885, *Works*, iv, 351.

[3] T. Carlyle, *Sartor Resartus*, 1838, in *The Works of Thomas Carlyle*, Centenary Edition, 30 vol, 1896–9, I, 153.

of the 'religious agnosticism' which had replaced the orthodox Christianity of his upbringing. There was no revelation of disbelief and, of course, no break with the Church. The 'Broad Church' attitude to certain dogmas, which Arnold had inherited from his father, gave way gradually to a more radically sceptical outlook. Arnold's exposure at Oxford to the more liberal world views of such writers as Emerson, George Sand, Carlyle and Goethe seems to have had its effect. The obituary which Tom Arnold wrote on his brother for the *Manchester Guardian* (18 May 1888) explicitly links his drift away from Christianity with his reading of Goethe, and this is indirectly confirmed by Arnold himself. In the essay 'Heinrich Heine' he wrote: 'Goethe's profound, imperturbable naturalism is absolutely fatal to all routine thinking; he puts the standard, once for all, inside every man instead of outside him. . . . Nothing could be more really subversive of the foundations on which the old European order rested; and it may be remarked that no persons are . . . so thoroughly modern, as those who have felt Goethe's influence most deeply.'[1] Goethe, then, had been for Arnold one of the 'dissolvents of the old European system of dominant ideas and facts', but he had been no 'acrid dissolvent'. It is not hard to see what Arnold meant by this. The German poet was no crude anti-Christian propagandist; his influence was more oblique. It was the spirit in which works like *Wilhelm Meister* and *Dichtung und Wahrheit* were written that impressed Arnold most strongly, for Goethe's attitude to Christianity was free both from hostility and from retrospective, regretful nostalgia. His works were written from a standpoint which took it for granted that the Christian revelation was not the literal or final truth, and his calm assurance and authority must have carried far greater weight with Arnold than any 'sceptical' biography of Jesus.

A direct consequence of Arnold's 'religious agnosticism' was the ethical uncertainty in which he now found himself. Put simply, the problem was to discover some firm basis for responsible conduct in the absence of the sanctions that Christianity had previously provided. The difficulty was not easy to resolve and Arnold's uncertainty is reflected in *The Strayed Reveller*, where a number of varying, and often contradictory, ethical positions are explored. The possibility of a hedonistic response to a world without God—or with Gods 'careless of our doom'—is considered in the poems 'Mycerinus' and 'The New

[1] *Essays in Criticism* (1865), *CPW*, III, 110.

Sirens', but only to be rejected. 'The Sick King in Bokhara' and 'Fragment of an "Antigone"' contemplate an alternative position, that of a moral law absolute in itself, requiring no watchful deity to enforce it. But the 'Law', the compelling necessity, which impresses the Sick King is an irrational one, and the prospect of life-long submission to unreason could have held no strong or permanent appeal for Arnold. Instead, he found a better solution to his difficulties in a moral position close to that of stoicism. The heroic repression of pain had a certain Byronic attraction for Arnold which is evident in one of his earliest published poems, 'To a Gipsy Child by the Sea-shore'. Even Mycerinus, Arnold hints, may have been a stoic in disguise. Not until the poem 'Resignation', however, was Arnold able to give his stoicism a more mature and less self-conscious form.

'Resignation' shows that this picture of Arnold searching for a 'new' morality is in one important respect an over-simplification. Arnold was not a moral philosopher. His interest in the ethical basis of conduct was not theoretical but practical and deeply rooted in his personal life. Nor was Arnold simply a man without religious faith, but more importantly a poet without a faith. The question which confronted Arnold was not simply 'how to act', but rather 'how to act as a poet', and it was with respect to this second question that Goethe was helpful to him. The stoicism that Arnold sets out in 'Resignation' is of a relatively serene and untroubled kind. He contrasts a life of fierce resolution and activity with one 'freed from passions, and the state/ Of struggle these necessitate' and argues that the second of these states is more appropriate for a poet.[1] From his high vantage point above the agitated life of humanity, the Poet is able to survey the course of mankind. The Poet is a man set apart from others; he understands action and suffering, but he takes no part in them. He is above the strife and because he does not envy what he sees, his separateness causes him no pain:

From some high station he looks down,
At sunset, on a populous town;
Surveys each happy group which fleets,
Toil ended, through the shining streets,
Each with some errand of its own—
And does not say: I am alone.[2]

[1] *Poems*, 85.
[2] *Poems*, 90–1.

This conception of the Poet was almost certainly suggested by *Wilhelm Meister*, a work whose large, liberal view of human life had struck a sympathetic chord in the young man:

> Look at men, how they struggle after happiness and satisfaction! Their wishes, their toil, their gold, are ever hunting restlessly; and after what? After that which the poet has received from nature,—the right enjoyment of the world. . . . Now fate has exalted the poet above all this, as if he were a god. He views the conflicting tumult of passions; sees families and kingdoms raging in aimless commotion. . . . He has a fellow-feeling of the mournful and the joyful in the fate of all human beings.[1]

The Goethean position of calm detachment from human affairs suited Arnold so well because he was by temperament distrustful of emotional agitation. The word 'feverish', which is one of Arnold's favourite epithets, has strongly negative associations in his poetry and is nearly always linked with the emotional turmoil of youth. Excitement is a form of weakness, whereas calm is tranquil strength. A part, at least, of this distrust stems from Arnold's almost obsessive preoccupation with the passage of time and the fleetingness of youth. Thus, the poet-hero of 'The New Sirens' spurns the delights of romantic love because they are transient, not because he considers 'thought' more important than 'feeling'. One suspects, however, that when Arnold first drafted 'Resignation' in 1844 or 1845 he had very little to resign himself to, and that his knowledge of turbulent passions derived from the novels of George Sand rather than from actual experience. It was not until his two encounters with the French girl 'Marguerite' at Thun, Switzerland, in the Autumn of 1848 and 1849, that Arnold learned from personal experience that self-mastery was easier to preach than to practise.

Arnold's difficulty is revealed in the letter which he sent to Clough from Switzerland at the time of his second meeting with Marguerite in September 1849. He wrote:

> What I must tell you is that I have never yet succeeded in any one great occasion in consciously mastering myself: I can go thro: the

[1] Carlyle's translation of *Wilhelm Meister*, Book II, Chapter 2, in *Works*, XXIII, 112.

imaginary process of mastering myself and see the whole affair as it would then stand, but at the critical point I am too apt to hoist up the mainsail to the wind and let her drive.[1]

The second—and final—parting from Marguerite, whatever its cause may have been, was acutely painful to Arnold, and unhappiness strengthened his determination never again to give free play to his emotions. The poem 'Stanzas in Memory of the Author of "Obermann"', which was begun by November 1849, confirms that two important tendencies in his mental and moral development were his wish to attain stoic detachment and his wish to avoid 'excitement':

He who hath watched, not shared, the strife,
Knows how the day hath gone.[2]

These two lines establish his preference for a poetry of 'distance' and objectivity to a poetry of self-destroying involvement such as he had briefly contemplated in 'The Strayed Reveller'. The 'Stanzas in Memory' end with the speaker bidding farewell to Obermann's 'unstrung will' and 'broken heart', but it was no mere character in a book that Arnold was painfully putting behind him. Rather it was a portion of his own mind and life.

The nature of Goethe's relevance to Arnold at this time is not immediately obvious, but Arnold's description of Goethe in the 1853 Preface as 'the greatest poet of modern times, the greatest critic of all times'[3] gives us a useful clue. The danger for Arnold after the failure of his relationship with Marguerite lay in morbid despondency and for his poetry in possible preoccupation with the theme of 'love gone wrong'. The reason why Goethe assumed such great authority as a critic with Arnold was that he diagnosed (the metaphor is suggested by Arnold himself) the young poet's situation with telling accuracy.[4] Arnold translated two essays of Goethe, 'Für junge Dichter' and 'Noch ein Wort für junge Dichter' into an (unpublished) note-book dated June

[1] *Letters to Clough*, 110.
[2] *Poems*, 134.
[3] *CPW*, I, 8.
[4] See 'Memorial Verses', *Poems*, 227.

1847.[1] These short essays are basically an indictment of romantic subjectivity and a refutation of the belief that poetry is a vehicle for self-expression. At first, argues Goethe, a poet's subjectivity is his source of strength, but once his 'inward, youthful contentment' begins to dwindle, morbidity sets in and he becomes a 'misanthropical hermit'. The poetic gift survives only in the man who can 'cheerfully renounce . . . early dreams, wishes and hopes, and the satisfactions of young romance', who 'nimbly recovers himself, who can gather some fruit from every season . . . who imposes silence on his own suffering'. The mark of a 'perfected life in its full development' is 'circumspect wisdom'. Nothing could have been more appropriate to Arnold than Goethe's exhortation to a young poet to ask himself at every poem 'if it contains an actual experience, and if this actual experience has furthered you'. 'You are not furthered', Goethe went on, 'when you keep bewailing over one you have loved, and lost through separation, faithlessness or death. . . . All this is good for nothing.' Goethe's message was clear. If the ability to write poetry was to be sustained beyond youth, then self-restraint, stoical renunciation and self-development were indispensable.

Arnold found Goethe's advice sound but hard to follow. It was necessary, as he later explained to Clough in 1853, to bar out 'all influences that I felt troubled without advancing me'[2] and one of these influences was undoubtedly the memory of Switzerland. The struggle to which Arnold subjected himself is evident from the poems 'Absence' and 'Courage'. Arnold was torn between a desire for a 'nobler, calmer train/ Of wiser thoughts and feelings'[3]—that circumspect wisdom which Goethe counselled—and a deep reluctance to give up the life of passion. In the penultimate stanza of 'Absence' Arnold seems to accept the necessity of rejecting the 'Once-longed-for storms of love' in favour of self-knowledge and knowledge of the world, but his renunciation of early wishes, dreams and hopes was anything but 'cheerful'. The indecision revealed in 'Absence' is evident too in 'courage'. The first stanza concedes the validity of Goethe's stoic counsel:

[1] See J. W. von Goethe, *Werke: Ausgabe letzter Hand*, 60 vol, Stuttgart and Tübingen 1827–42, XLV, 426–7.

[2] *Letters to Clough*, 129.

[3] 'Absence', *Poems*, 138.

True, we must tame our rebel will:
True, we must bow to Nature's law:
Must bear in silence many an ill;
Must learn to wait, renounce, withdraw.[1]

Nevertheless, the remainder of the poem attempts to justify a kind of Byronic dynamism on the grounds that it is at least 'dauntless' and resolute, whereas his present 'faltering course' is mere weakness. By rejecting the memory of Marguerite, Arnold was in effect choosing a life of 'Moderate tasks and moderate leisure. . . . Both in suffering and in pleasure'. The wisdom of the choice was hard to dispute:

No small profit that man earns,
Who through all he meets can steer him,
Can reject what cannot clear him,
Cling to what can truly cheer him.[2]

But the poem's title betrays Arnold's true attitude—it is only 'The Second Best'. He was unconvinced that the decision to suppress the turbulent parts of his temperament was really the right course, and by a bitter irony this uncertainty led him into that very state of morbid depression which it had been his main intention to avoid.

By a further stroke of irony, it was out of this same emotional state that 'Empedocles on Etna', the single indisputable masterpiece of Arnold's longer poems, was born. The poem's central concern is with the reasons for Empedocles's misery. His misery, it seems, is partly due to the hostility of his environment, for the great period of Greek religious philosophy is past and the influence of the Sophists has begun to prevail. He feels that 'great qualities' are trodden down by 'littleness united' (Act II, ll. 92–4). But the root cause is more fundamental than this, and lies within Empedocles himself: he has become enslaved to the 'imperious lonely thinking-power' (Act II, l. 376). In consequence he has destroyed the harmonious wholeness of being which enables the youthful Callicles still to take pleasure in existence. In this respect the character of Empedocles is a portrait of the man Arnold feared that he might become. A part of Arnold's strategy for curbing his emotional

[1] 'Courage', *Poems*, 141.
[2] *Poems*, 278.

self was rigorous intellectual effort. In 1850 he wrote to Clough: 'I go to read Locke on the Conduct of the Understanding: my respect for the reason as the rock of refuge to this poor exaggerated surexcited humanity increases and increases.'[1] Three years later the tune had changed dramatically: 'I feel immensely . . . what I have . . . lost and choked by my treatment of myself and the studies to which I have addicted myself.' And in another letter of 1853: 'I am past thirty and three parts iced over.'[2] By then he had realized what the search for calm had cost in terms of the power to feel.

Goethe's influence on Arnold's development at this point in his career was not an altogether healthy one, for his advice had encouraged Arnold to adopt a course of action that resulted in a restless and unhappy dissatisfaction with himself. It is true, however, that Arnold had slightly misconstrued the meaning of Goethe's words to a young poet. Goethe advises the young man not to dwell on experiences which trouble without advancing him, but Arnold took this 'advancing' in a strictly ethical sense. It is unlikely that Goethe intended his words to be taken in this way. He was thinking in much wider terms of the development, not of the moral character alone, but of the whole personality including the creative faculties. Arnold may not have felt advanced as a person by his experience in Switzerland, but, whether he knew it or not, he was advanced as an artist. The 'Switzerland' poems themselves are not Arnold's best work, but the deepening of feeling and insight to which they are witness, eventually lent weight to the tragic view of life which he held, unconvincingly in the 1849 volume of poetry, but with far greater authority in 'Empedocles on Etna'.

Arnold was perhaps too ready to equate those things which troubled him with those which hindered his development. He would have found it difficult to accept that an experience which upset his moral and mental equipoise could actually have been useful or beneficial to him as an artist, whereas to Goethe this notion would have appeared obvious. Arnold could have corrected his distorted interpretation of Goethe's advice by simple reference to the German's poetic practice. Much of Goethe's finest work (from the early *Werther* to the 'Marienbad Elegy' of 1823) is clearly the direct consequence of an unhappy experience in

[1] *Letters to Clough*, 116.

[2] See *Letters to Clough*, 136 and 128.

love similar to Arnold's with Marguerite. There is a great difference between Arnold's futile efforts to bar out the memory of Marguerite as an unhelpful influence, and Goethe's recommendations which were intended only to discourage that kind of repetitive preoccupation with inner suffering which cuts the poet off from the external world. Arnold never saw poetic creation as a means of exorcising those unwelcome spectres. For Goethe, on the other hand, the writing of poetry was always a therapeutic act, a way of liberating himself from the tyranny of strong emotion. He would have regarded Arnold's love for Marguerite and the pain which separation from her caused as perfectly legitimate subjects for poetry. The transformation of these subjects into poetry was indeed the only hope of crushing 'the seed of madness that lies in every separation'.[1] Arnold avoided 'madness' by suppressing the capacity for suffering, but in this way he ultimately killed his frail poetic gift.

It would be enormously helpful to know what Arnold's views about Goethe were at this time, the period of his most intense poetic activity, but unfortunately he was not so obliging as to leave us with a record of them. The essay 'A French Critic on Goethe' (1878) is too late to be of much use, for by then Arnold's admiration for Goethe had become somewhat cooler. However, by piecing together Arnold's scattered remarks about Goethe in letters and poems, it is possible to arrive at a fairly coherent picture. In the poem 'Stanzas in Memory of the Author of "Obermann"' Arnold identified the two moderns who, apart from Obermann, had 'attained . . . to see their way' (ll. 47–8) as Wordsworth and Goethe. Both poets suggested themselves to Arnold as models for his own development, but Wordsworth was here given short shrift: he had averted his eyes from 'half of human fate' (l. 54). On the other hand, Goethe's 'wide/ And luminous view' of life Arnold could not hope to 'emulate'. In 'Memorial Verses', the poem written on the death of Wordsworth, Goethe figures as the 'Physician of the iron age' (l. 17):

> *He took the suffering human race,*
> *He read each wound, each weakness clear;*
> *And struck his finger on the place,*
> *And said:* Thou ailest here, and here!

[1] See Goethe, *Italienische Reise*, 1816–29, in *Werke*, XXIX, 302.

He looked on Europe's dying hour
Of fitful dream and feverish power;
His eye plunged down the weltering strife,
The turmoil of expiring life—

. . . .

And he was happy, if to know
Causes of things, and far below
His feet to see the lurid flow
Of terror, and insane distress,
And headlong fate, be happiness.[1]

The 'Obermann' stanzas are not, of course, addressed to Goethe or Wordsworth, but to Senancour, and Lionel Trilling comments on this fact: 'Arnold saw him as the very type of the modern soul, more relevant than either Wordsworth or Goethe, for his icy clarity of despair is of more use, says Arnold, than either "Wordsworth's sweet calm" or Goethe's "wide and luminous view".'[2] But it is surely because 'icy despair' is of no use that Arnold turns his back on Obermann. 'Despair' might be the most appropriate response to the insane distress of expiring life in the 'Iron age' of European history, but it did not help. Arnold neither could nor wanted to retire to a mountain like a misanthropical hermit: 'I in the world must live" he says (l. 137), and to do this he needed, as he expressed it in a letter to Clough of 1849, 'a distinct seeing of my way as far as my own nature is concerned'.[3] The task of achieving a comprehensive view of life might well prove beyond him, but the impossibility did not absolve Arnold from the duty of endeavour. For Arnold's purposes Goethe might be less 'relevant' than Senancour, but, as a model of what a poet ought to be, he was of far greater 'use'.

There is a further element worth noticing in Arnold's picture of Goethe. His praise of Goethe in the 1853 Preface stressed his greatness as a critic, and it is Goethe's intellectual rather than his poetic stature which Arnold emphasizes in a letter of 22 September 1864, where he describes him as 'a great and powerful spirit . . . in the line of modern thought'.[4] There is here an interesting example of Arnold's tendency to

[1] *Poems*, 227–8.

[2] L. Trilling, *Matthew Arnold*, 4th edn, 1963, 85.

[3] *Letters to Clough*, 110.

[4] *Letters*, I, 239.

discern parallels between his own position as a poet and Goethe's. In the figure of Empedocles Arnold had expressed symbolically his fear that over-concentration on intellectual study had done great injury to his poetic gifts: Empedocles, who in his younger days had been like Callicles, is a lapsed poet. Arnold believed that Goethe had suffered in a similar way, for in 1860 he wrote to his sister, Frances: 'Goethe owes his grandeur to his strength in this [intellectual power], although it even hurt his poetical operations by its immense predominance.'[1] This picture of Goethe may not be altogether accurate, but its very inaccuracy is revealing. For Arnold, distrustful as he was of youth's feverishness, Goethe's strength lay in his powerful intellect: he knew 'causes of things' and was stoical in the face of suffering, detached from the turmoil of human affairs, surveying it—like the poet of 'Resignation'—from a lofty vantage point. During that period of unhappy emotional uncertainty between 1848 and his marriage to Frances Lucy Wightman in 1851, this conception of the Poet had considerable appeal for Arnold. But Empedocles discovered too late that detachment can easily become a tormented isolation. Arnold found in stoicism a certain joylessness which made it valueless as a creed to live by, and as he grew older it became steadily less appropriate to his situation. In January 1851 he wrote sadly to 'K' his sister Jane: 'The aimless and unsettled, but also open and liberal state of our youth we *must* perhaps all leave and take refuge in our morality and character; but with most of us it is a melancholy passage from which we emerge shorn of so many beams that we are almost tempted to quarrel with the law of nature that imposes it on us.'[2] Sensibly, Arnold did not quarrel with this law of nature. He accepted a post as Inspector of Schools and put himself in a position to marry. The marriage was a happy one and although the 'incessant grind in schools' was uncongenial, Arnold persevered.[3] The 'rebel will' was tamed.

Perhaps the most important contribution to Arnold's evolution of a philosophy less despairing than that expressed in 'Empedocles on Etna' was made by Spinoza. Arnold had probably read some Spinoza by 1847, but the first definite proof of his interest is the letter he wrote to Clough in October 1850: 'Locke is a man who has cleared his mind of

[1] *Letters*, I, 127.
[2] *Letters*, I, 14.
[3] *Letters*, I, 26.

vain repetitions, though without the positive and vivifying atmosphere of Spinoza about him. This last, smile as you will, I have been studying lately with profit.'[1] Arnold does not say what had prompted him to begin studying the philosopher, but his essay 'Spinoza and the Bible' (1863) supplies an answer. In discussing the sources of Spinoza's attractiveness for Goethe, Arnold comments:

> Spinoza first impresses Goethe and any man like Goethe, and then he composes him; first he fills and satisfies his imagination by the width and grandeur of his view of nature, and then he fortifies and stills his mobile, straining, passionate, poetic temperament by the moral lesson he draws from his view of nature. And a moral lesson not of mere resigned acquiescence, not of melancholy quietism, but of joyful activity within the limits of man's true sphere.[2]

Goethe had affirmed Spinoza's importance in very similar terms in *Dichtung und Wahrheit*.

> The mind who effected me so decisively and who was to have so great an influence upon me, was Spinoza. . . . I chanced eventually upon the Ethics of this man. What I read out of or into this work I could not say, enough that I found here what I needed to subdue my passions; a wide, free prospect over the physical and moral world seemed to open up before me.[3]

Clearly then, Goethe stressed the very kind of effect—restraining, calming—that Arnold felt he needed after the final separation from Marguerite. Arnold had read *Dichtung und Wahrheit* in 1849 so it is quite probable that he turned to Spinoza consciously desiring certain effects, and that he did so because of Goethe's experience. Certainly, it is difficult not to feel as one reads Arnold's description of Spinoza's influence on Goethe—*and any man like Goethe*—that his words have a personal application. The troubled poetic temperament could be calmed by confronting the rebellious will with a wide and grand view of nature: this was the message of Goethe's biography for Arnold. The

[1] *Letters to Clough*, 117.

[2] *Essays in Criticism*, 1865, *CPW*, III, 177.

[3] Part III, Book 14. See *Werke*, XXVI, 290–1.

resultant stoicism could be both joyful and active. If, therefore, Goethe's critical advice had at one point led Arnold into a slough of despond, the German poet's own life now suggested a way out of it.

Considering the extent of Goethe's importance to Arnold in the analysis of his own situation as a poet, Goethe's poetic practice exerted comparatively little influence on Arnold's actual poetry. Nevertheless, some influence there is. Trilling observed that Arnold's 'unrhymed, loosely-cadenced verse was modelled after Goethe's *Grenzen der Menschheit*' (*Matthew Arnold*, 143–4), but did not pursue the matter further. Metrically there are indeed striking similarities between Goethe's free-verse poems like 'Mahomets Gesang', 'Prometheus', 'Grenzen der Menschheit', 'Das Göttliche', 'Gesang der Geister über den Wassern' and Arnold's 'The Youth of Nature', 'The Youth of Man', 'The Future', 'Haworth Churchyard', 'Rugby Chapel' and 'Heine's Grave'. In each case the poem consists of unrhymed verse paragraphs of no fixed length; the line usually has three stresses but a varying number of syllables. But other features of the poetry need consideration too. There are, for example, similarities between Arnold's 'The Future' and Goethe's 'Gesang der Geister' which are so striking that mere coincidence can be ruled out. In general terms Arnold borrowed from Goethe the technique of what may be called 'explicit parable'. This technique involves the open statement at the beginning of the poem of a metaphor which the remainder of the poem pursues and develops. Arnold begins 'The Future' with an explicit statement of this kind:

A wanderer is man from his birth.
He was born in a ship
On the breast of the river of Time.

The second paragraph closes:

As is the world on the banks,
So is the mind of the man.[1]

Goethe uses the same method in 'Gesang der Geister', which begins:

[1] *Poems*, 263–4.

Des Menschen Seele
Gleicht dem Wasser:
Vom Himmel kommt es,
Zum Himmel steigt es,
Und wieder nieder
Zur Erde muss es,
Ewig wechselnd.

[The soul of man/ is like to the water/ from heaven it comes,/ to heaven it goes,/ and all again/ to earth it must,/ in endless alternation.]

The poem concludes with a return to the parable in a slightly modulated form:

Seele des Menschen,
Wie gleichst du dem Wasser!
Schicksal des Menschen,
Wie gleichst du dem Wind![1]

[Soul of man,/ how like to the water!/ Destiny of man,/ how like to the wind!]

The element of parable occurs in other of Arnold's poems. Though less explicitly than in 'The Future', it plays an important part in 'The Buried Life', where the 'river' is again used as an extended metaphor, and in 'Rugby Chapel' where the parable is introduced by a question:

What is the course of the life
Of mortal men on earth?[2]

Arnold's answer points to the aimless, 'eddying' lives that most men lead; he compares them to transient ocean waves that 'have swelled,/ Foamed for a moment, and gone'. Goethe manages the parable of 'Grenzen der Menschheit' in the same way:

Was unterscheidet
Götter von Menschen?

[In what do Gods/ differ from men?]

[1] *Werke*, II, 58–9.
[2] *Poems*, 447.

And his answer, like Arnold's, is an image of waves:

Dass viele Wellen
Vor jenen wandeln,
Ein ewiger Strom:
Uns hebt die Welle
Verschlingt die Welle,
Und wir versinken.[1]

[In this. That many waves/ before them pass,/ an eternal stream:/ us the wave lifts/ us the wave devours/ and we sink.]

This application by Arnold of a technique learned from Goethe appears to be fully conscious and deliberate.

There are suggestive similarities also between the 'Grenzen der Menschheit' and 'Das Göttliche' of Goethe, and Arnold's free-verse 'pindarics', 'The Youth of Nature' and 'The Youth of Man'. The relationship consists in the attempt made in all these pieces to achieve a calming conception of nature. In 'The Youth of Man' this attempt can be seen in Arnold's suppression of the personal emotion of grief at Wordsworth's death by emphasizing the permanence and superiority of 'nature'. The poem ends with nature proclaiming that, although men may perish, 'I remain'. In 'The Youth of Man' the same sublime view of nature is asserted:

We, O Nature, depart,
Thou survivest us! this,
This, I know, is the law.[2]

Once again an attempt is made to 'still' and to 'fortify' by contraposing the wilfulness of youth with universal necessity: it is 'law' that nature is permanent while men are transient. In 'Grenzen der Menschheit' and 'Das Göttliche' an identical confrontation takes place between Necessity and the human will:

Ein Kleiner Ring
Begrenzt unser Leben,

[1] *Werke*, II, 85.
[2] *Poems*, 251.

Und viele Geschlechter
Reihen sich dauernd
An ihres Daseins
Unendliche Kette.[1]

[A small circle/ limits our life,/ and many generations/ are linked perpetually/ on the infinite chain/ of their existence.]

And in 'Das Göttliche':

Nach ewigen, ehrnen,
Grossen Gesetzen
Müssen wir alle
Unseres Daseins
Kreise vollenden.[2]

[We must all complete/ the circles of our existence/ according to/ eternal, immutable/ great laws.]

Both 'Das Göttliche' and 'The Youth of Man' teach acquiescence. An essentially moral effort is reflected in a verse style which is plain and subdued but which, through its deliberate slow movement, enforced by the necessary pause at the end of each line, aspires to elevation and dignity. In both poems a parallel tendency is observable to produce statements of 'philosophical' truth and simple moral exhortation:

Edel sei der Mensch,
Hilfreich und gut!
Denn das allein
Unterscheidet ihn
Von allen Wesen,
Die wir kennen. ('Das Göttliche', ll. 1–6)

[Be man noble/ helpful and good!/ For in this alone/ he differs/ from all creatures/ that we know.]

[1] *Werke*, II, 85.
[2] *Werke*, II, 87.

'The Youth of Man' ends with the lines:

> *Sink, O Youth, in thy soul!*
> *Yearn to the greatness of Nature:*
> *Rally the good in the depths of thyself.*

Whether or not Arnold was consciously intending to reproduce the style of Goethe's free-verse philosophical lyrics is difficult to say positively, but it seems likely. At least, there cannot be much doubt that Arnold's attempt to curb the 'Romantic' self by confronting it with a wide and luminous view of nature was a self-conscious stratagem carried out in the full knowledge that it had already been successfully adopted by Goethe.

Between 1847 and 1853 Arnold steeped himself in Goethe's writings. The German poet was not primarily a critic or a theoretician of literature, and his views on poetry are not set out neatly in any one definitive work. 'Critical' statements are to be found not only in his essays on literature and art,[1] but are also scattered throughout his autobiographical writings, his long novel *Wilhelm Meister*, the records of his conversations with Eckermann and his letters to friends like Schiller and Zelter. Arnold probably had a better knowledge of these works than any other Englishman of his day. In spite of Arnold's literary-historical context, bobbing with his contemporaries in the wake of the great Romantics, his literary training from Rugby School to Oxford had a strong classical bias and this was greatly increased by the neo-Classical tendencies of Goethe's criticism. Even before his second visit to Switzerland in 1849, Arnold had expressed dissatisfaction with the subjective nature of his own poetry.[2] By 1850 or 1851 he had resolved to renounce personal confession as subject matter for his poetry. To his sister 'K', he wrote: 'More and more I feel bent against the modern English habit . . . of using poetry as a channel for thinking aloud, instead of making anything.'[3] The classical concept of the poet as 'maker' began to have an increasingly strong appeal.

Arnold was eventually provoked into a public statement of his views when a writer in the *North British Review*, David Masson, claimed that:

[1] See *Werke*, XXVII–XXIX, XLIV–XLVI.
[2] See *Letters to Clough*, 104.
[3] *Unpublished Letters*, 17.

'A true allegory of the state of one's own mind in a representative history, whether narrative or dramatic in form, is perhaps the highest thing that one can attempt in the way of fictitious art.'[1] To make matters worse Masson attributed the idea to Goethe and pointed to *Faust* as an example of it in practice. Arnold's reply was a straight rejection of Masson's point of view: 'An allegory of the state of one's own mind, the highest problem of an art which imitates actions! No assuredly, it is not, it never can be so.'[2] It was Masson's reference to 'narrative or dramatic' art which infuriated Arnold. His own experiments in these forms, 'Sohrab and Rustum', 'Balder Dead' and *Merope*, were attempts to find an alternative to poetry of self-expression. Masson's belief that his view of poetry was also Goethe's, Arnold knew to be mistaken. In conversation with Eckermann, for example, Goethe commented on Byron's play *Marino Faliero* in terms that strongly support Arnold's anti-subjective stand: 'The characters speak completely out of themselves and their situation, without any trace of the subjective feelings, thoughts and opinions of the poet. That is the right way.'[3] An even firmer rebuttal of Masson's argument is Goethe's remark that: 'As long as [a poet] expresses only his few subjective feelings he may not properly be called a poet at all; but as soon as he is able to take possession of the world and to express this, then he is a poet. Then he is inexhaustible and can always be new, whereas a subjective nature has soon expressed its little bit of inner self and eventually goes to ruin in mannerism.'[4] Goethe would not have denied that a poet's personality is conveyed by his poetry, but Masson was fundamentally in error in making self-expression the poet's aim. Goethe realized that the ideal of self-expression in art encouraged morbid introspection and that true objectivity consisted in the poet's vision being directed outwards. For Goethe, it was only through contact with the external world that the poet could enrich the content of his life and, ultimately, his art. Hence the great defect of most young writers lay in this: that the inner life which they sought to express

[1] 'Theories of Poetry and a New Poet', *North British Review*, XIX, 1853, 338.
[2] *CPW*, I, 8.
[3] See Eckermann, *Gespräche mit Goethe in den letzten Jahren seines Lebens*, ed P. Stapf, Berlin and Darmstadt, 1958, Part III, 10 March 1830, 751.
[4] See Eckermann, Part I, 29 Jan. 1826, 177.

lacked any 'content', any significance. The reason for the sharpness of Arnold's response to Masson is now clear. If Masson had been correct, it would have meant that the direction of Arnold's effort towards objectivity in epic and dramatic poetry was misguided and futile. The rationale of this effort had been supplied by Goethe.

Arnold was acutely conscious also of the relationship between a poet's social and cultural milieu and his capacity to produce poetry. A part of his own difficulties as a poet he attributed to the inimical environment of contemporary England. He complained to Clough: '. . . these are damned times—everything is against one—the height to which knowledge is come, the spread of luxury, our physical enervation, the absence of great *natures*, the unavoidable contact with millions of small ones, newspapers, cities, light profligate friends . . . our own selves, and the sickening consciousness of our difficulties.'[1] In the 1853 Preface Arnold inveighed against the 'spiritual discomfort' and the 'want of moral grandeur' which characterized the age, and in case any reader impressed by commercial and industrial progress felt inclined to demur, Arnold pointed calmly towards Goethe and Niebuhr and asked him to remember 'the judgements . . . [of] the men of strongest head and widest culture whom [the age] has produced'.[2] Arnold's historical consciousness was certainly fostered by the education he had received from his father, who had taught that history was mere antiquarianism if one did not apply the lessons of past ages to the immediate present. Carlyle, too, preached the miserable 'condition of England', and Arnold had early absorbed the message of 'Characteristics' and 'Signs of the Times'. But as the reference to Goethe in the Preface indicates, it was the German poet, the 'Physician of the Iron age', who seemed to have given the authoritative diagnosis of the times' ills:

> That creative state . . . through which alone anything great can flourish, is no longer possible. The critical journals appearing daily in fifty different places and the nonsensical claptrap they produce among the public will allow nothing healthy to grow. Whoever fails to detach himself completely from them and to isolate himself forcibly, is lost. . . . For a productive talent it is an

[1] Letter of 23 Sept., 1849, *Letters to Clough*, 111.
[2] *CPW*, I, 14.

> invidious mist, a falling poison which destroys the tree of his creative life, from the green crown of the leaves into the deepest pith and most hidden fibre.
>
> And then how tame and feeble life itself has become in the last few miserable centuries! Where will you find unhidden an original nature today. . . . This reacts on the poet, however, who has to find everything within himself while he is left stranded by everything outside.[1]

Sentiments like these were expressed frequently by Goethe in the last ten years or so of his life. They left their mark on the young Arnold.

Arnold was further indebted to Goethe in his analysis of the conditions under which the poetic talent *could* flourish. One of the central insights of the essay 'The Function of Criticism at the Present Time' concerned this very question:

> . . . the exercise of the creative power in the production of great works of literature or art . . . is not at all epochs and under all conditions possible. . . . This creative power works with elements, with materials. . . . Now in literature . . . the elements with which the creative power works are ideas; the best ideas . . . current at the time. . . . And I say *current* at the time, not merely accessible at the time.[2]

On the basis of this premise Arnold rested much of his argument concerning the importance of 'criticism' and its function in supplying poets with their 'materials'. Arnold discovered the idea in embryo in Goethe's discussion with Eckermann about the French poet Béranger. Goethe argued that in the Paris of the early nineteenth century, through the efforts of men like Diderot and Voltaire, there had been current for three generations such an abundance of intellect—*Geist*—that a talented writer could develop quickly and easily, in a way unthinkable in any less stimulating environment. Béranger had never attended a university, yet he was still able to produce a cultivated poetry of great delicacy and value. Goethe summed up his argument with the following remark: 'So, my good friend, I repeat: if a talent is to develop quickly and happily it all

[1] See Eckermann, Part III, 2 Jan. 1824, 560–1.

[2] *Essays in Criticism*, 1865, *CPW*, III, 260–1.

depends on there being current in the nation much intellect and solid culture.'[1] This conception of the poet's relationship to his cultural environment is basic to Goethe's thinking in these matters, and his criticism abounds with examples of a similar kind. Arnold, whose 'sickening consciousness' of his own predicament compelled him to an analysis of it, was not slow to take up and develop Goethe's suggestions.

In the 1853 Preface Arnold considers one of the problems confronting an artist living, as he believed himself to be, in an age of spiritual discomfort. The siren voices of critics like Masson urged false ideals. Where under such conditions was the artist to find models of sound practice? Arnold's answer to this question was Goethe's—with the Greeks. This would not be of much significance, were it not for the fact that both poets gave identical reasons for their preference of Greek to modern art. The Greeks, Arnold maintained, understood far better than we the importance of choosing 'worthy subjects', that is, subjects possessing an inherent human interest. No amount of skill expended on an 'intrinsically inferior action' would compensate for the initial disadvantage. The artist 'may indeed compel us to admire his skill, but his work will possess, within itself, an incurable defect'.[2] Arnold was here repeating a basic tenet of Goethe's critical teaching. The German poet continually emphasized the importance of subject matter with *content*. Without this, a poet could only produce, regardless of talent, 'a mere artistic trick rather than a work of art, which should be based on a worthy subject, so that finally the treatment will . . . reveal to us all the more fully the worth of the subject'.[3] Almost by definition, the range of truly 'worthy subjects' would be very restricted, and to both Goethe and Arnold it made excellent sense for the poet to follow the example of the Greeks in writing only on those 'actions' whose value was already proven. In practice, this argument led Arnold to write *Merope*, and to many that alone would seem sufficient proof of its inadequacy. Goethe's one use of a traditional Greek subject, the Iphigenia legend, produced a sort of masterpiece, but one which he never repeated. Few critics have mourned the loss.

The practice of the Greeks was exemplary in another important

[1] See Eckermann, Part III, 3 May 1827, 649.

[2] *CPW*, I, 4.

[3] See *Dichtung und Wahrheit*, Part II, Book 7, in *Werke*, XXV, 104.

respect: '. . . with them', Arnold argues in the Preface, 'the poetical character of the action in itself, and the conduct of it, was the first consideration; with us, attention is fixed mainly on the value of the separate thoughts and images which occur in the treatment of an action. They regarded the whole; we regard the parts.'[1] This distinction between the 'whole' and the 'parts', which has many implications, resolves itself into Arnold's insight that, given subject matter of intrinsic value, the essential stature of a work of literature depends upon the power of *architectonicè* which the poet has expended upon it, and not upon the poet's gift for producing delightful turns of phrase. Arnold had borrowed the notion of *architectonicè* from Goethe's essay 'Ueber den sogenannten Dilettantismus', which he had translated and copied into his 1847 note-book, and his definition of it as 'that power of execution which creates, forms, constitutes', follows Goethe's own words. Arnold explained the difficulty which his English contemporaries had in appreciating the importance of construction by pointing out that critics attached exaggerated value to richness of imagery and abundance of illustration, because the dangerous and misleading practice of 'those d——d Elizabethans', Shakespeare in particular, had become established as the poetic norm for English poets. Shakespeare's talent for felicitous expression was so striking, Arnold claimed, that it obscured his most important and characteristic gift—that of *architectonicè*. Arnold's feeling that Shakespeare was a risky model for a young talent to emulate, was in part instinctual, and in part rooted in his dissatisfaction with Shakespeare's romantic successors, Keats, Shelley and Tennyson. It was a feeling that Goethe shared. Both men were united in a conviction that the practice of the Greeks offered a far safer guide: 'With them, the action predominated over the expression of it; with us, the expression predominates over the action. Not that they failed in expression, or were inattentive to it; on the contrary, they are the highest models of expression, the unapproached masters of the *grand style*. But their expression is so excellent because it is so admirably kept in its right degree of prominence; because it is so simple and so well subordinated.' Kenneth Allott has pointed out that the characteristically Arnoldian phrase—the grand style—was used originally by Goethe when, in a description of the *Iliad*, he praised the poem for 'making use only of what is essential,

[1] *CPW*, I, 5.

in description and simile rejecting all decoration'.[1] But this is no isolated borrowing or chance echo. Arnold's reliance on Goethe in the critical formulations of the 1853 Preface was extensive, and the authoritative air of the essay undoubtedly stems from his awareness that in most of his opinions he had behind him the authority of the greatest critic of all times.

William Madden has suggested that Arnold found his distinction between the 'whole' and 'the parts' first made by Goethe in *Wilhelm Meister*.[2] This may be so, but Goethe's critical judgements refer to it so constantly that no single source really matters. Its wider implications for Arnold begin to reveal themselves in his letter to Clough of 28 October 1852. Arnold links his demand for 'great plainness of speech' in modern poetry to another requirement. Poetry, he argues, 'can only subsist by its *contents*: by becoming a complete magister vitae as the poetry of the ancients did: . . . it must not lose itself in parts and episodes and ornamental work, but must press forwards to the whole'.[3] This statement implies that modern poetry had been unfitted for its proper task because Christian culture had isolated man's religious instincts and ministered to them as a separate part of his constitution. Such a state of affairs, never satisfactory, was now serious. The decline of this culture had left both man and poetry incomplete. The nature of poetry's 'proper task' was explained by Arnold in his inaugural lecture 'On the Modern Element in Literature' (1857): '. . . it is to the poetical literature of an age that we must, in general, look for the most perfect, the most adequate interpretation of that age,—for the performance of a work which demands the most energetic and harmonious activity of all the powers of the human mind'.[4] It is to poetry that men must look for 'intellectual deliverance', for freedom from the bewilderment which they feel when confronted with the 'immense, moving confused spectacle' of the modern world. Ideally, poetry should make this spectacle intelligible, because its 'wholeness', that is, its harmonious integration of all elements of experience, derives from the wholeness of being that belongs properly to the poet. The root of modern man's

[1] See *Poems*, 595.

[2] W. A. Madden, *Matthew Arnold: a study of the aesthetic temperament in Victorian England*, Bloomington, Indiana 1967, 15.

[3] *Letters to Clough*, 124.

[4] *CPW*, I, 22.

suffering, Arnold believed, lay in the fragmentation of his being. For the Greeks of the age of Pericles completeness had been possible. The poetry of Sophocles represented 'the highly developed human nature of that age—human nature developed in a number of directions, politically, socially, religiously, morally developed—in its completest and most harmonious development in all these directions'.[1]

Goethe, too, applied the concept of wholeness both to the individual and to human culture in general, and for him no less than for Arnold, the example of the Greeks was crucial. In his essay on 'Winckelmann' (1805) Goethe wrote:

> By the expedient use of his individual powers man is capable of much; by the combined use of several powers he is capable of extraordinary things; but he will only achieve the truly unique, the wholly unexpected when his total powers combine simultaneously. This last was the happy lot of the ancients, particularly of the Greeks in their best period; we moderns are fated to exist in the first two states.
>
> If the healthy nature of man were to function as a whole, if he felt himself in the world as in a grand, lovely, noble and precious whole, if harmonious contentment granted him a pure and free delight, then would the universe, if it were conscious of itself, leap with joy at having arrived at its goal, and gaze with admiration at the culmination of its own life and development.[2]

But the conditional 'ifs' show that for modern man wholeness of being cannot be attained. Something had occurred since the time of Pericles to divide mind and heart. In the same essay Goethe wrote: 'Then, feeling and contemplation were not fragmented, that perhaps incurable schism in healthy human nature had not yet happened.' Goethe's diagnosis of modern ills was remarkably close to Arnold's.

The degree of Goethe's importance to Arnold in the decade after 1847 is difficult to overstate. For Arnold the German poet was, in the words of his friend Shairp, 'an oracle'.[3] He found Goethe's writings more than a repository of random ideas, he found a neo-Classical

[1] *CPW*, I, 28.

[2] See *Werke*, XXXVII, 19–20.

[3] *The Correspondence of Arthur Hugh Clough*, ed F. L. Mulhauser, 2 vol, Oxford 1957, I, 270.

poetic which suited his own particular needs and, so he thought, the needs of his age. Goethe's criticism helped Arnold to analyse his situation and to define his poetic ideals and aspirations. To discuss whether Goethe's influence was on the whole 'good' or 'bad' would probably be unprofitable, but it would be wrong to overlook the fact that this influence tended to confirm Arnold in his desire to produce a kind of poetry of which he was largely incapable. By stifling the intimate, personal voice of suffering in his poetry Arnold eventually stifled his poetic talent altogether. 'Dover Beach' and 'The Scholar-Gipsy' have 'the true voice of feeling', and few do not prefer them to the academic 'Balder Dead' or the stony *Merope*. After 1857 Arnold wrote little poetry and Goethe's importance for him underwent a relative decline. The fact that Goethe is quoted more often in the *Notebooks* than any other source except for the Bible and Thomas à Kempis can be misleading. So can the appearance of Goethe on his reading-lists throughout the 1860s, 1870s and 1880s. Arnold read and quoted Goethe, but from being 'the greatest critic of all times' in 1853 he had become eleven years later simply 'one of the greatest critics',[1] and in 1885 Arnold was able to speak of him as 'great' but also as 'the stiff, and hindered, and frigid, and factitious Goethe who speaks to us too often from those sixty volumes of his'.[2] Arnold's mature estimate of Goethe—contained in his fullest piece on the German poet, the essay 'A French Critic on Goethe' (1878)—was an ambivalent one: a 'double judgement' he himself called it. His comments on Goethe's artistic productions, with the exception of the short poems, are uniformly unfavourable. Even the first part of *Faust*—'undoubtedly Goethe's best work'—is too episodic, too fragmentary to 'produce a single, powerful total-impression', and *Faust II* he dismisses as 'mystification' and 'hieroglyphic'. Arnold ranks Goethe as 'the greatest poet of modern times', and yet he finds that it is not as a poet that Goethe truly excels, but rather as 'the clearest, the largest, the most helpful thinker of modern times'. The essay ends on a note of praise for Goethe 'as a clear and profound modern spirit, as a master-critic of modern life', but it is impossible not to detect the underlying coolness of Arnold's attitude. Furthermore, to be fair to Goethe, one must

[1] 'The Function of Criticism at the Present Time', 1864, *Essays in Criticism*, *CPW*, III, 259–60.

[2] See 'Emerson', *Discourses in America*, *CPW*, X, 167.

remark on the eccentricity of a judgment which concludes, as Arnold's does, that the true greatness of the German poet does not reside in his poetry but rather 'in the immense Goethe-literature of letter, journal and conversation'.[1]

The reason for this change in Arnold's attitude to Goethe seems not to lie in any discovery by Arnold of some new and displeasing aspect of the German poet's work, but rather in the development of his interests into areas where contemporaries like Renan and Sainte-Beuve had more to say. Arnold's occupation as an Inspector of Schools brought him into contact with problems very different from those which had occupied his thoughts in 1853, and gradually these assumed increasing importance. This interest in questions of a social and political kind was in no way new for Arnold but whereas previously he had sacrificed it in pursuit of 'detachment', he was now more disposed to follow his bent. Only the briefest account of Arnold's and Goethe's political thought will be necessary to show the profound dissimilarities between their respective outlooks.

With few exceptions Goethe's writings were apolitical and they were so by conscious choice. Essentially Goethe approved a rigidly hierarchic arrangement of classes in society and to democratic ideas he was, of course, hostile. If Arnold feared disorder and sought stability, it was a stability compatible with the recognition of the social changes inevitable with the passing of power to the middle class in his time. That strict conservatism made not for stability but was indeed a disruptive force Arnold had been taught too well by his father to doubt. He knew that the days of the aristocracy as a hereditary ruling class were numbered. It lacked the breadth of vision to understand or to direct the irresistible, historical movement towards a democratic society, and its almost exclusive possession of the land made social equality impossible. If the group historically destined to assume political power was clearly the middle class, the middle class as Arnold saw it was eminently unfitted for the task. In his essay 'The Future of Liberalism' (1880), Arnold described his notion of the inadequate civilization of the English middle class as the 'master thought' of his political writings. All his essays in social criticism can be seen as an attempt to shake the complacency of his middle class audience and to make them conscious of their deficiencies.

[1] *Mixed Essays*, 1879, *CPW*, VIII, 275.

In spite of the irrelevance to Arnold of Goethe's political thought, his social criticism can still be viewed as the wider application of an idea which he had derived from the German poet. The important distinction between wholeness and fragmentation in art had led Arnold to an analysis of the modern situation which concluded that one basic cause of man's discomfort lay in the overdevelopment of 'intellect' at the expense of 'feeling'. The balance could only be restored by the reintegration of the personality through the development of all its elements in a harmonious whole: from 'feeling and reason' to 'imaginative reason'. The effort at integration may be regarded as the driving force behind Arnold's social criticism. Civilization—the humanization of man in society—could only be achieved, Arnold argued, through the development of all the 'powers' which constitute human life: 'the power of conduct, the power of intellect and knowledge, the power of beauty, the power of social life and manners'.[1] In *Culture and Anarchy* Arnold groups these powers under the more famous categories of Hebraism (associated with 'conduct') and Hellenism (associated with intellect and beauty), and the malady of English civilization is diagnosed as a want of the latter; the middle class earned full marks for conduct but was marked down in sweetness and light. It followed that improvement had to be sought 'in the general harmonious expansion of those gifts of thought and feeling, which make the peculiar dignity, wealth, and happiness of human nature'.[2] Clearly, then, to talk of Arnold's integration of society, as some critics have done, can be misleading for the elements which he integrates are personal rather than social. Arnold's 'civilization' is essentially an internal condition of being. A society is civilized only in so far as its public life reflects this condition, venerates it, and makes it possible. The integration of human life in the individual was always Arnold's fundamental concern, and although his political essays stress the social context of this process, their continuity with his earlier poetic criticism cannot be mistaken.

Arnold's increasing interest in the social and political problems of the day in the 1860s accompanied his work as a critic of literature. But even in matters of literary criticism Goethe's influence was now less important than it had been in the past. Again, this was due in part to

[1] 'The Future of Liberalism', 1880, *CPW*, IX, 141.

[2] *CPW*, V, 94.

the social orientation of Arnold's interests. His literary criticism—in *Essays in Criticism* (1865) and *On the Study of Celtic Literature* (1867), for example—is often so concerned with aspects of English civilization that the distinction between literary and social criticism seems arbitrary. Everything of the first importance that Arnold learned from Goethe had been learned by 1860, and the development of his ideas on poetry after this year proceeded independently of the German poet. Occasionally one suspects that a particular idea or opinion advocated by Arnold may have derived from Goethe, but it is difficult to be sure in these isolated instances for Arnold's thought was now fed from so many different sources. When, for example, Arnold argues in 'The Function of Criticism at the Present Time' that criticism must regard 'Europe as being, for intellectual and spiritual purposes, one great confederation, bound to a joint action and working to a common result', one is conscious that Goethe's cosmopolitanism and his conception of a *Weltliteratur* may have influenced Arnold, but R. H. Super, in his note to the passage, points out that a very similar thought had been expressed by Renan too.[1] Of course, the ideas which Arnold expressed in the literary criticism of the 1860s and later were partly an elaboration, development or application of earlier insights which did owe a great deal to Goethe. The dialectic of the 'parts' and the 'whole' often figures centrally, if not obviously, in Arnold's literary essays. His disapproving judgement on Dante for the excessive cultivation of the spiritual side of his life, for example, and his censures on the intellectual deficiencies of Byron and the English romantics belong here. So too, though less directly, does his analysis of pagan and medieval religious sentiment; both types of religious sentiment placed too much weight on some particular element of human nature at the expense of others. Pagan religion forgot the importance of conduct and degenerated into moral laxity; medieval religion was incomplete because it neglected intellect and beauty. An adequate religion, therefore, would need to be a harmonious synthesis of all these 'powers'. The ancestry of these ideas in the 1853 Preface and the inaugural lecture of 1857 is not hard to discern for even where the application is quite new, their essential structure remains unchanged. Goethe is important here only as a part of this ancestry, but on the developments and changes in the Englishman's thinking Goethe's influence after 1860 was slight. It was Goethe's

[1] *CPW*, III, 284, 481.

'profound, imperturbable naturalism'[1] that Arnold thought so admirable and here, perhaps, in Arnold's emulation of this quality, is Goethe's most pervasive and least tangible influence to be found.

Arnold's strictures in *Culture and Anarchy* on the 'defective' religion of the middle class led in the 1870s to his major writings on religion: *St. Paul and Protestantism* (1870), *Literature and Dogma* (1873) and *God and the Bible* (1875). One cannot speak of Goethe as 'areligious' in the same way that one can speak of him as 'apolitical', but it is still the case that Goethe's religious views were unimportant as an influence on Arnold's theological writings. True, there are suggestive parallels between their respective religious positions—both had rejected the metaphysical and theological-dogmatic superstructure of Christianity while retaining the highest possible respect for its ethical content, and both behaved towards the established Christian churches without bitterness or rancour—but these parallels help to account neither for the evolution of Arnold's religious convictions nor for the particular form in which they are expressed. Goethe never defined his attitudes to Christianity at the same length or with the same fulness and coherence as Arnold. Having once abandoned Christianity, Goethe was frankly no longer concerned. Arnold was never unconcerned. Throughout the 1870s his labours were directed largely at a restoration of Christianity to a form that would be appropriate to modern needs, at removing whatever was unsound in it—miracles, faith in the divinity of Jesus and in the existence of a personal God—and at establishing what remained on the firm basis of experience. The claims made by religion would have to be capable of verification; 'verifiable', the word echoes and re-echoes through *Literature and Dogma*. The essential tenets of Arnold's religious position, and in particular his identification of 'God' with 'that stream of tendency by which all things seek to fulfil the law of their being'[2] owe little or nothing to Goethe.

What then remains of Arnold's claim, which I quoted at the beginning of this essay, to the effect that he had learned from Goethe 'ruling ideas' that were constantly with him? Surprisingly, the answer is: a good deal. There is probably no author to whom Arnold refers, or from whose writings Arnold more often quotes, than Goethe; this is true even of the longer works on religion. Arnold's motives are

[1] 'Heinrich Heine', *Essays in Criticism*, 1865, *CPW*, III, 110.

[2] *St Paul and Protestantism*, 1870, *CPW*, VI, 10.

various. Occasionally his references to Goethe are little more than a gesture of respect across the years to an author with whom he felt a strong affinity. Such is the case of his essay 'The French Play in London' (1879) whose title acknowledges Goethe's essay '*Das französische Schauspiel in Berlin*'. On other occasions a reference to Goethe serves Arnold as a rod with which to cow the unlettered Philistine. He berates the English middle class for its lack of intelligence and, lest any voice be raised in protest, he settles the matter with Goethe's remark to Eckermann, 'der Engländer ist eigentlich ohne Intelligenz'—'the Englishman, properly speaking, is without intelligence'. In other instances, however, the quotations are related to ideas which had profound importance for Arnold. The stanza beginning 'Stirb und werde'—Die and become—from Goethe's poem 'Selige Sehnsucht' was one of Arnold's favourite quotations; he wrote it out several times in his *Notebooks* and cited it often in his published writings. Arnold associated Goethe's lines with the idea of *necrosis*—a spiritual dying to the old self, and a resurrection to the new. But Arnold's original 'source' is, of course, not Goethe but St. Paul. Similarly, the idea of 'renunciation' expressed in Faust's ironic cry 'Entbehren sollst du! sollst entbehren!' which Arnold delighted to cite, had for him a fundamentally Christian significance which it did not have for the German poet. The concept of historical development as a necessary force, irresistibly changing and reshaping the forms of religion and thought, is central to *Literature and Dogma*. Arnold figures this development with the word *Zeitgeist*, or Time-Spirit, which he had borrowed from Goethe, but, as Fraser Neiman had shown, Arnold's use of the term has very little connection with its source in Goethe's essay on Homer.[1] Even after 1870, therefore, while it is still true that some of Arnold's 'ruling ideas' relate to or derive from Goethe, in their original context these ideas have a very different significance from that with which Arnold endows them.

'It is a mistake to think', Arnold says in 'A French Critic on Goethe' (1878), 'that the judgment of mature reason on our favourite author, even if it abates considerably our high-raised estimate of him, is not a gain to us.'[2] As Arnold gradually exchanged his role as a poet a little removed from the world for that of a critic deeply involved in 'life',

[1] See F. Neiman, *Matthew Arnold*, New York 1968, 113–35.

[2] *Mixed Essays* (1879), *CPW*, VIII, 255.

Goethe's importance for him diminished. The lines from *Torquato Tasso* which Arnold cites in *On the Study of Celtic Literature* are appropriate here:

> *Es bildet ein Talent sich in der Stille,*
> *Sich ein Character in dem Strom der Welt.*

[Poetic talent develops best in solitude,/ moral character in the stream of life.]

Ultimately, however reluctantly, Arnold put life before solitude, and moral character before poetic talent.

Selected Bibliography and List of Abbreviations

DAVID J. DeLAURA

THE LIST in §1 shows the edition used for reference in this volume, unless otherwise indicated. Throughout, place of publication is London unless otherwise indicated.

1. PRIMARY TEXTS AND LIST OF ABBREVIATIONS

CPW *The Complete Prose Works of Matthew Arnold*, ed R. H. Super. 11 volumes projected. Volume X appeared in 1974. Ann Arbor 1960– .

Letters *Letters of Matthew Arnold, 1848–1888*, ed George W. E. Russell, 2 vol, New York and London 1895.

Letters to Clough *The Letters of Matthew Arnold to Arthur Hugh Clough*, ed H. F. Lowry, London and New York 1932.

NB *The Note-Books of Matthew Arnold*, ed H. F. Lowry, K. Young, and W. H. Dunn, 1952.

Poems *The Poems of Matthew Arnold*, ed Kenneth Allott, 1965. In the 'Longmans Annotated English Poets' series.

PW *The Poetical Works of Matthew Arnold*, ed C. B. Tinker and H. F. Lowry, 1950.

Unpublished Letters *Unpublished Letters of Matthew Arnold*, ed Arnold Whitridge, New Haven 1923.

Works The Works of Matthew Arnold. 15 vol, 1903–4.

Commentary C. B. Tinker and H. F. Lowry, *The Poetry of Matthew Arnold: A Commentary*, 1940.

Buckler William E. Buckler, *Matthew Arnold's Books: Towards a Publishing Diary*, Geneva, 1958.

Abbreviations of Periodicals Cited

PMLA	*Publications of the Modern Language Association of America*	*UTQ*	*University of Toronto Quarterly*
PQ	*Philological Quarterly*	*VN*	*Victorian Newsletter*
RES	*Review of English Studies*	*VP*	*Victorian Poetry*
		VS	*Victorian Studies*

2. BIBLIOGRAPHIES AND CONCORDANCE

The Arnold entry in the *New CBEL* III (1969), by R. H. Super, is the most up-to-date collection of primary and secondary items. Super's edition of the prose works has a great deal of bibliographical and publishing information, as does Buckler, listed above. The Ehrsam and Deily bibliography includes lesser critical items and a valuable listing of reviews of Arnold's books.

Arthur Kyle Davis, Jr., *Matthew Arnold's Letters: A Descriptive Checklist*, Charlottesville, Virginia 1968.

Carl Dawson, ed, *Matthew Arnold: the Poetry*, The Critical Heritage, London and Boston 1973.

David J. DeLaura, 'Matthew Arnold', *Victorian Prose: A Guide to Research*, ed D. DeLaura, New York 1973.

T. G. Ehrsam and R. H. Deily, *Bibliographies of Twelve Victorian Authors*, New York 1936, rpt. 1968.

Frederick E. Faverty, 'Matthew Arnold', *Victorian Poetry: A Guide to Research*, ed F. Faverty, Cambridge, Mass. 1956, revised edn 1968.

Stephen Maxfield Parrish, ed, *A Concordance to the Poems of Matthew Arnold*, Ithaca 1959.

Thomas Burnett Smart, *The Bibliography of Matthew Arnold*, 1892, rpt. New York 1968.

3. GENERAL STUDIES

Edward Alexander, *Arnold and John Stuart Mill*, New York 1965.

Kenneth Allott, 'Matthew Arnold's reading-lists in three early diaries', *VS* II, 1959.

—— *Matthew Arnold*, Writers and Their Work, 1955.

Warren D. Anderson, *Matthew Arnold and the Classical Tradition*, Ann Arbor 1965.

Douglas Bush, *Matthew Arnold*, New York 1971.

E. K. Chambers, *Matthew Arnold: A Study*, Oxford 1947, rpt. New York 1964.

David J. DeLaura, 'Matthew Arnold and the nightmare of history', *Victorian Poetry*, Stratford-upon Avon Studies 15, ed M. Bradbury and D. Palmer, 1972.

H. W. Garrod, *Poetry and the Criticism of Life*, Cambridge, Mass. 1931.

Leon A. Gottfried, *Matthew Arnold and the Romantics*, Lincoln, Nebraska 1963.

R. H. Hutton, *Essays Theological and Literary*, 2 vol, 1871. Hutton has valuable comments in several of his other volumes of criticism.

D. G. James, *Matthew Arnold and the Decline of English Romanticism*, Oxford 1961.

J. D. Jump, *Matthew Arnold*, 1965.

Howard F. Lowry, *Matthew Arnold and the Modern Spirit*, Princeton 1941.

William A. Madden, *Matthew Arnold: A Study in the Aesthetic Temperament*, Bloomington 1967.

Matthew Arnold: A Collection of Critical Essays, ed D. J. DeLaura, Twentieth Century Views, Englewood Cliffs, N.J. 1973.

Patrick J. McCarthy, *Matthew Arnold and the Three Classes,* New York and London 1964.

J. Hillis Miller, *The Disappearance of God: Five Nineteenth-Century Writers*, Cambridge, Mass. 1963.

Fraser Neiman, *Matthew Arnold*, New York 1968.

Stephen Spender, *The Struggle of the Modern*, Berkeley 1963.

R. H. Super, *The Time-Spirit of Matthew Arnold*, Ann Arbor 1970.

Geoffrey and Kathleen Tillotson, *Mid-Victorian Studies*, 1965.

Lionel Trilling, *Matthew Arnold*, New York 1939, 1955.

Basil Willey, *Nineteenth Century Studies*, 1949.

4. STUDIES OF THE POETRY

Kenneth Allott, 'A background for "Empedocles on Etna"', *Essays and Studies by Members of the English Association* n.s. XXI, 1968.

Paull F. Baum, *Ten Studies in the Poetry of Matthew Arnold*, Durham 1958.

Charles Berryman, 'Arnold's *Empedocles on Etna*', *VN* No. 29, 1966.
Louis Bonnerot, *Matthew Arnold, poète*, Paris 1947.
Allan Brick, 'Equilibrium in the poetry of Matthew Arnold', *UTQ* XXX, 1961.
William Cadbury, 'Coming to terms with "Dover Beach"', *Criticism* VIII, 1966.
A. Dwight Culler, *Imaginative Reason: The Poetry of Matthew Arnold*, New Haven and London 1966.
J. P. Curgenven, '*The Scholar Gipsy*: A Study of the growth, meaning and integration of a poem', *Litera* (Turkey) II–III, 1955–6.
—— '*Thyrsis*', *Litera* IV–VI, 1957–9.
David J. DeLaura, 'Arnold, Clough, Dr. Arnold, and "Thyrsis"', *VP* VII, 1969.
—— 'What, then, does Matthew Arnold mean?' *Modern Philology* LXVI, 1969. Review of recent Arnold books.
A. E. Dyson, 'The Last Enchantments', *RES* n.s. VIII, 1957. On 'The Scholar-Gipsy'.
David L. Eggenschweiler, 'Arnold's passive questers', *VP* V, 1967.
T. S. Eliot, *The Use of Poetry and the Use of Criticism*, Cambridge, Mass. 1933.
John P. Farrell, 'Matthew Arnold and the middle ages', *VS* XIII, 1970.
—— 'Matthew Arnold's tragic vision', *PMLA* LXXXV, 1970.
R. A. Forsyth, '"The Buried Life"—the contrasting views of Arnold and Clough in the context of Dr. Arnold's historiography', *ELH* XXXV, 1968.
Walter E. Houghton, 'Arnold's "Empedocles on Etna"', *VS* I, 1958.
E. D. H. Johnson, *The Alien Vision of Victorian Poetry*, Princeton 1952, rpt. Hamden, Conn. 1963.
Wendell Stacy Johnson, '"Rugby Chapel": Arnold as a filial poet', *The University Review* XXXIV, 1967.
—— *The Voices of Matthew Arnold*, New Haven 1961.
Frank Kermode, *Romantic Image*, 1957.
G. Wilson Knight, '*The Scholar Gipsy*: an interpretation', *RES* n.s. VI, 1955.
U. C. Knoepflmacher, 'Dover revisited: the Wordsworthian matrix in the poetry of Matthew Arnold', *VP* I, 1963.
Murray Krieger, '"Dover Beach" and the tragic sense of eternal recurrence' (1957), rpt. in *The Play and Place of Criticism*, Baltimore 1966.

Gabriel Pearson, 'The Importance of Arnold's *Merope*', *The Major Victorian Poets*, ed Isobel Armstrong, 1969.
Linda L. Ray, 'Callicles on Etna: the other mask', *VP* VII, 1969.
Alan Roper, *Arnold's Poetic Landscapes*, Baltimore 1969.
G. Robert Stange, *Matthew Arnold: The Poet as Humanist*, Princeton 1967.
Lionel Stevenson, 'Arnold's poetry: a modern reappraisal', *Tennessee Studies in Literature* IV, 1959.
M. G. Sundell, 'The Intellectual background and structure of Arnold's *Tristram and Iseult*', *VP* I, 1963.
——'Story and Context in "The Strayed Reveller"', *VP* III, 1965.
A. C. Swinburne, 'Mr. Arnold's New Poems' (1867), *Essays and Studies*, 1875.
R. H. Super, 'Emerson and Arnold's Poetry', *PQ* XXXIII, 1954.

5. STUDIES OF THE PROSE

Flavia M. Alaya, 'Arnold and Renan on the popular uses of history', *Journal of the History of Ideas* XXVIII, 1967.
F. H. Bradley, *Ethical Studies*, Oxford 1876, 1927.
E. K. Brown, *Matthew Arnold: A Study in Conflict*, Chicago 1948.
—— *Studies in the Text of Matthew Arnold's Prose Works*, Paris 1935.
William E. Buckler, 'Studies in Three Arnold Problems', *PMLA* LXIII, 1958.
Vincent Buckley, *Poetry and Morality*, 1959.
A. O. J. Cockshut, *The Unbelievers*, 1964.
W. F. Connell, *The Educational Thought and Influence of Matthew Arnold*, 1950.
S. M. B. Coulling, 'The Background of "The Function of Criticism at the Present Time"', *PQ* XLII, 1963.
—— 'The Evolution of *Culture and Anarchy*', *Studies in Philology* LX, 1963.
—— 'Matthew Arnold's 1853 Preface: its origin and aftermath', *VS* VII, 1964.
David J. DeLaura, 'Arnold and Carlyle', *PMLA* LXXIX, 1964.
—— *Hebrew and Hellene in Victorian England: Newman, Arnold, and Pater*, Austin 1969.
—— 'The "Wordsworth" of Pater and Arnold: "The supreme, artistic view of life"', *Studies in English Literature* VI, 1966.

Robert A. Donovan, 'The Method of Arnold's *Essays in Criticism*', *PMLA* LXXI, 1956.
Fred A. Dudley, 'Matthew Arnold and Science', *PMLA* LVII, 1942.
John S. Eells, *The Touchstones of Matthew Arnold*, New Haven 1955.
Frederic E. Faverty, *Arnold the Ethnologist*, Evanston 1951.
N. N. Feltes, 'Matthew Arnold and the modern spirit: a reassessment', *UTQ* XXXIII, 1963.
L. E. Gates, *Three Studies in Literature*, New York, 1899.
F. J. W. Harding, *Matthew Arnold the Critic and France*, Geneva 1964.
W. J. Hipple, Jr., 'Matthew Arnold, dialectician', *UTQ* XXXII, 1963.
John Holloway, *The Victorian Sage*, 1953, rpt. Hamden, Conn. 1962.
Murray Krieger, 'The critical legacy of Matthew Arnold; or, the strange brotherhood of T. S. Eliot, I. A. Richards, and Northrop Frye', *Southern Review* V, 1969.
B. E. Lippincott, *Victorian Critics of Democracy*, Minneapolis 1938.
William A. Madden, 'The divided tradition of English criticism', *PMLA* LXXIII, 1958.
J. C. Major, 'Arnold and Attic prose style', *PMLA* LIX, 1944.
Patrick J. McCarthy, 'Reading Victorian prose: Arnold's "Culture and its Enemies"', *UTQ* XL, 1971.
J. B. Orrick, 'Matthew Arnold and Goethe', *Publications of the English Goethe Society* n.s. IV, 1928.
John Henry Raleigh, *Matthew Arnold and American Culture*, Berkeley 1957.
William Robbins, *The Ethical Idealism of Matthew Arnold*, 1959.
E. San Juan, 'Arnold and the poetics of belief: some implications of *Literature and Dogma*', *Harvard Theological Review* LVII, 1961.
Robert Shafer, *Christianity and Naturalism*, New Haven 1926.
Geoffrey Tillotson, *Criticism and the Nineteenth Century*, 1951.
—— 'Matthew Arnold's prose: theory and practice', *The Art of Victorian Prose*, ed G. Levine and W. Madden, New York 1968.
Alba H. Warren, Jr., *English Poetic Theory, 1825–1865*, Princeton 1950, rpt. New York 1966.
René Wellek, vol IV of *History of Modern Criticism, 1750–1950*, New Haven 1965.
Arnold Whitridge, 'Arnold and Sainte-Beuve', *PMLA* LIII, 1938.
Raymond Williams, *Culture and Society, 1780–1950*, 1958.
J. Dover Wilson, Introduction to *Culture and Anarchy*, Cambridge 1932.

Index

Prepared by Mrs. Brenda Hall, MA